Pierre Boulez

Pierre Boulez

Dominique Jameux

Translated by
SUSAN BRADSHAW

Harvard University Press
Cambridge, Massachusetts
1991

Printed in Great Britain
10 9 8 7 6 5 4 3 2 1

Originally published in French in 1984
by Librairie Arthème Fayard, Fondation SACEM, France

Library of Congress Cataloging-in-Publication Data

Jameux, Dominique.
  [Pierre Boulez. English]
  Pierre Boulez / Dominique Jameux; translated by Susan Bradshaw.
    p.   cm.
  Includes bibliographical references (pp. 394–7) and indexes.
  ISBN 0–674–66740–9
  1. Boulez, Pierre, 1925–   . 2. Composers—France—Biography.
I. Title.
ML410.B773J313 1990
780'.92—dc20
[B]   90–4715
                                                                CIP
                                                                MN

For S.

Contents

Acknowledgements

The author wishes to thank the various people whose observations have enabled him to write this book and, in particular, Susanne Tézenas, who put the archives of the Domaine musical (today deposited in the Bibliothèque Nationale) at his disposal, Jeanne Chévalier, who welcomed, followed the progress of, and gave kind support to the undertaking, and Michel Fano, whose friendship – and acquaintance with the subject – has been of infinite help.

He also wishes to thank the publishers Amphion, Heugel and Universal Edition for the documentary aid they have furnished.

At IRCAM, Nancy Hartmann and Astrid Schirmer have been unstinting in their help with the search for this or that piece of information: thanks are due to them also.

And finally, it gives him pleasure to be able to express his gratitude to Brigitte Masson for her encouragement of the project, and to Jean Nithart (Editions Fayard), whose skilful dedication to the problems of a difficult manuscript was equalled only by his patience in awaiting the outcome.

Foreword

Any serious biographer of Pierre Boulez inevitably faces the task of describing at least four separate, though interconnected, aspects of his professional life.

As composer, Boulez has written some thirty works, which have already earned him a place in musical history. Although the present volume concentrates mainly upon his composing career, I realize that this side of Boulez – the most important, indeed the most fundamental – is scarcely known: there are few recordings of his works, and his music is neither played nor studied as often as it might be.

Boulez is perhaps best known as a conductor. His reputation is established, he has a glittering array of honours, and his recordings are part of the history of interpretation – a history hardly less important than that of music itself, if indeed (as he himself has said), 'music scarcely exists except as direct communication'. Schoenberg, Webern, Berg, Stravinsky, Debussy, Bartók, Wagner, and the great orchestras of the world are there on disc to delight the ear and to satisfy the intellect. As a radical interpreter, Boulez has won successive battles in conservative strong-holds: *Wozzeck* and *Lulu* at the Paris Opéra, *Parsifal* and the *Ring* at Bayreuth, prestigious and eminently well-deserved posts in London, Cleveland and New York. But nothing is gained without sacrifice, and the fame of the conductor has somewhat eclipsed that of the composer.

At the outset, Boulez saw his literary activity only as an armed extension of his work as a militant composer – using his pen in a characteristically polemical manner in the tradition of a Berlioz or a Debussy: when the public appear intimidated by a new, even scandalous work, Boulez lashes out at their faintheartedness like an avenging archangel, with the authoritative censure of *Notes of an Apprenticeship*. And when the time came for him to take stock of the contemporary scene in his book, *Boulez on Music Today*, it was evident that he was not one to measure success by the size of his audience.

Finally, Boulez may be regarded as a political entrepreneur, his most controversial and equivocal role, demanding what are, essentially, 'back-stage' skills. He must not only make music himself, but encourage others to do so, and be able to organize performers. Having won over the public, he must retain their support. Furthermore, he must know how to 'operate' groups, ensembles or institutions as diverse as the Domaine musical, orchestras in London or New York, or IRCAM[1] in Paris. Boulez is undoubtedly a powerful man, but first and foremost a musician, whose power stems from his energy, his ability and his renown.

So I find myself faced with the task of talking about a musician who seems to comprise four distinct personae in one. It is noticeable how few composers in the past have adopted this fourfold way of life: of these, Schoenberg, Wagner and Bach can be considered only partly comparable. (Surprisingly, it was Schumann who – briefly – came closest to Boulez in the range of his activities.) All this, together with my own inadequacy, makes this book – the first in France[2] – seem something of a gamble. I have therefore drawn up the following guidelines:

1 I begin with a concise biography (up to mid 1984) which aims to collate as much factual information as possible. I have naturally talked to a number of people who knew Boulez before I did, but it is almost certain that there is information still to be obtained. Nevertheless, I believe my biographical portrait to be accurate at least in its essentials.

2 This is the biography of a public man. For the past twenty years or so (since about 1963), Boulez the public figure has been very much in the limelight, and his mastery of the interview has produced a kind of regular chronicle of his movements and motivations: I have drawn widely on these, with gratitude to the journalists involved.

On the other hand, I felt that, as an individual living today, Boulez had every right to be revealed only as he himself wished: few notes on his personal, private daily life will be found here – that is his business. There

1 Institut de Recherche et de Coordination Acoustique Musique, the music section of the Georges Pompidou Centre in Paris.
2 The only remotely comparable book I know of is *Boulez – Composer, Conductor, Enigma* by the American journalist Joan Peyser.

again, I think that what he himself allows to be seen is sufficient for the fidelity of the portrait.

3 The second part of the book consists of notes on the principal works. In a separate foreword I explain the spirit in which I wrote them and in which they should be read (see pp. 225–6).

4 The book concludes with an extensive documentation which I have endeavoured to make as comprehensive as possible. This will be of assistance first to the interested reader, eventually to my inevitable successors: like the work of the composer himself, this documentary biography is a 'work in progress'.

5 Throughout the writing of this book, I have had Boulez's unstinting help; he has allowed me ten or so fairly searching interviews, in addition to a multitude of informal meetings or other exchanges. But a tacit agreement prevailed from the outset, according to which the contents of the book were to be entirely my responsibility; they were not to be submitted for approval or imprimatur, nor even for a pre-publication reading: Boulez was to discover the contents of the book in the same way as the reader. The disadvantage of this is clearly that, since the remarks expressed here are mine and not his, our views on the interpretation of this or that approach or work may not always concur. As author, I claim the right to err – an understanding between us on any other basis would have been unthinkable. Moreover, the fact that Boulez was prepared to give me *carte blanche* is itself a facet of the portrait; I can only express my thanks – albeit with some anxiety.

This acknowledgement leads me to another: despite the difficulties I have encountered I have been sustained by listening to and dealing with the most remarkable music. To be sure, nobody writes a substantial book on a contemporary composer without a profound conviction – which he readily assumes may not be shared by all – that the composer in question merits such an expenditure of time. Even if I periodically distance myself from my subject, that in no way detracts from my fundamental and acknowledged admiration – nor from my gratitude for the musical enchantment in which ear, heart and intellect each play their part.

Saint-Etienne-le-Thillaye, January 1981
Loix-en-Ré, Paris, April 1984

PART ONE

TRAJECTORIES

CHAPTER ONE

Matrices
(1925–43)

Pierre Boulez was born on 26 March 1925, in the predominantly agricultural community of Montbrison in the Loire Valley.[1] His family lived above a small pharmacy at the far end of the rue Tupinerie, where many shopkeepers plied a modest trade. His father, Léon Boulez, who died in 1969, was an engineer who worked as technical director of a steel works. Catholic both by upbringing and conviction, he was an authoritarian figure, who was later to win the respect of many of his son's musician friends. Boulez's mother Marcelle (née Calabre) came from a socialist and agnostic background, but she too had been educated as a Catholic. An outgoing personality, she followed her son's career with interest, combining maternal pride with the scepticism of the uninitiated. They were as comfortably-off, united and stable a middle-class family as one could hope to find. There were four children: the first-born (also named Pierre) died after a few months in 1920; Jeanne, the beloved older sister, was born in 1922, Pierre in 1925, and Roger in 1936.

In 1929 the Boulez family left the flat in the rue Tupinerie to move into a house of their own at 46 rue Alsace-Lorraine. This was a small detached house, with a garden, set in a quiet little street in what might be described as the Neuilly district of Montbrison. The following year Léon Boulez brought back a radio set from a business trip to the United States: this was the first time that the young Boulez had heard any orchestral music.

---

1 Jean-Pierre Derrien gives Boulez's date of birth as 25 March ('Dossier Pierre Boulez', *Musique en jeu*, No. 1, Le Seuil, 1970).

He began his musical studies in 1931, when he and his sister both started to learn the piano; she was quickly outstripped, and family history has it that Pierre was capable of playing 'difficult' Chopin at the age of nine. He joined the seminary choir, which (amongst much rubbish) introduced him to a few more worthy items, including works by Josquin, Bach and Lassus.

He soon began to play chamber music with several much older local notables: their repertoire included trios by Haydn and Schubert, piano quartets by Mozart and Fauré, and the sonatas for violin and piano by Beethoven. Nearly fifty years later, Boulez still has fond memories of the Saint-Saëns Septet with trumpet.

Unlikely as it may now seem, in 1932 he started school at the Institut Victor-de-la-Prade, the little seminary of Montbrison. There was no choice, for Montbrison had neither *lycée* nor *collège* and the seminary was the only establishment for primary education in the town. Pierre Boulez received his entire education up to and including the *baccalauréat* in a one-time Ursuline convent, a tall, ramshackle building from which the nuns had been expelled by the revolution. He had to get up at 5.40 a.m. (he has remained an early riser) and, in the early-morning darkness, trudge up a steep slope exposed to all weathers, which in twenty minutes led him to the school.

For the next eight years he spent more than twelve hours a day in the strict, repressive, and over-devout atmosphere of a religious seminary, that nevertheless offered a sound education. To Célestin Deliège, who later questioned him on the predictable conflict between this religious education and his own philosophical convictions, Boulez replied with typical realism: 'When one is thirteen or fourteen one feels a bit isolated anyway, so one thinks only of making the best of things in relation to one's own life; in any case, I did not at the time suppose that the difficulties I had with the system were in any way connected with the validity or otherwise of the system itself.' And on the subject of religious practice in a boys' school, he remarked, 'What struck me most was a kind of mechanical attitude that had absolutely nothing to do with profound conviction; it was a parody, and when one is young one resents it the more because one is particularly drawn to life-styles that express conviction – later on, one learns somehow or other to adapt.'[2]

2 *Conversations with Célestin Deliège*, London, Eulenburg, 1976; originally published as *Par volonté et par hasard*, Paris, Le Seuil, 1975.

He was a brilliant pupil, particularly in chemistry and physics. His teachers describe him as diligent and strict with himself, always putting work first. His fellow pupils seem to have found him overbearing. His work table was always tidy, without unnecessary trimmings. 'Pierre was naturally disciplined rather than submissive', his sister recalls, and comments further that there was no malice in his nature.[3]

A fellow-pupil at the Institut Victor-de-la-Prade from 1934–40 evokes the surroundings and the climate. Paul Bouchet, today a lawyer in Lyons, remembers it as 'really a medieval world'. The following disconnected remarks are among his most striking recollections. Living locally, the Boulez family acted *in loco parentis* to Paul Bouchet, a boarder at the school. Latin and Greek were crammed into eleven-year-old heads – Latin was begun in the third term, when the children were only seven. An implicit understanding evolved between the two youngest in the class, which went beyond their common initials; this was a partnership between the extrovert and the introvert. There was no disciplinary dossier on either of them. Once a year, towards the end, there was a festive holiday organized by the *Rhéteurs* (the top form): this always caused great excitement, for it meant three days of relative madness. A move to democratize the proceedings met with virulent protest from the 'Hatchet Committee' (of which the two young friends were part) against the attempt to adulterate a proud tradition.

'We resented the total social control exercised from within,' notes Paul Bouchet, who remembers that Boulez appeared even then to be 'marked out, set apart': he did not seek to command, but nevertheless seemed 'one of the elect' – a fact which did not escape certain of those rare teachers gifted with the ability to awaken the spirit and to discover talent. The young Boulez was recognized for his intelligence and his obvious absolutist qualities: he was strongly urged to enter the training college for the priesthood. Although he would certainly have been a good recruit, he first demurred, then refused.

This then was the climate in which he passed the years from early childhood to adolescence. Future entomologists will doubtless find a way to track down the countless exploits, significant anecdotes and indiscreet reminiscences which will serve no purpose other than to deepen the mystery characteristic of all formative years.

3 Within the framework of a 'Pierre Boulez day', organized by *France-musique* in 1981, an amusing radio programme (produced by Claude Hermann and François Bréhinier) presented various memories of Boulez from his Montbrison days.

SAINT-ETIENNE (1940–1)

Pierre Boulez passed his *bachot* in July 1940. His studies had been uneventful, although he excelled in mathematics, towards which his feelings were ambivalent. While the ideals of logic and of perfection obviously gave him great pleasure, he grew to conceal his success in this field, sensing that it might be used to strengthen the argument that he, too, should pursue a career in engineering. Later he disclaimed all mathematical talent, when he found that his enemies were only too ready to describe him as 'the algebraic composer', 'the blackboard musician', and in other such flattering terms.

In the mean time, music was already becoming a dominant factor in his life. A year earlier, he had started going to Saint-Etienne, some thirty-five kilometres away, in order to take piano lessons from a more 'advanced' professor. 'Once a week', he told Jean-Louis de Rambures, 'I now went to take lessons from an old lady at Saint-Etienne; when the electricity failed, she lit the candles fixed to the piano, and it was by their flickering light that I first discovered the Beethoven sonatas, works by Debussy, Ravel, and so on.'

At the beginning of the 1940 academic year, he entered the private Saint-Louis boarding school in Saint-Etienne. Here the teaching, still narrow in outlook, was undertaken by monks. 'With the Jesuits of Saint-Etienne, literature stopped with Sully-Prudhomme, and music and painting played no part in the curriculum. While my friends found escape in devouring adventure stories, I covered my exercise books with music: I have never been interested in anything I could not take seriously.'[4]

In the summer of 1941, his application was rewarded with success in the second part of the *baccalauréat*.

LYONS (1941–3)

His sister provides a restrospective comment on this austere boyhood: 'When we were fifteen, we were both of us religious sceptics. Pierre never liked sport, and hated swimming in the limited space of a pool. He had no other particular likes or dislikes, but he enjoyed family holidays; we travelled throughout almost the whole of France during this period. He had some school friends, but friends were not all that important to him,

4 Conversation with Jean-Louis de Rambures (*Réalités*, April 1965). Boulez was mistaken – they were not Jesuits!

nor his relationships with them particularly intense. It was to me alone that he confided his activities, his hopes and his most private ambitions.'[5]

The following academic year, there was a perceptible change in the life of the future composer: at sixteen, he enrolled for a course in higher mathematics at Lyons – this time run by the Lazaristes of the *Cours Sogno*.[6] He went home every three or four weeks, but meanwhile, in this great metropolis, discovered the relative freedom of a new world, embracing contemporary culture and, of course, music. It was in Lyons that he heard a live orchestra for the first time and paid his first visit to the opera to see *Boris Godunov*. In 1942, while on a country holiday with his family at Saint-Bonnet-le-Chateau, he met the great Ninon Vallin,[7] who asked him to accompany her in arias from *Aida* and *La Damnation de Faust*. She proved a useful advocate in persuading Léon Boulez to withdraw his earlier objections and allow his son to go to the town conservatoire. But the selection panel missed the opportunity to do something worthwhile: Boulez was turned down after playing the first movement of the Sonata in A flat major by Weber – he nevertheless regards the piece with little rancour![8]

At the end of his first year in Lyons (1941–2), Boulez asked his father for permission to spend a further year there, in order to perfect his musical studies. At first, he was refused. Then, in June 1942, Jeanne got married, just as her brother was becoming increasingly alienated from his parents. Jeanne now interceded to persuade her father to agree to an extra year, and so Boulez began to study piano and harmony as a private pupil of Lionel de Pachmann, the son of Vladimir, to whom he had been introduced by Ninon Vallin (whose *répétiteur*, Violette Lubail, was Lionel's half sister). But Boulez was not altogether enchanted by Lyons, for he was made to enrol for a faculty course in the theory of mathematics – his first and only contact with the university world. Recalling his Lyons years in 1982, all he could find to say about it was 'I attended for three whole years'.

A word should be included here about the political and artistic climate prevailing at the time. These were the blackest years, the nadir of a

5 Peyser, op. cit., p. 24.
6 A religious establishment; the Lazaristes are priests of a lay religious order founded in 1625 by Saint Vincent de Paul.
7 Mezzo-soprano (1886–1961) whose real Christian name was Eugénie; she took part in the first performance of *La Martyre de Saint-Sébastien*, and was the much-favoured star of the Teatro Colón in Buenos Aires 1916–36.
8 An honourable precedent: in 1878, Debussy failed to gain a *premier prix* for piano with the same work.

ruthless war; Lyons, the centre of the Resistance, suffered severely from the rigours of the Occupation. It was during Boulez's second year there that the fiction of 'free' and 'occupied' zones was swept away by the Germans. While the young man and his family obviously regarded the activities of the occupying forces with scant pleasure, they do not seem to have been unduly perturbed by the issues. In this region of deepest France, the silence of the majority really did hold sway.

At the end of the year 1942–3, when Boulez was eighteen and the decision about his future could no longer be evaded or kept secret, he made up his mind to leave for Paris. One can imagine him tearing himself away from an exclusive contemplation of the great musicians of the past with the cry that he, too, would be a musician. But these musical ancestors were still for the most part unknown; today, Boulez remembers that the very first time he saw the name of Schoenberg in print was in Landormy's book *La Musique française après Debussy*, which he bought in Lyons, and which mentions *Herzgewächse*, Op. 20.

The break with his father, while undramatic, was evidently a reality – as was perhaps underlined by the objectivity with which it was accomplished. Nevertheless, the door was not finally closed to the possibility of reconciliation. So, in the autumn of 1943, Boulez found himself in Paris.

CHAPTER TWO

The Ancestral Age

'Everything threatens the life of a young man; love,
new ideas, the loss of his family. It is hard
for him to find his place in the world.'
Paul Nizan

'One has to understand what it is that one
wants to leave behind.'
Pierre Boulez

THE CONSERVATOIRE

Boulez arrived in Paris in the autumn of 1943 to embark on a serious study of music. In the event, he was to undertake two parallel courses of study during these apprentice years – the public and the private. Officially, he was a student at the Conservatoire, in the rue Madrid, an institution ruled with a fairly liberal hand by its recently appointed director, Claude Delvincourt. Boulez entered the Conservatoire through George Dandelot's[1] preparatory harmony class which, as may be imagined, provided him with a grounding in Georges Caussade's[2] *Treatise on Harmony*.[3] During this first year, however, he got to know Arthur Honegger's niece and, through her, was introduced to Honegger, composer of *Joan of Arc at the Stake*, and his wife, Andrée Vaurabourg: it was

1 Composer and teacher (1895–1975), professor of harmony at the Conservatoire from 1943.
2 Composer and pedagogue (1873–1936), professor of counterpoint and fugue at the Conservatoire and author of a Treatise on harmony (1931).
3 One of the principle textbooks used by Dandelot, together with his own 'Basses' and 'Chants donnés'; Boulez also worked from Reber and Dubois.

with the latter that he then set to work on a study of counterpoint which lasted until the autumn of 1945. Music is, after all, a perpetual entwining of vertical and horizontal gestures – a fact which, since Schoenberg, seems obvious to every intelligence attuned to present-day musical reality. It should nevertheless be noted here that the parallel teaching of harmony (or the 'vertical science of chords and their movement') and counterpoint ('the study of superposed melodic lines') is considered to be beyond the bounds of official teaching which, particularly in France, is by tradition harmonic. Boulez was a brilliant counterpoint pupil; Mme Vaurabourg kept and later framed a particular 'Conduit à huit voix' which now hangs in her drawing-room and must be more or less his earliest known work.

In 1943 and 1944, Boulez undertook further private tuition, this time piano lessons with Mme François, Jean Doyen's[4] assistant. Although he worked hard, when he applied for entry into her advanced class at the Conservatoire, playing the first movement of Beethoven's Sonata, Op. 111[5] – he was faced with a setback: admirable pianist as he is, Boulez was considered to lack the necessary ability.

At the start of the 1944 academic year, Boulez began studying with Messiaen; this was to be his first encounter with the master who was to have such a profound influence on him.

OLIVIER MESSIAEN

I should here explain what Messiaen stood for during this period immediately after the war. Intellectually, culturally and even emotionally, it was a time of deprivation. But whilst the world seemed to be undergoing radical changes, musical life in the rue Madrid continued to go round as if nothing had happened.

Messiaen combined the prestige of the composer with that of the performer. He had made his name before the war, notably as co-founder (with Yves Baudrier, Daniel Lesur and André Jolivet) of the group Jeune France,[6] but above all as the composer of several works – among them the *Préludes* for piano (1928–9), *Offrandes oubliées* and *L'Ascension* for orchestra (1932 and 1933), and latterly of a work composed and first

4 Pianist (1907–82), pupil of Marguerite Long at the Conservatoire and her successor from 1941–77).
5 Debussy too tackled this work for a Conservatoire competition in 1876 – without success.
6 Established in 1936 on the initiative of Yves Baudrier, this group proposed a return to music of a more spiritual nature in opposition both to the 'diversionary' aesthetic of Les Six and to the intellectualism attributed to Germanic composers. It ceased its activities in 1939.

performed in a prisoner-of-war camp, *Quatuor pour le fin du temps*. He had also been resident organist at the Trinité church since 1931 and, by virtue of this, the composer of several works for the instrument. And lastly, the teaching methods he employed at the Ecole Normale de Musique had, since 1936, given an indication of the means he was later to favour – like the group sight-reading class he used as an outlet for his insatiable musical curiosity. This was the man that Boulez met: a practitioner of the art of composition, a composer experienced in interpretation, a seeker, an imparter of knowledge – almost akin to Boulez himself. Since his return from captivity in 1941, he had been in charge of a harmony class at the Conservatoire – which he quickly turned into one for the broader study of music and of sound in general: here he enthusiastically analysed not only classical masterpieces from *Don Giovanni* to *Pelléas*, but Gregorian chant and the music of the great polyphonic composers of the Renaissance, as well as Hindu modes and birdsong. In 1942, the publication of *Technique de mon langage musical* brought him recognition as a theoretician in addition to his threefold status as composer, performer and teacher, and in 1943, the Egyptologist Guy-Bernard Delapierre put his Paris apartment at Messiaen's disposal so that, as a parallel to his official teaching at the Conservatoire, he could take selected pupils for courses in musical analysis on a more informal – if no less exacting – basis.

Messiaen's comprehensive, two-tier teaching system was to be experienced by an entire generation of composers. Those who were fellow students of Boulez at the time included Serge Nigg,[7] Jean-Louis Martinet,[8] Maurice Le Roux,[9] Yvette Grimaud – a remarkable pianist[10] who was to give the first performance of four of Boulez's early works for the instrument – and Yvonne Loriod.

To clarify the chronology: Boulez first got in touch with Messiaen in 1944; he was at the time a member of Dandelot's preparatory harmony class, which he left having learnt almost nothing. He then took private lessons with Messiaen in September 1944, to prepare himself for the compulsory entrance examination to the Conservatoire (which he passed

7 Composer (born 1924), pupil of Messiaen and Leibowitz, in 1959 he founded an association for progressivist musicians inspired by 'socialist realism'.
8 Composer (born 1912), pupil of Koechlin, Messiaen and Leibowitz.
9 Composer and conductor (born 1923), pupil of Messiaen and conductor of much contemporary music.
10 And composer too, notably of *Chants d'espace*, which makes use of quarter-tones.

in October). The following month he began to attend Messiaen's supplementary but more important course in Delapierre's apartment.

Relations between Messiaen and Boulez were volatile, and it was not until many years later – in the sometimes unreliable context of an official tribute – that Boulez gave his admirable explanation of exactly what it was that the master awoke in the pupil.

I do not much care for veterans' reminiscences, but I should like to recall an experience that must have been shared by many others, both before and after me – that sudden feeling of attraction to a master of whom one knows, with an inexplicable sense of certainty, that it is he, and only he, that is going to reveal you to yourself. This is a kind of magic exercised partly by his music, but also by the power of his personality, by his immediate appeal and by the overwhelming force of his example. This chosen master acts as a stimulus by his very presence, his behaviour, his very existence and the glimpses that he gives of what he demands of himself. He sees and listens, understands the clash in the pupil's personality as he tries to discover himself in a fog of contradictions and resentments. The master is prepared to accept ingratitude and injustice, rebuffs and rebelliousness, if these reactions mean the momentary loss of the pupil in order to establish him firmly as an original, independent personality. Attention and detachment are needed for this, and a sense of the adventure of preparing all the details of a long voyage without knowing its destination, a desire to set out for goals that are never clearly defined. Giving an example is as necessary as learning to forget it: 'Throw away the book I have taught you to read and add a new, wholly unexpected page!'[11]

That is the legend. As for history, it is riddled with astonishing misunderstandings. If Boulez is in fact crediting Messiaen with throwing open a window on the world of music, he soon makes a point of listing what he does and does not find particularly interesting with regard to the composer of the *Thème et variations* for violin and piano (1932) – the only work of Messiaen's that Boulez knew in 1944. Its exotic sound-world is typical of the composer; its overridingly rhythmic propositions will be shown later. But Boulez does not and never will subscribe to the idea of using imports from the Far East in Western music. The question of Boulez's attitude is nevertheless a delicate one, since he – like Messiaen and other composers of the time – is quite ready to regard so-called exotic music as a possible source of enrichment for the sound-world under exploration. Boulez often speaks of the vivid impression made on him by the Japanese Noh theatre, and a work like *Le Marteau sans maître*

11 Talk given at the Paris Opéra on 10 December 1978, on the occasion of Messiaen's seventieth birthday (printed complete in *Orientations* by Pierre Boulez, trans. Martin Cooper, London, Faber, and Harvard University Press, Cambridge, Massachusetts, 1986).

explicitly insists on the assumption of certain non-European traditions, particularly with regard to timbre. But he rejects the adoption of exotic formal procedures, as well as the notion of ideological integration. However, he is a realist, and he readily admits that the use of non-European music is the final misadventure of a musical neo-colonialism! Perhaps this stretches one's credulity, but the significant thing is that he adopts a position whose very severity implies a balance: while accepting that a knowledge of these kinds of music is essential, he regards their wholesale integration into our musical vocabulary as impossible. 'Frankly, Messiaen never really interested me all that much.[12] In my opinion, his frequent use of rhythms extracted from Greek or Indian rhythmic systems creates a problem: it is very difficult to incorporate fragments of an alien civilization into one's own work. I thought this even at the time; we have to invent our own vocabulary according to our own norms . . .'[13]

Any discussion of Boulez's early period must include mention of the *Trois Psalmodies* for piano (1945); although the composer later disclaimed them, they give occasional hints of the kind of precipitous violence he inflicted on the instrument in his early sonatas, together with turns of phrase and sonorities that seem to come straight from Messiaen – and even Jolivet.[14]

Both Messiaen and Boulez show the same ambivalence when it comes to rhythm. Nevertheless, it was from Messiaen's rhythmic researches that Boulez was to develop his own rhythmic grammar. Once again, Messiaen sought to combine analytical research – such as his early analysis of the rhythmic character of *The Rite of Spring* – with the compositional practice of his own *Mode de valeurs et d'intensités* (discussed later). It was during Messiaen's supplementary classes that the best of the Conservatoire students, free from all academic worries, had time to pore over the masterpieces for which he had given them such a voracious appetite.[15] Boulez began his own analysis of *The Rite of Spring* on the basis of Messiaen's ideas, but he advanced them to a point of extreme system-

---

12 Boulez is here referring to Messiaen's theories on rhythm and especially to his interest in Indian rhythmic systems.

13 *Conversations with Célestin Deliège*, p. 13.

14 A recording made by Yvette Grimaud of the *Trois Psalmodies* is to be found in the archives of the Institut National Audiovisuel (LO 13691). The work lasts 13'30". The first of the pieces has an incantatory quality, the second is gentle and romantic in the manner of Webern and the third is an *ostinato* akin to Ravel's *Le Gibet*.

15 The first works Boulez remembers being analysed: *Ma Mère l'oye* and *Petrushka*.

atization.[16] It was in this class too that he discovered Debussy's *Jeux*, then almost unknown and seldom studied, as well as *Wozzeck* and the early works of Schoenberg.

Schoenberg was to be the subject of the first real disagreement between Messiaen and Boulez. As Messiaen remembers: 'When he came to the class for the first time he was charming. But he soon turned against the whole world: he thought that everything was going wrong with music until, a year later, he discovered serialism and became a passionate convert, deeming it the only viable grammar!'. Messiaen would readily speak about Schoenberg and Berg, but with a fairly lukewarm attitude to dodecaphony. He was not after all a serial composer; or perhaps he was too much of one, as his *Mode de valeurs et d'intensités* will show. It therefore fell to someone else – in an intense, short-lived and violent exchange of ideas – to reveal to Boulez a whole musical continent then regarded in France as barbarous.

Meanwhile, he ended the academic year 1944–5 with a brilliant *premier prix* for harmony. The next year he joined Simone Plé-Caussade's[17] course in fugue; it was a prison from which Boulez duly escaped. He was called to order and words were exchanged between professor and pupil: 'All right, expel me then', Boulez taunted. This was no way to obtain a prize for fugue, especially as he had been behind a petition putting forward Messiaen's name as professor of composition. Years later, all that seems to remain of this teaching is his sour recollection of presenting Simone Plé-Caussade with a fugue exercise in the style of Bartók's *Music for strings, percussion and celesta*, and of her saying: 'There's nothing wrong with Bartók – but true enlightenment comes from the old masters.'

In 1944, travel was almost impossible, and Boulez spent the summer holidays in Paris; the following year he was able to return to Montbrison. The summer of 1946 was spent peacefully, recovering from an attack of appendicitis and renewing his resources; it was a time for reflection on the excitement of the year just past, and for cycling.

---

16 'Stravinsky remains', 1952. Included in *Notes of an Apprenticeship*, New York, Knopf, 1968 (originally published as *Relevés d'apprenti*, Paris, Le Seuil, 1966).
17 Pianist (1897–1986), pupil of Alfred Cortot, married to Georges Caussade whom she succeeded (1928) as professor of fugue at the Conservatoire.

RENE LEIBOWITZ

René Leibowitz's influence upon Boulez was as crucial as their subsequent parting was dramatic. Leibowitz could have passed for Schoenberg's most faithful disciple had he not exercised his ministry retrospectively. Nevertheless, essentially he must be credited with introducing 'Schoenberg and his school'[18] to Paris, thereby determining Boulez's musical direction (and that of a whole generation).

It was in Claude Halphen's house in February 1945 that Boulez first heard the Quintet, Op. 26, conducted by Leibowitz. In his own words, 'It was a revelation; the work obeys no tonal laws, and in it I found a harmonic and contrapuntal richness and a capacity for development and extension of a kind I have never found anywhere else.'[19] After this, he and a group of students from Messiaen's class went in search of Leibowitz. Detailed analysis sessions then took place every Saturday morning: 'The first work we analysed was the Symphony, Op. 21, by Webern; I was very impressed by this and made a copy of it, since the score was not then available.'[20]

This serial apprenticeship was as brief as it was passionate. It was practical too: in December 1945, Leibowitz conducted a Schoenberg concert in the hall of the old Conservatoire at which Boulez played the harmonium part in *Herzgewächse* (sung by Lucienne Trajin). But it was not long before a rift began to develop. Leibowitz was a deeply committed Schoenbergian, whereas Boulez was just discovering Webern – for him, the composer most effective in pushing the serial system to its extremes, and in reaching 'fertile ground', without ever giving the impression, as Schoenberg did, of wishing to pause or cast a backward glance. Neoclassicism was considered the enemy; and so it happened that, one evening in 1945, in the Champs-Elysées theatre[21] – birthplace of *The Rite of Spring* – a tremendous uproar punctuated a performance of Stravinsky's *Danses concertantes*. Boulez was conspicuous among the hecklers, although it was soon rumoured that Leibowitz himself was behind the demonstration.

Such collusion was short-lived, for this was a turning point for Boulez. He had already absorbed everything he really needed to learn from others:

18 From the title of his book, Janin, 1946.
19 Peyser, op. cit., pp. 32 and 33.
20 Antoine Goléa, *Rencontres avec Pierre Boulez*, Paris, Juilliard, 1958, pp. 27–8.
21 Comédie des Champs-Elysées: a small theatre with about 600 seats, housed in the same building in the avenue Montaigne as the Théâtre des Champs-Elysées, built by Perret in 1913.

an interest in Messiaen's rhythmical grammar, his non-European culture, and his keyboard writing, but also a sense of their limitations; and from Leibowitz a recognition of the principle of the twelve-note series and its importance. However, for Boulez, serialism is more a question of a way of thinking than of a repressive juggling with twelve pitches; fundamentally, what he dislikes about the series is its very dodecaphonicism. This Graeco-antiquarian vocabulary means little to him, and Leibowitz's mechanical handling of the pitches could only, in Boulez's view, lead to academicism – as indeed with many composers of the period. With his desire for strict control over the pupil, Leibowitz seemed to be re-enacting the didactic relationship between Schoenberg and his class – an approach which only succeeded in alienating Boulez. By the time of the First Sonata (1946), the break was already complete, and the unfortunate Leibowitz was thereafter never referred to by Boulez without qualification or accusations, of which that of pedantry was the least wounding.[22]

BARRAULT-RENAUD

In 1945, at the age of twenty, Boulez passed his army medical board at the town hall in the Panthéon, although those born in 1924 and 1925 were not to be drafted that year. Instead, he turned his thoughts to the question of earning a living.

On 1 January 1945, he moved from his room in the rue Oudinot where he had lived since September 1943, and which he had paid for with the mathematics lessons he gave to the son of the house. He sought the help of a small-time coal merchant who transported all the papers, manuscripts, notes and books belonging to the young composer by hand-cart. Boulez followed this Hoffmannesque turn-out on foot, all the way from the seventh to the fourth *arrondissement*, through a Paris still drowsy and deserted after the New Year's festivities. Boulez had found two communicating fourth floor[23] *chambres de bonne* in the rue Beautreillis in the Marais – and this was to be his base until he left for Germany in 1959. A contemporary photograph shows the premises: a narrow bed, a small desk, and manuscripts spilling over on to the floor. African masks hung on the wall alongside Klee reproductions, while the shelves held works of

22 An animosity which, years later, was temporarily laid aside in saluting Leibowitz's complete lack of interest in financial gain: like Messiaen, and like Schoenberg before him, he asked nothing from his gifted and impecunious pupils.
23 A taste for heights: since 1977, Boulez has lived on the thirteenth floor of a Paris apartment block.

Rimbaud, Mallarmé and Joyce: in short, Boulez's aesthetic and intellectual preoccupations were already echoed by his surroundings.

On the other hand, the musical substance of his professional activity was rather different from what was to follow: he was the *ondiste* at the Folies-Bergères! In other words, he was a virtuoso on the currently popular ondes martenot which, with its terrifying animal-like wail, was used to provide a cheap and effective form of incidental music for the theatre. Nevertheless, it was through the ondes martenot that Boulez was to meet Barrault.

Jean-Louis Barrault and Madeleine Renaud[24] had just caused a stir by leaving the Comédie-Française to found their own company at the Marigny theatre[25] (then directed by Simone Volterra). A production of Hamlet, in the French translation by Gide, was to have incidental music by Honegger, scored for wind, percussion and ondes martenot, and as Boulez had kept in close touch with Honegger, it was as a player that he was first introduced to Barrault. The production went well, and Barrault immediately recognized the exceptional qualities of his musician. His description of love at first sight is still famous:

Boulez arrived, all of twenty years old; we liked him straight away. Prickly and charming as a young cat, he was unable to conceal a very pleasant, shy disposition. We discovered an affinity between us, and he soon became popular: he was definitely 'one of us'. At the time, he acted abrasively, 'with all claws out', sparing hardly anyone; he was caustic, aggressive, occasionally irritating, and apparently ill at ease. When one officiates at one's own birth, as is the lot of the artist, it is normal to experience both the infant's fears and the mother's sufferings . . . But behind this antisocial, almost anarchic front, we sensed the extreme modesty and underlying sensitivity of an exceptional temperament . . . From these early contacts, we rightly guessed that we were witnessing the dramatic birth-pangs of Boulez the creative artist. He was inhabited, possessed, and his frequently cutting remarks were defensive; we were well aware of it, and liked him the more.

Realizing the young composer's enormous potential, Barrault meanwhile named Boulez his musical director. So began (1946) a form of collaboration which can still be seen to work with magical effect on certain concerts given by the Ensemble InterContemporain . . . At

24 Jean-Louis Barrault (born 1910) and Madeleine Renaud (born 1900): a famous theatrical couple who left the Comédie-Française to found their own company; this was established first in the Théâtre de Marigny (1946–56), then in the Théâtre de l'Odéon (1958–68), and lastly in the Théâtre d'Orsay – before returning to the Champs-Elysées and its present home in the Théâtre du Rond-Point.
25 Grand Marigny/Petit Marigny: the Théâtre du Grand Marigny is situated on the Champs-Elysées; it opened in 1925.

twenty-one, Boulez was not only freed from all material worries but, more importantly, was able to make contact with the craft of the working musician in all its aspects: arranging, transcribing, rehearsing, conducting, travelling, planning and organizing. He could be seen conducting the music of Honegger, but also that of Sauget (which he hates), of Poulenc or Auric (to which he is indifferent) – even of Tchaikovsky or Offenbach. He bestowed equal care on all, assiduously debunking the notion of the legendary conductor figure: 'I generally arranged ten or twelve minutes of music, mostly fanfares or something of the kind; and occasionally there was a half-hour mime show. Although this meant I went to the theatre every evening, it left the day free for my own work.'[26] In fact, Boulez was beginning to compose a lot, though not for Barrault (apart from the incidental music to the *Oresteia* of Aeschylus in 1955).

So from 1946 to 1956 he was either in the pit at the Marigny or on tour, bringing to every undertaking the same rigorously disciplined approach he was later to apply to more elevated projects. It is essential for a composer to have a practical apprenticeship of this kind, in order to balance his more abstract intellectual inclinations; this was something else he owed to Barrault.

He got on well with the musicians, but was by no means easy-going. Theatre music is notorious for being badly performed, particularly from the rhythmic point of view; in 1981, Boulez gave a concert performance of Mahler's *Lied von der Erde* with an opera orchestra that had recently played the work for the ballet, and found the situation unchanged in this respect. At twenty, he was neither patient nor prepared to adopt a resigned attitude: he would beat time violently on the shoulders of perpetual offenders, and rumour has it that the furnishings of the pit once suffered at the hands of the enraged composer.

THE ROAD TO FREEDOM

At the time of the Liberation, Parisian musical life was not without paradox. In the midst of its procession of horrors, the German occupation by no means signalled the cessation, or even a curtailment, of cultural life – rather the reverse. 'The theatres were full', Boulez notes. 'People were unable to travel, so everyone rushed to the concert halls; I even had difficulty getting in to a concert given by my own professor. In fact, the Germans brought high culture to France.' This was a dangerous state-

26 Peyser, op. cit., p. 52.

ment: many musicians exasperated by the shallowness of easy-going artistic practice in France were thrown off balance by German musical tradition, particularly between the two wars – Alfred Cortot was just one such casualty. For younger musicians, Germany was certainly the enemy – but an enemy which succeeded devilishly well in the domain it held most dear. The ideal would have been to introduce into France some of the essential seriousness traditional to the music of the Germanic countries in order to wipe out both the frivolity (of Les Six) and the tepid humanism (of Jeune France) characteristic of certain French music, before turning against the wretched inspirers, who, with their vilification of Mahler, the Second Viennese School and others, had attempted to stifle the very creativity they had unknowingly introduced.

Thanks to Darius Milhaud, Schoenberg had certainly been played in France this side of 1925, but he had never been accepted as part of the musical establishment. On his way into exile in 1933, he had merely passed through France; nevertheless, he took the opportunity during his brief stay to return to the Jewish faith. Ostensibly, the die was cast: atonality, serialism and dodecaphony were already considered *passé*, and unlikely ever to find a following in France.

Little more was known of the work of other pioneers – of the more demanding scores of Bartók, of Varèse or the best Stravinsky, or for that matter, Ives: Paris had become the province of the world. There was a musical intelligentsia, of course, but that now centred around Nadia Boulanger, an exceptional musician and a very effective teacher who made her coterie the rallying-point for Stravinskyan neo-classicism.

Perhaps this makes it easier to understand the upset caused by the (literally) 'open-necked' teaching of an Olivier Messiaen or by the innovative strictness of a Leibowitz. An apprentice musician needs to learn from both the radical and the reactionary beliefs of such teachers, and later, to detach himself from their influence. Understandably then, Boulez was to experience an abiding sense of musical isolation, intensified by the relative mundanity of his daily life. This was the price to be paid for an essential freedom.

CHAPTER THREE

The Lyric Age

(1946–50)

'Become what you are.'
André Gide

It has become something of a long-standing cliché to accept that Boulez's musical trajectory – starting with an austere strictness inherited from Schoenberg and more especially from Webern – was later (from around the time of *Le Marteau sans maître*) to be amended in favour of a more seductive sound and an ever-increasing formal flexibility. Quite apart from the fact that this so-called evolution gives a misleading impression of Boulez's present-day approach (*Répons* is not really the result of a more relaxed attitude), the cliché can easily be disproved: Boulez's early works have a marked lyricism and an almost ultra-romantic vehemence, while the period from 1950 to 1952 is like a severe interlude, effectively brought to an end by *Le Marteau sans maître*.

This widespread misunderstanding of the perspective stems from the fact that – with the exception of the Second Sonata – the main works of the first period are now rarely played. It is true that the technical difficulty of these works, together with Boulez's predilection for revising, or even withdrawing them, has rendered them less accessible: they remain like diamonds in a glass case, with a certain aura of mystery.

THE FIRST SONATA FOR PIANO

Before his regular job with Barrault, Boulez the virtuoso ondes martenot player accepted free-lance work wherever he could find it, and not only at the Folies-Bergères. This was how he came to meet Maurice Martenot who organized a musical evening in the winter of 1946, at which Boulez himself gave the first performance of his First Piano Sonata. Among those present were the composers Nicholas Nabokov[1] and Virgil Thompson, and the conductor Roger Désormière (who was later to become Boulez's esteemed friend).

This was not exactly the first work by Boulez. He had already composed a Quartet for ondes martenot (afterwards rewritten as a Sonata for two pianos), a set of Variations for piano left hand, the *Notations* for piano dedicated to Serge Nigg (which were later to give rise to an orchestral work) and the *Trois Psalmodies* already mentioned. These received their first performance on 12 February 1945, when Yvette Grimaud recorded them for the radio, despite the fact that the composer had by then disowned the work: 'At the time I wrote the *Trois Psalmodies* I did not even know that serial music existed – even though I clearly sensed the need for it. Today, I just want to forget that these pieces were ever written; they have never been published, and never will be – at least not with my permission.'[2]

In 1946, it was again Yvette Grimaud who was the first to play the First Sonata in public following the private première given by the composer. Composed conjointly with the *Sonatine* (see below), this was the first important work by Boulez to be heard in Paris. One can imagine the astonishment produced by this relatively short work whose virtuosity, particularly that of the second movement, always makes such a strong impression. If one considers contemporary works in this genre, for example, Prokofiev's Seventh Sonata (1947), or the Sonata by Dutilleux (1946–8), one can appreciate the distance separating the aesthetics of the music of the young Boulez from those of even the most advanced practitioners of the time.

A description of the work's fundamental ideas will be given later. I shall here concentrate on the kind of thinking on which it is apparently based. Traditional sonatas are principally concerned with conflict, arising from the juxtaposition of contrasting themes, tonalities and movements. Though manifestly different in kind, the First Sonata of Boulez exploits similar tensions, through its two contrasted movements, the dual aspect of

---

1 American composer (1903–78) of Russian origin, pupil of Busoni; as secretary general to the Congress for Cultural Freedom he organized a twentieth-century music festival (1952) which included the first performance of *Structure 1a*.
2 Goléa, op. cit., p. 20.

its dodecaphonic series, its two-note motifs, two kinds of writing (strict and free), two tempos (slow and fast), and so on.

THE *SONATINE* FOR FLUTE AND PIANO

Though it predates the First Sonata, the *Sonatine* for flute and piano became known much later: after a more or less private first performance in Brussels in 1947 (by the flautist Jan van Boterdael and the pianist Marcelle Mercenier), it was not until 1957 in Darmstadt that the marvellous Severino Gazelloni and David Tudor were publicly to reveal this youthful work by the leader of the European avant garde. Afficionados of serialism were astounded by it.

Within a formal design adopted and interpreted by Schoenberg (in *Pelléas*, the First String Quartet and the *Chamber Symphony*, where the separate sections of a whole sonata are encapsulated within the framework of a single sonata-form movement), the *Sonatine* is another example of the combination of deliberation and exuberance which marks all great works. Serialism is here strict and more personal by turn. In essence, Boulez retains the notion of the series as a reservoir of motifs, intervals and functions from which he freely constructs both his horizontal statements and his vertical attacks. Furthermore, he incorporates silence, as well as strongly contrasted dynamics, and exploits the difference between the monodic instrument and its polyphonic partner. The shrillness of the one is answered by the violent outpourings of the other which, according to the composer's own words on the work, 'is the very instrument of delirium'. The expressive markings (*Très librement* . . . *appuyé* . . . *très marqué* . . . *violent* . . . *précis et sans pédale, sans nuance* . . . *avec humour* . . . *subito* . . . *en éclaboussures* . . . *heurté et violent* . . . *de plus en plus tourbillonnant* . . . *arraché* . . . *très brusque* . . .) convey the emotional tenor of the work, and also offer some insight into the preoccupations of the volatile young composer.

RENE CHAR

It was then that Boulez encountered René Char, first his poetry, soon in person. Since three important works were to result (*Le Visage nuptial, Le Soleil des eaux* and *Le Marteau sans maître*), Char is clearly a crucial figure in the composer's artistic development.

René Char was born in 1907, one short generation before Boulez, and spent his childhood in Névons, the family estate in the Vaucluse countryside. Fatherless from the age of eleven, he grew up in an atmosphere of financial hardship. In 1924, he came across the early surrealist manifestos (the First Manifesto, in the review *La Révolution surréaliste*) and became a camp follower of the movement he was to join formally in 1929. That same year, he published his first collection of poems (little of his earlier work has survived). Entitled *Arsenal*, this included 'Bel édifice et les pressentiments', later to be used by Boulez in movements 5 and 9 of *Le Marteau sans maître*. Char then received a visit from Paul Eluard, met André Breton in Paris, and went to Spain to see Salvador Dali. He had a hand in founding the review *Le Surréalisme au service de la révolution* in 1933, but grew away from the movement after 1934. In the interim, he published numerous poems of a surrealist kind, such as 'L'Action de la justice est éteinte' (which gave Boulez 'L'Artisanat furieux' for movement 3 of *Marteau*) in 1931, and in 1932 'Poèmes militants' (which contained 'Bourreaux de solitude', movement 6 of *Marteau*).[3]

The pre-war years were marked by physical and moral struggle against the menacing forces of Fascism in France, and Char fought with his literary fists against the leagues of the extreme right in 'Chien andalou' (1931). It was in 1938 that he finished *Le Visage nuptial*, a sequence of five lyric poems entitled 'Conduite', 'Gravité', 'Le Visage nuptial', 'Evadné' and 'Post-Scriptum'. First published in *Cahiers d'art* in 1944, the cycle was reprinted in the collection *Seuls demeurent*, published by Gallimard in February 1945, before being included in the still larger collection, *Fureur et mystère*, brought out by the same publisher in 1948.

Written after the war, *Le Soleil des eaux* was prompted by the poet's belief in the need to struggle against the invader (no longer the German, but a similarly alien invasion of the rights of the fishermen and the inhabitants of the little village of Isle-sur-Sorgue)[4] and by his love of nature in its unique capacity to persuade, even to enable, man to stand up to adversity. Written in 1946, this 'Spectacle pour une toile de pêcheur'[5] was produced for the radio by Alain Trutat, who enlisted the services of the almost unknown Pierre Boulez to write the music. Boulez did so, and the radio work was first broadcast in April 1947. The

3 *Le Marteau sans maître* is the title of a collection published by Editions Surréalistes in July 1934 and which, among others, includes 'Arsenal', 'L'Action de la justice est éteinte' and the 'Poèmes militants'.
4 A small area in the Vaucluse, on the river La Sorgue; its 13,000 inhabitants are known as Les Ilois.
5 Char's subtitle indicates the simplicity of a décor provided by the sails of fishing boats.

composer then salvaged part of the music and, taking two Char poems that had nothing directly to do with the work as it stood ('Complainte du lézard amoureux' and 'La Sorgue', which he already knew from the collection *Les Martineaux*, published in 1950), he started to set 'La Sorgue' from scratch, and grouped the two under the heading of *Le Soleil des eaux*.

The chronology of Char's three groups of poems is by no means identical to that of the three works by Boulez. It is difficult to explain in a few words what it was that attracted Boulez to three rather different periods of the poet's productivity. His verse has been described as 'solar', even 'sultry':[6] rock-hard and resolute, it is expressed in words of strength and violence that roll off the tongue. That is very true, but it explains little. Often questioned about this poetic encounter, Boulez always replies in one sentence: what he found most important in Char was the extreme condensation of his images – a whole world reduced to a single word or phrase. This is certainly true of *Le Marteau sans maître*, less so of *Le Soleil des eaux* (which leans towards the incantatory in 'La Sorgue'), and only partially true of *Le Visage nuptial*, which opts for a form of rhetoric. It is by examining the texts of the poems themselves that the reader will get an idea of Char's world, or at least that part of it that Boulez makes use of. There is a fine article by Boulez which was printed in the daily newspaper *Libération*,[7] and written to mark the publication of Char's complete works in *Pléiade*. In it, Boulez stresses the immediacy of his first encounter with Char at the age of twenty-one. This is the complete text:

It often happens that the discoveries crucial to one's own definitive character catch one unawares, taking one's breath away; they cause irreparable havoc – needed and even longed-for at the same time as they lash out at you. It is impossible to imagine this catastrophe occurring at any time other than when you least expect it. Without paying much attention, you gaze idly at some poems on the page of a newspaper, and suddenly, you recognize yourself: there, in front of you, this illuminating paragraph seems simultaneously to take possession of you and to increase your potential, your grasp and your power beyond anything you had dreamed possible.

This form of expression relates to you without possible compromise; it questions you in the depths of your innermost being and yet reveals nothing of which you were not already aware: it shows you as you are, transmutes you into an integral identity of your own. I was responsible to it before knowing it: the knowledge made me responsible to myself and to my as yet undefined self. One may well find the time to specify these affinities with more reflective hindsight, but

6 By Boulez himself, *Conversations with Célestin Deliège*, p. 43.
7 24 June 1983.

this explosion is followed by an inner silence which expands beyond all expectation, then by an irrepressible and violent force hurling you beyond limits which no longer seem acceptable. How rarely are face-to-face encounters capable of unleashing such affinities!

What more priceless gift is there than this involuntary upheaval! It teaches you the fundamental requirements, it imprints within you a precision and an integrity, it upsets your internal compass points and turns them upside down; it does not subjugate, but liberates a wild, joyous energy intoxicated with its new existence. Certainly, all this is juvenile – but that is how it has to be! Time for reflection will be here soon enough – because this emotional upheaval, once provoked by an outside agency, has now to be sought only within yourself.

But there remains a strong signal from this remote transmitter which reaches you through electric impulses in the brain: confidence and a feeling of unity renewed by the silent and sovereign pact of an undertaking which develops and increases. The relationship is no longer as dazzling as it was at first, nor can one expect it to be; but it is refined and transformed into a profound consensus, unrelated to any particular instant. Proof is superfluous; this presence can be detected anywhere and everywhere. The relationship is imperceptibly transformed: there is a certain electric impulse at the centre of your own abundant proliferation. No, this is not two narrations for a time superposed, neither is it a graft or an osmosis, nor even a carrier wave. It is much more like a continuing contravention of limits and of substance.

The final paragraph is addressed to Char himself. Happy the ageing poet who can be restored to the world by inspiring such free and affectionate reverence from a richly gifted junior. Mallarmé was to be the poet of adulthood, when Siegfried was prepared to become master of his destiny: Char is the poet of the twenty-one-year-old hero, bounding into the forest in search of himself.

LE VISAGE NUPTIAL

Taken at face value, Le Visage nuptial is a parable of love. Its five formants describe an almost operatic episode: the anxious awaiting ('Conduite'), the spiritual meditation and inner concentration on the beloved ('Gravité'), the heady sharing of the encounter ('Le Visage nuptial'), the serene, already somewhat detached calm that ensues ('Evadné'), and finally, the loneliness that inevitably returns ('Post-Scriptum'). This progression, representing the first level of poetic meaning, is translated by Boulez into a work lasting about half an hour and comprising five sections of unequal length.

But before coming to the music, it might be as well to go a little further into the text of the poem. I do not myself agree with the hypothesis put forward by one of the most discerning of Char's scholarly commentators, who sees the symbolism of *Le Visage nuptial* as reflecting 'the marriage between the poet and the poem'.[8] Thus interpreted, it is in fact all too easy to see Boulez's choice of Char's poem as the first trace of an attitude that would eventually lead him quite naturally to Mallarmé. However, it seems to me that there is nothing in Char's text to justify this interpretation. The text is hardly lucid. *Le Visage nuptial* contains various interrelated images, sometimes reflecting an erotic, almost crudely stated reality, sometimes the naturalistic symbols which pervade all Char's work and which nourish, fertilize and finally staunch the flow of the expression of love. If every poetic undertaking is an attempt to establish a link between the intimate minutiae of the self, and the surrounding world, whether that of a starlit night, or of human communication, then the poetry of Char would seem to be founded upon the purest classical tradition.

The history of the work falls into two distinct stages. In its early form (1946) it was scored for soprano and contralto soloists, two ondes martenot, piano and percussion. It may be said in passing that this scoring, unchanged, might well have allowed the work to figure more regularly in concert programmes than it does in its enlarged version, even that the original score was more in keeping with the intimate character of the work and its text. The fact remains that Boulez withdrew the first version and, between 1951 and 1952, re-cast the work for the same two soloists, adding a chorus of female voices and substituting a large orchestra. It was in this form that the work was first performed in 1957.[9]

1 'Conduite'. In a *mezza voce* introduction, the chamber orchestral colouring derives from subdivisions affecting almost the whole of the large orchestra. The music is preparatory in feeling, almost in the manner of an improvisation, and the normal singing voice is used. Serial statements in this movement are fragmented into cells and short motifs, only rarely appearing as an organized whole – as, for instance, towards the conclusion, where the voice (unaccompanied except for a few unobtrusive punctuations from a Chinese cymbal and a cello harmonic) pronounces the invocatory 'O Bien-aimée'.

2 'Gravité'. Subtitled 'the entombed', this movement is slower and longer than the preceding one, with reduced orchestration and a percussion group whose emphasis is more on resonance (xylophone, vibraphone)

8 Mary Ann Caws, *L'Œuvre filante de René Char*, Paris, Nizet, 1981, p. 62.
9 The *Pléiade* edition wrongly gives 1956.

than on hammered, tapped or stroked sounds. The poem still tells of waiting, but with an anticipation exacerbated by an almost painful – occasionally feverish – desire. The erotic imagery of Char's text led the composer towards a greater complexity, allowing him to be intentionally cryptic. This movement includes quarter-tones, here used by Boulez for the first time to obfuscate the sound. In the same way, the voice varies its expression from speech to song, in imitation (almost inevitable, at the time) of Berg. The superposition of identical statements sung in different ways is used to increase the density of the musical sound still further, and the varied enunciation of the chorus (from humming to articulated words) provides an admirable counterpoint to the solo line.

3 'Le Visage nuptial'. This eponymous central movement of the work is the longest and the most highly charged: a vivid realization of a successfully consummated love. Near the beginning, a beautiful vocalise for the sopranos and altos of the chorus on the words 'J'aime' defines the preoccupation central to the movement as a whole. The rapturous quality of the scoring explodes in a huge final *crescendo* – beyond the expression of speech for either chorus or soloists.

4 'Evadné'[10]. Here, simple speech is employed throughout. The writing excludes the real soloists, and replaces them with a group of five sopranos and five altos drawn from the chorus, who are required to murmur rather than sing. The movement outlines the different roles of the two processes at work here: the exterior world (of the orchestra) versus the interior (of the solo voices).

5 'Post-Scriptum'. This is the conclusion, in which loneliness returns. Soloists and chorus are again present, but now supported by an orchestra reduced to strings and percussion. The sundering of the couple and the inevitable return of solitude is underlined by some inspired orchestration, fuller than in the first movement. The strict canon employed here demonstrates a 'principle of reality' which the violently subjective, hallucinatory state of the preceding episodes seemed designed to avoid. Again, the use of quarter-tones plays a part in the progressively more evanescent quality defining the harmonic spectrum of the movement. This most eloquent of the composer's works ends with the words 'Ecartez-vous de moi, qui patiente sans bouche.'

---

10 Greek mythology has preserved two Evadne figures. One is a character from the mythology of Asia minor: the wife of Kapaneos, one of the 'Seven against Thebes', she threw

THE FIRST PERFORMANCE OF *LE VISAGE NUPTIAL*

The work was given its first performance on 4 December 1957, as part of the *Musik der Zeit* series in Cologne. The great Hermann Scherchen had been engaged as conductor but, after seeing how well Boulez coped with coaching the chorus, he felt compelled to ask the composer to direct his own work. This was the first time that Boulez had conducted a symphony orchestra: the evening was effectively to announce the betrothal of Boulez to the world of orchestral performance.

There was a large audience, the orchestra were captivated, and the occasion was a resounding success. Such French critics as had bothered to make the journey discovered both an early work by a now famous composer and an unusually civilized musical environment which they found delightful: they enjoyed the novelty of observing rehearsals in the surroundings of a large radio station. Antoine Goléa notes that 'Boulez directed the work with incredible precision, but also with all the consuming passion that it demands', – and he goes on to praise the performance of the soprano Ilona Steingruber (who had sung in the first performance of Webern's *Cantata II* in 1950). Claude Rostand placed the work in relation to its period: 'The sumptuous instrumental and vocal textures of *Le Visage nuptial* are certainly very different from the extremely spare and refined music Monsieur Boulez is writing today', and he described the vast musical outpourings of the new work by citing the name of Richard Strauss.

Until now, the fate of the work has been a curious one. It appears that the first performance of the earlier version should have been given by Roger Désormière in 1952, but he fell ill; the second version then had to wait six years for its first performance, so that what was heard in 1957 was a work anchored to the Boulez of more than ten years earlier. It is now seldom performed – certainly not by Boulez, who declares himself dissatisfied with the orchestration. 'At the time, I had no orchestral experience', he often said later. It was programmed for the 1981 Paris Autumn Festival, and Boulez started rehearsals but then gave up for the same reasons. He then let it be understood that, as soon as *Répons* was finished, he would at last make the necessary revisions. (The first complete performance of this revised version was finally given at the Royal Festival Hall in London on 23 November 1989 by Phyllis Bryn-Julson, Elisabeth Lawrence and the BBC Symphony Orchestra, conducted by the composer.)

herself into a blazing fire in pursuit of her beloved spouse. The other Evadne was the daughter of Poseidon, beloved of Apollo.

THE SECOND SONATA FOR PIANO

One masterpiece was closely followed by another, for in 1948, Boulez wrote his Second Sonata, unquestionably one of his finest works. I have devoted considerable space to this milestone of the twentieth-century piano repertoire (see pp. 240 ff.), if only because there are so few pianists willing, or technically equipped, to measure themselves against it. A work whose lineage can be traced from late Beethoven (especially Op. 106), through Liszt (in *Mazeppa* rather than the Sonata), and to the early works of Boulez himself (in the *Sonatine* and the First Sonata), the Second Sonata gives the deceptive impression of adopting a relatively conventional articulation in the clear design of its four movements. This decision seemed to relieve Boulez of the need to justify form in relation to style, and the writing is consequently much freer. A completely personal kind of serialism prevails here, as he explained to Goléa: 'This Sonata is a blunt denunciation of the dodecaphonic starting point and of the formulae deriving from it. No initial series are to be found here,[11] either on the level of pitch or that of rhythm; relatively brief note cells now serve to support true rhythmic themes, here worked and developed according to the principles expounded by Messiaen.'[12] Let me follow Boulez's remark by saying that the strict writing in the Sonata is in no way at odds with its volatile moods which seem to mirror the composer's own personality, in its admixture of aggression, fury and exuberance, ultra-sensibility, modesty and charm.

There are three particularly outstanding moments in this Sonata. The first occurs at the beginning, in the form of an outburst that seems to seize hold of the keyboard, changing its very nature, thrashing it in every direction and dominating it with a passionate intensity. As if taken by surprise, the piano at first resists, but soon yields to a second theme in steady chords, which Boulez likens to the second subject of Beethoven's *Waldstein* Sonata.

My second example is from the slow movement. After the somewhat dry, almost ironic, exposition of an undecorated initial proposition, a commentary develops – a 'trope', as Boulez calls it, rather than a variation of a theme. This seems to unfold spontaneously as the movement progresses. Here, the piano is tamed, open to exploration. Unexpected sonorities, often widely contrasted in register and dynamics, seem strikingly inevitable. The quest continues – an ancient quest for a strange

11 This is not right; see p. 242.
12 Goléa, op. cit., p. 82.

and hitherto unknown region: the Sonata also lends itself to an erotic reading. Occasionally, progress comes to a halt; a pause acts as a landmark, then secondary 'troping' develops, differing in dynamic intensity, pace and register from what has gone before. Another pause, and the progress resumes. A sense of ineluctable conclusion, capable of producing a powerful elation in the listener, will only be experienced when one is thoroughly familiar with the work.

And finally, to the last page of the Sonata, where Boulez has dispensed with all superfluous indications, as if in a postscript. The fugue has done its work and the composer is alone with his keyboard. The tempo is fractured, time interiorized. This page functions not only as a coda to the movement but as a conclusion to the work as a whole. A group of four notes is repeated six times, to form a cryptogram of significance only to the composer. What matters to the listener is that this is the final stage of an immense reflection. Here the piano is familiar, unobtrusive, always correct; it speaks in an undertone, letting silence gradually encroach upon space in the certainty that words are no longer needed.

The Second Sonata was by no means received with universal acclaim, as Hélène Jourdan-Morhange's[13] review (*Ce Soir*, 11 May 1950) testifies:

I do not understand it. I am one of those listeners who still craves what the Greek philosophers called 'the moral strength of music'. It was Aristotle who noted the relaxation of facial expressions when a great work was being played. The audience the other evening scarcely radiated well-being – it was in turmoil. Anger and laughter were on the verge of erupting, but the listeners were unusually polite since, after this half-hour of boredom or revolt they did not even whistle; in this respect they were much more restrained than Boulez's young followers, who noisily left the hall as music returned with Schumann – at the hands of two charming pianists, Jacqueline Bonneau and Geneviève Joy.[14]

THE YOUNG COMPOSER IN PARIS

Boulez was now approaching his twenty-fifth year and, at an age when others were still students, he was his own master, and soon to become recognized by some of his peers. He lived alone in the rue Beautreillis, playing host to illustrious visitors, like Cage, launching the Domaine

13 Musicologist (1888–1961), violin pupil of Enesco, friend and pupil of Ravel, writer of numerous articles.
14 Jacqueline Bonneau (born 1917) and Geneviève Joy (born 1919): famous two-piano duo, active between 1945 and 1970; Geneviève Joy, a pupil of Yves Nat, later married the composer Henri Dutilleux.

musical (1954), and above all, writing the great masterpieces of the period.

Each evening, Boulez worked with Barrault, broadening his own theatrical experience and making many friends, including Claudel (with whom he was to enjoy a lasting intellectual relationship). Boulez particularly enjoyed the company's foreign tours, although they meant that he was rarely able to attend first performances of his works – except when he was, of necessity, involved as a performer (a somewhat surprising state of affairs which he now dismisses as the inevitable consequence of his engagements with Barrault).

These commitments were rather restricting, and effectively prevented him from taking part in Parisian musical life – for which in any case he felt no particular enthusiasm. When I asked him whether he went to concerts at the time, he replied: 'I was busy in the evenings with Barrault.' However, he attended all possible orchestral rehearsals, especially those of the Orchestre National – whose conductor, Désormière, was soon to become a respected friend.

Boulez was more interested in the plastic arts and in literature than in the music on offer from the Parisian musical establishment. As always with him, his reactions to aesthetic encounters were lightning fast and decisive: 'The first time I saw a picture by Klee I was absolutely fascinated by the power of his invention – and many things crumbled to dust at a single stroke' he said to Célestin Deliège,[15] adding that, in 1947, he had discovered Klee, Kandinsky and Mondrian, and 'immediately sensed that these were three absolutely fundamental figures in present day painting'. In 1949, there was a Joyce exhibition at La Hune, the famous bookshop in the Place Saint-Germain des Près, and this fired him with enthusiasm because with Joyce 'technique and narration are one and the same thing', and because Joyce uses a different narrative technique specific to each chapter.[16] Boulez read *Ulysses*, as well as *The Castle* by Kafka – of which he spoke enthusiastically in a letter to Yvette Grimaud. In another letter dating from the summer of 1948, he listed his summer's reading, 'higgledy-piggledy, but in chronological order: Dostoevsky, Nerval, Gogol, Rimbaud, Lautremont, Kleist, etc . . .'

The summers were usually spent with his family, either in Montbrison, or in the Moravan, or the Haute-Savoie (where 'the hotel was a hideously petit-bourgeois gathering of idiots'). Summer was always the time for a

15 *Conversations with Célestin Deliège*, p. 36.
16 Peyser, op. cit., p. 80.

renewal of resources, expressed in terms of a genuine love of nature and of a distaste for the 'artificial atmosphere' of Parisian life.

He also read scores, including Beethoven's *Missa Solemnis*, in which the 'awe-inspiring power of a supreme being' fascinated him. And he continues: 'Coming face to face with this terrifying Mass proved the downfall of some of my all too limited conceptions though I need hardly say that the religious standpoint had nothing to do with it.'

Yvette Grimaud, the heroic, enthusiastic and talented performer of his piano works during this period,[17] was one of the quite small circle of Boulez's friends – those who noisily and with a guilty lack of interest in Schumann left the hall of the Ecole Normale after she had played the Second Sonata. True, this circle was to see some changes. In the beginning it consisted of his one-time fellow-students from the Conservatoire: Serge Nigg, Antoine Duhamel,[18] André Casanova[19] and Jean-Louis Martinet. Then, as his own musical principles began to crystallize, the musicians tended to drift away – sometimes after violent disagreements, from which Boulez has never retracted. The 'family' group then made way for artists and writers; these included the painter Bernard Saby, later to design the programme covers for the Domaine musical and who meanwhile discussed Webern at length with Boulez; the writer Armand Gatti who, before turning to theatrical militancy, provided Boulez with the text for a 12-part chorus, *Oubli signal lapidé* (commissioned by Marcel Couraud,[20] composed, and then withdrawn from circulation); the writer Pierre Joffroy, author of a strange book on a repentant Christian SS man, *Un espion pour Dieu*; Paule Thévenin,[21] a friend from the early days and still a loyal supporter, who made him read Artaud; and Pierre Souvchinsky,[22] who was older than the others, and who helped the composer enormously

17 *Notations* and *Psalmodies* (dedicated to Yvette Grimaud) at the Tryptique, 12 February 1945; First Sonata, RTF, 1946; Second Sonata in the concert hall of the Ecole Normale de Musique, 29 April 1950.
18 Composer (born 1925), son of the writer Georges Duhamel and pupil of Leibowitz, his interests lean towards music theatre and the cinema; he is director of a music school in Villeurbanne.
19 Composer (born 1919) and an early disciple of Leibowitz.
20 Choral conductor (1912–85), founder of the vocal ensemble which bears his name and which gave many first performances of modern works between 1944 and 1954.
21 Writer, specialist on Artaud; it was she who collected the Boulez articles which make up *Notes of an Apprenticeship*.
22 Musicologist (1892–1985) of Russian origin, friend of Stravinsky, then of Boulez – particularly with regard to the Domaine musical; editor of the collection *Domaine musical* published by Rocher.

in various undertakings (see chapters 4 and 5). The family circle was narrow, but relatively secure, and united by their common experience of adversities encountered in the outside world.

Despite these friendships, Boulez's complete musical isolation must again be emphasized here. This arose less from the criticism his works encountered than from a creative loneliness: he was the only one of his stature amongst his contemporaries. He did not even have the support of Messiaen – whom he had deeply offended by referring to the latter's *Trois petites liturgies* as 'brothel music', and remarking that the Turangalîla Symphony made him 'vomit' (in both instances because of the ondes martenot!); when the opinion is expressed in less bucolic terms it becomes: 'Messiaen does not compose, he juxtaposes.'[23] As we have seen, dealings with colleagues of his own generation were no easier – the distance between them was just too great. Boulez was in fact 'the first and the only' composer of his generation – as Maurice Le Roux noted. Jean Barraqué could perhaps have claimed a place on the same level had he not been in some way too musically close to Boulez; the collision between these two stars was to produce strong but ultimately sterile sparks.

BOULEZ THE WRITER

The composer's first important writings date from this period. While Boulez is neither a musicologist nor a true theoretician (*Boulez on Music Today* is an unfinished project*), nor yet a musical historian, his essays and other articles have created what amounts to a specific genre that has, in turn, inspired the writing practices of musicologists themselves. His writings show an acute awareness, at once subjective and informatory as to the future of music in the twentieth century. Boulez writes for reasons that are alternately polemical and intellectual: because of his desire to wage war upon the animosity and musical philistinism to be found in professional circles, and because writing was a parallel creative activity to composition, offering a mirror – a kind of testing-ground – for the concepts he was seeking to define. These early essays also attest to his lifelong determination to teach the French about music.

23 He was to say the same thing about Varèse.
*   Since continued – albeit on a less technical level, in a series of lectures on form delivered at the Collège de France between 1978 and 1988 and published under the title of *Jalons (pour une décennie)*, Paris, Christian Bourgois, 1989.

'PROPOSITIONS'

'Propositions'[24] was written in 1948 for the specialist review *Polyphonie*, and it takes stock of Boulez's rhythmical preoccupations following *Le Visage nuptial*, the *Sonatine*, the recently composed Second Sonata, and even the famous Symphony (since lost, but mentioned and even illustrated in the article). Boulez here discusses the question of how to establish a rhythmic organization as comprehensively worked out as the organization of pitch in the dodecaphonic system.

After having trapped the unfortunate Leibowitz in an obscure argument, Boulez points out the new rhythmic preoccupations of some of the twentieth-century classics. Again taking the example of Stravinsky as his starting point, he outlines his own future analysis of *The Rite of Spring* by pointing out the various rhythmic 'terracings' at the beginning of the 'Sacrificial Dance'. He notes Bartók's use of central European folk music rhythms and its influence in breaking the rigidity of the classical metric system, and dismisses Jolivet as a monodist bent on exploiting irrational rhythms such as the triplet. It seems to Boulez that Messiaen's most valuable contribution to this question lies in his exploitation of a rhythmic grammar based on the notion of added values (of which the dotted note in classical music is an embryonic example) as applied to the notes of a given motif. Boulez ends this panoramic assessment by underlining his opinion that, compared to Webern, the rhythmic writing of Schoenberg and Berg[25] is superficial in its exaggerated reverence for classical models.

Boulez then proceeds to analyse some of his own recent works – though in such a way as to exclude the uninitiated. He describes rhythmic refinements far too complex to be appreciated by the ear, and which would seem to justify his reputation as a 'blackboard musician', were it not for the statement of his aesthetic preoccupations with which the article ends: 'Why try for such complexity? In order to match the expressive variety of dodecaphony with an equally atonal *rhythmical* element.' And he emphasizes his opinion that, in this respect, Varèse's development of rhythm is far too limited as a result of its attachment to an outworn polyphony.

Was this a paradox? As if to forestall the accusation mentioned above,

24 *Notes of an Apprenticeship*, pp. 61–71.
25 Boulez did not at the time seem much in sympathy with an idea like that of Berg's *Hauptrythmus*, nor with the relationships that may be established between rhythmic and harmonic structures – as for instance in *Wozzeck* (the first of the two B flats in Act III, scenes 2 and 3). It was Michel Fano who, in 1952, was to draw attention to the prodigious richness of Berg's score in this respect.

Boulez then makes a hyper-expressionist declaration of personal faith: 'I have my own reason for giving so important a place to the rhythmic phenomenon. I feel that music ought to be emotionally exciting, seductive, and overwhelmingly relevant – along the lines suggested by Antonin Artaud, rather than in the sense of a mere ethnographical reconstitution of the image of civilizations more or less remote from our own.'

'INCIDENCES ACTUELLES DE BERG'
('PRESENT-DAY ENCOUNTERS WITH BERG')

Later that year, *Polyphonie* published the first of a series of historic articles on musical aesthetics. One after another, these Boulez essays were to prove invaluable to a whole generation of lovers of twentieth-century music – both as listening guides, and as a yardstick for assessing the great composers of the century (then scarcely known) within the historical context of musical development.

What he disliked at the time was surely the mixture of styles, the eclectic gestures, and exaggerated expressiveness. Later, he will be seen to revise his judgement. It seems likely, however, that this article reflects an essential part of Boulez's view of Berg – a view which revealed an emotional incompatibility only rarely to be found between Boulez and the two other Second Viennese composers, Webern and Schoenberg.

Written on the occasion of an exhibition of Austrian music in Paris, the article on Berg is all tactful restraint. Boulez pays homage to the composer of *Wozzeck* as an authorized member of the Second Viennese School, simply remarking on the quality and evident consistency of Berg's writing. He even goes so far as to salute the 'outstanding moments' to be found in the central trilogy of *Wozzeck*, the *Chamber Concerto* and the *Lyric Suite* – though mainly in order to underline the 'qualitative differences in musical material' to be found even in the midst of these works: the waltz in the first movement of the *Chamber Concerto*, the 'exasperating sentimentality' of the *trio estatico* from the *Lyric Suite*, or the banality of the military march in *Wozzeck*, not to mention the tango from the aria *Der Wein*, or the serial harmonization of the Bach chorale in the Violin Concerto – where he rejects the 'unacceptable hiatus' arising from the cross-fertilization of tonal and dodecaphonic systems.

What he disliked at the time was surely the mixture of styles, the eclectic gestures, and exaggerated expressiveness. Later, he will be seen to revise his judgement. It seems likely, however, that this article reflects an essential part of Boulez's view of Berg – a view which revealed an emotional incompatibility only rarely to be found between Boulez and the two other Second Viennese composers, Webern and Schoenberg.

I have remarked elsewhere[26] that Boulez's attitude towards Berg at the time was dictated partly by a still embryonic knowledge of the latter's

26 Dominique Jameux, *Alban Berg*, Paris, Le Seuil, 1980, p. 7.

output, but above all by the tactical need to counter the attempts made by the more traditionally minded contemporary musicians to re-establish the image of Berg as the most approachable of the Second Viennese composers, and the one most obviously attached to some form of romantic expression.

Much later, when he no longer felt obliged to attack him on stylistic grounds, Boulez was to discover the true Berg – initially through conducting his music: the adversary was then overcome. He could thereafter enjoy the complexity of Berg's writing and musical thought, his Proustian narrative art, and his sense of being 'in a labyrinth', with which Boulez could identify – even though he always seemed to maintain a certain distance from the emotional aspect of the Bergian musical spectrum.

'TRAJECTOIRES' ('TRAJECTORIES')

In the third article of this period, dating from 1949,[27] Boulez adopts the stance of 'professor of non-academic music' – a role he was to fulfil, at any rate in the eyes of the French public, for the next thirty-five years or so.

This provided a good opportunity to settle his account with modernism and modernity.[28] Subtitled 'Ravel, Stravinsky, Schoenberg', the article takes as its starting point the similar instrumentation of Ravel's *Trois Poèmes de Stéphane Mallarmé*, Stravinsky's *Trois Poésies de la lyrique japonaise*, and Schoenberg's *Pierrot lunaire* – works which, moreover, all contribute to the mythology of a twentieth-century musical renaissance. In this respect, the first two composers were influenced by the third. Boulez shows how the innovatory aspects of these works can conflict with the need to preserve an outmoded system – in this case, that of tonality. 'Within a still-coherent tonal system, there is an undercurrent of shock arising from its disintegration.' In 1912, Ravel's own discovery of Schoenbergian atonality (as described by Stravinsky!) led him into the snares of polytonality, or towards the hedonistic abyss of timbre.

Stravinsky's first reaction to the impact of *Pierrot lunaire* was one of repugnance: he did not hold with the romantic style of Schoenbergian melodrama and Boulez found it hard to disagree with him on this point. But 'having rejected the poetic aspects, he [Stravinsky] rejected the

27 *Contrepoint*, No. 6, 1949; in *Notes of an Apprenticeship*, pp. 242–67.
28 Modernism is here to be understood in the sense of fashionable, accessory – a deviation from true modernity.

technique', resulting in a simplistic style, incapable of providing the basis for a truly new language. (Boulez is here referring to *The Rite of Spring*, which demonstrates nothing more than 'a revolutionary reappraisal of rhythm'.) And he regards Stravinsky's neo-classical detour in the same negative light in which, before the war, Stravinsky himself would have dismissed Schoenberg.

This important article outlines a basic history of twentieth-century music, including that of Boulez himself. It deserves to be quoted in full, but I note only his denigration of Ravelian 'hedonism' and of Stravinsky's 'instrumental tics' (which Adorno calls 'piquancy'). Curiously, Boulez speaks of Wagner in relation to Mussorgsky, whom he regards as having 'demolished the whole bloated romanticism exercised by the man from Bayreuth',[29] and he refers to the 'staggering poetic beauty' of the Russian composer's music.

But the main interest of the article lies not so much in its presentation of Boulez's view of some of his illustrious predecessors as in its circumscription of the limits he attributes (in 1949) to the true modernity of Schoenberg – the composer he contrasts with them. Boulez's dialectic first praises Schoenberg for rejecting the mistaken solutions once favoured by his colleagues, and then criticizes him for subscribing to what was, by 1948, already an outdated concept.

He emphasizes that the counterpoint in *Pierrot lunaire* is of 'the most traditional, almost the most academic kind', noting that there is nothing here of the organic, almost 'uterine' relationship between language and structure. In this respect, Boulez's opinion has not altered. Webern's music went much further in this direction: speaking on an independent radio station in 1983[30] Boulez explained that, for him, Webern is like a diamond – not the diamond 'that is placed on the finger of an elegant woman', but one that is used to cut glass, admired for its incisive edge. Webern's serialism 'cuts'; it relates to the very architecture of a work, particularly its form, while Schoenberg's serialism is only an 'ultra-thematicism'; the series is nothing more than a theme,[31] and does not penetrate the sound-space as a whole. Hence Schoenberg's return to old forms – marches, minuets, waltzes, gigues, and so on – between the two

29 Today, recordings by Boulez of both *Boris* and *Tristan* make it possible to compare the extent of his commitment *vis-à-vis* the two works; he would seem to be stylistically closer to the music of the one, emotionally closer to the libretto of the other!
30 Conversation with Robert and Bruno Serrou, Radio Notre-Dame, 26 March 1983.
31 It is true, for instance, of the *Variations*, Op. 31.

wars: 'The novelty of the language itself has done nothing to change the mode of thought that preceded it.'

It is obviously very much a matter of 'Penser la musique aujourd'hui' (which became the simple yet powerful title of the book published in English as *Boulez on Music Today*). The article 'Trajectoires' comprises both a written criticism of Schoenbergian serialism – which Boulez was to develop in 'Schoenberg est mort' (1951) – illustrated with reference to his own Second Sonata and *Structures*, Book 1.

The literary Boulez wrote essentially for his own peers. The excellent specialist magazine *Polyphonie* published these authoritative guidelines, which were invaluable to contemporary composers. When these articles were collected together by Paule Thévenin in 1966, they seemed somewhat dated in the light of the composer's own evolution. Despite its poor sales, however, the anthology is masterly in presenting the quintessential Boulez.

LIVRE POUR QUATUOR

Two important works from the period from 1946–50 remain to be discussed. The first – *Le Soleil des eaux* – has already been mentioned and will be further examined later. The other – *Livre pour quatuor* – seems something of an enigma.

To start with, it was effectively withdrawn from circulation until very recently. It was written immediately after the Second Sonata (from which it borrows some of the material for its slow movements). In theory, it has six movements – movements I, II, III and V dating from 1948 and 1949, while movement VI was composed in 1959. But movement IV seems to exist only in the abstract: according to Boulez, it is to be a combination of movements I and II. The fact remains that it has never been played, and is not included in the score published by Heugel in 1960. Moreover, this score is unusual in that it does not entirely correspond with the only commercial recording of the work as played by the Parrenin Quartet – not only because the Parrenins omit the even numbered movements II, IV (obviously) and VI, but because in the course of rehearsals for a recording made at Baden-Baden in 1959 in full collaboration with Boulez himself, the players changed a lot of the more awkwardly written passages with the composer's blessing. He even asked Jacques Parrenin to leave him his copy of the score so that he could look at it again for himself. Similarly, it is difficult to be specific about the dates of a definitive first performance, since the work can be given with practically any number of movements.

To take things in order. It was between 1948 and 1949 that Boulez composed a work which he called *Livre pour quatuor*, not String Quartet. He had just read Mallarmé's 'Igitur', and it is possible that the idea of a 'Livre', with detachable, even permutatable pages was already taking shape in his mind. On the other hand, it seems that the concept of a book whose successive chapters would be even further enriched by the experience of preceding ones was already present; hence the idea of movement IV as the sum of movements I and II in *Livre pour quatuor*. (This idea was later applied to the Third Sonata.)

The earliest version of *Livre pour quatuor* has been available since 1949, when movement V was often played on its own by the Hamman Quartet in Germany. The Parrenins gave what was probably their first performance of it at a Domaine musical concert at the Petit-Marigny on 3 February 1956, when they played movements I (a and b) and II, though it was not announced in the programme. In 1959, at another Domaine concert, they again played the first three movements, and they recorded the odd-numbered movements I (a and b), III (a, b and c) and V on disc (see above). As the years went by, Boulez became convinced that the appalling difficulties of the writing presented a serious obstacle. In 1968, he began a version for string orchestra – of which only movements Ia and Ib are so far complete (see p. 149) – while the Alban Berg Quartet seem recently to have persuaded him also to revive the quartet version.

Boulez's first work without piano, *Livre pour quatuor* is inscribed as part of the history of Western quartet writing which – from Haydn to Berg's *Lyric Suite* – has always striven to produce maximum differentiation of timbre and instrumental gesture from within the extreme homogeneity of the string quartet sound. The various known movements of *Livre pour quatuor* allow for a variety of playing methods, both as regards attack (*col legno, pizzicato, sul ponticello*), and continuity.

The relationship between detached and sustained sounds is essential to the organization of the various contrasting sections of the work: the lyricism of Ia, the importance of silence and of small motifs in Ib, the presence of a cantus firmus in each voice in turn in IIIa, the relative opacity and the problems of both performance and audience accessibility in II, the density of texture and again of polyphony in IIIb (with its astonishingly abrupt end), the more concerted and developed character of IIIc, the flexible three-part counterpoint, punctuated by the *pizzicato* of the fourth instrument, in V – and so on.

All in all, the quartet vibrates with remarkable energy, even if its approach makes it one of Boulez's least communicative works. Its energy is often implicit rather than forcibly demonstrated in terms of an expressionist outburst: in comparison with the explosive ultra-romanticism of the Second Sonata, *Livre pour quatuor* assumes the unmistakably intimate character of chamber music.

THE FIRST PERFORMANCE OF *LE SOLEIL DES EAUX*

This period is brought to a close with a major work, *Le Soleil des eaux*, which started life in 1946 as incidental music (see p. 257) for a radio production. Having amassed material surplus to the broadcast, Boulez kept the title and constructed a completely new diptych around two of Char's poems.

Although somewhat cryptically connected (the first six notes of the series of the first movement are exactly the same, closely transposed, as the first six of the second movement), the two movements are very dissimilar – and it is this difference that makes them complementary.

The fourth, definitive version is scored for soprano soloist, mixed chorus, and orchestra. The first movement, 'Complainte du lézard amoureux', is set to fluid, almost nonchalant music, lingeringly reminiscent of the sonorities of Messiaen. A four-note melodic idea is prominent within the generally fragmented motivic texture of the writing. It is left to the voice to establish continuity through its ability to adapt both to an ornamental style ('Chardonneret, reprends ton vol / Et reviens à ton nid de laine') and to a soft-spoken percussiveness ('Tu n'es pas un caillou du ciel'). Despite its considerable rhythmic complexity and many problems of intonation, the movement gives the impression of an overall *rubato* perfectly in keeping with the ephemeral image of a natural world in which the lover can still bask in song.

'La Sorgue' has the effect of completely disrupting this serenity: biting, inflexible, vertical and harmonic, the second part of the work contrasts with the almost indolent tone of the opening movement. Here, the antagonistic struggle of the fishermen is expressed musically in terms of the energy of a determined minority that was closely in accord with Boulez's own moral outlook. If the argument now seems a purely ecological one, to Char it was a symbolic fable of the Resistance versus the occupying forces. Boulez, who certainly disapproved of the pollution of rivers, and even more strongly resented foreign oppression, was to transmute the rights of the struggle against these tangible realities into a Nietzschean parable of power and combat, thus presenting an ideological antiphony between the carefree existence of the first movement and the struggle for life of the second.

In 'La Sorgue' the sequence of the choral writing is in keeping with the atmosphere of the whole piece. It begins with the sopranos, 'bouche fermée', followed by the men's speaking voices (with the pitches at first approximately notated, later becoming more defined), then four-part writing (sometimes sung, sometimes spoken), and finally, four-part singing. The soprano solo enters late in the movement ('Il n'est de vent qui ne fléchisse'), and then continues with a passionate intensity. The work ends with a succession of four massive block chords, *tutti* and *fortissimo*, preceding the final *diminuendo*. The use of dislocated phrases and protracted syllables foreshadows the treatment of the voice in the *Improvisations* from *Pli selon pli*.

The second version of the work – *Soleil des eaux II* – is scored for three vocal soloists and chamber orchestra. Of extraordinary originality in the context of post-war France, it had an historic first performance marking Boulez's entry into official musical life. This was an entry made by the main door: the first concert version of the work was premièred by Roger Désormière and the RTF orchestra on 18 July 1950.

The event was memorable, as Maurice Le Roux recalls. The hall was not packed on this July evening – most Parisians were sunning themselves at the seaside – but nevertheless, an extraordinary tension reigned: it felt like some kind of enthronement. A small group of friends eased Boulez's pre-concert nerves by chanting: 'We're off to hear *Le Soleil des eaux*-. . . rmière!' (sic). The distinguished vocal cast included Irene Joachim, Joseph Peyron and Pierre Mollet, and the work had an immense public success, even though the French critics were conspicuous by their absence. It is, however, worth quoting the professional opinion of one Bernard Gavoty:[32]

I turn now to the performers of *Le Soleil des eaux*, and to them I say: 'Unfortunate victims of a capricious tyrant who has caused you to suffer without giving us the least pleasure in exchange for your heroic efforts! What then are you thinking about – you, Irene Joachim, Pierre Mollet and Joseph Peyron – as you stand there, armed with your resolutely unsingable scores?' Of Mélisande, of Pelléas or Fortunio?[33] I would like to believe it – just as I can imagine the taste of fresh water on the parched tongues of the damned! For my part, I reflect on the remarkable

32 Music critic (1908–81) who, under the name 'Clarendon', wrote for *Le Figaro*; lecturer to the JMF, incumbent organist at Saint-Louis des Invalides, author of books and articles on music.
33 By Messager.

gifts so unthinkingly squandered by a young mathematician, of so many useless blunders outside the realms of scientific truth. Pierre Boulez's Sonata aroused our curiosity last winter;[34] a pity, I think, that that anagramatic puzzle did not comprise a more amusing solution! A pity that its equation, too full of unknowns, did not allow for the conclusion that $X = 1$! Was it perhaps merely a youthful error? But *Le Soleil des eaux* has not proved any more illuminating. How eminently deplorable useless music is![35]

All in all, a splendid conclusion to a notable début.

34 The Second Sonata, which had had its first performance the preceding 29 April.
35 *Le Figaro*, 3 August 1950.

CHAPTER FOUR

'Eventuellement'

The inevitable move towards
total serialization
(1949–52)

'Blackboard musicians' was an insult often hurled at those composers who seemed, after the war, to be moving towards a highly calculated form of writing. Barely decipherable scores, photos of courses given at Darmstadt and elsewhere – in which Stockhausen or Boulez, chalk and duster in hand, are shown setting out some indecipherable hieroglyph or other on the blackboard – as well as articles and analyses filled with figures: all these have given positive credence to the idea that music has become a mathematical affair, full of esoteric explanations for those with powerful intellects, limited sensitivity, and a lack of emotion. The musical world has lost touch with its composers. In short: these criticisms reflect the basic discontent of music-lovers with the contemporary creative scene.

This view of things is evidently more applicable to Boulez than to others. Both his past as a budding mathematician and his sober demeanour set him apart from the traditional image of the romantic composer – an image that Stockhausen for example, assumes so well; then there is the prematurely receding hairline of the scholar, his clear, dry manner of speaking, his already published writings and his dodecaphonic affiliation, all of which contribute to this unfavourable image. After the little-known, unusually lyrical works of the late 1940s, the intervening years before the composition of *Le Marteau* resemble a self-contained interlude, which invites further investigation. But superficially at least, Boulez, with his 'calculated' music, conforms all too easily to the negative stereotype with which his detractors would attempt to identify him.

Boulez has a tendency to announce his plans prior to acting upon them. On this occasion he was to state his intentions in an important article, published in 1952, which is summarized here in order to illustrate that this short but decisive period in his career amounted to something of a gamble.

'EVENTUELLEMENT'[1]

To establish the ineluctable nature of Schoenberg's 'revolution', the article first criticizes 'dodecaphonicism' for the doctrinaire way it is taught, and then attacks its critics, who – in the name of freedom and clarity – refuse to submit to its discipline. The following extract is well known: 'Any musician who has not experienced – I do not say understood, but in all exactness, experienced – the necessity for a dodecaphonic language is USELESS. For his whole work is irrelevant to the needs of his epoch.' And he reminds those who (in 1950) still speak of the 'arbitrariness of the series' that it was part and parcel of development even within the tonal system: 'It is not a decree; it is an authentication'.

Nevertheless, Boulez thinks that while the Viennese made a good start in exploiting successions of pitches, they remained much less assured in the field of rhythm – and he compares this retarded aspect with the efforts of Stravinsky or Messiaen who, conversely, handle the organization of pitch in a somewhat 'rudimentary' manner.

It seems that Boulez's purpose at the time was to lay the foundations of a grammar which would encompass the various parameters of sound – pitch, duration and rhythm, timbre and attack, and dynamics – according to a system later to be called total serialization. Thus he goes on to define the duration series (should it perhaps be called dodecachronic?) by establishing a list of twelve durations, increasing progressively from the demi-semiquaver to the dotted crotchet. (See p. 271.) Taking the instrumental terminology of *Polyphonie X* (still on the work-bench) as illustration, he then outlines the intersection of pitch and duration and the cells that could be derived from it.

At this point, he pays homage to two composers – the one expected, the other now somewhat surprising: Messiaen and Cage. 'They alone are the exceptions that I pointed out in the language's acquisitions after Webern, Stravinsky, Berg and Schoenberg. The first through his discoveries in the rhythmic domain, the second by his prospecting among complex sounds, sounds complexes, and also in the rhythmic domain.' Boulez sees

1 Published in *La Revue musicale*, 1952, reprinted in *Notes of an Apprenticeship*, pp. 146–81.

Messiaen's well-known contribution to this area as an extension of certain of Berg's discoveries, such as *Hauptrythmus*,[2] where rhythmic writing is released from its dependence on the polyphonic or melodic aspect – and he finds the perfect phrase to express just what he himself owes to Messiaen in this respect: that is, 'a rhythmic disquiet'.

(As for Cage, it should be remembered that Boulez was then in the thick of a theoretical flirtation with the composer of the *Sonatas and Interludes* for prepared piano of 1946–8.[3] The latter's sound complexes were understandably of interest to Boulez because of the way in which they demonstrated the break with traditional chromaticism. And Boulez showed a sympathetic curiosity in observing Cage's handling of the huge charts on which he wrote his own series – moving from one to another by means of procedures borrowed from the methods of the I-Ching. Boulez was equally interested in an approach which conceived rhythmic structure in terms of numerical relationships 'without the intervention of the personal factor': this theme of impersonality can be seen at work in *Structures*, before returning in a guise more characteristic of the Mallarméan 'operator'.)

He then reveals what he has learnt from his recent experiences in the *musique concrète* studio (see p. 48). Again, he sees these as offering the potential for the strict treatment of certain problems relating to the long-sought 'inclusive grammar of sound' and (notably with regard to durations) for 'realizations' more perfect than with human interpreters,[4] rather than merely regarding them as an amazing source of preposterous or unbelievably wonderful sounds. And this is what sets him apart from the French 'concretists'.

To sum up, he poses the central question to which he had never ceased to refer: that of the relationship between intellectuality on the one hand, and sensibility and creativity on the other. And he attacks those who accuse him of sacrificing the latter to the former: 'If the creator is inadequate, there is a rush to treat him [the composer] with contempt as a theoretician, clockmaker, etc. If the creation is good, there is an equal rush to assert that it is not the theoretician who should enlist agreement, that

2 A fundamental rhythmic structure – a succession of accented or non-accented notes and silences – which can be applied either to melodic sequences or to changes of metre (cf. *Lulu*, Act I, the death of the Painter).
3 Cage's works up to 1934 (including *Xenia* and *Two Pieces*) were for 'normal' piano; the first pieces for prepared piano date from 1938 (*Bacchanales*) and 1943 (*Amores*).
4 The trump card of the machine – as Boulez was fondly to recall when, thirty years later, he introduced Giuseppe di Giugno's 4x machine at IRCAM.

his theories are not very important, given that he has produced a beautiful work.' He also pleads the cause of music in which expression will be 'intrinsically linked to language' and in which research and creativity will go hand in hand: 'Otherwise it remains only laughable anecdote, noisy grandiloquence or morose libertinage'. And he ends by echoing the sentiments of Verlaine and Barbey d'Aurevilly: 'The heart, [is] an organ that takes precedence over all others.'

THE FIRST PERFORMANCE OF *POLYPHONIE X*

During the winter of 1950–1, Heinrich Strobel, who was head of music services at the Südwestfunk in Baden-Baden and artistic director of the Donaueschingen Festival (founded in 1921), came to Paris in order to introduce himself to Boulez. Arriving at the rue Beautreillis, he found the latter hard at work on a score mysteriously entitled *Polyphonie X*. Muffled up against the cold, calmly composing in his usual cramped handwriting, Boulez was surrounded by sheets of manuscript paper on which the serial organizations he was using were carefully noted in a whole range of different coloured inks. Like many others, Strobel was captivated by the mixture of severity and charm in the twenty-six-year-old composer, and immediately decided to include *Polyphonie X* in the programme for the next festival in the little Black Forest town – where it would have its first performance under the direction of Hans Rosbaud.

Lasting just over fifteen minutes,[5] the work is scored for eighteen solo instruments, divided into seven groups:

1) piccolo trumpet
   E flat clarinet
   cor anglais

2) oboe
   bass clarinet

3) flute
   bassoon

4) piccolo trumpet
   alto saxaphone
   horn
   trombone

7) viola 1
   viola 2
   double bass

6) violin 2
   cello 2

5) violin 1
   cello 1

5 Exactly 16' 30" in the recording of the first performance.

The symmetry of the groups on either side of the central quartet (4) is quite intentional on Boulez's part. The work comprises three sections, corresponding to the three basic tempi: *modéré souple, assez lent* and *vif*. Starting with an explanation of the title, Boulez reveals his own design as follows:

X is simply X, neither a letter of the alphabet, nor a number, nor yet an algebraic symbol. It is rather a graphic symbol. I called this work *Polyphonie X* because it contains certain structures which intersect in the sense of augmentations and diminutions arising from their encounter, as well as similarly conceived rises and falls in the sound, and finally a series of rhythmic cells which intersect in like manner. It is moreover these cells which comprise the main ingredient of the work on the structural level.[6]

On another occasion he gave an example of how the initial instrumental groupings are altered during the course of the piece: 'For instance, an instrument from group 7 will be linked to group 6, or one from group 5 to group 4, and so on. And at the end, unlike the way it looks in the score, all the groupings are inverted – which is to say that they too obey the same general phenomenon.'[7]

One should not forget that the interplay of permutations and of transferred sounds in *Polyphonie X* obeys both a preliminary 'plan' and a decision to 'loosen' the original attachments between one parameter and another. All this is very abstract, and even the title of the work seems to suggest that it was actually part of a preparatory examination for entry to higher education in mathematics. And since Boulez's knowledge of handling a purely instrumental ensemble – used here (1951) for the first time – was still rudimentary, the work posed formidable problems for performers and audience alike. Antoine Goléa drew attention to a high trumpet passage, played fortissimo across gaping intervals and with abrupt contrasts between *legato* and *staccato*, which was as perilous to play as it was ungrateful to listen to. But such affronts to conventional instrumental idioms were inevitable the moment the work became subject to a preliminary permutational plan that was both abstract and restrictive.

The audience reaction to this problematic work was less than favourable. Antoine Goléa was there: 'Those who experienced this Donaueschingen première will remember the scandal as long as they live. Shouts, caterwauling, and other animal noises were unleashed from one half of

6 Goléa, op. cit., p. 139.
7 Conversation with Dominique Jameux, *Musique en jeu*, No. 16, 1976, p. 34. Note in passing Stockhausen's title *Kreuzspiel* or *Crossplay* (1951).

the hall in response to applause, foot-stamping and enthusiastic bravos from the other.'[8] Gone are the happy days when such battles were still waged in concert halls!

Boulez was absent, detained once again in London by his touring activities with Barrault. He did three things: he sent a congratulatory telegram to the gallant Hans Rosbaud and his players, listened to the Südwestfunk tape, and decided to withdraw the work until such time as it might one day be rewritten. 'I have in fact looked at it again, or at least I have thought about it, and I find that the judgement I made at the time was absolutely correct: that is to say, the problems posed were the right ones, but they were resolved in much too perfunctory a manner – the principles and ideas went in the right direction, but their development was too schematic to be effective.'[9]

Although the work is harsh upon the ear, it nevertheless has a sort of edgy alacrity that is not without a strength of its own. It is best consigned to the limbo of other Boulezian scores awaiting redemption.

AN APPRENTICESHIP IN THE MUSIQUE CONCRETE STUDIO:
THE TWO ETUDES (1952)

A chronological point: when Boulez composed *Polyphonie X* in the summer of 1951, the first *Structure*, the famous *1a*, had already been written in the spring of that year; the two others were to follow after *Polyphonie X*. But before discussing the work for two pianos, the most important of its period, it would be as well to consider two other contemporary works marked with the same seal of experimentation and dissatisfaction.

Pierre Henry[10] was one of Boulez's fellow students at the Conservatoire, and it was he who, some years later, took Boulez along to Pierre Schaeffer's *musique concrète* studio and introduced him to its director.[11]

8 Goléa, op. cit., p. 140.
9 Conversation with Dominique Jameux, *Musique en jeu*, No. 16, 1976, p. 33. Some years later, in conversation with Célestin Deliège, Boulez blamed the shortcomings of the Conservatoire education system – but he just as clearly implicates the 'abstract design' of his own work: 'The instrumentalists are there merely to play the notes which fall within their own registers . . . It was an intermediate work and suffers from theoretical exaggeration' (*Conversations with Célestin Deliège*, op. cit., p. 58).
10 Composer (born 1927), pupil of Messiaen and Nadia Boulanger; worked with Pierre Schaeffer at the Studio d'Essai de la RTF and 'invented' *musique concrète*.
11 This was not the first contact between the two: in 1947–8, Schaeffer needed someone to record a few chords and, at Barrault's request, Boulez made the recording with the players from the theatre [as communicated to the author].

Schaeffer was a sceptical (even autodestructive) engineer/polytechnician, eager to search for understanding of his own epoch through his thoughts and actions. He was joined, for varying periods of time, by many composers sharing his curiosity as to the nature of sound.

Two events were that year to give positive encouragement to this musical research. The first was technical, with the introduction to France of the tape-recorder and the phonogene: the one substituted magnetic tape, which could be edited at will, for direct recording onto flexible disc, the other made possible the mechanical variation of speed and thus of pitch, so that it was no longer necessary to brake manually or to 'tinker' at random. Together they meant that practically the whole arsenal of modern technical means was already assembled. Secondly, as if to officialize this new state of affairs, Schaeffer founded the Groupe de Recherche de Musique Concrète (the GRMC), installed in the premises at 37 rue de l'Université, which he had occupied since 1949.

Like IRCAM in years to come, this group included semi-permanent members and also welcomed probationers – who came initially to learn about the techniques and available materials and were then invited to produce works of 'taped music', as it was then called. Between 1951 and 1952, these probationers included Boulez, Stockhausen and Barraqué. There were many others, more or less within the orbit of the serialists, including Maurice Le Roux and Yvette Grimaud.

So it was at the GRMC that Boulez composed his two *Etudes* – although these are in no way 'concrete', since they are concerned with the treatment of instrumental sounds played on the cello. The first, *Etude sur un seul son*, sets out to attain the maximum sound dispersal from a minimum amount of material (almost in the classical manner of Chopin's Study Op. 10 No. 2, a hundred and twenty years on!). What one hears is a chord, stretched and distorted within a reverberation reminiscent of a disused factory; incorporating bands of silence, it is gradually formed into an intermittent pedal bass, with sporadic decorations coming from this side or that. Of a similar duration, *Etude II* or *Etude sur sept sons* displays the 'extra-terrestrial' character seemingly inevitable to taped music in these exploratory years, with objects crashing to earth like meteorites and bizarre sounds which quite quickly reveal themselves as simply having been played backwards – all in a predominantly medium register which gives this *Etude* a more restrained feel than the first.

However, the significance of what is perceived by the ear is, undoubtedly, less important than the historical significance of these two *Etudes*. They were to influence future developments by their very limitations – for

Boulez had met with the machine and found it wanting. Magnetic tape certainly allowed for duration to be organized with great precision (a point emphasized in 'Eventuellement') but, for the rest, the tools were far too rudimentary for his liking. His endeavours in this sphere were few (only *Poésie pour pouvoir* in 1958 and '. . . *explosante-fixe* . . .' in 1971) and largely disappointing until he began work at IRCAM. In fact, as long as the machine was limited to production – either of transformations (*musique concrète*) or even of actual sounds (electronic music) – without leading to new and valuable compositional strategies, Boulez was to remain unfailingly scornful; his attitude was to remain unchanged until the advent of the computer.

For the time being, conflict between him and Schaeffer was unavoidable. The latter was not a trained musician. His preoccupations were both physical (the constitution of a sound and its practical manipulation, fabrication – even just tinkering with it) and metaphysical (man's interest in the meaning of sound, the signs of its manifestation and its communicative function). Boulez, meanwhile, regarded the machine as a means of realizing his ideal of an integrated serialism. He could only be indifferent to Schaeffer's humanist preoccupations and exasperated by what he saw as the prevailing amateurism of the GRMC, as well as by the practice of collecting and classifying harvested sounds without any real syntactical purpose.

This conflict was frequently violent: 'I am not the least attracted by this flea-market of sounds' was one of the least offensive phrases used publicly with regard to the activities of Schaeffer and his friends – including Pierre Henry, who nevertheless went through some kind of structuralist, and even serial, phase with his *Antiphonie* (1950–2).[13] This animosity was to have practical results. As he recalls with some amusement today, Boulez felt himself the bearer of more important tidings than the wretched tinkerings of the GRMC: 'From the height of my Sinai I sent down quite a number of lightning flashes.' The composers of the GRMC united against him and the situation could only be resolved in one of two ways: by a Boulezian putsch taking power and using the machines for their own ends, or by an ordered withdrawal. The latter course prevailed.

12 Michel Chion, *Pierre Henry*, Fayard/Sacem, 1980, p. 42.

STRUCTURES FOR TWO PIANOS BOOK I

On 4 May 1952 at the Comédie des Champs-Elysées, a three-and-a-half minute work was performed by an oddly-assorted duo: Messiaen and Boulez gave the first performance of the celebrated *Structure 1a* as part of a concert of twentieth-century works organized by UNESCO. The small hall was full, and somewhat restless. The handbag of an enraged female critic was sent flying towards the head of a more enthusiastic male colleague. It seemed that Boulez, now very much his own master, had regained the support of his former teacher who was not afraid to risk his name by lending his talent; the coldness of earlier years – caused by Boulez's iconoclastic attitude and exacerbated by disagreeable proclamations – was thus publicly erased. Stravinsky, who was in the audience, found the work arrogant (according to Robert Craft) but expressed interest in its composer.

These two hundred or so seconds have become legendary. Few contemporary scores have so often been quoted, referred to and analysed: Ligeti, Roman Vlad, Donald Mitchell, Marc Wilkinson and Edward T. Cone are just some of the well-known specialists who have each added to the impressive body of analytical literature provoked by this one piece.

Structure 1a is seldom played and still less often listened to; any discussion of the work centres around the essential fact that it systematically develops a programme from a minimal amount of initial information. This information comprises a series that Boulez – here seeking the maximum 'impersonalization' – took from Messiaen's *Mode de valeurs et d'intensités.*[13] With the means and in the manner characteristic of its own composer, this was a work which itself attempted a kind of total serialization of the various sound parameters as early as 1949, so that Boulez's borrowing was evidently deliberate.

Boulez immersed himself in this concept, stretching his experiment to the limit. In 1977, he told Célestin Deliège that 'To quote Barthes, I was experimenting with "an expressive nadir".' And he recalls that he had originally intended to call *Structure 1a* 'At the Frontier of a Fertile Land' – the title of a picture by Klee which he later used for one of his own articles, in 1955.

The procedure was obviously to start with the given series and to apply

---

13 Like Berg who, in order to demonstrate the advances in musical language over the past twenty-five years, chose a series composed by his pupil and friend H. F. Klien as material for his twelve-note song, 'Schliesse mir die Augen beide'.

the serial principle to pitches, durations, dynamics and 'attacks'. But it was not a matter of wholly automatic music, partly because the possibilities were not completely exhausted, and also because the choice of register – a fundamental element of the keyboard writing which often transcends the level of the pitches themselves – was left to the composer. Like Klee's picture, which is composed solely of horizontals and obliques, *Structure 1a* is limited both in its resources and in the treatment of its material. Boulez adds that 'The circumstances of its composition are another story, but the piece was composed very fast, during a single night, because I wanted to exploit the possibilities of a given material and to see how far one could pursue the automatism of musical relationships without allowing individual choice to intervene other than on really very basic levels of organization – that of density, for instance.' Density is to be understood here simply as the number of polyphonic voices (each representing one of the forty-eight possible versions of the initial series) superposed in each of the eleven sections of *Structure 1a*. The organization of these densities has the twofold advantage of involving the composer once more, and of being quite perceptible to the listener, thus providing formal landmarks. My attempt at analysis (pp. 269 ff.) rests entirely on this notion, and effectively succeeds in demonstrating a very simple antiphony of the verse/response kind.

Structures 1b and *1c* were written later (after *Polyphonie X*) and they progressively reduce the part played by automatism, thereby increasing the role of the composer. The three *Structures* of Book 1 were first performed on 13 November 1953 in Cologne by the faithful Yvette Grimaud together with Yvonne Loriod – not yet the wife of Olivier Messiaen but one of his closest disciples – so the occasion was something of a 'family affair'.

The work had enormous repercussions. The evident virtuosity of the performers on the two pianos (needed both for a density and continuity of sound which would have been impossible on a single instrument) made up for the austerity of expression. It is, incidentally, a sign of Boulez's greatness that he was able to arrive at a full-blooded composition instead of what might have been a mere document. Today, Book 1 sounds almost like Brahms.

BOULEZ, CAGE AND STOCKHAUSEN

It is amusing to find that the period of Boulez's most extended theoretical research into integral calculation coincides with that of his closest friendship with John Cage, the musician–poet of chance, contemplation and improvisation.

John Cage arrived in Paris in 1949 for his first visit to the French capital since his student days at the Conservatoire as a pupil of Lazare-Lévy in the 1930s. He had come a long way since then, first in the California of his birth, then in the east. He came under the influence of Henry Cowell (famous for his invention of the cluster, for using the inside of the piano, for inserting egg shells between the strings of the instrument, and so on), who sent him to study with Schoenberg. Recently settled in Los Angeles, Schoenberg gave free but unavailing lessons in harmony and composition to the penniless, charming, but intractable young musician, from 1934 to 1936. In 1937, Cage, who had already composed a number of scarcely Schoenbergian works, settled in Washington as pianist for a dance course, invented the prepared piano, went to New York, met Merce Cunningham, discovered Satie and developed a passion for Duchamp.

At the outbreak of war, he was receiving instruction from Suzuki, who taught him Zen Buddhism at the prestigious Columbia University. Between 1946 and 1948, Cage wrote his *Sonatas and Interludes* for prepared piano. First performed by Marc Ajemian at New York's Carnegie Hall in January 1949, the work was very well received: the National Academy of Arts and Letters offered Cage a thousand dollar bursary and the Gulbenkian Foundation added another two thousand four hundred. He then set out for Europe, and one of his first visits on arriving in Paris was to the rue Beautreillis.

The two men got on well together: Cage was charmed by Boulez's intelligence, force of personality, and his systematic and pioneering attitude; Boulez was in turn attracted by the freshness of outlook and reaction of his American visitor. Many years later, when this closeness had long since disappeared, Boulez remained constant both in his judgement of the man and in his retrospective interest in the prepared piano. In about 1976, despite the truly archetypal nature of the dichotomy between their respective styles of music-making, the conductor of the New York Philharmonic could be seen directing a work entitled *Apartment House*, by the celebrated composer–mycologist.

In December 1949, a very fashionable soirée was organized at the house of Suzanne Tézenas – to whom Boulez had recently been introduced by Pierre Souvchinsky. There were at least a hundred invited guests, including artists, writers, society women, and even musicians. The hostess's venerable piano had to suffer all kinds of attentions with a view to producing a more brilliant sonority – including pins, nails, erasers, and even glassfuls of cognac on the strings; Cage vouched for his experiment, saying that he always left an instrument in a better state than when he started.[14] That evening, Boulez gave a splendid and affectionate speech introducing the composer of *Sonatas and Interludes,* not forgetting to mention that Cage had been a pupil of Schoenberg. The newcomer was welcomed with open arms.

Boulez also introduced Cage to Messiaen, who invited him to come and give a demonstration to his Conservatoire class. Cage also made the acquaintance of Boulez's small circle of friends: the poet and future playwright Armand Gatti, the painter Bernard Saby, the writer Pierre Joffroy, and the indispensable Pierre Souvchinsky. Cage repaid Boulez for his many kindnesses by introducing him to the publishers Amphion and Heugel – who were later to share the publication of Boulez's early works.

When Cage left for the USA at the end of three months, the two composers continued to communicate by post. Two astonishing letters written by Boulez in 1952 bear witness to this correspondence.[15] In them, he expounds upon the total serialization of *Polyphonie X* and *Structure 1a.* Looked at today, this seems a puzzling, even eccentric thing to have done: it is hard to see what could possibly have interested Cage in this computerized passion, harder still to understand Boulez's indulgence towards the contemplative tinkering of *Sonatas and Interludes.* But both were reaching for an absolute. In 1951, the depersonalization sought by Boulez in *Structure 1a* came close to the concept of chance that Cage had yet to adopt for himself – just as Boulez's understandable curiosity as to the nature of sound was leading him in a new direction (taped music). This explains his interest in the prepared piano which, many years later, enabled him specifically to condemn 'this necessary misappropriation of instrumental integrity' in order to demand the means for an authentic acoustical research that would benefit from the contributions of contemporary science – in other words, IRCAM. Furthermore, it has been suggested that, on a psychological level, Boulez's involvement with Cage was both pleasurable and stimulating, since it offered a valuable opportunity for exchanging ideas with an avant-garde musical culture completely divorced from his own European heritage.

Around 1950, Cage discovered the *Book of Changes,* a collection of Chinese divinations from the *Grande époque* given to him by Christian

14 Peyser, op. cit., p. 61.
15 Since printed in *Orientations,* London, Faber; USA, Harvard University Press, pp. 129 ff.; originally published as *Points de repère,* Paris, Christian Bourgois, 1981.

Wolff – a new acquaintance who formed part of the circle of Cage's American friends, together with David Tudor, Earle Brown and Morton Feldman. In 1951, he began his *Music of Changes*, in which the drawing of lots played an important part. This was the start of a process whereby the introduction of chance into the act of composition (or, perhaps, the depersonalization of the composer) was to attain proportions unacceptable to a composer such as Boulez. This was, effectively, to mark the parting of the ways between the two men, both musically and theoretically. Boulez finally severed the connection with his article 'Aléa' (1957) and the open-form works that went with it, which demonstrate Boulez's own very distinct concept of the composer/performer relationship.

The case of Stockhausen was altogether different. Without any doubt, Boulez's encounter with the German composer was a more important musical experience than any other contact on the contemporary music scene. Stockhausen came to Paris in 1951, when he joined Messiaen's class and first met Boulez. He came across Boulez again during a period of study at the GRMC, which he left with his *musique concrète Etude*. The two composers agreed on many issues: they had the same fundamental interest in Schoenberg and Webern (rejected by the GRMC), the same desire to found a new language based on strong theoretical hypotheses, the same respect for the traditional *métier* of the composer and the performer – and the same reciprocal esteem. The Stockhausen of 1951 (and for many years to come) was one of the rare musicians spared Boulez's criticism, and Stockhausen, it seems, has never denigrated the music of Boulez.

These were the beginnings of an international community which, until 1955, seemed to monopolize the contemporary musical establishment with a style which – despite marked and abiding differences – could be seen as 'international' (a characteristic of the great sixteenth-century polyphonists, as Claude Rostand has noted). Boulez, Stockhausen, Nono and Berio were sometimes referred to as 'the Darmstadt generation'. This Utopian ideal of a unified language lasted only a few months – a year or two at the most; otherwise, it could have proved remarkably powerful.

'SCHOENBERG EST MORT'

It could perhaps be argued that this international community was in some way turned in upon itself, with audience relationships becoming something of a side issue. I would have liked to ask Boulez at the time whether these composers saw themselves as an integral part of a larger musical life.

Boulez's reply in 1984 is a resounding 'no'. Nowadays, he is intimately in touch with his time and with musical life world-wide; then, he was part of a 'family unit' occupying a completely ghetto-like position in relation to the global musical establishment. There were really two kinds of music: theirs, and the rest. Yes, they knew that Bayreuth had reopened (1951), and even perhaps that a revolutionary producer (Wieland Wagner) was dusting off the works of his famous grandfather – but they were totally indifferent: the generation of great classical performers (Schwarzkopf, Lipatti, Karajan), sociological and psychological changes in listening habits (especially since the development of the long-playing record) were not even thought about. This was in no way due to narrow-mindedness on the part of these remarkable composers, who were thoroughly conversant with the contemporary artistic languages of literature, painting and the theatre. They were, after all, only about twenty-five years old and in a polemical position *vis-à-vis* the classical musical establishment. Consequently, in their search for a means of expression resolutely adapted to contemporary needs, and which they themselves had evolved, they sought protection in their struggle by assuming a supreme indifference to the 'events' of the time.[16]

Nevertheless, the death of Schoenberg in Los Angeles, on 13 July 1951, prompted Boulez to provide less an obituary than an analysis. It marked the limits of his own Schoenbergianism at this stage of his life, though at the same time, it is fair to say that he spoke on behalf of all composers of his generation. 'Schoenberg is dead' is the title of a celebrated article written for the English magazine *The Score* (published in France in *Relevés d'apprenti* in 1958).

The article was less important for its content than for its effect. At the time, Schoenberg was really a thing of the past for Boulez – from his point of view too closely connected with Messiaen and more particularly, with Leibowitz, just as he himself was turning first and foremost to Webern. It was certainly necessary to note the importance of Schoenberg's work, especially up to 1914, as well as its stylistic limits with regard to form, rhythm and timbre (despite *Klangfarbenmelodie*, the 'melody of tone colours'). The article received a lot of publicity and its title – scarcely

16 Such transferred alliances – in which innovatory musicians chose the company of equally maligned artists and writers in preference to that of their colleagues in traditional music – had been in operation since before the First World War, when the establishment of the Akademischer Verband für Literatur und Musik brought Viennese musicians into close touch with such figures as the architect Adolph Loos, the painter Gustav Klimt, the poet Peter Altenberg and the polemicist Karl Kraus.

questionable in itself – caused a scandal because of its ambiguity. Today, it is hard to imagine the effect of 'Schoenberg is dead' upon contemporary readers: some found it inspiring, whilst others were profoundly shocked. It caused a particular furore in America, where the works of the Austrian composer – latterly an American citizen – enjoyed all the esteem appertaining to the idea of the avant-garde within the ghetto-like university structure. Nevertheless, the article is significant in that it indicates the evolutionary point reached by Boulez's own musical reflections.

His criticism hinges on the Schoenbergian concept of the series itself, starting with the Five Piano Pieces, Op. 23 and the *Serenade*, Op. 24. In Boulez's view, the series was for Schoenberg only a contemporary form of the theme; it was established merely in order to control a chromaticism inherited from Wagner. 'The confusion between theme and series in Schoenberg's twelve-note works is sufficient evidence of his inability to foresee the sound-world that the series calls for'; it is in no way thought of as being capable, by its very nature, of giving rise to a new type of structure.[17] 'Any logical relationship between the serial forms themselves and the structures derived from them was generally absent from Schoenberg's considerations: hence his relapse, after the period 1920–5, not only into academic musical forms (the quartet, quintet, variations, and so on) but into easily anticipated stylistic mannerisms, harmonic acquiescence and rhythmic poverty. Only certain aspects of timbre remain innovatory.

He explains that the Schoenbergian impasse was reinforced rather than attenuated during the composer's American period, which coincided with the distressing but logical 'revaluation of harmonic polarity and even of tonal functions'; faced with this, the lone and humble star of Webern shines with undiminished brilliance. Webern's ability to 'generate structure from material' (the philosopher's stone that Boulez has drilled away at up to and including IRCAM) seems both the most advanced (though, in truth, the assertion is somewhat debatable: the *Symphony*, Op. 21, the Quartet, Op. 22, the *Variations*, Op. 27, and even the second *Cantata* also depend on pre-existing formal schemes) and the most likely to indicate possible lines of development, micro-intervals and total serialization in particular. The tenor of the article, or rather its point, is well known: 'Neither gratuitous insolence nor a mealy-mouthed complacency have

17 For my part I prefer to speak of an atmosphere. Thus the atmosphere of Webern's *Symphony*, Op. 21 is by no means the same as that of Schoenberg's exactly contemporary *Variations*, Op. 31.

any part to play in an adjustment based only on an implacable logic exempt from weakness or compromise. So, with neither a foolish desire for scandal, nor yet any hypocritical modesty or pointless melancholy, let us not hesitate to write the words: SCHOENBERG IS DEAD.'[18] In other words: Schoenberg is dead, we must strive to live.

18 There were other less inevitable epitaphs: 'The final expression of a putrifying culture formed in contempt of normal man – of a sick culture which glories in being both insuperable and inaccessible to healthy emotions' (Serge Nigg on Schoenberg, *Guide du concert*, 16 November 1951). This was the 'Zdhanovian' (socialist–realist) period of Boulez's one-time fellow pupil from the Messiaen class who has since become a perfectly honest man!

CHAPTER FIVE

A Door Opens

From the birth of the Domaine musical
to the first performance of
Le Marteau sans maître
(1953–6)

Boulez was now almost thirty. He was far from unknown, but his fame was still largely limited to avant-garde circles. The formidable composer–communicator of future years had yet to achieve recognition from his public.

The years 1953–6 were to give him two opportunities for doing so. In 1954, Boulez conceived, created and succeeded in establishing the Domaine musical; the following year, the première of the symbolically titled *Le Marteau sans maître* was a *succès de scandale*, earning him his rightful place in the concert world. By the end of this short period, the composer appeared fully equipped for the future.

In 1953 Boulez was still Director of Music for the Barrault company. This involved working daily with the players as the humble 'in-house' composer, as well as performances and tours, and friction with the intellectual world both in Paris and abroad; it also marked the end of his apprenticeship in the art of masterminding an evening in front of an audience. It was then that he proclaimed 'it is time for our generation to prove itself with a series of chamber music concerts which will serve as a means of communication between contemporary composers and a public interested in its own century'.[1] This was the first serious attempt since Wagner to set up such an organization – although the Society for Private Musical Performances founded by Schoenberg in Vienna shortly after the First World War comes closer in certain respects to the undertaking of the Domaine musical than does the example of Bayreuth. Boulez's motives in organizing the Domaine were quite clear: since new music was not

[1] Peyser, op. cit., p. 109.

performed in France (or if it was, it was played badly), he aimed to establish a new repertoire as part of Parisian musical life, based on the criterion of supreme performance quality.

One needs only to glance at the concert programmes of the day to realize how astonishing they were. The main outlet for the broadcasting of contemporary music, the French radio (then under the direction of Henri Barraud), congested its wavelengths with composers who, in Boulez's view, in no way represented any of the really innovatory trends. The great composers of the time were thought to be the neo-classical Stravinsky, Milhaud, Honegger, Poulenc, Dallapiccola, Martinů and Menotti – not to mention the importance accorded in France to the estimable talents of Marcel Delannoy[2], Marcel Landowsky[3], Jean-Michel Damase[4], Claude Arrieu[5] or Claude Delvincourt.[6] Of the Second Viennese School, and Webern in particular, there was almost no trace. This was contemporary music in the JMF[7] fashion of yesteryear! The great symphony orchestras, the record producers – then at the start of their systematic exploration of the repertoire, thanks to the advent of the long-playing disc – and the concert organizers were certainly in no hurry to move into dangerous territory.[8] As to the level of performance at concerts given by ostensibly 'enlightened' circles (like that of Leibowitz) or specialist groups, there are no recordings from which to draw any conclusions. Listening recently to a tape of a contemporary radio recording of Berg's *Lyric Suite*, however, I have to admit that it took some time to recognize the work being played! In other words, everything seemed to justify Boulez's determination to come to grips with the problem of finding a platform for the really new music, and of performing it well.

The saga of the Domaine musical can be outlined briefly as follows:

2 Composer (1889–1962), pupil and friend of Honegger.
3 Composer (born 1915), pupil of Honegger and Director of Music at the Ministry of Cultural Affairs from 1966–74.
4 Composer and pianist (born 1928).
5 Composer (born 1903), she carried out important musical functions within the radio from as early as 1946.
6 Composer (1888–1954), Director of the Paris Conservatoire from 1941–54.
7 A youth and music organization giving concerts and lectures directed in particular at schools and universities; founded by Roger Nicoly in 1941, the movement became an international federation in 1945. At its height (in about 1957), the French Jeunesses Musicales could count on something like 200,000 members in 290 centres. Contemporary music was then always approached somewhat warily.
8 The apathy and complacency of the broadcasting media, the inertia of the large associations, the laziness and conformity of star performers, the timidity or irresponsibility of record producers: is the situation so very different in 1984?

amid general hostility, a clique of young musicians – with the sectarian self-assurance of the just, and tightly grouped around the Robespierre figure of Boulez – first asserted itself and then gradually got the upper hand. The undertaking is too closely linked to Boulez himself to omit any of the remarkable circumstances in an attempt to separate legend from history.

THE CONCERTS AT THE PETIT-MARIGNY (1954)

Fired with enthusiasm by both the musical and human qualities of Boulez's personality, Jean-Louis Barrault and Madeleine Renaud were easily convinced by his arguments. They then made the following generous proposal: four times a year, on days when there were no performances in the theatre itself, the small hall in the attics above the Grand-Marigny[9] would be put at his disposal, the initial costs to be born by the Renaud-Barrault company. The concerts took the provisional name of the Concerts du Petit-Marigny, and the first season (1953–4) presented four such events: on 13 January, 24 February, 24 March and 10 April, 1954.

The programmes for this first season are self-explanatory (pp. 71–2). They followed the principles of programme-building as laid down by Boulez in a foreword to the inaugural season, which I quote here almost complete:

We wish to establish three levels of activity.

1 The reference level is to include works which, either in their stylistic leanings or as concepts, have a particular relevance for our own time; hence the isorhythmic motets of Machaut and Dufay, the chromaticism of Gesualdo and the formal inspiration of *The Musical Offering* by Johann Sebastian Bach.

2 The educational level is to include contemporary works that are still little known, even though they must be regarded as having played an essential role in musical evolution (Stravinsky, Bartók, Varèse, Debussy). Although almost totally ignored in France, the works of the New Viennese School, and of Webern in particular, are no longer the cause of abstract controversy; nevertheless, their performance will give them a reality they now enjoy everywhere except in Paris.

3 Then there is the level of research, or even, of discovery. This aims to place within the clearest possible historical perspective recent works by composers who

9 Throughout its various peregrinations, the Company had always retained the idea of the two theatres, 'not so as to place successful plays in the one and difficult works in the other', as Jean-Louis Barrault recently stated, but 'because you don't put a Cranach on a large wall, nor a Rubens on a medallion!'. The Petit-Marigny opened in 1952 and planned from the outset to include concerts as part of its programme.

are at least artistically honest, if not manifestly talented, masters of their art, and whose integrity is a guarantee of their essential creativity.

He concludes with a word on the 'conspicuously international' scope of the undertaking as well as on the principle of repeating performances; and he notes that a number of the relevant scores are to be published by Julliard.

Boulez was invited by French radio to announce the start of his new series during a news broadcast on 4 January 1954. Not yet accustomed to improvising in front of the microphone, he drew a piece of paper from his pocket and gave a somewhat stilted account of the above text.[10]

L'Artisanat furieux

The concerts took place in a hall with inadequate ventilation, 280 uncomfortable seats,[11] and curtained walls which all too easily muffled the sounds of Webern's minimalia! The programmes were of interminable length owing to the fact that Boulez imagined everyone to share both his insatiable appetite (which was sometimes true) and his powers of endurance (which was often false). Antoine Goléa gives a lively description of these early concerts:

Right from the first, there was a tremendous crush in the hall of the Petit-Marigny. Of course it was a small hall, holding three hundred people at a pinch. But there has to be a beginning to everything, and what counts in this kind of affair is not so much the initial size of the audience as its quality and the current of excitement created. This current of excitement was undoubtedly there right from the start. In the depths of winter, in the mud and melting snow of the Champs-Elysées gardens, long queues of applicants, most of them young, formed in front of the theatre box-office for each of the concerts. Very soon, people had to be turned away; in the second year, between a hundred and a hundred and fifty were disappointed on each occasion, after the hall had been filled to the brim. Oh, that hall! There were no proper seats, only benches – each theoretically designed for a certain number of people but with no allowance made for the corpulent. In the end, at least a third more were squeezed in, demonstrating astonishing goodwill on the part of an audience consumed, if not by sacred fire, at least with curiosity. There were people sitting or standing in the doorways, at the sides, at the foot of the platform – even on the platform itself when there was room. Winter or summer, it was unimaginably hot: an advertisement in the programme proclaimed that the hall was heated by 'infra-red tubes provided by the Quartz and Silicon Society' – and the temperature was around 27 degrees Celcius. At the intermission we crammed onto the narrow staircase, trying to get out into the fresh air, but hardly had we got

10 INA, Lo 1379.
11 Later to serve as a cinema.

to the bottom than it was time to go back – so short were the intervals, owing to the inordinate length of the programmes.[12]

The concerts were extremely long. 'I had to learn about the timing of a concert as I went along', Boulez says today. His own remarkably high threshold of concentration, and his proselytizing zeal made him some-what oblivious to reality; in addition, he rarely made allowances for the time taken to arrange the platform, in relation to the length of the pieces themselves.[13] Nevertheless, all those who were there confirm that the audiences were extraordinarily silent, attentive and enthusiastic. Michel Fano[14] likens the atmosphere to that of a rite, or a ceremony. The fact that it was mostly a subscription audience suggests an unusual affinity between organizers and public; the early Domaine concerts were received with a mixture of admiration and disconcerted amazement, as opposed to the whistles and howls traditionally associated with anything new.

What was most striking about these early days of the Domaine musical was the extraordinary mixture of worldly-wise professionalism and militant idealism. The wordly wisdom was the result of being financed by private patronage. As Barrault said to Boulez over a pint at the theatre bar at the end of the first season: 'My friend, the concerts are all very well, but I can't go on like this!' It was not simply a matter of opening up the theatre four times a year, but of meeting the instrumentalists' fees, and defraying the other expenses.

As mentioned earlier, Boulez had known Suzanne Tézenas since 1948 and it was she who organized an effective patronage (partly sustained by a large fortune inherited from North Africa) that protected the enterprise against total insecurity. The name 'Domaine musical' was adopted at the start of its second season, and the association was immediately able to engage the most distinguished performers and to offer them sufficient rehearsal time to achieve the best possible results.

Even now, the musicians remember the promptness with which the president of the Domaine appeared backstage with his little envelopes at the end of each concert. Boulez was realistic enough to know the importance of ministering to the morale of the troops, even those most committed to the cause.

12 Goléa, op. cit., pp. 186–7.
13 There has been no improvement; the concerts of the Ensemble InterContemporain are occasionally guilty of the same thing even today.
14 Composer (born 1929), pupil of Messiaen and one of the early members of the Domaine musical; later became more interested in cinema, producing taped sounds for several films by Alain Robbe-Grillet. He presently teaches at the Institut National Image et Son.

These troops were recruited from amongst the best instrumentalists – whom he had got to know through conducting them day after day in the pit at the Marigny. Nowadays, he points out that their loyalty to the undertaking was based mainly on their confidence in one who was also able to procure work for them. Gilbert Amy notes that Boulez had discovered how little satisfaction these eminent musicians gained from their daily work in large orchestras or from thankless sessions in the Marigny pit, and that they were more than ready to devote their time, enthusiasm and ability to a more inspiring cause. Soon musicians as remarkable as Guy Deplus (clarinet), Serge Collot (viola), and others were associated with the Domaine.[15] Thirty years later, these players still recall the far from ideal circumstances of their rehearsals in some back room at Heugel, as well as the unsatisfactory ratio between time spent and remuneration received. In particular, Guy Deplus, who was also a member of the orchestra of the Garde Republicaine, remembers the ironic smiles of his colleagues when he used to tell them he was off to the Domaine – for a session of 'that kind of music'.

Even at this early stage in his conducting career, Boulez was able to capitalize on his excellent rapport with the players. Their relationship was based on an unusual combination of camaraderie and immense mutual respect. 'We had known him for a long time', Guy Deplus told me. 'We were on Christian name terms, and when we didn't agree we told him so in no uncertain terms. But he was so musically cultured, he knew so well what he wanted and why, that we were invariably forced to go along with him.'

The audience might well have said the same, for Boulez gave freely of himself, and it was difficult not to respond. His determination to provide his backers with value for money was admirable. Right from the start, the Domaine needed a *répétiteur*, and later, a conductor, manager, secretary, platform steward, programme-note writer and treasurer: Boulez combined all these functions. Inclined by nature to think that things go best when he attends to them himself, he became the veritable jack of all trades of his enterprise. These days, he recalls with some amusement: 'I did absolutely everything; I was the librarian and I wrote the programme notes, as treasurer I collected the cheques and took them to the bank myself. I really did everything, from A to Z.'

15 Jacques Castagnet, flute; Claude Maisonneuve, oboe; André Rabaud, bassoon; André Fournier, horn; René Albin, trombone; Pierre Doukan and Luben Yordanoff, violins; Jacques Cazauran, double bass; Claude Helffer, piano; and many others, too numerous to mention.

No member of his subscription audiences could fail to be impressed by this extraordinary level of activity. Paule Thévenin explains that 'He was unsparing of himself, displaying so much energy and organizational ability in order that all might go well, that we could not deny him support.' In short, the organizer and his public were, for once, admirably matched.

The audience of the Domaine

The Domaine succeeded in establishing an audience by appealing to four different population groups – a principle Boulez later applied to other undertakings at IRCAM, Bayreuth, or in New York.

First, there were the 'society ladies', who were to provoke general sarcasm, and to infuriate Bernard Gavoty (alias Clarendon). Dressed in their compulsory mink coats, they rolled up in Cadillacs which were parked in front of the Odéon,[16] alongside the mopeds of the students. They may have been rich, but at least they put their money to good use. Boulez was aware of what he owed them, and was in no way allergic to their expensive attire: 'I have never understood the kind of inverted snobbery which has it that those who wear mink necessarily have cloth ears.' To the critic Emile Vuillermoz,[17] who was soon to find fault with this part of the audience, he said that 'quite frankly' he found these women 'much nicer to look at, their judgements more worthy of consideration and far less pretentious than those of certain professional critics'.

On the benches alongside the moneyed upper crust sat the younger members of the audience and the students; it was they who queued for hours for these concerts, who were ready to absorb enormous quantities of unknown music and who had refused to ignore Boulez at a time when nothing in their educational background could have drawn them to him. Years later, it was they who chanted 'BOU-LEZ, A PA-RIS'!' when the exiled composer made an appearance at the Salle Pleyel; and even now, it is the composer's younger admirers who dominate the ranks of the IRCAM subscription audience. Irrespective of changing fashions, Boulez can rely on them.

Then there were the professional musicians – at least, those who considered themselves to be more or less abreast of the times. Representa-

16 A theatre founded in Paris in 1797; when the Barrault-Renaud company moved there in 1959 it became the Théâtre de France, then in 1971 it was re-named the Théâtre de l'Odéon.
17 Musicologist and critic (1878–1960); editor of La Revue musicale and author of numerous books and articles.

tives of the generation preceding Boulez's own were few in number: Georges Auric, Nadia Boulanger (who hated it, but came nonetheless), Darius Milhaud and, of course, Olivier Messiaen – whose support and participation to some extent protected the Domaine from accusations of musical Bolshevism. Most significantly, there were the young serial musicians, composers and instrumentalists alike; suffocating in the desert of French music, they drank in the atmosphere of the Domaine musical like flowers the morning dew. Sometimes these composers were given the chance to hear their own music played, and played well. For such tremendous opportunities, Michel Fano, Gilbert Amy, Betsy Jolas (a later recruit) and Jean-Claude Eloy[18] are grateful even today. 'It was the end of the tunnel', explains Michel Fano, and when Gilbert Amy was asked what the Domaine meant to a young composer he replied 'Almost everything'.

And lastly, there was the intelligentsia. The Domaine attracted a crowd of writers, philosophers and artists, including such prominent subscribers as René Julliard,[19] Nicholas Nabokov, Louis-René des Forêts,[20] Armand Gatti, Pierre-Jean Jouve,[21] André Schaeffner,[22] Henri Michaux,[23] Marcel Brion[24] and M. and Mme Henri Gouin, the directors of Royaumont. A random glance at the list of subscribers from these early years yields many other well-known names: the physician François le Lionnais, Henry-Louis de la Grange,[25] Vladimir Fedorov,[26] François Wahl,[27] Daniel Charles,[28]

---

18 His ex-pupil after the latter had referred to the 'hegemonic' character of IRCAM – so leading to the controversy which arose around 1978–80.

19 Publisher, notably of the *Cahiers Renaud-Barrault* in the early days.

20 Writer (born 1918), author of an occasional series of articles for the NRF and of *Le Bavard* (1946).

21 Poet and writer (1887–1976), author of a book on Mozart's *Don Giovanni* (1942) and, in collaboration with Michel Fano, of *'Wozzeck', ou le nouvel opéra* (1953).

22 Ethnologist and musicologist (1895–1981), founder of the ethnological department at the Musée de l'Homme in Paris in 1929 and author of studies on Debussy and Stravinsky, amongst much else.

23 Poet (1899–1984); Boulez based *Poésie pour pouvoir* on one of his texts.

24 Writer and aesthetician (1895–1984), author of novels and fantasy tales as well as of studies on German romanticism.

25 Musicologist (born 1924), author of a monumental monograph on Gustav Mahler (3 volumes, Paris 1973–84).

26 Russian historian and musicologist (1901–79), custodian of the library at the Conservatoire, then at the Bibliothèque Nationale; author of a book on Mussorgsky (1935) and president of the International Music Council at UNESCO (1964–6).

27 Writer and philospher (born 1925), associated with the Tel Quel group; literary director to Editions du Seuil.

28 University lecturer and aesthetician (born 1935), pupil of Messiaen at the Conservatoire, specialist on John Cage; head of the music department at the University of Paris VIII and author of *Temps de la voix*.

Mme André Malraux – and even the composers Henri Sauget, Giuseppe Englert and Iannis Xenakis.[29]

Oddly enough for a composer alleged to have suffered his worst setbacks in his own country, Boulez immediately succeeded in hitting upon a formula that was the *sine qua non* for musical success in France: he formed an alliance with the artistic and academic intelligentsia. It would only have taken Jean Cocteau to complete this cosy (even traditional) family scene! (Ironically, as Maurice Le Roux reports, the prophet of Les Six did actually attend the Domaine's inaugural concert, resplendent in flowing cape and striped waistcoat: the very embodiment of the 'eternal avant-garde'.)

The journalists

Much can be learnt about the state of musical France at the beginning of the fifties from an exhaustive study of the stimulating, instructive and well-contrasted press reviews of the time – always bearing in mind that these writers would inevitably have subscribed to one of three opposing groups: the licensed enemies, the active supporters, and the indifferent.

The enemies were led by Clarendon, whose long-standing hostility towards Boulez has earned him several incongruous nicknames. Adopting this same antagonistic stance, he warned his *Figaro* readers of what would await them if they ventured to set foot in the Domaine; toning down his remarks when addressing the JMF, he was no less voluble in trying to dissuade the music-loving youth from risking adventure. 'I would say that the atmosphere is more than serious' he wrote, referring to the 'roll-necked sweaters, frayed collars, unkempt hair and lynx-like eyes' of a section of the audience on the look-out for possible hecklers – who in turn risked being 'torn to pieces'. The traditional image of an obedient student youth had been superseded by 'the activity of a religious sect' attending a 'black mass'. He speaks of hearing the Webern *Bagatelles*, apparently for the first time, and a quintet by Pousseur which he 'would not wish on his worst enemy'; Berg's *Lyric Suite* 'spreads a little balm on the wounded heart' but he suspects this music to be somewhat heretical in the eyes of those who programme it here. These were some of the more inane remarks from one by no means lacking in intelligence.

Other critics were no more benevolent, adopting a heavily ironical tone; on the subject of Varèse's *Density 21.5*, Marc Pincherle[30] wrote that 'As

29 And the painters André Masson, Vieira da Silva, and others.
30 Critic and musicologist (1888–1974); president of the French musicological society from 1948–56 and author of numerous works, particularly on the violin.

regards the density of the music, the decimal point could well be moved back a place.' In an account in *Le Monde*, the economist and part-time critic, Pierre Drouin, reckoned that Nono's work 'is more closely related to the morse alphabet than to musical notation'. Adding his voice to the free-for-all, the redoubtable José Bruyr[31] also attacks Webern for his 'sharp, sour grace-notes, cries as of frightened mice, sonorities as attractive as cold pee – all giving the impression of being there as the result of a "random cast of the dice", to quote the eighteenth-century dictum'. The collection of absurd remarks about the Domaine is seemingly inexhaustible.

But the allied camp made up for quantity by quality. This camp included literary writers on music like Marcel Schneider, lovers of literature like Louis-René des Forêts and, above all, the two most astute music critics of the day, Claude Rostand and Antoine Goléa. The first, who writes mainly for *Le Monde*, is both a connoisseur and a defender of serialism; the second, who divides his vehement judgements between *Témoinage chrétien* on the left and *Carrefour* on the right, combines unquestionable competence with an eloquent enthusiasm. His relations with Boulez have not always been entirely untroubled – the *Entretiens* ingenuously include a letter from Boulez which is almost outside the bounds of common courtesy – but Goléa permits Boulez the ingratitude of the great.

Eventually, the commonest press reaction was discreet restraint: one may not like what one hears, but one has to show a semblance of objectivity – better to be on the safe side, since Boulez can prove a terrifying adversary! The first season's concerts were announced and later reviewed in *Le Guide du concert* under the name of Claude Chamfray. He gives credit to the new enterprise for its existence and salutes the old music in the programmes; for the rest, he speaks of Nono's work as a 'laboratory' product of 'abstract, withered, dehydrated and dehydrating' music – and again uses the term 'abstract' with regard to Stockhausen. This was to be the commentator's 'stock-in-trade' from now on. Mean-while, the critics made up for a lack of enthusiasm towards the works themselves by their almost fulsome praise of the unanimously acclaimed performers.

---

31 Belgian music critic (1889–1980), contributor to numerous publications, including *La Revue musicale*; author of a book on Brahms (1965).

The programmes, 1954–6: a preliminary evaluation

So things continued. If the critic was less than enchanted, he got used to it; in the end he will be regarded as having played no part, either positive or negative, in the rise of the Domaine. This had its own audience, its supporters, and its *modus operandi*. The first three seasons were held at the Petit-Marigny, with the number of concerts increased to six for the 1954–5 season. These took place on Saturdays at 5.30 (again, starting in the second quarter of the season, with the first concert on 12 February, the last on April 27), or in one case, a Sunday at 11 o'clock (6 March, preceded by a short talk by Boulez on the Blaue Reiter exhibition at the Maeght Gallery.[32] Another, on a Monday evening in March, was held at the Trinité church,[33] filled to overflowing for a Messiaen concert. *La Chronique* reported that the crowd pressing for entry to the church was such that the Master was almost prevented from reaching the organ loft: he had to prove his identity and explain that he needed to warm up the organ in advance, before reluctantly being allowed through.

The following season returned to the original format of four concerts, beginning on 10 December. Their unqualified success meant that each one now had to be given twice: on Saturdays at 5.30, repeated on Sunday mornings at 11 o'clock.

The list of works presented speaks for itself. In 1964, the *Cahiers Renaud-Barrault*,[34] which offered a regular platform to Boulez and his friends, provided a statistical summary. It included the first performances of works soon to become classics by Barraqué (1956), Cage (1956), Eimert (1955), Fano (1954), Henze (1956), Messiaen (1954), Nono (1954 and 1955), Pousseur (1955), Stockhausen (1954 and 1955) and others. The 'enlightened' composers of the past included Machaut, Dufay, Gesualdo, Gabrieli, Monteverdi, Bach, Mozart and Beethoven. And lastly, there were an impressive number of works by the Second Viennese School, headed by Webern, as well as great twentieth-century classics by composers such as Debussy, Ravel and Stravinsky – who were certainly not ignored by traditional concert life, but whose music was to become more broadly understood through the Domaine's performances of

32 A contemporary art gallery founded in 1946 by Aimé Maeght (1906–62); in 1954, with his wife Marguerite, he set up the Maeght Foundation at Saint-Paul de Vence.
33 Eglise de la Trinité: a church in the nineteenth *arrondissement* of Paris where Messiaen became incumbent organist in 1930.
34 Quarterly review of the Renaud-Barrault company that first appeared in 1953; originally published by Juilliard, later by Gallimard.

unjustly neglected works like Ravel's *Frontispice*, Stravinsky's *Pribaoutki* or Debussy's *En Blanc et noir*.

It is a remarkable fact that no work by Boulez was ever premièred at the Domaine concerts. Several important works of his were played there, of which some (*Structures* Book 1, and *Le Marteau*) had not previously been heard in France. But clearly, Boulez did not regard the Domaine as a launching-pad for his own compositions.

Despite accusations of sectarianism, the second surprising factor was the fine balance achieved between firmness of purpose and open-mindedness – contradictory requirements that an enterprise of this kind had to reconcile. As the years went by, the broadening of the Domaine was to lead to more emphasis being given to the second than the first, but in the early years, Boulez kept his pledge to define an aesthetic while keeping an ear open to the pulse of the world.

'RECHERCHES MAINTENANT' ('*PRESENT-DAY SEARCHINGS*')

Written in 1954, during the first season of the Domaine musical, this short article was a key to Boulez's compositional strategy at the time.[35] It was in fact a critical approach to strict serialism, both from the point of view of the organization of the various parameters as well as that of form (he also hints at instrumentation, but does not deal with it here).

Examining the concept of dodecaphonicism – which 'clearly displays its garden of Greek roots' – Boulez seizes on the example of Webern in order to point to the need for serial realignment: 'Webern had organized nothing but pitch; one [now] organizes rhythm, timbre, dynamics; everything is fodder for that monstrous polyvalent organization which must be quickly brought under control unless one wishes to be condemned to deafness.' To be aware of the danger is in this respect to guard against it. He notes that total serialization has its own contradictions: based on the continual variation of the different parameters, it generates 'a total absence of variation on a more general level' – in other words, 'monotony'. The key question with regard to musical composition (and, one is tempted to add, analysis) had already been perceived: that of the relationship between what is written and what is actually heard. Boulez thus arrives at the proposal 'to seek a dialectic that will place each moment

---

35 *Notes of an Apprenticeship*, pp. 21–6. This article first appeared in the *Nouvelle Revue Française*, a monthly review devoted to literature and criticism, founded in 1909 by a group of writers led by André Gide and others.

Concerts at the Petit-Marigny (1953–4)

First Concert (January 13 1954)

1 *The Musical Offering*   J. S. Bach
   (realized by Vuattaz)

2 *Polifonica, Monodia, Ritmica*   L. Nono
   (first performance)
   Kontrapunkte   K.-H Stockhausen
   (first performance)
   Concerto, Op. 24, for 9 instruments   A. Webern

3 *Renard*   I. Stravinsky
   with J.-L Barrault (in the mimed role of Renard),
   Jean Giraudeau, Bernard Lefort, Xavier Depraz,
   and an ensemble of solo players directed by
   Hermann Scherchen

Second Concert (February 24 1954)

1 Group of Pieces   G. Dufay
   Three Satires, Op. 28   A. Schoenberg
   (first performance)
   Marcel Couraud Vocal Ensemble and an
   instrumental ensemble directed by Marcel Couraud

2 *Suite*, Op. 25   A. Schoenberg
   Variations, Op. 27   A. Webern
   Sonata, 1926   B. Bartók

3 *Cantéyodjayâ* (1948)   O. Messiaen
   played by Y. Loriod
   Ile de feu I (1950)
   Mode de valeurs et d'intensités (1949)
   Neumes rythmiques (1949)
   Ile de feu II (1950)
   these four works played by O. Messiaen

4 Three Madrigals   G. Monteverdi
   Two Madrigals   G. Gesualdo
   Entflieht auf leichten Kaehnen, Op. 2   A. Webern
   Two Songs for Mixed Chorus, Op. 19

Third Concert (March 24 1954)

1   *En Blanc et noir*   C. Debussy
    Astrid and Hansotto Schmidt-Neuhaus
    Six Bagatelles, Op. 9   A. Webern
    New Vienna String Quartet
    Four Pieces, Op. 5   A. Berg
    Guy Deplus, clarinet, Paul Jacobs, piano

2   Sonata No. 2 for Violin and Piano   B. Bartók
    Luben Yordanoff, Paul Jacobs
    Pièces en Trio   M. Philippot
    (first performance)
    Quatre Chants russes   I. Stravinsky
    Trois petites chansons
    Trois histoires pour enfants
    Pribaoutki
    Jean Giraudeau, instrumental ensemble directed by
    Serge Baudo

3   *Frontispice*   M. Ravel
    Sonata for Two Pianos   M. Fano
    (first performance)
    Astrid and Hansotto Schmidt-Neuhaus
    Lyric Suite   A. Berg
    New Vienna String Quartet

Fourth Concert (April 10 1954)
at the Grand-Marigny

1   *Octandre*   E. Varèse
    Serenata   B. Maderna
    Five Pieces, Op. 10   A. Webern

2   Ricercar from *The Musical Offering*   J. S. Bach
    Chansons de Bilitis   C. Debussy
    (incidental music version)
    reciter Madeleine Renaud
    Grosse Fuge (for string orchestra)   L. van Beethoven

3   *Chamber Symphony*, Op. 9   A. Schoenberg
    conducted by H. Scherchen

of a composition between a rigorous total structure and a momentary structure subject to free will'.

The second part of the article is devoted to the problem of form, and consolidates the direction of this 'research'. Boulez did not consider that external formal modifications had done anything to upset the traditional concept of form as such:

Even when the most essential contemporary works reject formal classical schemes, they do not really abandon at all a general idea of form which has not varied since the development of tonality. A musical work is made up of a series of separate movements; each of them is homogeneous in both structure and tempo; it is a closed circuit (a characteristic of Occidental musical thought); balance among its different movements is established by a dynamic distribution of tempos.

He is critical of this idea of a single, definitive interpretation of form, and looks to the advent of a musical work 'in which this separation into homogeneous movements will be abandoned in favour of [a] non-homogeneous distribution of developments. I demand for music the right to parentheses and italics . . .' (here he is anticipating the very device to be used in *Trope*!). And he continues by demanding 'a notion of discontinuous time, thanks to structures that will be bound together rather than remaining divided and airtight': *Le Marteau sans maître* is not far off. He ends with an indication of the concept that opens up the whole poetic expression of the Third Sonata itself, calling for 'a sort of development in which the closed circuit will not be the only solution envisaged'.

In this way, 'Recherches maintenant' seems like a written statement of fact that invokes 'Eventuellement' (1952) before announcing 'Aléa' (1957); these are the three crucial moments within the composer's own trajectory.

LE MARTEAU SANS MAITRE: A MAGNIFICENT SCANDAL

The years 1954 and 1955 were fully occupied, not only with the launching of the Domaine musical and the execution of various bread-and-butter tasks, but more particularly, with the completion of the important score on which Boulez had worked for the past two and a half years. This is a symbolic work, whose title was to impart a certain notoriety at the time. Like *Les Misérables* or *Les Grandes Baigneuses*, *Le Marteau sans maître* has now become an accepted part of the vernacular, to the extent that the work eclipses its composer, and the title the work itself.

The dramatic circumstances surrounding its first performance served a purpose. The new work was designed for the Donaueschingen Festival of 1954, marking Boulez's first important entry into what has been called the Nation of Concerts – although this was a nation without frontiers which, in the Europe of the 1950s, was characterized by a kind of international style. It so happened that the première had to be postponed owing to the illness of the proposed guitarist. Boulez took advantage of this delay to revise a number of details: in addition to more minor improvements, he lengthened certain notes, slightly expanded the scoring of the first movement, and added a ninth movement as finale.

A good opportunity for the first performance then arose in June 1955. The International Society for Contemporary Music (ISCM) was that year to be held in Baden-Baden at the suggestion of Heinrich Strobel, director of music at the Südwestfunk, and a devotee of Boulez. It remained only to obtain the agreement of the French section of the ISCM – without whose sanction nominees were denied the honour of representing their country at this event. The French section declined: thanks to them, Boulez found himself on the same exalted level as Berlioz and Debussy, who had also been exposed to the harassment of the Philistines after the gods had already given their blessing!

Heinrich Strobel's enthusiasm for Le Marteau had already fired him to arrange fifty rehearsals with Hans Rosbaud. With a reflex action which was more legitimate than legal, he decided to go further: as the result of a little arm-twisting, the Südwestfunk (the inviting authority) was persuaded to withdraw from the organization of the session.

In this way, Le Marteau sans maître had its triumphant première on 18 June 1955, with Sybilla Plate (then the seventh Valkyrie at Bayreuth!) as soloist. The French contingent made a dignified exit from the hall, although certain of its members were later to rally round. As for the audience, it withheld none of its enthusiasm: it was 'an instant and sensational success', as Goléa notes. Meanwhile, history has done the French committee the favour of forgetting its constitution.

LE MARTEAU SANS MAITRE (1954)

For the third time, Boulez showed a striking loyalty in resorting to Char – but this time a very different Char. Unlike the erotic, almost romantic lyricism of Visage and the sunlit warmth of the poetic symbolism of Soleil, the poems which form the literary basis of Marteau belong to another creative period of the poet's life – the period from 1930 to 1934 which, in his own words, constitutes 'the irreconcilable domain of Surrealism'. The exact chronology of the texts set by Boulez is described on pp. 22–5.

The text of the three poems chosen is striking in its concision: a few phrases, or rather successions of words; a few words, hardly more than phonemes. To 'interpret' them poses formidable problems, which even the best of Char's scholarly commentators seem in no hurry to confront. Perhaps it is not even necessary. It might be simpler to take note of the particular evidence offered; when incorporated into a relatively long piece of music (one of Boulez's longest works), the concision of the poetry – with its absence of punctuation, except for the final full stop – seems in some way immersed in the musical flow. One becomes aware of many striking characteristics: the use of the initial capital letter, sometimes conventional, ('Pérou'), sometimes according to arbitary requirements ('L'Imitation', 'Balancier'); the repetition of certain words ('tête', 'che-vaux-cheval'); the iterative allusion of certain others ('cadavre', 'morte'); the elision of over-indicatory articles or verbs; the sole rhyme; the assonance of 'Bel édifice'; the alliteration of 'Bourreaux' or, at the beginning, of 'L'Artisanat'. But above all, there is the extraordinary power of the images presented, the flint-like hardness of the chosen vocables, and the magnificent balance of lines which bring enchantment to the simplest utterance.

Boulez chose three texts as the three crucibles of his personal poetry. Setting the poems within an instrumental commentary, and 'doubling' the third in the manner of Couperin or Rameau, he organized a succession of nine movements dedicated to exploring the relationship between a sung text and the sea of the surrounding music. In doing so, he presented himself with an age-old musical problem which, in this instance, led him to return to a seminal twentieth century work and, if possible, to transcend its expression. The work in question was, of course, *Pierrot lunaire*.

From Pierrot lunaire to Le Marteau sans maître

The reference to *Pierrot lunaire* is 'intentional and direct', as Boulez explained in 'Dire, jouer, chanter' – an article[36] dating from 1963 which is in fact the scripted and somewhat elaborated version of a talk given on a number of occasions when the two works were presented in the same concert.

36 Published in *Cahiers Renaud-Barrault*, No. 41, 1963; reprinted in *Orientations*, pp. 330–43.

In fact the parallels are both direct and indirect. In the direct sense, both cases involve a succession of relatively short movements for voice and a small instrumental ensemble whose composition changes with each movement:

Pierrot	Marteau
voice	voice
flute (+ piccolo)	flute
clarinet (+ bass clarinet)	vibraphone
violin	xylophone
viola	viola
cello	guitar
+ piano	+ percussion

Both composers arrange the movements to form three cycles: Schoenberg's twenty-one movements make up three cycles of seven movements each, while Boulez surrounds two of his sung poems with instrumental 'settings', the third being repeated in its 'double'.

It can be seen that the four vocal and five instrumental movements of Boulez's three cycles are interlinked (cf. 'Recherches maintenant', pp. 71–3 above). The linear succession of the nine movements makes the first version of 'Bel édifice' the centre of the work, with the other eight movements symmetrically arranged around it. The composer has outlined the links between the movements of each cycle: the three commentaries on 'Bourreaux de solitude' form a single movement, itself 'directly linked, from the formal point of view' with the vocal movement. (One could perhaps regard the recognizably 'triptych' aspect of 'L'Artisanat furieux' as an unconscious homage to the passionately detailed work of the religious painters of the Middle Ages.) The first version of 'Bel édifice' is a form in itself, while its 'double' brings elements of all the preceding movements into play – so serving as a finale in which all the instruments are employed. And lastly, in another direct reference to Pierrot lunaire, Boulez's third movement for voice and flute is an instrumental quotation of Schoenberg's seventh movement, 'Der kranke Mond'.

Le Marteau sans maître will be examined in some detail later on (see pp. 285 ff.). For now, I would like to draw attention briefly to Boulez's allusions to 'exotic' musical cultures, and to the specific use of serial technique.

I CYCLE OF 'L'ARTISANAT FURIEUX'	II CYCLE OF 'BOURREAUX'	III CYCLE OF 'BEL EDIFICE'
1 Avant 'L'Artisanat furieux'		
2	Commentaire I 'Bourreaux'	
3 'L'Artisanat furieux' (with voice)		
4	Commentaire II 'Bourreaux'	
5		'Bel édifice' (with voice)
6	'Bourreaux de solitude' (with voice)	
7 Après 'L'Artisanat furieux'		
8	Commentaire III 'Bourreaux'	
9		Double of 'Bel édifice' (with voice)

From the breaking with 'the closed circuit of Western music' to the approach of serialism

On hearing *Marteau*, one is immediately struck by its genial sound, its expressive consistency, and by the undeniably non-European aspect of its design. Boulez's allusion to 'exotic' music is again intentionally direct, arising from his choice of instruments: 'the xylorimba is a version of the African balaphone, the vibraphone is a reference to the Balinese gamelan, and the guitar is reminiscent of the Japanese koto'. He nevertheless guards against a possible misinterpretation of these sound relationships: 'as such, neither the style nor even the use of the instruments has anything to do with the traditions of these different musical civilizations' – any connections are more akin to reminiscences and quotations than to functional borrowings. Still less is there any attempt at a sharing of spiritual preoccupations; in this respect, Boulez marks the limit of his non-European adaptations – a limit distinct from that of Stockhausen, or later, of Jean-Claude Eloy.

In fact, Boulez's repeated declarations as to what African or oriental civilizations might have contributed to his own style (or to that of Western music in general) are very ambiguous. For example, the ritualistic aspect of the second movement of *Marteau*, or the bell-like sounds of the seventh, certainly show that these influences have been absorbed by the composer: immediately, the quotation becomes relative. Incidentally, Boulez's ideas on musical time or on the necessary (and here ignored) 'contemplation of sound' later to be expressed in *Eclat* or *Rituel* may produce admirable works, but it would be hard to imagine them coming from the pen of a composer not entirely versed in Western techniques. So the question remains open.

This 'breaking of the closed circuit of Western music' – to return to an expression that is a kind of leitmotif with Boulez – is in any case completely in step with the composer's reconsideration of serialism in *Marteau*. The seductive sound of the work is not solely dependent on the incredible mastery and sensitivity of the scoring – which has provoked the malicious to label Boulez as a latter-day Ravel; neither does it depend solely on the 'piquancy' (to borrow Adorno's expression apropos Stravinsky) produced by such exotic colours. It rests above all on a more relaxed expression – vocal as well as instrumental – that is the direct result of a completely absorbed language: with *Le Marteau sans maître*, Boulez has completed the arsenal of his expressive means. The work is in no way less 'serial' than its predecessors (*Structures* and *Polyphonie X*) – a misinterpretation largely encouraged by journalistic comment. In one sense it is more so: serialism has imploded through an accumulation of internal energy. Disregarding the idea of dogmatic strictness, and starting from the fundamental rule of non-repetition and variation, Boulez has invented derived procedures which he handles with supreme elegance – in much the same sense as a mathematical solution may be described as elegant or not, rather than merely right or wrong. Exclusively musicological analyses of *Marteau* (like that of Piencikowski) have already taken sufficient account of this: it will suffice to summarize them in the chapter devoted to the work later on. What is important is that Boulez, at thirty, was thereafter master of the means of his alchemy: he had transformed disparate linguistic elements into a 'transparent and gilded' whole, through the hammering of 'l'artisanat furieux', and had achieved a 'psychological and formal liberation'.[37] Once again René Char sums up the innumerable constraints facing both poet and musician: 'The dejected, symbolic side of Man is always shackled, but now his prison is that of freedom.'

Le Marteau sans maître becomes part of the repertoire

The Baden-Baden performance of *Marteau* was repeated a month later at the Aix-en-Provence Festival; directed by Gabriel Dussurget[38] and Roger Bissonet, this was the only international festival apart from the specialized Donaueschingen to include programmes of the best contemporary music alongside those devoted to Mozart and Campra.[39] The credit for this must again be given to Hans Rosbaud, who excelled in both repertoires, and who usually travelled with the Südwestfunk orchestra as part of his luggage.

It was then that the French critics discovered – or, in the case of Goléa and Rostand, rediscovered – the work, now preceded by the explosive reputation it had acquired at its tumultuous première. The predictably loyal Claude Rostand acclaimed the artistry and rock-hard beauty of the stones (pierres) in a score composed of 'crystal, diamond or flint'. He also noted that flint is 'the symbolic emblem chosen by René Char to describe his output as a whole', before going on to underline the classical and wholly French vein of inspiration in the new score – a classicism that included Debussy, of whom Boulez was the direct heir.[40] But the reaction of Marcel Schneider is still more interesting. At Aix, he disliked *Marteau*. He did, of course, acknowledge the impressive work done by all concerned in the fifty or so rehearsals at Baden, while chastizing Sybilla Plate for her poor French pronunciation. He then went on to discuss the score itself. He dismissed Boulez's contrapuntal skill, saying that 'he now counterpoints noise instead of notes', and even considered that the composer showed a nostalgic yearning for electronic music. Schneider was presumably referring to the percussion, which transported him to 'the Peking Opera'. There followed a long description of the Chinese (?) character of the instrumental ensemble and, as the end of the article approached, he no longer hid the feelings of boredom induced in him by the monotony and by the sheer length of *Marteau*. If Boulez wanted to

---

37 I here paraphrase what Mary Ann Caws has to say about *Marteau* in *L'Œuvre filante de René Char*, p. 55.
38 Founder of the Aix-en-Provence Festival in 1948.
39 Composer (1660–1744), born in Aix-en-Provence.
40 *Carrefour*, 27 July 1955.

immerse the listener in exoticism, that was fine, but why had he chosen to set Char? 'I have read and re-read *Le Marteau sans maître*, and I can discover neither the spirit nor the sentiment nor, above all, the lyrical strength, clarity and simplicity of René Char's poetry in a score assembled like a fragile clockwork mechanism – in this erudite pulversation of sound corpuscles where the human voice adds a jarring note, alternately anachronistic and offensive. It seems as if "Monument to a Chinese Musician" or "Composition opus such and such" would have been a more appropriate title.'[41] And yet, Schneider was a man of cultivated sensibility, and generally well-disposed towards Boulez.

Nine months later, his views were to change. *Marteau* was given at the Domaine on 21 March 1956, this time with French performers, and Marie-Thérèse Cahn as soloist. The gallant ensemble included Serge Collot, whose appearance as viola player on three recordings conducted by Boulez (Cahn, Desroubaix, Minton) is a splendid example of loyalty. At the Domaine it was Boulez himself, still little experienced in this field, who conducted. Marcel Schneider had now had time to reflect. He admitted frankly that he had changed his mind, showing himself receptive to its balance and lucidity: '*Le Marteau sans maître* is a traditionally French work, its stylistic logic and penetrating intelligence putting it in line with Rameau. The skilful choice of instruments and the flexibility of their use is reminiscent of Stravinsky's *L'Histoire du soldat*, or *Renard*. These are first-rate recommendations, and there is no doubt that *Marteau* will likewise become a classic.'[42]

In any event, the work itself was a success. In the months following the Baden-Baden première it was enthusiastically received wherever it was heard – whether in Vienna, Zurich, Munich, London, New York, or Los Angeles. Stravinsky could be counted among its most celebrated admirers, greeting it as the masterpiece of new music. Suddenly, Robert Craft was persuaded to conduct *Marteau*, and he even made a somewhat inflexible recording of it. It is fascinating to follow the evolution of a single contemporary piece through its performance on disc, and *Marteau* is one of the rare works with enough different recordings to permit this.[43]

There have even been attempts to choreograph it. I have not seen the

41 *Combat*, 23–4 July 1955.
42 *Combat*, 27 March 1956.
43 Such a comparison was made with Boulez's help and in his presence during an analysis broadcast on France-Culture; the Yvonne Minton recording (the most recent) is striking for its impression of serenity and natural facility.

ballet based on a synopsis by Serge Popesco[44] and premièred on 10 November 1965 by the Bucharest Opera Ballet, although I know the one by Maurice Béjart. First performed at La Scala, Milan in 1973, this has become one of the Company's classics; it is an intelligent spatial representation of both the instrumental structure of the work (with certain dancers present or absent from particular sequences, in line with the presence or absence of instruments within the work itself), and its dynamic and kinetic energy. Musicians scarcely need the materialization of the images supplied by the dance, but it certainly presents a real means of introducing undeniably difficult music to a public larger than one would normally expect at our exalted contemporary music ceremonies.

Today, *Le Marteau* sounds oddly dated compared to a work like *Pli selon pli*. Like Char's text itself, the oriental tolling of the music sounds to me like a signal from another planet: *Le Marteau sans maître* definitely belongs to the past.

FROM THE *SYMPHONIE MECANIQUE* TO THE *ORESTEIA*

Two relatively minor but interesting works appeared during the years 1955–6.

In 1955, largely for financial reasons, Boulez composed the music for *Symphonie mécanique*, an experimental film by Jean Mitry. Lasting some fifteen minutes, this remarkable production was a hymn to the 'art of precision' of our mechanical age. Using filming techniques involving magnification, it shows various objects, apparently with a life of their own – for instance, bottles on an assembly line – in such a way that the significance of the object is dissolved: it becomes abstract through a process that might almost be described as musical. Boulez quickly composed an appropriate score, with instrumental sounds reworked and transformed at the experimental studio of the GRMC – to which he still had access.

That same year, Barrault's director of music presented him with evidence of a more essential art by composing incidental music for the *Oresteia* of Aeschylus (given in the translation by André Obey).[45] This incidental score consisted of about a quarter of an hour's music spread

---

44 Rumanian choreographer who worked at the Bucharest Opera, emigrating to the United States in 1965 following the first performance of his ballet *Le Marteau sans maître*; he committed suicide shortly afterwards.
45 Writer (1882–1975) who worked with Jacques Copeau at the Théâtre du Vieux Colombier; translator of the *Oresteia* by Aeschylus.

over the three hour spectacle. It was written for voice, chorus, and an instrumental ensemble of six players. The pianist Paul Jacobs acted as *répétiteur* for this work, which bore witness to Boulez's friendship with Barrault. When Boulez raised his baton, the players were sometimes heard to snort with disgust at music which to them sounded outlandish as well as being rhythmically difficult.[46] I recently asked Boulez if this was the occasion he beat time on the shoulders of his players and he replied 'Yes, both for the *Oresteia* and for *Christophe Colomb* . . .'.[47] Even if still smarting from the effect, the players doubtless relish the memory of the distinction thus conferred.

THE END OF AN ERA: FROM THE PARTING WITH BARRAULT (1955) TO INTERNATIONAL RENOWN AS A COMPOSER (1955–7)

At the end of the 1954–5 season Boulez ceased to be musical director to the Barrault company – partly owing to lack of time, but also for psychological reasons: a turning point had been reached in the relationship between celebrated elder and promising junior, making it difficult for the director of the Domaine musical to remain as pit conductor at the Marigny. As a leaving present, Boulez gave Barrault the score of the *Oresteia*, his first piece of incidental music.

It was in any case a question of a change rather than a rift between them. The Domaine was there to maintain a more than cordial *entente*, and Boulez's move to the Salle Gaveau in 1957 was merely a temporary one: when the company found new premises of its own in the Odéon theatre in 1959, it was once again able to accommodate the Domaine.

By this time the Domaine itself was well under way. In February 1956, a concert of works by Debussy, Bartók, Pousseur, Berg and Webern was so successful that Antoine Goléa announced in *L'Express*: 'Pierre Boulez at last has a public'.[48] In April of the same year, the French première of *Le Marteau sans maître* placed the work alongside songs by Webern, Nono's

---

46 First given at the Bordeaux Festival, the production offended Jean-Jacques Gautier, the theatre critic of *Le Figaro* notably because of its incidental music: '. . . I must avow that what they have the nerve to call the music of Pierre Boulez seemed to me an abominable magma of discordant sounds – and that the sheer quantity of pretentious noise is ear-splitting even to the least sensitive. It is a gross insult to a distinguished public. Anything resembling a right note is driven out, hunted down, systematically banished and exterminated' (*Le Figaro*, 14 June 1955). It should also be noted that the translation of the *Oresteia* (by Paul Claudel) used by Darius Milhaud played no part here – despite what may be read elsewhere.

47 A play by Claudel for which Darius Milhaud wrote the incidental music in 1928.

48 *L'Express*, 8 February 1956.

Incontri, and Stockhausen's *Kontrapunkte*; the reception given to the Boulez work has already been noted.

At this time, Boulez's principle musical contact was with Stockhausen. Though the two musicians were linked by a sort of reciprocal deference, their opposing aesthetic viewpoints were even then being revealed, with Cage as the subject, if not the pretext, for disagreement. It was at Stockhausen's instigation that, in May 1956, David Tudor played parts I and II of *Music of Changes* during the yearly Darmstadt summer course. Graciously in attendance at this private concert were Boulez, Maderna and Nono. At the end of the performance, there was a brisk exchange of opposing views between Stockhausen and Boulez as to the importance one should accord to indeterminacy and chance, and whether the limit had been reached. Doubtless planning his *Klavierstück XI* at the time, Stockhausen was a maximalist; Boulez, then contemplating his Third Sonata, was more circumspect. This marked the beginning of a parting of the ways from the artistic and social points of view, but did not affect their professional esteem: in December of the same year, Boulez presented a carefully prepared performance of *Zeitmasse* at the Domaine, preceded by an analysis (though it is true that there is nothing in this particular work to offend Boulez).

Meanwhile, in October, *Structures* Book 1 had been given at Donaueschingen by Yvonne Loriod and the composer, preceded by Debussy's *En Blanc et noir*. This was at a time when the two musician–pianists were only too happy to tour Germany as a means of making some money – their recitals including works for solo piano by Messiaen and Boulez, played by Yvonne Loriod.[49] Claude Rostand was present in Donaueschingen, and, in *Le Monde*, openly proclaimed his admiration for the duo:

> Their performance of the Debussy had an extraordinary rapport, in style both analytical and intense, aided by a firm and supple technique and a muscular, incisive and powerful sonority: no swooning here – this was playing of steely quality, just as well suited to the enigmatic Debussy piece as it was to the superb *Structures* by a young composer who is now one of the outstanding personalities of the contemporary French school.

All this gave a definite impression that, in 1957, a new phase was about to begin. Boulez was recognized in France, but spent much of his time elsewhere. Few premières of his works were given in his own country; the Domaine carried on, but without promoting the composer's personal

---

49 The same programme formula was to be proposed for the NDR series 'Das neue Werk', Hamburg, 1957.

interests. He was beginning to be better known internationally than in France, and had perhaps reached the point where it was time to move on. This is certainly the implication of a contemporary article which sums up his progress to date, and hints at directions soon to be taken – directions which in fact represent a substantial revolution within his compositional style.

'TENDANCES DE LA MUSIQUE RECENTE'[50]
('DIRECTIONS IN RECENT MUSIC')

This article bridges two historical stages. It first summarizes the major musical developments of the century – this amounts to something of a subjective history of music as seen by Boulez at the time. Then it projects itself towards the future birth of an electro-acoustic technology to an extent that would not have been inappropriate in an inaugural IRCAM booklet or even as a programme note for *Répons*.

The contributions of Stravinsky and the Second Viennese School are reassessed: with the former, the survival and even the strengthening of 'elemental poles' freed the mind for the development of rhythm; with the latter, the series was conceived to the detriment of formal preoccupations and only achieved its full potential with Webern, who was to make it an essential 'fibre' (Boulez's expression) of the whole sound-space.

The works of Varèse shed a particular light on the evolution of music: a preoccupation with the phenomenon of sound *per se*, 'the structural use of dynamics', the highlighting of the percussion with its avoidance of equal temperament; (Boulez criticizes both the latter and the octave-based scale which, in its various organizations, dominates our music). From this point of view, Cage's interest in percussion and in scales not based on the octave places him in a direct line of descent from Varèse.

Boulez then returns to Webern, 'the threshold of contemporary music'; it was Webern who tried as far as possible to 'reduce' linguistic articulation to its solely serial functions and who, because of this approach, was led to abandon the question of rhythm: it is here that Messiaen comes in, and Boulez underlines just how much the concept of total serialization is indebted to the composer of *Mode de valeurs et d'intensités*.

(Here, I digress for a moment. This cavalier view of twentieth-century music is both striking and persuasive; it has all the clarity and sequential

50 *La Revue musicale*, 1957; *Notes of an Apprenticeship*, pp. 224–32.

logic of Boulez's then subjective teleology. But are things really so simple? In any case, this is a musical twentieth century deserted by Debussy, Bartók, Berg, and others.)

'The final goal for discovery is that of the non-tempered sound-worlds'; so writes Boulez in a postlude to his note on Messiaen. The second part of the article develops this point in depth. The author again sets out from John Cage's experiment with the prepared piano which, at the time, he saw not as a tinkering with timbre but as a craftsmanlike attempt to alter the four components of piano sound: duration, amplitude, frequency and timbre. Even earlier than this, the Webern of the *Klangfarbenmelodie* discovered that orchestration did not have a merely decorative value but 'formed part of the structure itself; it is a particularly effective way of relating and combining pitches, durations and dynamics'. With a remarkable prescience, Boulez draws attention to a truth that computer research was many years later to confirm: namely, that timbre is not in fact the fourth parameter of sound, but a function of the three others.

In other words, today's means of progress lies in the use of the machine! It alone allows for a real extension of serial thought (which Boulez, as we know, does not confuse with dodecaphonic technique) to include all components of the sound-world. Certain of his phrases have a curiously futuristic ring:

Instrument construction is one of the major obstacles to the development of a musical idea based on non-tempered intervals . . . It is now possible to assess the extent to which it has become a matter of urgency to collate all the research done, to broadcast the discoveries made, and to extend the means of an already acquired technique . . . [Musical thought] finds itself in need of a particular realizatory means at the very moment when electro-acoustic techniques are able to furnish them . . . Important researches into the intrinsic qualities of sound remain to be undertaken; perfected apparatuses, manageable and essential to the composing of such works still have not been built. Nevertheless, these views are not so utopian that they can be ignored; it is even probable that the increasing interest aroused by the epiphany of an unprecedented, unheard-of sound-world will only hasten the solution. Let us wish, modestly, to be the first artisans.

CHAPTER SIX

From the Open-form Work
to Mallarmé's *Livre*

'Everything in the world exists to give rise to a book.'
Stéphane Mallarmé quoted by Jacques Scherer[1]

'To love what one will never see again.'
Alfred de Vigny

Enough has been said, written, debated, and even composed on the polemics of the open-form work and the meaning of the term. Various other expressions have been used in an attempt to arrive at a satisfactory definition: the aleatory work, controlled chance, the mobile work, and so on. None is really as convincing as the 'open-form work', which even in its most general sense indicates less a technique than an attitude of mind, less a result than an approach, less the aesthetic of a work than its compositional ethic.

Boulez was one of the principle actors in this saga; nevertheless, we should here acknowledge a chronological paradox. Boulez's compositional path twice crossed with that of Mallarmé, and in each case, the objective was quite simply that of artistic creation itself. But the two works are each nurtured by very different literary material. In the first case, Boulez had recourse to poems that are arguably among Mallarmé's most successful, but which call for the utmost understanding if they are to reveal any of their esoteric quality: this confrontation was eventually to give rise to *Pli selon pli* (1957–62), the subject of the next chapter.

In the second case, Boulez came across the author of 'Un Coup de dés'

---

1 '*Le Livre*, instrument spirituel', *La Revue blanche*, 1 July 1895.

for the first time when he himself was already deeply immersed in a compositional project – and even then he discovered Mallarmé only through the illumination of a particular work by a third person: in 1957, Jacques Scherer published a version of the *Notes* that Mallarmé left concerning the preparation of the *Livre* – an unfinished project which represents the very culmination of his poetic inspiration. The chronologies of the two artists are thus reversed, with the prototype of the open-form work represented by the Third Sonata (1957) predating the poetic transmutation attempted in *Pli selon pli*. And in this case the challenge posed does not involve the single and arduous objective of discovering a meaning from a text and then attempting to create a sound equivalent. Instead, Boulez offers a mirror image of the writing itself and of the object – whether book or score – resulting from it. The approach is, if you like, much more radical.

BOULEZ VERSUS STOCKHAUSEN

On 26 September 1957, during the season of concerts organized by the Kranischstein Institute at Darmstadt, Boulez played his latest work: the Third Sonata for piano. This makes ample use of an 'opening up' process, in which the performer is given a certain latitude as to the choice of material and, in particular, to the order in which he plays it. Coming from a composer who had always presented a picture of himself and of his music as belonging to a particularly controlled and supervised world, the event caused a sensation. The eminently authoritative, almost mechancial composer of the notorious *Structure 1a* and the meticulous (but no less imperious) musician–poet of *Le Marteau sans maître* seemed to be approaching new shores.

Two months earlier, this time during the closing concert of the International Summer School at Darmstadt, Paul Jacobs had given two successive interpretations of Stockhausen's *Klavierstück XI* (separated by pieces by Webern and Juan Hidalgo – the future founder of the post-Cageist group Zaj!). This is a remarkable piece in which the pianist plays with a certain degree of indeterminacy: the music is written on a single, huge sheet divided into nineteen 'structures' – each endowed with its own tempo, dynamics, 'attacks', and nuances. The performer starts with whichever structure his eye lights upon, and proceeds to play it in the most neutral way possible – without nuance, at a regular tempo, within a moderate and consistent dynamic, and so on. At the end of this, his glance turns, again theoretically at random (though habit soon tended to be a problem!), to another of the nineteen structures, endowing it with performance characteristics not of its own, but of those indicated by the preceding one. And so the work proceeds. It is apparent that there are many possible versions of *Klavierstück XI*, especially as the performer can, if necessary, omit one or more of the nineteen structures: any Hewlett-Packard should demonstrate that there are at least a million versions! To the seasoned professional listener, it was obvious that the work Paul Jacobs repeated later that evening in no way resembled the one he played at the start of the concert.[2]

Some of the other pieces in the series of *Klavierstücke* – like *Klavierstück VII* – represent a sort of apotheosis of almost unrealistically precise stipulations, forcing the performer into a veritable strait-jacket; compared to these, the sudden freedom conferred on the interpreter in *Klavierstück XI* was hailed as revolutionary.

Was the prophet of this revolution Boulez or Stockhausen? From the autumn of 1957, this question was to be the subject of much conjecture. Those who championed the German composer alleged chronological priority; those in favour of Boulez replied that while it was possible to appreciate the aesthetic of the French composer in various ways, it was difficult to imagine his being dictated to by a research programme. All the same, one has only to know how slowly Boulez works to realize that the overall concept of the Sonata must already have been formed by the time Stockhausen finished his *Klavierstück XI*. Besides, the arguments are largely academic, particularly since this idea of a reconsideration of the role traditionally allotted to the performer – by introducing a measure of indeterminacy into the progress of the work itself – had been in the air for some time, and Boulez's 1957 revolution was the result of a specific development of the ideas fundamental to Western notated music.

IDEAS IN THE AIR

Without wishing to overstress the point, however precise a traditional score may be, it leaves a margin wide enough for the performer to put his own seal on it through the interplay of tempos, dynamics, colours and phrasing – even the decision to make this or that repeat (as can be heard in

2 In *Rencontres avec Pierre Boulez*, Antoine Goléa gives a spirited account of the evening. In fact, *Klavierstück XI* had been premièred by David Tudor in April 1957 at the Carl Fischer Hall in New York; for health reasons, Tudor was unable to travel to Europe, and Paul Jacobs then had less than two months to familiarize himself with the work (Peyser, op. cit., p. 125).

certain performances of Beethoven's Fifth Symphony by Boulez himself). In fact, since printing began, the history of music really seems to have depended upon the composer/performer relationship. As notation became better differentiated and perfected, so the composer attempted progressively to reduce these interpretative liberties – as in the music of Ravel, which goes a long way in this direction.

The limits of the undertaking are obvious. If, for instance, music descriptive of nature and gusts of wind wishes to suggest a feeling of improvisation, must it necessarily stipulate an absence of precision? At the opposite extreme were those composers who relished the discovery of total serialization and who were to overload their scores with peremptory, sometimes frenzied, indications, the multiplicity of which cancelled out the very possibility of obeying them. Some sections of the Second Sonata, or of *Le Marteau sans maître* verge on the impracticable from this point of view. When the composer's requirements resulted in too many specific instructions, the actual performances tended inevitably to result in what might be described as '*rubato* interpretations'.[3]

One also needs to consider another factor, which is at the heart of the process of serial writing itself. As Ivanka Stoianova[4] shrewdly observed, 'the serial statement brings about a particular fusion between difference and repetition within the sound texture'. By dint of demanding non-repetition, the serial organization of a finite number of elements of pitch and duration paradoxically establishes a kind of non-repetitive pattern. Boulez has already been seen to treat the series in a predominantly mechanical manner: hence the fragmentation, variation, and the displacement of values at work in a post-serial score like that of *Le Marteau sans maître*. The minor adjustment involved in handing over responsibility for effecting this dislocation of the system to the performer was doubtless part of Boulez's actual serial thinking.

This endogenous revolution was in line with contemporary thinking – particularly that of American composers. However, it should be pointed out that with Boulez, the aesthetic of the open-form work seemed influenced by the Americans (Cage, Brown, Feldman) only because it

3 Faced with the same situation, Kagel gave it dramatic form: the stipulated frenzy he inflicts on his performers pushes them into a state of permanent anxiety, almost of distress – a psychological circumstance that provokes the tension characteristic of his best works (*Acustica, Match, Der Schall* and others).
4 In the study devoted to 'La Troisième sonate de Boulez et le projet mallarméen du *Livre*', *Musique en jeu*, No. 16, 1974, pp. 9–28, reprinted in *Geste, texte, musique*, (UGE, 1978), pp. 120 ff.

represented a reaction against what he regarded as an open invitation to total abdication.

The reader should refer to what has been written about Cage,[5] or about American trends in general, in order to assess what Boulez was so ruffled by. The various procedures brought into play (throwing dice, drawing lots, the use of radio programmes, scores that could be read in any direction, and much else) were to cast general suspicion on the notion of a pre-established text with which the performer had no option but to comply. The fact that the performer is now invited to take part in the compositional process means that the composer has to relinquish a share of his rights, either in the interests of aleatory procedures or to allow the performer more freedom of movement.

It is important to note that the platitude which claims that the discovery of the open-form work arose from a libertarian reaction against the iron grip imposed by the serial system was invented after the fact: either because, once again, the open-form project was inherent in the system of total serialization itself, or because the American composers had had occasion to feel themselves 'got at' by the European serialists of the 1950s. In fact, this so-called liberation served rather as an excuse for those composers – particularly the Europeans – who felt ill at ease with serialism, and wished to extricate themselves from it in an honorable manner.

The year 1957 can be regarded as symbolic for Boulez: matching actions to words, he wrote an article which spoke of the new spectre of chance now haunting the musical world.

'ALEA'[6]

This is one of Boulez's most difficult but most important articles. He begins by pointing out two uses of chance, both tending towards one general direction. The first of these is inadvertent chance, where 'the event arrives as it may, uncontrolled by the composer (voluntary absence, though not meritorious, resulting from impotence), BUT inside a certain established network of probable events, it being very necessary for chance to dispose of some sort of contingency.'

5 For example, *Pour les oiseaux* by Daniel Charles, Paris, Belfond, 1976; and in particular, the article on John Cage in *Documentary Monography in Modern Art*, edited by Richard Kostelanetz, New York, Praeger Publishers Inc., 1970. Other editions appeared in England (Penguin Press, 1971) and Germany (DuMont, Cologne, 1973).
6 *La Nouvelle Revue Française*, 1 November 1957; *Notes of an Apprenticeship*, pp. 35–51.

This disinterested chance is the opposite to automatic chance, where the composer aims at achieving 'the most untouchable objectivity. Schematization simply takes the place of invention, the imagination strains to give birth to a complex mechanism that is then charged with engendering microscopic and macroscopic structures until the exhaustion of possible combinations has indicated the end of the work.'

Boulez saw this last attitude as a somewhat fanciful concept: the more one seeks to expel the arbitrary, the more present it becomes. Hence the move in a direction that involves awarding arbitrariness a compositional value in itself: 'Notation will become sufficiently – but subtly – imprecise, to allow the passage through its mesh – a diagram of a hypothesis – of the interpreter's instantaneous and changing reflection. One *could* prolong this silence, one *could* suspend this sound, one *could* accelerate, one *could* . . . at every moment . . .'

Boulez sets what he calls 'controlled chance' against what he describes as the miscalculations of the century. Using the image of a 'sort of multi-circuited labyrinth', he again asserts the rights of the composer to exercise his discretion, not in the sense of a hedonistic reinstatement, but as an inalienable criterion for the compositional act – authorizing the composer to change the style of writing adopted at the start if he feels the need to do so. Here he takes the example of Hindu music – he could as well have referred to jazz – which combines some kind of structural *formant* with on-the-spot improvisation. For Boulez, the possibility of introducing a degree of chance lies in this interaction between 'two textual determinants, the one strict, the other open to interpretation', because he insists that total improvisation leaves more room for cliché and automatism than for spontaneity and true invention. (On this point he has never changed.)

I have done no more than present a very simplified outline of Boulez's position; the text of 'Aléa' itself is much more subtle and articulate. The reader will still find it useful today because, even if its concerns are dated, it poses compositional questions that are nonetheless crucial and almost unvaryingly present. Some particularly interesting points arise. Boulez, a composer descended from Schoenbergian serialism, unexpectedly shows himself much less concerned with the logic of pitch than with that of register and interval; he also outlines the vocabulary of a work, such as the notion of the 'terraces of options'[7] adopted *in toto* in *Constellation—*

7 Nevertheless, in noting (and with reason) that 'even on the highest level, the *ossia* is by no means the last word in invention', Boulez provides ammunition against himself: in practice, the *ossia* is well and truly the only possibility left to the interpreter (cf. the end of *Don*, *Structures* Book II and, in particular, *Domaines*).

Miroir; and lastly, in relation to the performer, he appears optimistic that the future will further modify the real possibility of semi-open devices so as to include more than one or two players – a matter yet to be followed up.

MALLARME'S LIVRE

The boundary lines are thus well defined. The open-form work will exploit chance, but in a genuinely controlled way. In fact, Boulez was to set up a system of options which would serve the purpose of 'opening' the work. At this or that moment in performance, the interpreter finds himself faced with a choice: he can elect to go this way or that, to play this structure or that, or neither – to follow this path now, or later. Taken as a whole, the meaning of the message is not altered by the permutation of its constituents. Rather like a mobile, the object remains the same even if a breeze displaces its 'formants'.

The discovery of Mallarmé's *Livre* can be regarded as pertaining to this concept of supervised freedom. As early as 1866, Mallarmé (then aged twenty-four) indicated in a letter to Théodore Aubonel that he had 'laid the foundations of a magnificent work', and shortly afterwards, forecast that it would take him a good twenty-five years to compose the five books envisaged. In fact the forecast proved optimistic. Mallarmé began work on his *Livre* in 1873, but made slow progress. Twelve years later, in 1885, he became convinced that it was destined to remain incomplete, and proposed to reveal only 'a finished fragment as an example of its glorious authenticity, while giving an outline indication of the remainder, which a whole lifetime would not suffice to complete'.

From 1894, he was able to work at it more continuously, devoting his mornings to 'this old pool of dreams', as he called his work-to-be, and the afternoons to his poetry. The compilation of the fanatically specific notes making up the general outline of the work occupied all the latter years of his life. Mallarmé died in 1898, at the age of fifty-six; pledged to a poetic existence since about 1862, his short life had thus been almost entirely obsessed by this astonishing project of the *Livre*.

When he died, Mallarmé's family handed over to Henri Mondor[8] a blue loose-leaf folder containing the outline of the future *Livre*, and Mondor

---

8 Surgeon and writer (1885–1962), member of the Academy of Science, author of works of literary criticism on Mallarmé and Valéry, editor of the *Pléiade* volume on Mallarmé (1945).

sent the manuscript to Jacques Scherer who published this collection of two hundred and two sheets in 1957.

Frankly, it makes heavy reading. It takes little or no account of the fascinating research possibilities, or of the richness of choice that the *Livre* ought to offer. But it has to be remembered that these are only working notes, not the *Livre* itself – of which the famous poem 'Un Coup de dés' might well have been the first chapter to come.[9]

It is the poetic project which is important here rather than the non-existent *Livre* in itself (which might in any case never have come into being) or even the notes left by Mallarmé. This is explained both in the course of his correspondence and in the two articles which form the basis of the substantial preface to Scherer's edition – which I have drawn upon here.

The writing

The writing itself refers to an infinity, which needs to be expressed in a form corresponding to its essence. The words printed on a white page effectively symbolize an inversion of the fundamental concept of a heavenly nocturnal canopy, with cloudless stars standing out against a dark background. The relationship between the two may be likened to that between a photograph and its negative.

Variability

It is obvious that this pursuit of infinity cannot be limited by the linear, unidirectional and fixed ordering of the ordinary book. The truly literary expedient is to enable the constituents of the book – pages, phrases, verses (if there are verses), words, and even letters – to be moved freely and imaginatively, but not arbitrarily, within the *Livre* itself.[10] The movable sheets do not only prompt multiple permutations, they demand to be read from right to left, to be omitted and repeated in changing successions. Mallarmé himself said: 'Despite the impression of being fixed, the book becomes mobile as a result of this permutational play – from death, it comes to life.[11]

9 Such is in any case the hypothesis of Guy Michaud in *Mallarmé*, Hatier, p. 200.
10 Scherer, Preface to Mallarmé's *Livre*, p. 57.
11 Ibid., p. 191.

Performance

This variability, which effectively turns a fixed number of elements into an infinity[12] (hence the capital letter of the *Livre*) in itself suggests performance. The *Livre* is not understood unless it is performed, and this is one of the most important things it has in common with music, which 'scarcely exists except as direct communication' (Boulez). Mallarmé's meticulous plans for his *Livre* included not only physical details, relating to the thickness of the book itself, the number of symbols on the page, and the distribution of its chapters, but also the crucial premise that it should be read in public. Mallarmé's Tuesday reading sessions in the rue de Rome generally took place in front of an audience of twenty-four persons, with the reading divided into two parts, separated by an interval; successive versions of incomplete sections of the *Livre* were presented two at a time. As interpreter of an object both absolute and infinite, Mallarmé suppressed his own personality in a ceremony that was by turn theatrical and ritualistic: he was no longer author, nor even interpreter; he was priest to the believers, and 'operator' of the *Livre* itself.

'SONATE, QUE ME VEUX-TU?'
(*'SONATA, WHAT DO YOU WANT OF ME?'*)[13]

I have summarized as succinctly as possible the whole of the 'idealized' material governing the *Livre* which becomes the explicit model for the open-form work as represented by Boulez's Third Sonata. As regards the theatrical aspect of the performance of the *Livre*, and its financial side (much talked about in the notes), there I would refer the reader to Scherer's preface, since these points, important though they may be for the project itself, are much less so for the purpose of grasping the fundamental ideas behind this astonishing encounter between Mallarmé's *Livre* and Boulez's project for a mobile form. The whole question of the *Livre* will be examined further when we come to discuss the problem such forms were to pose for Boulez, and for others.

Several years later, when the Third Sonata had already begun its quasi-autonomous life as symbolic of a new age – as seen in the work of Boulez and other serial composers – he wrote a remarkable article compiling an

12 On combinatory analysis, see p. 102.
13 An article on the Third Sonata in *Médiations*, No. 7, Spring 1964, pp. 61–75, reprinted in *Orientations*, pp. 143–54. This is the original French version of the article 'Zu meiner III Sonate', translated by H.-K. Metzger, *Darmstädter Beiträge*, Mainz, 1960.

aesthetic of the open-form work with the detachment and clear-sighted-ness he always brought to such undertakings.

In it he asks: 'Why compose works destined to be changed with each performance?' And he underlines the current discrepancy, as he sees it, between an energetic renewal of vocabulary on the one hand, and on the other, a certain laziness with regard to form.

Literary influences play a greater part in this awareness than do musical ones. Boulez cites the example of Joyce, with whom 'the novel . . . looks at itself from an external, objective point of view', and of Mallarmé, through whom 'thought has become an end in itself, its main justification being an essentially poetic quest'.

Using his knowledge of oriental music to make the point, he criticizes the concept of a work as a unique object whose straightforward repetition excludes all potential for surprise. He sees the work of the future more as a 'labyrinth' where, as in Kafka's short story *The Burrow*, 'it adopts a number of possible itineraries in which, with the aid of an extremely precise plan of action, chance can play the part of a last-minute shunting device'. Later, Boulez liked to quote Butor's example of Venice as the ideal, a town in which the same goal can be reached by different routes.

In this way he immediately distances himself from total indeterminacy 'where the same phenomenon is applied to any organizable thought, in any style, to the point of absurdity'. Indeterminacy can only be partial and controlled; it requires directions for use, some sort of code and, for the composer, a re-questioning of the graphic organization of classical scores. In fact, each *formant* of the Third Sonata introduces control devices peculiar to itself. Boulez here takes the example of the poem 'Un coup de dés' which, through its typographical arrangement on the page, suggests a musical organization concerning the relationship between sound (the letter) and silence (the space). The layout also suggests hierarchies, dominant motifs, recurrences, symmetries, dynamics (the consistency, character, thickness and thinness of the lettering) – even a 'cantus firmus' (as in the 'Texte' section of *Trope* from the Third Sonata), where the words of the famous line 'Un coup de dés jamais n'abolira le hasard' ('a dice-throw will never abolish chance') are distributed from page to page with all their common resonances and verbal harmonies.[14] For Boulez, as

---

14 A similar correspondence between the basic material and the nature of the text can be observed in another of Mallarmé's activities: having remarked that the dimensions of an envelope are just right to contain a quatrain, Mallarmé was in the habit of writing the name and address of his correspondents in verse. The legibility of such addresses rested to a large

for Mallarmé, graphic invention must always be strictly dependent on structure: 'We have already seen certain experiments where, despite the elegant design, commendable in itself, there is no fundamental re-casting which would impose an exigency for total transformation.'

It was when thinking along these lines, and when he had already 'completed the essentials of his self-imposed task', that Scherer's book appeared: 'For me, this was a revelation, in the strongest sense of the word.' The idea of multiple routes, reversible and variable, with an *ad hoc* typographical format, on separate sheets, was to fuel the work in hand, to take charge of it ideologically and theoretically so that it could move towards open-form works in which the composer – without relinquishing his own responsibilities – offers the interpreter (the 'operator') the chance to exercise his own imaginative faculties.

The article ends with a description of the main formal principles governing each of the five separate 'formants' forecast for the Third Sonata, as well as those governing the work as a whole. He concludes:

Form is becoming autonomous and tending towards an absolute character hitherto unknown; purely personal accident is now regarded as an intrusion. The great works of which I have been speaking – those of Mallarmé and Joyce – are the data for a new age in which texts are becoming, as it were, 'anonymous', 'speaking for themselves without any author's voice'. If I had to name the motive underlying the work that I have been trying to describe, it would be the search for an 'autonomy' of this kind.[15]

THE THIRD PIANO SONATA (1956–7): SOLUTION AND PROBLEMS

The elimination of the content of a work

The material of the Third Sonata is wide-ranging and extremely rich. Pianistically, Boulez achieves a full and iridescent instrumental sonority analogous to that of *Le Marteau*. The use of the entire keyboard compass is even more assured than in the Second Sonata, particularly in the use of harmonics. Furthermore, the whole range of resonances, 'attacks', registers and hand clusters, together with a generally extreme virtuosity, offer a rewarding challenge to the interpreter.

Nevertheless, it is not possible to discuss the presentation of the Sonata

---

extent on a correct pronunciation of the text (which had been syntactically transformed, with words and phrases reversed, etc.). The postmen must really have appreciated this.

15 A dream of anonymity represented by opposing practices: the anonymity of Cage's fortuitous choice, of the borrowed series in *Structure 1a*, and now of the anonymous text.

without a brief description of its form (see pp. 299 ff.). As with Boulez's other open-form works, there is a danger that it will be drained of some of its strictly musical meaning by attempting to analyse the devices upon which it is based. To say that is not however to express any fundamental reserve as to the principles of the work. In other words, Boulez had only to look to Mallarmé on this very point. Jacques Scherer rightly points out that Mallarmé's eloquent, precise, even meticulous notes on the external appearance of the separate sheets of the *Livre* and on the rules for its 'reading', throw little light upon its content. 'Very few pages of the manuscript', he writes, 'are devoted to what the *Livre* has to say. Reflections on its structure are pursued in depth, those on its content barely sketched.'[16] In any case, even the slightest suggestion of a means of access to the content is only the more fascinating, and Scherer's attempts in this respect comprise the most valuable part of his Preface.

Some analogies

Everyone knows the Beethoven sonatas or the Chopin waltzes. As to the former, we take for granted that their first movements, for instance, will be heard as a succession of bars and of sections exactly as foreseen by the composer himself. One would therefore expect any well-known pianist to launch into the Appassionata at bar one and continue up to the final double bar of the opening Allegro. Authoritative commentators have disclosed that, as usual, this movement comprises an exposition and its repeat, a development and a recapitulation – four sections as clear to the listener as they are to the reader of the score. If by chance an enterprising interpreter should decide to begin the sonata with its development, followed by the recapitulation and then by the exposition and its repeat – and the next day he were once more to change the point at which he began the work, but still so as to play the four sections in the same circular succession, this would be the Beethovenian equivalent of Boulez's *Trope*, the second 'formant' of the Third Sonata.

The fourteen Chopin waltzes are usually played in the printed order. A performer may nevertheless decide to group them otherwise, arranging them according to taste, while taking account of the contrasting characters of each waltz, the suitability of their succession according to key, contrasting tempos, and so on. One such experiment took place in Besançon on 16 September 1950, when Dinu Lipatti presented his own

16 Scherer, op. cit., p. 125.

sequence of the fourteen waltzes.[17] What he did with the fourteen units of Chopin's text is exactly what Boulez proposes the performer should do with the meticulously composed structures of 'blocks' or 'points' in *Constellation*, the third 'formant' of the Third Sonata.

Such comparisons do not, in themselves, prove anything, and these examples probably contain more differences than analogies. But the differences themselves provide the most fertile ground for discussion, since it is the character of the abnormal (in the first case) or the far-fetched (in the second) that marks the innovatory in Boulez's approach to variability: by constructing a work within which the concept of time will be different from that of chronological time.

The polemics of the open-form work

What is so striking about the open-form work in general is that its artistic orientation has a direct bearing on the form of the work itself. Irrespective of the aesthetic success or otherwise of the work in question, this gives rise to polemics – in the highest meaning of the word. The Third Sonata has never aroused much controversy in respect of its aesthetic qualities. On the other hand, the debate launched in France as to the new problems posed by the open-form work (which cannot have escaped the composer himself) was such as to affect not only present or future pronouncements on the notion of variability but future compositional practice. I have come to the conclusion that, with the Third Sonata, Boulez entered upon a period of research which, in turn, led to a period of crisis, defined by a awareness of the inevitable problems of the open-form work. This crisis was eventually resolved some twenty-five years later, with *Répons*. Apart from *Pli selon pli*, which arises from another important Boulez tradition (although it, too, includes provision for optional procedures), all the works of this period are symptomatic of an ambivalence pushed to extremes: *Structures* Book 2, *Eclat*, *Domaines* and *Rituel* all demonstrate the inherent problems of the open-form work.

The open-form work and the various protagonists in the musical game

The musical game involves various participants. Each reacts to the open-form work in a different way, though some are, perhaps, less crucial in determining the final outcome. Nevertheless, music publishers, copyright societies and record producers are certainly involved; for example,

17 It could even be said that Lipatti chose to omit one of the 'structures' from his programme, since he left out the fourteenth waltz, deeming he no longer had the strength to play it as he would wish.

Universal Edition were not exactly thrilled by the graphic design of the Third Sonata, and in particular, by the use of two colours for *Constellation–Miroir* – whose publication was consequently delayed. Copyright can cause problems: should one remunerate the composer alone, or include a fee for the performer, since the latter's contribution both to the structure and the duration of a work must, to some extent, be acknowledged? And lastly, there is the question of the record producer, who must ultimately fix for all time the outcome of a momentary decision, by issuing one version of a work paradoxically defined by the multiplicity of its possible readings. No company has so far recorded different versions of the Sonata; perhaps some far-sighted video producer will one day hit upon the form (or the format!) which will allow everyone to compose his or her own version of the Third Sonata from previously recorded material, in line with Boulez's instructions for use.[18] But joking apart, there are three major human components to this musical game: composer, performer and audience. And the fourth element is debate.

The performer

One can speculate as to whether the performer of the Third Sonata feels more creative, or less inhibited by routine than when he tackles the Second Sonata. It would be interesting to know whether he regards the 'multiple choice' aspect of the work as affording too few (or too many) permutations, and whether he feels capable of conveying the difference between two successive performances of the same work. There is also the possibility that the open-form work may have changed his relationship with the composer.

This is what Claude Helffer has to say:[19]

In theory, I ought to play the work differently each time. In practice, I do not, because I believe that a certain rapport is established between a personality and the possibilities offered. So how did I arrive at playing it as I do today? Proceeding cautiously, the first thing was to discover the possible routes. Basically, each sequence has to be worked at separately before joining them together. Little by little, one comes to link two or three sequences, with the subjective feeling that one such link is more logical than another. In this way you arrive at a particular route which enables you to get from beginning to end. After three or four attempts I was satisfied with the routes I had chosen and no longer had any desire to search for different ones. Before starting to play *Constellation–Miroir* I now have three

18 This is the gamble of the hypothesis of interdependence on which Michel Fano is currently working, specifically with regard to Boulez's open-form works.
19 In *Musique en jeu*, No. 16, 1974, p. 29.

possibilities in mind – routes for which I have already provided. But this does not prevent me from sometimes taking an unplanned path on the spur of the moment.

In short, his approach is both balanced and empirical. Those who perform this work do somehow experience a sense of real freedom underlying their intentions – even if this freedom does not reside in exactly the direction the composer had envisaged. It is almost as if the performer goes through a process of familiarizing himself with the work which is not dissimilar from the way he might approach a Beethoven sonata for the first time. But whereas coming to terms with a conventional work would normally involve matters of nuance, tempo, phrasing, atmosphere and touch, here, he has to search out routes within the work itself. It is not simply a question of more, or less, freedom: Claude Helffer playing Boulez's Third Sonata is no more free than Boulez conducting Beethoven's Fifth. He is free in a different way – at least in the sense that he is responsible for determining the overall design of the work. And yet this work is in some ways more resistant to interpretation, since the formal reshaping it allows from the outset can inhibit the performer's response to the essentially musical issues involved.

The change is thus more subtle than one imagines. The ideal of variability seems somewhat hollow: the performer chooses what he feels to be a satisfactory version and generally sticks to it.

The audience

The question arises of whether the audience is attuned to the distinctions and choices offered by the open-form work, and whether such an awareness sharpens audience response. It would be easy to dismiss this notion out of hand, thus obscuring the more tenuous, fragile, problematic (but at the same time more perceptible) bonds between an audience and the open-form work. It may be that listeners are generally little aware of alterations to the sounds with which they are presented: probably even less in the case of the Third Sonata than of Stockhausen's *Klavierstück XI*. But perhaps they are sensitive to a certain tension revealed in the playing, and to the fact that they are being confronted not simply by the image of a composed work but by the composition of the music itself. My own experience as a listener bears this out: at the same concert where Claude Helffer first played the Third Sonata, then talked about it, with examples, before playing it a second time, the atmosphere was completely different from that of a traditional recital – even one of contemporary music. But there we are touching on the phenomenon of music itself.

Debate

The open-form work was a qualified success with the three principle participants in the musical game but it was an unequivocal success as a topic for discussion by various other involved parties, namely the critics, analysts, musicologists, writers of notes for programmes or record sleeves and of monographs on Boulez. Even Boulez himself has had occasion to perfect his formulae and moreover, to clarify his thinking during the course of many interviews.

In the thirty or so years that the open-form work has been part of our musical culture, it has brought about many irreversible changes in the relationship between a work and its composer, performer, and audience – changes which are fundamental to the music of our time.

The composer

What is striking about Boulez's discussion of the open-form work is the discrepancy between the forcefulness of his ideological explanation (literary comparisons, the freedom of the performer, changing attitudes to the work itself, the disappearance of the composer in favour of the anonymity of the 'operator') and the realistic self-effacement of his purely musical description. The composer remains the composer; by entrusting the performer with certain organizatory powers in connection with the material, he is not relinquishing his authority but investing it. As author of the limits of his own creation, he is putting himself in the god-like position of allowing an element of free will, without which his creation would cease to exist. Thus, the composer's potential is vicariously increased.

There are other ways in which the relationship between performer and composer have been affected. Boulez only really knows the performers he conducts, towards whom he shows infinite attentiveness and patience; but the solo performer (whether of the Third Sonata or any other solo work – the open-form nature of the former is not a factor) prompts only a polite detachment, not to say absent-minded indifference. Friendly and obliging, he went so far as to help Claude Helffer (on all fours!) to get his bearings in relation to the complicated signalling system of *Constellation* when, to begin with, its huge sheets were laid side by side on the floor – but that was all. He offered no comment on the aesthetic merits of this or that solution, and was even less disposed to applaud or criticize. What is interesting is that this structural attitude overlooks the characteristics of the works themselves; and that, in this respect, the open-form work is no more privileged than the rest.

The relationship of the composer to these kinds of works and his attitude toward the concept of open-form is much more inward, even conceptual in itself. In writing the Third Sonata, Boulez was not so much creating a mobile object as posing the problem of its variability. 'The interest lies not so much in comparing two aspects of a work as in sensing that it will never have a definitive image. It is a matter of amplifying the true nature of the work.'[20]

In other words, the open-form work is valued for its potential. The trace it leaves on the paper, even in an appropriately elegant graphic form, is no more than an analogue of the work itself, just one of its possible incarnations – even if it is one that can, in turn, give rise to sub-incarnations, represented by the different versions produced by the contingencies of performance. We are here in the realm of pure theory, which invites a deeper investigation of what is perhaps pretentiously called the 'ontology of the open-form work'.

The open-form work: from the incomplete to the whole

'I find it increasingly difficult to think of works as being merely fragments' – so Boulez declares in 'Sonate, que me veux-tu?'. Coming from a composer who has made the work-in-progress a way of life and half of whose output is regarded as incomplete – either to be finished (*Eclat/ Multiples*, the Third Sonata and, at the time of writing, *Répons*), revised (*Le Visage nuptial, Livre pour quatuor*, '. . . *explosante-fixe* . . .') or modified, (*Rituel, Domaines*) – the paradox is obvious. What he also challenges is the idea of a catalogue in which a number of separate and completed works accumulate in their autonomous and dead perfection. The 'work in progress' calls for extension, proliferation, subdivision into others; it is his own vast equivalent to the *Livre*, forming a single, open-ended, all-encompassing project.

It is at this point that a true philosophy of permutability is built up, which seemed at that time to invade Boulez's thinking. The open-form work adopts various aspects: optional points of entry, as in *Trope*; optional routes, as in *Constellation*; optional moments, as in *Structures* Book 2; and optional direction (forwards or backwards), as in *Domaines*. Ultimately, however, all these possible changes lead back to simple permutation.

20 *Conversations with Célestin Deliège*, p. 83. Compare that other Boulezian declaration, somewhat prior to the problem of the open-form work: 'Realization implies an abolition of what might be, in other words, the suppression of chance – not forgetting that chance itself plays a part in this suppression' ('Auprès et au loin', *Notes of an Apprenticeship*, p. 188).

Combinatory analysis clearly shows how permutation comes close to infinity. In the five complete volumes envisaged, Mallarmé's *Livre* can claim to aim at totality only because it is based on the permutability of its pages – the progression of possible permutations for a given number of objects being exponential.

As previously mentioned, there are nineteen structures in Stockhausen's *Klavierstück XI*. Since certain of them can be omitted, the number of possible permutations is significantly increased. Similarly, if the five *formants* of Boulez's Third Sonata were not subject to relatively constraining rules for linking one to another, there would be not eight but a hundred and twenty possible 'macro-versions' of the Sonata – without even taking account of the different 'micro-versions' that may be constructed from internal variations of the *formants* themselves.

It is then that the composer's decision (which Boulez calls choice) intervenes in order to avoid the reintroduction of chance as the result of an uncontrollable number of possibilities (here classed as any figure between zero and infinity). 'Chance as such is of no interest; it has no place in an aesthetic project, which essentially rejects it. Chance can only lead to components or samples, its only significance is statistical: that is, statistically speaking, the chance of having one interesting thing in a million.'[21]

How these decisions are to be taken is the crux of the problem of the open-form work, and it is doubtful whether the answer will have any bearing upon its function. The most that could be said is that this permutational fantasy tends towards mechanical interpretation of a slightly naïve kind in the less inspired works such as *Domaines*. Jacques Scherer remarks that the comic effect of Molière's phrase 'Belle marquise, vos beaux yeux'[22] is due to the fact that no directional variation is attached to its possible permutations, and that its content is both banal

---

21 *Conversations with Célestin Deliège*, p. 84.
22 This is a quotation from Molière's comedy, *Le Bourgeois Gentilhomme*. The newly rich, middle-class M. Jourdain aspires to the style and manners of the aristocracy. To this end he engages a number of teachers. He has written a billet-doux to a certain Marquise with whom he is in love, and wants to know the best way in which the message can be expressed: 'Belle Marquise, vos beaux yeux me font mourir d'amour'. When his teacher suggests that it needs some elaboration, M. Jourdain insists that just those words are to be used, and asks for the different ways in which they may be arranged. The teacher then enunciates the various permutations of which the phrase is capable: 'D'amour mourir me font, belle Marquise, vos beaux yeux . . . Vos beaux yeux d'amour me font, belle Marquise, mourir . . . Mourir vos beaux yeux, belle Marquise, d'amour me font . . . Me font vos beaux yeux mourir, belle Marquise, d'amour . . .'. At the end, M. Jourdain asks which is the best, and when he is told

and weak. He suggests taking a phrase rich in poetic resonance like the famous:

Un coup de dés	jamais	n'abolira	le hasard
I	2	3	4

– which, when chopped up into semantically meaningful elements, gives four permutational entities, and thus twenty-four possible permutations of unequal 'interest'. The example is all the more convincing in that, besides the differences in intensity arising from this or that permutational solution, the 'operator' declaiming the various solutions will have the full range of vocal resources at his disposal (accentuation, deceleration, acceleration, rhythm and weight) in order to add subtlety to his 'reading'.

The options offered by the Third Sonata are closer to the example just quoted than to the line by Molière. The aesthetic success of the open-form work thus risks being dependent on its place in a permutational scale bounded by these two types of text: in other words, musically speaking it depends on the quality of the material. From this point of view, the Boulezian open-form work inaugurates nothing radically new in terms of aesthetic approach, and in this respect its fascinating organizational device is no more than a superstructure.

The open-form work: from the whole to the dual option

By deliberately rejecting the possibility of infinite increase, the Third Sonata – written by a composer who aims above all at the possibility of realization – makes the figure 2 the centre of its system, so that 'infinity' contracts into 'alternative'. This realization unfolds inevitably within the given time-scale, so that each instant – imagined as separated from preceding and following instants by a negligible time-lapse – offers the performer the choice between two, and only two, actions at any given point: to change or not to change; to play the structure offered or to omit it; to play this one on the outwards route, that on the return (or the reverse); to move from left to right, or right to left. The Mallarmé-influenced composer of 1957 is preparing for the advent of the computer – which recognizes only zero and one. For me, the Boulez who conceived the Third Sonata has much in common with the Boulez who was later to design *Répons*, even if the resolution of the two works is completely different. Or rather, the new line of thought initiated by the Third Sonata

it is the phrase he himself wrote, he exclaims: 'And to think I got it right first time without having done any studying!'. (Footnote by Michael Purser.)

(notwithstanding the formal problems these innovations were to create in successive works) can finally call upon the resources of technology to resolve the underlying problem of the open-form work.

The suppression of the optional within time

We come now to the final part of the process. Performers have encountered the reality of choice, though it assumes a transient significance within the musical flow. This is because the dimension of time is so crucial in music. The plastic arts understand time only in terms of the duration involved in contemplating an object, irrespective of whether this object is static or mobile: the works reveal themselves within a time controlled by the viewer.

The literary work is to some extent dependent on the time taken to read it, but this is an accommodating time that may be suspended, interrupted, slowed down or accelerated. It allows for pauses, choices, and is reversible: some works can be read discontinuously and in several directions – particularly if, as in Mallarmé's *Livre*, the graphic lay-out lends itself to this approach.

The musical work does not have the advantage of these temporal freedoms. A piece of music is always heard, even played, within the unidirectional dimension of time. All procedures for upsetting this temporal arrangement are themselves caught up in the inexorable progress, over which no one – composer, performer or audience – has any control. Graphic design is misleading and, as Ivanka Stoianova notes: 'the musical elements to which it gives rise can in no way bear imprints of the visual labyrinth.[23] This, I believe, is really the final frontier of the brilliant but ultimately impossible undertaking of the open-form work.

23 *Musique en jeu*, No. 16, 1974, p. 26.

CHAPTER SEVEN

The Kindred Spirit

Mallarmé: Pli selon pli

When I began this undertaking, I intended to make Boulez's most famous work – *Le Marteau sans maître* – the central focus of the book, thus acknowledging that this important classic provides the most characteristic portrait of its composer. But as work on the book progressed, it seemed to me that it was not *Marteau* but *Pli selon pli* which was more truly representative of Boulez. I have already discussed the reservations which the Char-inspired work provokes today. To explain the precise nature of the deep understanding that links Boulez to Mallarmé will not be easy. Apart from certain similarities of background and temperament, they seemed to share a common attitude at the outset of their creative lives, when coming to terms with their separate callings. 'There is a need for poetry to be inaccessible, for poetry whose sense will at first escape the reader', writes Guy Michaud of Mallarmé; and he continues: 'this is because he was already aware that this concept of poetry exactly matched the demands of his own character, which combined and often found itself in confrontation with poetic insight, haughty reserve, and a desire for perfection'.[1] Is this not equally true of Boulez? But since this fraternal affinity is supposedly allied to a particular work, it is necessary to trace within the Mallarmé text itself the world of images and preoccupations that has given rise to a fundamentally parallel experiment on the part of the composer.

Such an undertaking is perhaps even more crucial than with Char. The text of *Marteau* is certainly obscure, but its affiliations with Surrealism inevitably make its interpretation subjective – whereas the hectoring tone

---

1 Guy Michaud, *Mallarmé*, Paris, Hatier, 1953 (re-issued 1970), pp. 20–21.

of *Soleil*, and the ardent lyricism of *Visage* offer the sympathetic reader material that is more immediately comprehensible. On the other hand, faced with a Symbolist poet whose output covered the last forty years of the nineteenth century, it is essential that one should arrive at an adequate level of understanding, precisely *because* of the difficulties involved. The ideal of a specific use of vocabulary and syntax demands some degree of deciphering before the meaning can be grasped.

Since Mallarmé clearly exerted a profound influence upon Boulez, it is perhaps worth examining their common preoccupations in some depth. The writings that Boulez has offered us on the subject are few, and far from satisfying. He has spoken about Mallarmé in numerous interviews, but his remarks remain general. For instance, in conversation with Célestin Deliège, he observed, 'What fascinated me about Mallarmé from my own position was the extraordinary formal density of his poems . . . Mallarmé tried to rethink the fundamentals of the French language.'[2] There is no article in *Notes of an Apprenticeship* comparable to the one about *Marteau* entitled 'Dire, jouer, chanter' and, more conclusively, nothing which explains his interpretation of Mallarmé's masterpiece. A lecture on *Improvisation II*, given at Strasburg in 1961 and only recently published,[3] sheds interesting light on the piece, particularly from the instrumental point of view. But again, there is nothing about his reading of the text, or about a possible similarity between the semantic content of the work itself and its musical progress. It is therefore left to us to discover Mallarmé's world, and the exact nature of the imagery and syntax that attracted Boulez.

A DIFFICULT GENESIS

Pli selon pli is a central work, standing as a turning-point in Boulez's career. It can be regarded as marking the successful outcome of the period between 1945 and 1960, during which he had written a number of articles, as well as a succession of works of varying significance. The actual composition of *Pli selon pli* was a lengthy and complex process; disregarding for the moment the most recent reworking of *Improvisation III*, it may be seen that the work went through no less than five separate stages, before arriving at the form in which it exists today:

2 *Conversations with Célestin Deliège*, p. 93.
3 'Construire une improvisation', *Orientations*, pp. 155–73.

1. In 1957, Boulez composed two *Improvisations sur Mallarmé* for soprano and percussion ensemble: 'Le vierge . . .' and 'Une dentelle s'abolit'. These two pieces were published separately[4] and may be separately performed.[5]

2. In 1959, he added *Improvisation III*, 'A la nue accablante tu' for soprano, small instrumental ensemble and a large group of percussion. This third *Improvisation* was first performed in Baden-Baden on 10 June 1959, by Eva-Maria Rogner and the Südwestfunk orchestra, conducted by Hans Rosbaud.

3. Also in 1959, he began *Tombeau* – after Mallarmé's 'Tombeau' (de Verlaine) – for soprano and large orchestra. This took three years to finish, and was first performed in part in Donaueschingen on 17 October 1959, and then, again in Donaueschingen, in its totality on 20 October 1962, with Eva-Maria Rogner, the Südwestfunk orchestra and Hans Rosbaud. This performance was given as part of the complete *Pli selon pli* (see No. 5 below).

4. In 1960, a provisional première of the complete work included *Don*. (Originally a piece for solo piano, it had been reworked for soprano and piano, based on Mallarmé's 'Don du poème', and first performed in this form in Cologne, on 13 June 1960, by Eva-Maria Rogner and the composer. This was followed by the three *Improvisations* of 1957–60, and then the incomplete version of *Tombeau*.

5. From 1960, the work was further modified. *Don* became a piece for large orchestra, balancing the completed version of *Tombeau*; together, these two movements flanked the three *Improvisations*. The first of these, 'Le vierge . . .', now exists in a second, large version, in order to balance the third when the work is given in full.[6] This definitive version of the whole was first performed in Donaueschingen on 20 October 1962 (see No. 3 above).

This complicated genesis was contemporary with that of the Third Sonata, a work which illustrates a different aspect of the connection between Mallarmé and Boulez. Though the two works are stylistically dissimilar, both exemplify the search for a new syntax relating to the form

4 UE 12855 ('Le vierge . . .') and UE 12857 ('Une dentelle s'abolit'), 1958.
5 First performance by Ilse Hollweg and members of the NDR Symphony Orchestra, conducted by Hans Rosbaud, Hamburg, 13 January 1958.
6 UE 16641, 1977.

of a work – an idea which is both delightfully ambiguous and dangerously ambivalent.

The title: Pli selon pli

On 18 February 1890, Mallarmé delivered a lecture in Bruges, during a tour of Belgium in honour of Villiers de l'Isle-Adam, who had died the previous year and was, like Mallarmé himself, a 'Wagnerian' poet. His sympathetic hosts were members of the Cercle Excelsior of Bruges. It was in honour of this new association, echoing his friendship with the deceased poet, that Mallarmé wrote the sonnet dedicated to the town of Bruges (see Appendix).

One should, perhaps, pause to consider the challenging expression 'pli selon pli', which occurs in the poem's fourth line, and whose vital significance is revealed in a note by Boulez: 'In the poem in question, the words "pli selon pli" are used by the poet to describe the way in which the mist, as it disperses, gradually reveals the architecture of the city of Bruges. In a similar manner, the development of the five pieces reveals, "fold upon fold", a portrait of Mallarmé himself.'[7]

I propose to go still further, and suggest that the reader faced with Mallarmé's text is, *mutatis mutandis*, in the position of the interpreter of Boulez's score. The successive stages involved in reading the poem are not unrelated to certain of the more striking characteristics of the musical expression of *Pli selon pli*. The reader is referred to the Appendix (p. 398) of this book for a more searching analysis of Mallarmé's poems.

The creative myth

Some of the greatest composers in the history of Western music appear, at least from external evidence, to have written music spontaneously and naturally. This may indeed be a gross simplification of the true circumstances in which their works came into being, but on the face of it, their apparent facility for composition would seem to attest to a creativity unfettered by the constraints of self-doubt. Others, however, have an attitude towards composition that might be described as 'Promethean': they compose self-consciously, and are perpetually faced with the problem of their own creativity – sometimes even inhibited by the very circumstances that called their music into being, or by their awareness of what will come to be written in the future. Beethoven, Mahler and

7 Sleeve note for CBS recording (Boulez 1), reprinted in *Orientations*, p. 176.

Schoenberg were among those who suffered such doubts, and for whom the creative process was often painfully demanding.

I believe that the artistic convergence of Mallarmé and Boulez represents a sort of reconciliation of the latter attitude – not only because the two created works mirror each other, but also because the very questions posed by the works are like a leaven, acting upon the linguistic material, the very syntax and formal apparatus of the work itself. For Boulez as for Mallarmé, the word 'poetry' is understood in the etymological sense of 'making'. The poetic act does not consist solely in producing a poem, but in reflecting upon the nature of the poem, and on the nature of creativity itself.

With Mallarmé, this preoccupation is evident in the texts already seen; it is also a permanent feature of his work, thwarted as he was by the 'demon of impotence'. Many traces of this may be found in 'Igitur', 'Hérodïade', 'L'Azur', and in twenty other sonnets. It lies at the root of his anxious search for the one punctuation mark indispensable to the sense, for just the right word – whose sense may escape both a superficial and a literal interpretation. It is responsible for the occasionally distorted, disjointed or elliptical syntax, intensified by the poet's distrust of the unreliability of day-to-day language. Ultimately, it explains his preoccupation with the *Livre* and its remarkably specific organization.

However, it seems to me that the 'Mallarmé work' composed by Boulez gathers up the threads of this anguished and truly obsessional dream, and arranges them with even greater concentration. Is this the sophistication of the poet or the affection of the composer? We are here faced with something approaching the tragic. *Pli selon pli* is the musical treatment of an essential self-questioning which the composer has always endured but which from 1957–60 took on a particular, almost intolerable intensity. And if one allows that *Pli selon pli* was the start of an undeniable compositional crisis (which began in earnest in 1962 and seems to come to an end only with *Répons*, 1981–4), one can calculate the risk involved in this 'portrait of Mallarmé' – the sub-title to a score which, more than any other, is a 'portrait of Boulez'.

. I append three brief notes as a provisional conclusion to this chapter:

1. Work on the hypothesis of a profound understanding between poet and musician has only just been begun and still needs to be fully articulated. My conviction is that, on Boulez's part, this rapport was established at least partly subconsciously, although the connection is now arguably more explicit.

2. It is not possible to draw up a table of direct correspondences between possible textual meaning and compositional gesture. The interested reader should now refer to the chapter on the subject (pp. 310 ff.), where the topic is explored in more detail.

3. On a wider level, one can begin to appreciate why Boulez was drawn to these particular poems: what he has had to say on the subject of the creative myth helps us to understand his preoccupation with the *Livre*. In considering the essential ambivalence of its structure, Boulez has found the means of expressing his own creativity. Thus, the Third Sonata and *Pli selon pli* might be regarded as complementary solutions to the same question.

CHAPTER EIGHT

Interludes

(1957–62)

Having examined Boulez's important new approach to the open-form work, and his connection with Mallarmé in some detail, one should now consider the period which now seems to constitute a kind of interlude: it extends from his departure for Germany in 1959, to the official beginning of his career as an orchestral conductor, in 1963.

The word 'interlude' is perhaps misleading, since there was no lessening of activity or pressure in Boulez's life. In the first place, he had to produce definitive versions of his two most important works of the period – the Third Sonata and *Pli selon pli* – while finding himself at the very centre of the controversy unleashed by the open-form work itself. At the same time, his move to Germany at the beginning of 1959 and the start of an international career did not alleviate practical problems, notably those concerning the Domaine musical (of which he remained director until 1967) which had entered a new phase in its development with its move to the Odéon in 1959. And finally, he was starting on several important works, including *Poésie pour pouvoir*, *Structures* Book 2, and *Figures–Doubles–Prismes*, while a substantial amount of teaching (at Darmstadt, Basle and Harvard) and writing (articles for the *Encyclopédie Fasquelle* and *Boulez on Music Today*) continued to enrich his professional life.

Nevertheless, it seems to me that this impressive list of activities cannot be regarded as central to the development of Boulez's career. 1958–62 can be seen as the period between his leadership in the field of post-Webern serialism, and his provisional escape from composition into conducting – and an entrepreneurial energizing of musical life that was to last for ten years. At thirty-five, Boulez had reached a turning point.

THE MOVE TO BADEN-BADEN

In June 1958 Boulez arrived in Baden for a two-week stay in order to finish his new work, *Poésie pour pouvoir*. He had been invited by Heinrich Strobel, who was director of the music department (the Musikabteilung) of Südwestfunk, and therefore in a position to make available to Boulez the equipment of a good radio station for the purposes of a 'mixed' work such as *Poésie pour pouvoir*. Boulez booked in to a nearby small hotel, taking his meals with the Strobels. Though he had been engaged to teach at Darmstadt that summer, he withdrew in order to catch up with work on *Poésie*, scheduled to be performed at Donaueschingen in the autumn. Perhaps symbolically, he was replaced at Darmstadt by John Cage.

Returning to Baden at the end of the year, he stayed this time in the servants' quarters above the Strobel's apartment, spending Christmas and New Year with them.[1] At the beginning of 1959, he signed a contract with Südwestfunk, giving them first refusal of his new works and agreeing to conduct concerts of twentieth-century music. This meant he had to live in Baden-Baden, so becoming composer in residence and a member of GEMA, the copyright association of German composers; this last affiliation gave rise to an unfortunate problem which, despite goodwill on both sides, still occupies SACEM to this day.[2]

His departure from France dismayed his followers, and aroused mixed feelings and much cynicism among his enemies. Boulez himself explains:

I left Paris because, on the organizational level of musical life, stupidity was even more prevalent there than elsewhere. France had completely lost its importance: there was no progress – the only composer of international significance was still Messiaen, the rest unexportable folklore. It had become the kingdom of artistic chauvinism, with the Sunday symphony concerts akin to the social life of the 1880s and the Opéra forming part of the Grand Tour – much like the Folies-Bergères. Not once did the RTF ask to broadcast my Domaine musical concerts . . .[3]

Boulez's grievances were only too evident: he could have added to the list, and indeed did so in many future interviews. Today it requires an effort of the imagination to conjure up the climate of the time – with contemporary music meagrely or indiscriminately funded, no specialized

1 Peyser, op. cit., pp. 138–9.
2 Note that prior to this date Boulez was not registered with any copyright society – a fact that does nothing to facilitate the task of documentation.
3 Conversation with Jean-Louis de Rambures in *Realités*, April 1965 – one of Boulez's best interviews.

festivals, and his own reputation somewhat tarnished. With its established musical tradition, the situation in Germany was quite different, although insofar as it concerned contemporary art, this tradition had fallen into disrepute during the Hitler era. Everything remained in a state of collapse until the Marshall plan enabled a nation yearning for freedom and for a world-wide culture – particularly its young people – to make a relatively rapid recovery. The concept of contemporary music had in fact already produced several *ad hoc* organizations (Donaueschingen dates from 1921), and the German federal system allowed for a number of radio stations – as opposed to the single one in France at the time – all of them disposed to broadcast really modern music: not only SWF in Baden-Baden, but NDR in Hamburg and WDR in Cologne (to mention only those relevant to the context of our discussion).

Moreover, German orchestral players took their work seriously, and Boulez, always appreciative of assiduity, had no reason to be biased against them at that time (as he was later to be, following regular dealings with English and American orchestras).

Boulez first found lodgings at the pension Rubens, where he stayed for a year before renting the top floor of a huge hillside villa. Outwardly, his house was much the same as any other in this delightful spa town; its interior was something else. Those visiting the Baden exile entered a living room furnished in the style of Mies van der Rohe – with a designer television set, a profusion of modern lamps and small drawings and paintings by Miró, Klee, Giacometti (a portrait of Stravinsky), Vieira da Silva and several others of similar calibre on the walls. In the corner of the main room was a bar at which Boulez showed himself a capable and attentive host and – before the medical profession advised him against strong drink – well able to keep pace with his guests. On the second floor was a large grand piano, books and scores, but no hi-fi equipment: once they are made, he shows absolutely no interest in his own recordings. The proximity of the Black Forest provided many opportunities for Boulez to indulge his passion for walking. Working conditions could hardly have been more propitious.

POESIE POUR POUVOIR

Henri Michaux's *Poésie pour pouvoir* is a collection published by Drouin in 1949 (with illustrations by M. Tapie) including 'Je rame', a blank verse poem of about forty-five lines that provides the literary material for Boulez's work. This uses only about twenty lines of the poem – inasmuch as a figure can actually be given for a text whose progressive submersion within the texture is one of the work's fundamental characteristics (as in the final movement of *Le Marteau sans maître*). Michaux's text celebrates the loved one's submission to the beloved; it is a poetic experiment that aims at extremes, through a mixture of the immediate and the obscure.

Written in 1958 for instruments and a five-track tape, Boulez's score has suffered a curious fate. The instrumental music, which involves three groups of players,[4] is crisp, brilliant, and with a cutting edge somewhat akin to that of *Polyphonie X*. The tape comprises both electronic sounds produced by oscillators and the electronically transformed sounds of fragments of Michaux's poem as recited by Michel Bouquet: Boulez recently declared himself still generally unhappy with regard to his whole treatment of the literary text.

Each morning, Boulez worked on the tape at SWF, leaving the afternoons free for the instrumental score. The electronic sounds are violent, biting and harsh; with their 'celestial' sonorities spiralling in all directions, they reflect the idiosyncrasies of all tape music of this somewhat protracted period. The colour and vitality of the tape nevertheless takes into account the declamatory and incantatory nature of the text. Boulez was extremely dissatisfied with the result – essentially because of the incompatibility of instrumental and electronic sounds, and because the tape did not produce the results he had envisaged. For all that, *Poésie pour pouvoir* – like Stockhausen's *Gesang der Jünglinge*, one of the first examples of 'mixed music' – began to explore two directions that were to prove important for Boulez: the instrumental-electronic sound continuum, and the spatialization of sound.

Following these early attempts, the disparity between instrumental and electronic languages was to make Boulez more wary about the whole subject of mixed music (irrespective of whether the instrumental music was also recorded). 'The one consists of a codified harmonic language with a very precisely stratified pitch system, which remains unquestionably powerful, however oppressive it might be felt to be. In electronic, or electro-acoustic, music on the other hand there is no trace of this organization; so that the passage from the one to the other suggested that the two had no point of contact.'[5] Boulez relied on the percussion as a means of reducing the gap between the two kinds of sounds: although

4 Two orchestras and a group of soloists.
5 Conversation with Dominique Jameux on the subject of *Polyphonie X* and *Poésie pour pouvoir*, as part of a forum on contemporary music held on 10 December 1973; published in *Musique en jeu*, No. 16, 1974, and reprinted in *Orientations*, pp. 199–202.

clearly answerable to instrumental language, it was also potentially able to participate in the electro-acoustic world by means of the elimination or elision of pitch contours, resonance, or special effects. The percussion thus mediates between the two worlds – a role it resumes in later works, whether purely instrumental (like *Doubles* or *Rituel*) or similarly mixed ('. . . *explosante-fixe* . . .' and *Répons*).

Boulez considered the spatialization of sound as indispensable to any electro-acoustic project. He has a horror of taped music which has its audience seated inanely in front of a row of loudspeakers. 'I have always been painfully embarrassed by the resemblance to a crematorium cere-mony, and found the absence of action a redhibitory vice.'[6] What action did he have in mind? Essentially, a use of space amounting almost to a spatial *mise-en-scène* of the taped sounds. *Poésie pour pouvoir* needed two conductors, one (Hans Rosbaud) to direct the main flow of the music, the other (Boulez himself) the subsidiary details. The three orchestral groups were arranged on platforms rising in a spiral in front of the audience – which had the speakers behind it, placed high up at the back of the hall, so that the furthermost instrumental platform (containing a few solo instruments) was at the same height as the first row of loudspeakers.

This spatialization of the sound was both spectacular and rudimentary because, to be fair, the tape was outclassed – the machinery used to produce it was insufficiently complex and integrated. The realization of this particular dream would have to await other equipment – notably the halaphone, as used in '. . . *explosante-fixe* . . .' and more especially in *Répons*. One is tempted to say that in 1958, these spatial relationships were years in advance of the means available to produce them. Boulez realized this and, after a single performance, consigned his work to a sort of no man's land, from which it escapes only by means of a poor recording.[7]

BOULEZ AS TEACHER

During these years, Boulez accepted various teaching jobs, most signifi-cantly in Germany (Darmstadt), Switzerland (Basle) and the United States (Harvard).

6 Forum, 10 December 1973 (see note above).
7 Notably in the course of this forum and, more recently, during an evening at IRCAM devoted to Boulez's 'work with machines' – and to *Répons* in particular.

Boulez had been to Darmstadt for the first time in 1952, not as a teacher, but to introduce his recent electro-acoustic *Etudes* and to hear Yvonne Loriod play his Second Sonata.[8] He did not return until 1956 when, at the invitation of Wolfgang Steinecke, he gave lectures in analysis (as did Stockhausen and Nono). That same year, Severino Gazelloni and David Tudor gave the first public performance of the *Sonatine*: written ten years previously, this had such a success that they had to repeat it as an encore. Boulez returned to teach at Darmstadt in 1959, 1960, 1961, and 1965.

A word about the Darmstadt myth. Observers and critics of contemporary music vie with each other in their admiration of 'the Darmstadt generation' – with particular reference to Boulez. Ironically, during Darmstadt's reputedly greatest era (1950–55) he did not actually attend the courses, being on holiday elsewhere at the time. From then on, he kept his distance from what already gave the impression of being a seedbed of academicism. What is more striking is that he should have returned so often in later years, when the summer courses had effectively ceased to present the more or less unified stylistic front of which he had been the undisputed leader. Steinecke died in 1961 and all the old stagers of the great Darmstadt period met again at the funeral; Boulez gave an address and had difficulty concealing his emotion.

It was Paul Sacher, founder of a string ensemble devoted largely to modern music, who authorized the invitation sent to Boulez to teach analysis and composition (for two days a week during the academic year) at the Basle Academy of Music, where other courses were run by Pousseur and Stockhausen.

Over the years he had numerous pupils, but the real disciples stand out. At Darmstadt there had been Cornelius Cardew, Richard Rodney Bennett* (who gave the first performance of the First Sonata in England), Gilbert Amy and Jean-Claude Eloy; in Basle, his pupils included Heinz

---

8 Antoine Goléa (op. cit., pp. 67 ff.) gives a lively and somewhat subjective account of the history of Darmstadt – where a series of courses and concerts were founded soon after the war by Wolfgang Steinecke with the help of the cultural director of the allied occupation forces, the American, Everett Helm, and the mayor of Darmstadt, Ludwig Metzger. It started from a broad stylistic base (Fortner, Henze, Hindemith), though a visit from Leibowitz in 1948 fairly soon caused Darmstadt to edge towards Schoenbergian, then post-Webernian serialism. It was there (in 1951) that Scherchen directed the first performance of the 'Dance round the Golden Calf' from *Moses und Aron*, and that the early works of Stockhausen and Nono were heard for the first time. There too, in 1950, Goléa introduced the recently recorded *Le Soleil des eaux*.

* This is misleading: Bennett was Boulez's first-ever pupil in Paris, 1956–8. (Trans.)

Holliger, Claude Lefebvre and Paul Mefano. Boulez's classes were to give rise to *Boulez on Music Today*.[9]

The teaching was based on analysis, and Boulez himself analysed the great works of the century, including those of the Second Viennese School (a gigantic analysis of Webern's *Cantata* No. 2 remains unfinished to this day), together with his own scores and those of his pupils. He was a demanding teacher, hard to pin down; he hated the idea of disciples, believing that a student could learn all he needed to know from a professor in eight days, and aware that analysis is a practice both inescapable and deadly.

Lastly, Boulez was invited to give classes, seminars, and lectures on composition at Harvard University for three or four months during the spring of 1963 in order to fill in the gaps in American knowledge of twentieth-century music.

MINOR WORKS

Three minor works date from this time. *Strophe* (1957) was a work for flute, intended to be accompanied by a small instrumental ensemble. The soloist was to change position within the ensemble (anticipating *Domaines* by some ten years) but only the flute part was written, and the idea was jettisoned. *Marges* (1962–4) was planned as a work for small percussion ensemble (for the Percussions de Strasbourg) but only a draft outline exists. On the other hand, *Le Crépuscule de Yang Koueï-Feï* (1957) was successfully concluded. This was music for a radiophonic work by Louis Fauré, produced by Alain Trutat – who had shown similar insight over *Le Soleil des eaux*, and who once again asked Boulez to write the music. Yang Koueï-Feï was a Chinese poet, a contemporary of Li-Tai-Po of Mahler's *Lied von der Erde* fame. Boulez's instrumental score experiments with the kind of material to be used in *Improvisation I* and *Pli selon pli*, with a singing voice (Ginette Guillaumat) entwined with the text (spoken by Roger Blin and Monique Mélinand).[10]

THE FASQUELLE ARTICLES (1958)

It is not surprising that Boulez should have become involved in writing articles for a dictionary. This was not to be the normal, run-of-the-mill compilation; for one thing, the project was ambitious: it was intended to

9 See the following chapter, pp. 130–1.
10 INA 9506 (3-box set); first broadcast on France-Culture, 6 October 1957.

produce an encyclopaedia which made a clear statement of position, rather than confining itself to statistics. Furthermore, this undertaking (headed by François Michel)[11] was to be conspicuous for the outstanding quality of its contributions, which were not only well-informed but which showed personal commitment and an up-to-date view of the area under discussion.

When Boulez came to review the twentieth-century composers he regarded as significant, he was able to produce definitive studies in terms basic to his own language. The result is not merely a work of reference but a real expression of opinion. If some of his articles – for instance, those on Berg, and on the series – might have been differently drafted today, that is both healthy and understandable. One contribution deserves special mention: in just a few pages, he provides a masterly analysis of the position of another kindred spirit: Claude Debussy.[12]

THE RECEPTION GIVEN TO *PLI SELON PLI*

This transitional period in Boulez's career included the many incomplete premières of *Pli selon pli* – whose five movements underwent various versions which were first performed separately (see chapter 7). Re-reading the press reviews of the time (and in particular those by Antoine Goléa and Claude Rostand), one can clearly assess the effect of Boulez's growing international reputation and his importance as a rising orchestral conductor. One could cite as an example the concert in Donaueschingen in October 1959, which included the first performance of the still incomplete *Tombeau*. As it happened, Prince Egon de Furstenberg had died in April, and the opportune Boulez première was to have been given together with two other commemorative pieces, by Stravinsky (*Epitaphium*) and Wolfgang Fortner; these were to have been played at the start of each of three symphony concerts given by the Südwestfunk orchestra and the Domaine musical (who had been invited especially for *Tombeau*). Then Hans Rosbaud, who should have conducted the two SWF concerts, fell ill three weeks before the festival, and Strobel had urgently to find a replacement. Thus Boulez inherited one of the two orchestral concerts (the other, a Webern programme, fell to Rosbaud's assistant), and had quickly to learn works by Petrassi, Berio and Haubenstock-Ramati. In the second half, he took up the challenge of the advertised programme, and

11 Musicologist (born 1916), editor of the Fasquelle encyclopaedia of music.
12 A list of articles is given under the heading of Documentation; all of them are included in *Orientations*.

directed a glittering performance of *The Miraculous Mandarin* which earned him some twenty curtain calls. With the Domaine, his own *Tombeau* was scarcely less of a triumph.

Pli selon pli was established in the contemporary repertoire version by version. In 1961, *Don* was still a splendid piece for piano solo (which Boulez himself had played in Cologne the year before), based on material very different from that of the final orchestral version. Commenting on the still incomplete first performance of the whole work at the Domaine in March 1961 (following the performance in Donaueschingen), Claude Rostand drew attention to the impact produced by a work that everyone recognized as having far surpassed the experimental stage:

I have frequently commented upon the fact that, while Boulez is often played abroad, he is almost never heard in France – and he very rarely allows his own works to figure in the programmes of the Domaine musical. Thus his music is almost unknown, both to the public and to the stay-at-home critic. It was doubtless this state of affairs that accounted for the lively sense of surprise that one could feel in the hall the other evening during the performance of *Pli selon pli*. There was nothing in this work approaching the relatively experimental quality of the scores often heard at these concerts: we were here in the presence of an accomplished work of art – and one which adopted none of the aggressiveness of the avant garde.[13]

From *Le Marteau sans maître* to *Pli selon pli*, and as Boulez embarks gently but firmly upon his career as a repertoire conductor, the idea of a Boulezian classicism in gestation has definitely been gaining ground.

BOULEZ AS RECITALIST

Despite his growing reputation as a composer and the recent discovery of his conducting prowess, Boulez's financial position was still relatively insecure. He was of course no longer director of music with the Barrault company, and the monthly payments from Baden were rather modest. Making a virtue of necessity, he gave a series of two-piano recitals, mostly in Germany, with Yvonne Loriod as his partner. Their programmes were almost always the same: *En blanc et noir* by Debussy, followed by *Structures* (before 1961 Book 1 alone, subsequently with the addition of Book 2) and, in the second half, works by Messiaen played by Yvonne Loriod.

In this way they appeared in Hamburg (as part of the series Das neue Werk), at Donaueschingen in 1957, and at the Domaine. After their

13 *Carrefour*, March 1961.

concert at Aix in 1958, Goléa exclaimed in *L'Express*: 'What a pianist this Boulez is!'. No discs have survived as evidence of such evenings, although there are some radio tapes.

STRUCTURES BOOK 2 (1956–61)

Having just mentioned the second book of *Structures* for two pianos, I will discuss it briefly, even though, twenty years on, it does not seem to me to represent so important a compositional landmark as neighbouring works, notwithstanding the fact that it falls so pleasantly upon the ear.

As mentioned earlier (see pp. 51–2), *Structures* Book 1 (1952) comprises three pieces whose extremely calculated conception was to lead to the development of total serialization. This course of action places the onus of responsibility firmly back on the composer – except in the case of the first piece, which consisted merely of the impersonal development of a programme applied to a given material.

Ten years later, Book 2 sets out with a different intention. It comprises only two pieces, called 'chapters', lasting eight and a half, and ten and a half minutes respectively.

The first chapter might be described as conventional. The two piano parts are not only fully notated but the many tempo changes are dictated by the composer himself, except where the second piano is instructed to follow the cadenza-like freedom of the first, or vice versa. Thus the whole piece is underpinned by a certain kind of reciprocity which involves each pianist tuning in to the other. The writing is explosively brilliant, very dynamic, and makes ample use of the registers of both instruments. Since the arid sonorities of 1952, Boulez had composed *Le Marteau sans maître* and the Third Sonata, and was now immersed in *Pli selon pli* (of which the keyboard version of *Don* might be thought to foreshadow this second book of *Structures*). In other words, Book 2 is infinitely more attractive to listen to. With its Lisztian brilliance, coupled with overtones of Albéniz, the work evokes something of Messiaen at his best, though with a sharper edge.

The second chapter is quite different. In terms of instrumental give and take, it begins like the first: thus, after an initial two-note chord from the first player, the second has to select one of two groups of notes which are either mixed or juxtaposed. The first player then proceeds with his written text, after which the two players are brought together in a stricter, fast-moving chordal passage.

Two and a half-minutes later everything changes – as a connecting passage of trope-like options intervenes to launch the first player upon a game of different possibilities; the second player remains subordinate until the end of the piece, his role dictated by the way in which his partner chooses when or how to play a particular figure. This device, appallingly overloaded with instructions, defies description; a careful reading of the score (rather tiresome in the abstract) shows that its verbal complexities relate mainly to the terms and conditions for alternative choice.

Needless to say, the various results are all much the same to the listener. As with other mobile works, the effectiveness of this variability is dependent not on the listener's perception but on his awareness of being confronted with an open-form work, and on the state of tension it induces in the performers – with the incidental advantage that the performance is given an interestingly 'dramatic' aspect.

This second chapter is divided into various sequences that are susceptible to permutation and which may be summarized as follows:

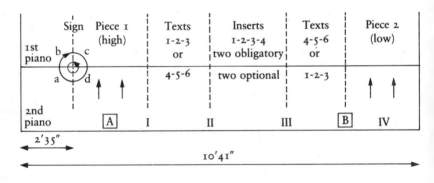

Starting with the signal indicated above, two 'Pièces' – one in a high, the other in a low register – frame the chapter as a whole. Six 'Textes' are grouped in threes after Pièce 1 and before Pièce 2: the first player chooses either to play Textes 1, 2, and 3, followed by 4, 5 and 6, or vice versa. At the centre of this symmetrical arrangement are four 'Encarts' or 'Insets', two of which are obligatory and two optional – so giving three hypotheses but numerous solutions. The vertical arrows in the diagram are by way of a descriptive indication of the alternatives offered to the second player in terms of the choices made by the first; there are many other such alternatives.

In conclusion, it is impossible to speak of the aesthetics or the energizing properties of the musical composition itself because the aesthetic values of the various options are interchangeable. The beauty and interest of the music are overshadowed by its directions for performance.

On the other hand, one is once again struck by the way in which the vastness of purpose (and of the theoretically conceivable solutions) is cancelled out by the simplicity – even the paucity – of the decisions offered. From this point of view, it would seem that works like the Third Sonata or *Eclat* offer choices that are both more numerous and more subtle, while the opportunity for limited freedom in *Structures* Book 2 is more akin to that of *Domaines*.

On a historical level, its performances were enthusiastically received. Book 2 was premièred in Donaueschingen on 21 October 1961 by the composer and Yvonne Loriod. Together with Book 1, it was later to constitute one of the most successful items in the repertoire of the celebrated duettists Alfons and Aloys Kontarsky.

FIGURES–DOUBLES–PRISMES

Figures–Doubles–Prismes is an expansion, dating from 1968, of the work entitled *Doubles* first heard ten years earlier. At that time, the Association des Concerts Lamoureux, directed by Igor Markevitch, had commissioned Boulez to write a piece for symphony orchestra. The gesture was an altruistic one. Twenty years ago, these now moribund associations provided the only excitement in Parisian musical life. Their concerts generally included a modest number of first performances, among them a still more modest number of works by avant-garde composers. On this occasion it was Markevitch himself who decided to take the plunge and to commission a work from the leader of the new music.

Boulez stuck to the terms of his contract with regard to the total strength of the orchestra, but he arranged it on the platform of the Salle Pleyel in a decidedly unorthodox manner, arguing from the apparently logical maxim that new music needed a new orchestral layout. He did not compose at any great length: but, while *Doubles* lasted a mere eight minutes, the setting up involved in the unusual seating plan (which was rearranged during the interval) took a good fifteen. The audience was fidgety before the work even began and indignant afterwards: the piece had hardly seemed to justify so much effort. The ingratiating Clarendon jumped at the chance to entitle it 'the game of musical chairs'.

This little story had a particular significance. In 1958, the avant-garde composer was tolerated within the 'ghetto' of the Domaine musical as long as he did not leave it to begin an assault on the hallowed temples of serious music. Doubtless Boulez found the experience salutary: in order to change the attitude of an audience, one had first to conquer it on its own ground – namely that of established orchestral masterpieces. Even so, the work itself has been unjustly neglected by promoters and publishers alike.

Briefly, *Figures* represents an initial statement of the material, scored for a large orchestra divided into fourteen groups: three woodwind, four brass and five string groups, arranged in alternate rows, with six percussion players (vibraphone, celesta, timpani, harp, xylophone and various unpitched percussion) placed between them – an organization reminiscent of both *Rituel* and *Répons*.

The title of *Doubles* refers to the duplication of certain elements (as in *Le Marteau sans maître*), and that of *Prismes* to the shimmering light of one figure reflected upon another by process of imitation and variation, by distortion of motifs or sequences, and so on. The work has a kind of expressive violence that is redolent of Varèse or – certainly by August 1968 – of the composer's own interpretations of Mahler and Berg. As an important stage in the reconsideration of the symphony orchestra by contemporary composers in general (undoubtedly hastened in his own case by his conducting activities), *Figures–Doubles–Prismes* later prompted Boulez to define his views on both the work and the modern orchestra. He described the former as

a series of variations for large orchestra – a sort of montage of different forms, each embedded in the others. Unlike *Eclat*, this is a work of fixed parameters, because a large orchestra reacts like a collective and not like a group of individuals; to be manoeuvrable, an orchestra must be given straightforward roles – only a smaller group of players can accommodate the instantaneous interplay of reactions within the limits of controlled chance.[14]

These three descriptive characters form a continuous whole that is a straightforward expansion of the original *Doubles*, comprising four different 'movements'. Almost in the manner of a symphony, the first is forceful, fast, and with a strong rhythmic pulse, the second a dance-like scherzo of the menuet kind, the third is slow and the fourth short, vigorous and simpler in style.

The complete version was premièred on 13 March 1968 by the Residencie Orchestra of The Hague, conducted by the composer. Antoine Goléa describes it as 'a farewell to Webern', while Jacques Longchampt appears to appreciate its 'dynamism' and a 'tough though not inhuman lyricism that shows a sort of lofty but coolly undemonstrative intensity

14 Interview with Maurice Fleuret, *Nouvel Observateur*, 23 February 1966.

much in the style of the man himself'.[15] Claude Rostand repeats his deep appreciation of Boulez's music in saying that this is 'one of the most personal, most subjective of Boulez's works', and he goes on to emphasize the 'sharp reliefs', 'mysterious explosions', 'breathless pulsations' and 'extraordinary instrumental quivering that skims across the entire orchestra'.[16] Clarendon was exhausted by the sheer level of sound and remarked on a 'certain monotony'.[17] It fell to Martine Cadieu[18] to give an idea of the overall temperament of the work: 'It is a changing panorama, altogether glowing and vigorous, consumed by heat and scarred by sharp-edged shadows like a Cézanne landscape, rugged, durable and intense, without the least hint of sadness.'[19]

15 Le Monde, 15 March 1968.
16 Le Figaro littéraire, 25 March 1968.
17 Le Figaro, 15 March 1968.
18 Music critic and writer, contributor to Lettres françaises, author of a short book on Boulez (see Bibliography).
19 Lettres françaises, 20 March 1968.

CHAPTER NINE

Boulez the Conductor (1)

(1963–70)

Between 1963 and 1973 Boulez emerged as one of the great orchestral conductors of our time, to a point where this image came near to eclipsing that of the composer in the eyes of public and press alike. These dates should obviously be regarded as representing Boulez's most active conducting period to date, since he had of course conducted before and after this decade – notably at Bayreuth for the *Ring* cycle, between 1976 and 1980.

Once his reputation as a conductor was fully established, his career in this field took off at lightning speed, as he found himself in charge of some of the most prestigious organizations: at Bayreuth, in London, Cleveland, and New York – not to mention the many short-term appearances with well-known orchestras in Berlin, Amsterdam or Los Angeles.

This also marked the beginning of his career as an entrepreneur. Still in exile from France, Boulez spent periods of several months at a time in English-speaking countries giving concerts, but above all directing the day-to-day life of an orchestra – with all the administrative, cultural, psychological and even 'political' responsibilities that implied. 'The organization of musical life interests me much more than being a conductor' he told André Calas,[1] and in numerous interviews he repeatedly emphasized his readiness to use his official influence (whether in London or New York) to revitalize musical life in a way that would focus more upon the great twentieth-century classics, and upon contemporary music.

Moreover, apart from his reputation as 'the greatest musician of our

---

1 In one of his most stimulating interviews, included in 'Lectures pour tous', July 1969.

age' – as declared by a glowing publicity hand-out[2] – the image we have of Boulez today was definitely formed during these ten years: that of a global, even archetypal, man of music – a modern pedagogue, closer than any other to achieving a remarkable conjunction of musical thought and action.

During these years of fame as a conductor, there were rumours that his compositional activities had hit a ten-year crisis akin to that of Schoenberg. To some extent, the catalogue denies it: two important works were to emerge from this period, the one relating to Boulez the conductor (*Eclat* and *Eclat/Multiples*, still admittedly incomplete), the other pointing to the future director of IRCAM ('. . . *explosante-fixe* . . .', still, in the composer's view, unsatisfactory). In addition, two other successfully completed works – *Domaines* and *Rituel* – were premièred in 1968 and 1975. In my opinion these are less experimental, but the quality of their formal presentation has assured their public success. Indeed they are indicative of a change in Boulez's public image, resulting from his break-through in the direction of the general music lover, as opposed to merely a specialized audience. A fifth work, the original and admirably organized *cummings ist der Dichter* (1970), preserved the tradition of uncompleted works while Boulez was finishing the ambitious and problematic *Figures–Doubles–Prismes* (1968). Add to this the bonus of part of *Livre pour quatuor* now rescored as *Livre pour cordes* and, all things considered, this was a reasonable record for a period of crisis.

THE MAKING OF A CONDUCTOR (1945–63)

Boulez conducted from early on and did so in very modest circumstances: he gained his earliest experience in the thankless surroundings of an orchestra pit, directing incidental music not of his own choosing and with players who were sometimes excellent, sometimes not. However, material considerations apart, Jean-Louis Barrault did Boulez a great service: without his daily work at the Marigny, Boulez might have remained the 'cerebral' composer his enemies are only too ready to condemn.

The second stage of this self-education was the Domaine musical. To summarize: this was his apprenticeship in establishing audience-relations through contemporary music, as well as the basis of his future role as a conductor specializing in the great twentieth-century classics (even though he was for the moment confined to directing chamber works by

2 CBS promotion material, 1970.

the Second Viennese composers, by Bartók, Stravinsky and Varèse). Confronted by complicated modern scores fraught with pitfalls for instrumentalists and public alike, he learnt to interpret, to communicate through gesture, and to create a sense of visual order – in short, to acquire a technique.

Beyond that, it was simply a matter of opportunity; the early episodes already mentioned (the première of *Le Visage nuptial* in Cologne in 1957, the concerts of the Domaine in London the same year) were followed by first engagements in Vienna, Berlin and Amsterdam.

PARIS, 1963: FROM *THE RITE* TO *WOZZECK*

Suddenly, two events intervened: Boulez was called upon to direct two major twentieth-century works with two of the most prominent musical institutions in Paris – the Radio and the Opéra.

The radio orchestra, the Orchestre National, had been one of the great orchestras of its time, particularly under conductors like Klemperer, Désormière or Inghelbrecht; and Boulez now gave a memorable account of *The Rite of Spring* at the Théâtre des Champs-Elysées on 18 June 1963, the fiftieth anniversary of its first performance in the same hall. It was an electrifying interpretation, and Boulez was lauded as a great conductor by the whole of music-loving Paris. As the *Le Monde* review by Jacques Longchampt put it:

What a splendid display Boulez gave us! Very upright, very self-possessed, controlled, but always ready to pounce, the powerful head bearing down onto the neck, he conducts without a baton, using gestures of a truly luminous clarity – not like a kneader of clay, but with a kind of perfection akin to the wide, soaring movements or delicate arabesques of birds in flight. The fingers are as expressive as in a study by Dürer or Leonardo – sometimes outspread, thumb and index finger touching in the form of a ring, sometimes closed together, the hand very straight, cutting in the vertical position, calming and protective in the horizontal.

It is true, indeed well known, that Boulez conducts with his bare hands, disdaining what he refers to as the 'one-armed pirate-hook' of the familiar baton. Finally the critic salutes his 'poetic precision' – a felicitous expression that underlines both his complete avoidance of vague histrionics as well as an accuracy that is never drily prosaic.

To sum up, it was a complete success with everybody, including – most significantly – the orchestral players, who gave him an ovation. The all-Stravinsky concert had been characteristically well planned by Boulez. He had omitted the *Four Norwegian Moods* in favour of shorter, more decisive works to go with *The Rite*: the *Quatre Etudes*, *Le Roi des étoiles*, the *Symphonies of Wind Instruments* of 1920 and that rather curious work, *A Sermon, a Narrative and a Prayer* (first heard in Paris in 1961). These works still form the basis of Boulez's Stravinsky repertoire today. A studio recording of *The Rite* and the *Etudes* conjures up the atmosphere of this hugely successful concert, on his first commercial disc.

In autumn of that year, Georges Auric, who was then the administrator of the Opéra, had pledged himself to organize the first performance of *Wozzeck* at the Paris Opéra.[3] As a frequenter of the Domaine musical, this ex-member of Les Six approached Boulez, who had never yet conducted an opera of any kind. Boulez accepted, on two conditions: that the work should be given in the original language (a fact that amazed the critics), and that he should have thirty-five rehearsals – 'A number that only became legendary', notes Jean-Pierre Derrien, 'because the demand was so exceptional here'.[4] The conditions were agreed, and Boulez brought to this new challenge all his proselytizing zeal, and a passionate desire to succeed.

Wozzeck opened on 27 November to a distinguished audience including several government ministers, amongst whom Malraux – victim of a recent accident – stood out by virtue of his white sling. The occasion was an overwhelming success. Long applause greeted the production by Jean-Louis Barrault, the décor and costumes by André Masson, the performances of Helga Pilarczyk (Marie) and Heiner Horn (Wozzeck), and above all, Boulez's musical direction; the standing audience chanted the names of both composer and conductor – the latter finally saluting the auditorium in front of an already deserted pit by raising his arms, hands together like those of a victorious boxer.[5] Ten performances played to capacity, and to an average box-office return of three and a half million old francs each evening. Berg was selling as well as Verdi.

Journalists were already aware of a conducting style that was always to

3 *Wozzeck* had been given for the first time in France at the Théâtre des Champs-Elysées on 2 and 3 May 1952, with Karl Böhm directing the Vienna Philharmonic Orchestra and with Christel Goltz as Marie and J. Herrmann as Wozzeck. There was another production, in German, this time by the Munich Opera, given first at Strasburg in 1959, then in Paris, at the Théâtre des Nations, in 1960. In 1962 the Lyons Opéra presented it in French, but with German singers (including Toni Blankenheim and Elsa Cavelti), under the direction of Richard Kraus.
4 The Boulez dossier in *Musique en jeu*, No. 1, 1970, p. 120.
5 Report by Maurice Croizat, *Paris-Match*, No. 767, 21 December 1963.

mark Boulez's performances in the Wagnerian (the *Ring, Parsifal*) or post-Wagnerian (*Wozzeck* in 1963, *Lulu* in 1979) vein: 'Always attentive to the balance between voice and instruments', wrote Claude Rostand for a German radio station, 'he unleashed the latter with intensity during the purely symphonic episodes, setting before us a transparent, clear orchestral sound – shimmering with the subtle and disturbing effect of shot silk. There was nothing excessive, heavy, no inappropriate distortion of the musical text.' And he additionally remarks on the extent to which Boulez had earned the liking and respect of the orchestra – which had made it a custom to applaud its conductor at some length at the end of each rehearsal.

A disc of the production was made in 1966, on the occasion of its revival at the Opéra and with substantial changes in the cast: Isabel Strauss was a rather insipid Marie, Walter Berry a somewhat approximate Wozzeck. The less pleasing development was that, following the triumphant early performance, a discrepancy began to emerge on each occasion thereafter between his scrupulous direction of the orchestra, and an attitude to vocal casting that was often dangerously casual.[6]

The Rite and *Wozzeck* were two successes which relieved the usual monotony of the Radio and the Opéra. The conquest of these two bastions of the musical establishment delighted his supporters, who tended to revel in controversy. Whilst they saw it as a great advance in Boulez's career, his enemies dismissed it as no more than a salvage operation.

BOULEZ ON MUSIC TODAY

As mentioned earlier, from 1960 onwards Boulez taught at the Musikakademie in Basle, giving courses in analysis and composition, and conducting the orchestra in contemporary works; he also taught at Darmstadt, where the instruction was geared more towards composition. As a link between his compositional preoccupations and a concept of

6 It is worth noting the extremely circumspect article by Antoine Goléa. At the time suspected of being somewhat anti-Boulez, in 1966 he was as enthusiastic as his colleagues with regard to this recording. In *Musica*, No. 145, April 1966, a comprehensive article concerning Boulez's increasingly multifarious activities explains Goléa's reservations not only as to the vocal casting of *Wozzeck* but as to a form of direction 'whose uncertainty was to have a progressively adverse effect on productions'. At the time, he had praised the earlier performances.

conducting based on analysis and on structural expectations, he undertook to publish a kind of theoretical treatise outlined as follows:

1 General Considerations ⎫ published in 1963 as *Penser la*
2 Musical Technique   ⎭ *musique aujourd'hui*
3 Form (given at Darmstadt in 1963)
4 Notation (given at Darmstadt in 1963 under the heading of 'Time,
   Notation and Coding')
5 Aesthetics
   (a) Aesthetics and the Fetishists (1961)
   (b) Style and Function (1961, published in *Tel Quel*[7], 1963)
   (c) The Need for an Aesthetic Direction (1963, published in
       Mercure de France, 1964).

Boulez on Music Today (published in London, 1971) remained a work in
progress (with certain articles published, others not) until the appearance
of *Orientations*,[8] a collection of Boulez texts which more or less fulfils the
initial purpose.*

The two studies published in 1963 (in paperback – the publisher was
not that brave) are totally inaccessible to the uninitiated, and relatively
abstruse even for musicians! In order to benefit from *Boulez on Music
Today*, one has to have analysed serial works, those of Boulez in
particular. However, certain remarks – like those on the priority given to
methods of investigation and of research into the technical attainments
themselves (p. 142), or those describing the extreme difficulty of establishing a continuum of timbres (p. 64), or again on the necessary relationships, in Western music, between pitch and transposition (p. 42) – directly
anticipate the preoccupations of the director of IRCAM ten years later,
and are still relevant. A vehement and controversial foreword takes the
form of a dialogue between Boulez and his *alter ego*, offering a penetrating
view of the composer.

---

7 A quarterly review concerned with theoretical research into questions of language;
founded in 1961 by Philippe Sollers and published by Le Seuil, ninety-four issues appeared
up to 1982. It was for *Tel Quel* that Boulez wrote 'Le Gout et le fonction', reprinted in
Orientations. *Tel Quel* was also the name given to a collection of books – including the
original French editions of *Notes of an Apprenticeship* and *Conversations with Célestin
Deliège*.
8 *Points de repère*: texts collected and introduced by Jean-Jacques Nattiez, Bourgois, 1981;
English translation entitled *Orientations*, London, Faber, and Harvard University Press,
Cambridge, Massachusetts, 1986.
* See translator's footnote on page 33.

ECLAT

In 1964, Boulez was dividing his time between Baden-Baden, where he lived and worked, Basle, where he taught, Paris, where he was still director of the Domaine (now at the end of its 'heroic' phase), and the conducting engagements which were starting to come in.

Elsewhere, André Malraux – who had once declared to the tribune of the Assembly that he was not prepared to do anything for music in France – requested a national commission to enquire into the problems of music. Boulez was introduced to the commission's president, Jean Biasini, by Gaeton Picon, Director General of Arts and Letters, and contributed to its work by writing a letter to Malraux. However, three years later the draft conclusions of the commission had still not been acted upon. The affair was to have a spectacular sequel in 1966 and again in 1968: this was the beginning of the complex saga of Boulez's relations with the French musical establishment – of which more will be said later.

On 26 March 1965 Boulez gave the first performance of *Eclat* in Los Angeles, during one of the Monday Evening Concerts organized by Lawrence Morton and often likened to the Domaine. Boulez was forty, and to mark the event he offered the world a masterpiece: his *Eclat* for fifteen solo instruments, composed the previous year, was a 'beautiful meteorite' that lasted a mere eight minutes; but it was to constitute only the first stage of a 'multiple' rocket head.

The work will be considered in more detail on pp. 335 ff. Quite apart from its euphoric sound resulting from its particularly Boulezian instrumentation, achieved with a Ravel-like brilliance and mastery, the work is important on at least three counts.

In the first place, it is a work not only with but for conductor. The device governing *Eclat* requires its conductor not merely to perform the work, with all the usual problems of interpretation, precision and expression, but actually to construct it, to take his bearings and to choose from among the options open to him, and to interact with his instrumental ensemble like a concerto soloist. Moreover, for the ensemble, the immediacy of gesture and the quickness of reaction it demands is a powerful musical stimulus.[9]

9 Michel Fano's remarkable film devoted to *Eclat* was broadcast on 10 April 1977 (TF1, a co-production with the INA, in Mildred Clary's series, 'Leçon de musique'). By means of an enlightening commentary delivered by Boulez to the players, this clearly shows the 'instantaneously dramatic' aspect of the work. The same commentary can be heard on the cassette of *Eclat* issued by IRCAM in conjunction with Radio-France.

Secondly, in some respects the work represents the optimum instrumental version of the Boulezian ideal of the open-form work. Its system of options, permutations, and of the variability of one element within a more fixed global structure makes *Eclat* both the continuation and the direct outcome of the Third Sonata. Boulez was to come up against serious performance problems when he tried to transfer these principles to a larger instrumental group, as in *Rituel*: the open-form work remains a chamber music formula.

Finally, the euphoric sound already referred to (and for which Boulez has a particular aptitude) has a certain ambivalence. It ensures the success of the work, brilliantly demonstrating the composer's mastery, and thereafter, his powers of persuasion with orchestral musicians. But it may legitimately disturb those who respect Boulez, causing them to question whether so distinguished a composer should be content with success on this level alone. As for his enemies, they assume a paternalistic satisfaction at this improvement: 'He's getting there', they say.

THE LEARNING EXPERIENCE: BOULEZ IN BASLE

In 1965 Boulez was invited to Basle to give courses in orchestral conducting. It is unlikely that this invitation was extended in order that a sensational baton technique (which, after all, he does not have!) might be admired, or that he should pass on some interpretative message concerning composers of the past; its purpose was rather to enable him, by means of physical gesture, to establish a visible connection between the truth of the works and the demands of interpretation, for the benefit of aspiring conductors.

It is this aspect which is remembered by one of his pupils, Michel Tabachnik (himself a conductor and composer), who attended the Basle courses between 1967 and 1971.

What was striking was to see that his interpretation came from his strict, very French, very Debussyish analysis . . . In class, he used always to conduct facing his pupil, so that one never knew what the pupil gave of himself because Boulez was directly in front of him! There were concerts at the end, and this was the first time the pupil was confronted with an orchestra . . . What I have never seen with other conductors is his ability to convey through gesture the analysis he had just given . . . In class, he would analyse a piece for us and then make us conduct it gesturally in terms of the analysis . . .[10]

10 During a Forum on Contemporary Music organized by the review *Musique en jeu* and held at the German cultural centre in Paris on 10 December 1973. The film, *Boulez, chef*

Briefly, this reiterates the view that music has no existence until communicated in performance.

The Basle courses were also instructive and educative for Boulez himself; in French, the verb 'apprendre' means both 'teach' and 'learn'.

BAYREUTH, 1966

During 1965 and 1966 Boulez's name began to feature more often on concert bills. In 1965 a musical retrospective took place in Edinburgh; he conducted several of his own works, but also some Beethoven. That same year, there was a spectacular Stravinsky evening at the Paris Opéra which coupled the names of Boulez and Béjart in a programme which included *The Rite, Renard* and *Les Noces*. But then came a more pressing demand which, when accepted, was to give real impulse to the international career of the conductor: Boulez was to conduct at Bayreuth.

The idea of a collaboration between Wieland Wagner and Boulez took several years to effect. During the whole of his artistic life Wieland Wagner had been confronted with a dearth of conductors able to respond to his dramatic requirements with the requisite lightness, flexibility and febrile intensity. He had heard Boulez conduct at a concert in Munich as early as 1963, and suggested that he should come to Bayreuth to direct *Tannhäuser*; this was to be Wieland Wagner's second production of a work he had first produced in 1961 and which, for the following two years, had been under the musical direction of Wolfgang Sawallisch. Boulez turned down the offer; he was not enough of a 'Wagnerian' in the accepted sense to consider conducting a work he regarded as relatively insignificant – neither was he foolhardy enough to take the risk of making his début at Bayreuth with a work of this nature. He was then offered the chance to conduct *Tristan* at Bayreuth on some future occasion, and to try it out in advance at the world trade exhibition in Osaka in April 1967.

But things turned out differently. On 25 October 1965 came the death of Hans Knappertsbusch, who had been almost the sole conductor of *Parsifal* since 1951, despite his reservations about the production. '*Parsifal* has been orphaned: would you like to conduct it next year at Bayreuth?' was the content of the telegram immediately sent to Boulez by Wieland Wagner. Boulez accepted.

The musical world received the news of this projected collaboration

d'orchestre, was shown during the evening (Filmography No. F 16) and I myself interviewed Michel Tabachnik (text published in *Musique en jeu*, No. 16, 1974, pp. 31–2).

with great scepticism. With the exception of *Wozzeck*, Boulez had never conducted an opera, and had given no sign of being particularly interested in Wagner. The Bayreuth Festival was (and still is) an event which takes place under the watchful scrutiny of conservative hard-liners; furthermore, it was difficult to imagine *Parsifal* as a work which, from the dramatic and spiritual point of view, could possibly interest the young, avant-garde, revolutionary – even Bolshevist – composer.

Nevertheless, to be summoned to Wagner by Wieland – and specifically to work with the latter – was obviously a major opportunity for Boulez. In the event, this was not to be, at least not at Bayreuth. There was a poignancy about the year 1966 for Wieland Wagner, who was then at the height of his creative talent (and, incidentally, of his renown). His career had started, fittingly, in Bayreuth, and he subsequently worked in various opera houses as a much sought-after producer. Although certainly overworked, he was doubtless reasonably content as well as productive. It is impossible not to be reminded of the Mozart of 1791, or Berg of 1935, whose bursts of creative activity show an ominous sense of urgency. In 1966, Wieland Wagner staged *Wozzeck* for the first time in Stuttgart. Professionally unaccustomed to modern music, he returned the score to Erich Schafer, director of the Opéra, three times before finally accepting – mainly to please Anja Silja.[11] Ironically, he had never had such a unanimous and immediate success. In March he produced *Der fliegende Holländer* in Hamburg, and the following month *Wozzeck* in Frankfurt, again with Anja Silja, but this time also with Boulez. The décor was stark and melancholy, realistic for Marie's environment, fantastic for that of Wozzeck – the couch on which the doctor examines him was an instrument of torture, the captain's chair a terrifying throne. Though this production was only a qualified success with the public, Boulez was its most loyal supporter. It was a meeting of like minds; Boulez wrote in 1967:

During the short time of our acquaintance, I felt no need to exchange many words with Wieland Wagner. We very soon understood one another and words would have seemed superfluous to both of us. This happens with people whose chief characteristic is a kind of magnetism, and in my own case these are practically the only people with whom I feel myself to be in instinctive agreement. Short as it was, this collaboration with Wieland Wagner served to draw my attention to a world that I had not been immediately prepared to regard as important or of presentday interest – the world of opera.

11 Geoffrey Skelton, *Wieland Wagner, the Positive Sceptic*, London, 1971.

Wieland Wagner then went to Rome for a production of *Salome* before starting to rehearse in Bayreuth – where he had to revise his new 1965 *Ring* as well as returning (yet again) to the task of *Parsifal*, in a quest for perfection that was almost obsessive. It was then that he experienced the first symptoms of lung cancer and had to go into hospital. The dress rehearsals for *Parsifal* went ahead without him, or rather, without his physical presence, since – with the help of tape recorder, teleprinter and secretary – he followed the shaping of events as closely as possible from his hospital bed in Kulmbach. This gave rise to a correspondence between him and Boulez which kept him informed as to the progress of his production. The *Parsifal* of 1966 was to be more theatrical than religious, more dramatic than mystical. 'It is odd' wrote Boulez, 'that celestial sweetness has never been much of an inspiration to either musicians or poets; thoughts of eternal bliss seem only to have given them ideas of a vaguely boring kind! . . . I would like to try to avoid drowning in this excessive sweetness by focusing upon the insubstantial nature of the orchestral sound; I have not yet succeeded – too many fleshy, chubby angels still remain.' And he tells Wieland he will visit him after the first night 'so as to give you a beginner's first-hand impressions'.[12]

Boulez's *Parsifal* was a brilliant success. French reactions were, generally speaking, good, even if the *Figaro* critic did not pass up the chance to introduce a sour note. 'A curious *Parsifal*' Clarendon called it, feigning admiration for the superlatively well-organized Boulez, 'master of his own reflexes and able to do as he wishes', so that he could more effectively drive home his final point: 'Music is not made with reason, but with the heart. For this, it is necessary to have one.'

Not surprisingly, Claude Rostand expressed himself in quite different terms. His is an interesting review,[13] describing from as early as 1966 the aesthetic approach to orchestral conducting that Boulez was always to implement at Bayreuth – and was to use again, as it stood, for the subsequent *Ring*. Having recalled the potentially hazardous circumstances of the undertaking – with Boulez untainted by contact with any previous performances of the work and lacking orchestral experience, together with the fact that directing at Bayreuth was something special – he enthusiastically salutes 'one of the most extraordinary, most beautiful and most profoundly poetic performances of *Parsifal* imaginable'. He

12 Letter of 24 July 1966, published in the *Programmheft Parsifal* from the 1973 Festival; reprinted in *Musique en jeu*, No. 22, 1976, p. 103.
13 *Le Figaro littéraire*, 4 August 1966.

remarks that, unlike those of his celebrated predecessors, Boulez's conception was animated not by a romantic eloquence but principally by his knowledge of Webern and Debussy. His refreshing tempos no longer recall the divine breadth of a recent past, 'which gave the impression that there was time for the metaphysical grass to grow between the notes'. (In the Richard Wagner Museum (Wahnfried) there is now a table giving the timings of the acts since the first performance: in brevity, Boulez follows hard on the heels of Richard Strauss, while the slowcoaches add at least as much as a quarter of an hour to the first act. These include Hans Knappertsbusch, of course, not to mention Arturo Toscanini – in his case doubtless in order to make it 'more Germanic'.[14] Rostand notes that the tension created by faster tempos brings to the fore the idea of a chain of events that is in fact fundamental to Wagner. And he finally draws attention to an 'analytical interpretation' that ensures the extreme transparency of the orchestration, always conceived in terms of chamber music, and that rejects all 'pathos superimposed on a score sufficiently expressive in itself'.[15] The German and international press were equally captivated. 'Bayreuth has found a conductor', wrote K.-H. Ruppel in the *Süddeutsche Zeitung*, readily comparing the French musician to the redeemer himself, now that the Knappertsbusch–Amfortas regime had had its day.

Bayreuth may have found a conductor, but it had lost its producer and, above all, its inspiration. Wieland Wagner died in Munich on 17 October 1966. For the *Trauerfeier*, the coffin was placed on the Bayreuth stage as Boulez directed the orchestra in the Prelude to *Parsifal*. Without wishing to add excessive poignancy to an already sorrowful occasion, I will merely say that – in the sphere of the collaboration between producer and conductor alone – we have lost much more than the cherished projects themselves (they had planned to do *Pelléas*, *Don Giovanni*, and doubtless the *Ring* and *Boris*). Some of these may follow, with other producers. But it is the potential of a team formed from an eminently musical producer

---

14 Act 1: Pierre Boulez,   1hr. 37'
         Richard Strauss,   1hr. 38'
         Rudolf Kempe,   1hr. 50'
         Arturo Toscanini,   2hrs. 10'
'As the conductors who directed at Bayreuth were generally on the aged side, they found it difficult to hear the singers on the stage, so that they slowed down in order to follow them instead of forging ahead' (an interview with Boulez in 'Lectures pour tous', July 1969).
15 'Since the composer's intentions are revealed as explicitly as possible within the musical text itself, any attempt to achieve a better "rendering" risks becoming caricature' (Pierre

and a musician with a passion for the theatre which was thus lost. Would the Bayreuth set-up – for better or worse unchanged – have been able to withstand the shock of two such personalities? Would they together have succeeded in achieving what was later, despite everything, to prove abortive: in other words, in establishing a real technique for modern operatic performance? Would Bayreuth have been open to the desirable sacrilege of including works other than those of Wagner? These questions must now remain forever unresolved.

THE TRAGI-COMEDY OF BOULEZ'S RELATIONS WITH FRENCH OFFICIALDOM

Boulez conducted *Parsifal* at Bayreuth in 1966, 1967, 1968 and 1970. At the invitation of George Szell, he had in March 1965 been guest conductor with the Cleveland Orchestra, among the best orchestras in the world. With them, he conducted programmes of twentieth-century classics, and the invitation was renewed for four weeks in 1967. Then, through the intervention of William Glock, Boulez had his first contact with the BBC Symphony Orchestra, conducting them at three concerts in 1965 at the Carnegie Hall in New York. Two years later, he toured with the same orchestra in Czechoslovakia, Poland and Russia.[16]

During this period, he was still living in Baden-Baden. Because of pressure of work – and doubtless disturbed by the rumours circulating about him in Paris – he resigned from the Domaine at the end of the 1966–7 season. (Gilbert Amy took over responsibility for the now celebrated institution until, in 1973, he put an end to an experiment that had definitely fulfilled its purpose.)

In 1966 the letter Boulez wrote to Malraux on the subject of the hypothetical reorganization of French musical life was relegated to the ministerial archives; while one may surmise the tenor of its contents from many interviews on the matter, it remained unanswered. Or rather, after a good deal of uncertainty and pressures of all kinds, the reply was oblique and disappointing – at least for Boulez: the composer Marcel Landowski was nominated head of the governing body for new music. Not that Boulez was in any way a candidate for the post, but one might have

Boulez, 'Chemins vers *Parsifal*', DG brochure; text several times reprinted – see Bibliography).

16 An amusing film was shot on this occasion, showing a jovial-looking Boulez, wearing a cap, and countering the attacks against modern music made by the press with a smile – making him look a good ten years younger.

thought that his central proposal – to recast the five Paris symphony orchestras as two groups forming a vast pool of variable strength and complementary disposition – would logically have led to a situation whereby the best French conductor would have conducted the best French orchestra. Apart from the fact that it meant that the minister had read Boulez's letter without much interest, the nomination of Landowski strengthened Boulez's deep-seated conviction that music ought to be controlled by an able and music-loving administrator rather than a composer inevitably called upon to play down his own involvement, and who, in such a position, could not fail to appear anything other than creatively disillusioned with himself.

In short, Boulez felt he had been swindled. He confided his indignation to the *Nouvel Observateur* in a famous diatribe entitled 'Why I say NO to Malraux'. Apart from his expression of contempt addressed to the minister, to his director of music and theatre, and to the president of the National Music Committee (then Jacques Chailley), his basic argument concerned the 'profile' desirable in one responsible for music. Such a person would necessarily control a wide field of cultural restoration – including theatre, exhibitions, and everything which could thus involve 'a young audience, as new in its social make-up as in its aesthetic aspirations'. He declared himself henceforth unwilling 'to collaborate with anyone, from near or far, in France or abroad, belonging to official musical organizations', adding that, in adopting this strictly personal position, he in no way implicated the honorary president of the SAMP.[17] He ended his article with a hint of regret: 'Is the only future in store for us one of lamentation, bitterness and desertion?'.[18]

Like certain of his other postures, Boulez's reply appears astonishingly sharp in retrospect, and he himself soon realized that the time for such aggression had passed. But one can no longer be unduly charitable towards his attitude to esteemed (and in any case dedicated) musicians: there is something juvenile about these personal and extremely discourteous onslaughts. Having said that, the fact remains: it is quite simply scandalous, even tragic, that French musical officialdom waited until 1972 before offering a substantial opportunity to the only practitioner of truly international stature (who was by then forty-seven). As Director General of Arts and Letters from 1961 to 1966, Gaeton Picon was to have

17 Which he has been since 1965. The General Secretary of the Syndicat des Artistes Musiciens de Paris was Arthur Haneuse.
18 'Farewell then, Herr Boulez!' was the remark flung at him by Jean Hamon while, for his part, Clarendon denounced the 'Hitlerian methods' of the Director of the Domaine musical.

inside knowledge of this early affair, and he describes the situation clearly, while diagnosing the ill: 'We have offered Boulez nothing – that would have been to exceed our function; as befitted our role, we asked him merely for his ideas on musical reorganization. The interest he took in this work and the obvious excellence of his suggestions made us simply hope that, in one way or another – though certainly not as a functionary – he would be able to help towards their realization, so giving him a reason to return to France.' And he concludes ruthlessly that 'the fact that the policy advocated by Boulez was impracticable does not mean that it was not the best, simply that, in France, the circumstances for the best do not exist.[19]

ACT II: THE VILAR–BOULEZ–BEJART PLAN

The curtain rose again almost immediately on the second act of this tragi-comedy. Meanwhile, the Bayreuth success was affirmed. In the hope of extricating the Paris Opéra from its fundamental crisis – defaulting audiences, unreliable standards, union disturbances, extravagant costs – Malraux asked Jean Vilar, founder of the TNP, for his ideas on a possible reform of this gargantuan establishment. Vilar immediately requested the commissioning of a 'troika' well informed in the matters of music and dance – including the two illustrious exiles, Boulez and Maurice Béjart (then in Brussels). 'I accepted because of Vilar himself', Boulez told *L'Express* (which again referred to him as Monsieur Boulez). The readers of this newspaper learnt that he considered selling Chagall's 'flying saucer' from the ceiling of the Palais Garnier to the Americans in order to pay for one more good production.

At the same time, appropriately enough, one of his best known interviews appeared in *Der Spiegel*; this was entitled 'Sprengt die Opernhäuser in die Luft' – which can be translated more or less as 'Devil take all opera houses'. This entertaining article begins by reporting on the endeavours of the would-be modernists (Henze, Schüller, Blacher and others) who, with the aid of electronic gadgets and other devices, thought they were making something new out of music that was in fact conventional. Kagel and Ligeti were credited with interesting ideas which unfortunately came to nothing because their theatrical ignorance could not conceal a thinness of musical purpose. Abroad, the situation was deemed hardly more encouraging – whether at the Metropolitan Opera,

19 *Le Monde*, 7 August 1969.

which had for years seemed indifferent to matters of production, or even in Hamburg, where the Administrator, Rolf Liebermann, was treated with a studied politeness. As to the Paris Opéra, this was nothing more than an 'ill-kept museum' – an obligatory tourist stop between the Folies-Bergères and the Invalides. The interview casts interesting light on Boulez's operatic tastes (Wagner, Mozart, Mussorgsky, Debussy and, of course, Berg) as well as on his own plans for a much discussed collaboration with Jean Genet on a text yet to be written.

Such was his frame of mind as he prepared to work with Vilar and Béjart. Apart from the fact that it indicated the future direction of a reformed Opéra, he was attracted to the 'troika' for its declared willingness to treat the matter within the larger framework of cultural experiments stemming from popular theatre, and was furthermore committed to the idea of moulding the aesthetic tastes of a new public.

Together with its administrative and budgetary appendices the scheme submitted to Malraux filled three large volumes, taking the form of a committed and willingly offered set of options: 'Even if not to everyone's taste, even if it gives every appearance of being sectarian, the existence of a determined long-term policy on the matter gives artistic undertakings – both public and private – the means of avoiding the shipwrecks, quicksands, or the disastrous tradition of routines that constantly threaten to bring experimentation and inventiveness to a standstill, leading to the abandonment of style, to a thinly disguised lassitude, and even to a neglect of the best . . .' (p. 3). The main points of the scheme were the disbanding of the Opéra-Comique, the renunciation of one part of the repertoire, and the quantitative equality of ballet and opera – but most important of all, the abandonment of the principle of an alternating repertoire (with a different show each evening) in favour of a small number of different productions each season, including first performances. Thus the first season was planned to have three French operas (both parts of Les Troyens, and Pelléas et Mélisande), two classical works (Gluck's Orfeo and Mozart's Don Giovanni) and two modern ones (Schoenberg's Moses und Aron, and a Berio première). Each production was naturally to be carefully rehearsed, and to be given a dozen or so times with an unchanging cast, and with Liebermann's presence essential to the future policy. The scheme also foresaw a reform of administrative and artistic structures, notably through the setting up of a working committee (which later came into being), and the creation of an important organizing sector, with a mission of obvious simplicity: 'to court, to welcome, and to inform the public'. A financial balance was to be established between an

80% subsidy, an increase in the number of performances and a diversifi-
cation of activity – including orchestral and chamber music concerts, and
outside events at the TNP or the Palais des sports.[20]

Some of these ideas were to be put into effect gradually, by subsequent
administrators of the Paris Opéra – notably Rolf Liebermann. With his
professional experience and his qualities of leadership, he managed for
seven years (1973–80) to bluff his way in concealing the fact that the state
of affairs was desperate. One would like to think that a scheme as
coherent, if not identical to that of the Vilar–Boulez–Béjart project, might
determine the future destiny of the new Paris Opéra presently being set up.

For the success of the 1967–8 undertaking could only have been
appreciated retrospectively, and by proxy, owing to the shattering 'events'
of 1968. As for Boulez, he watched things from a distance, partly in
Germany, partly in Cleveland, and partly at his house in Saint-Michel
l'Observatoire. (He openly declared at the time that his relations with his
own country were of the vacational, touristic kind – thereby revealing all
the scorn of northern man for the frivolity of the south.) He would not
have minded a successful radical revolution, and given the opportunity,
declared himself a 300% Marxist–Leninist – at the same time calling for
hordes of red guards to set fire to opera houses! But this imperturbability
is also the result of scepticism: he had ceased to believe in revolution a
long time ago, particularly this one – whose spontaneous nature in his
view deprived it of all serious intent, particularly in the cultural domain!

No doubt it was different for Vilar, who did not in any case support de
Gaulle's clamp-down at the end of May. With little warning to his two
associates, he protected his leftist conscience from compromise by
withdrawing from the hypothetical Paris Opéra; Boulez and Béjart had no
choice but to follow.

BOULEZ AND THE BBC SYMPHONY ORCHESTRA

'Eight days later, a representative of the BBC came to offer me the artistic
direction of its symphony orchestra', Boulez announced in *L'Express*. The
representative in question was William Glock, thanks to whom Boulez
had had a connection with the BBC for the past three years. Glock had
heard of his resignation from the Vilar project and knew that Boulez was
free to consider the offer. In June, he made a flying visit to The Hague,

20 The main outlines of the project were published in the review *Musique en jeu*, No. 14,
1974, pp. 110–11.

where Boulez was conducting the Residentie Orchestra, and there asked him if he would agree to succeed Colin Davis, whose contract was due to expire at the end of 1969. Boulez accepted, on condition that, exceptionally, a means be found to enable William Glock (then approaching retirement age) to remain alongside, in overall control of the orchestra.

Preceded by a long engagement period, the marriage of Boulez and the BBC was highly successful. For anyone fortunate enough to have seen him working with and conducting orchestras as different as those of Bayreuth, London, New York, or Paris, there can be no doubt that the relationship between Boulez and English musicians is a special one. It seems to depend on two things: a liking for work well done and for telling jokes – an ability that Boulez possesses to a surprising degree. I have attended dozens of rehearsals with the BBC. Each time, I have been struck by the speed with which he switches from an atmosphere of intense seriousness, concentration, and patience on the part of both players and conductor, to one of relaxation. Boulez intuitively senses the moment when tension needs to be relieved – by joking with the timpanist, by taking an early break, by moving away from the passage being rehearsed before coming back to it, by gossiping for thirty seconds with the front desks of the strings, or by releasing the players before the end of the allotted time if possible (as it often is). It goes without saying that this works both ways: work must begin the second he raises his hands; the English players are quite disciplined enough to stop the moment he asks them, not to talk in between times, and to pick up again without forgetting where they are. All these are details almost too trivial to mention, but together, they amaze and delight the continental witness, who can recall hundreds of rehearsals with French orchestras!

There is moreover something mysterious in Boulez's elective affinity with English musicians which results not from the language (learnt swiftly during his tenure), nor yet from the exceptional qualities of the orchestra itself (ultimately to be surpassed by others), nor even through any special tradition of mutual friendliness. One might more easily say that Anglo-French musical relations were clouded by a grain of reciprocal contempt – certainly unjustified on the part of the French. Boulez always felt he had room to breath in London; the style of English life seems to suit him, with its idiosyncratic mixture of routine and disregard for certain conventions.

There is, of course, an explanation of a more musical kind. The BBC SO is a splendid orchestra and one especially involved with twentieth-century music: it was for this reason that the arrangement was made for Boulez to come and to expand its repertoire to include the Second Viennese School,

Stravinsky, Bartók, Mahler and Debussy, as well as more recent composers, including the English. A statistical survey of the years 1963–72, when Boulez was only partly in control, reveals that the orchestra played two hundred modern works, twenty per season – a proportion that was maintained during the following five years. The English musical press, one of the best in the world, was generally more than sympathetic to the authority wielded by the French conductor, who was for his part aware of the richness and diversity of London musical life, with five excellent symphony orchestras. For his part, he gave concerts in glamorous venues like the Royal Festival Hall, but also at the Round House – a disused locomotive shed endowed with a quasi-Elizabethan circular layout, a good acoustic, and an informal atmosphere.

A final word on Boulez's anglophilia: perhaps his austere nature, counteracted by his taste for *badinage*, found something to admire in the spectacle of a country economically embarrassed, but nevertheless determined not to cut back on one essential. Like Boulez himself, the English were prepared to devote to music a truly Churchillian energy and application.

The three-year contract with the BBC, signed in January 1969, took effect from January 1971, and was to be renewed in 1974. It included reference not only to the work of conducting, both in London and on tour, but more particularly, to the responsibilities of an artistic director: programme planning, supervision of orchestral players, the engagement of soloists and guest conductors, and the arrangement of rehearsals. Boulez was new to the job, but clearly had all the qualities needed to excel at it. He left Tchaikovsky and Dvořák to colleagues more experienced in this kind of repertoire, politely but firmly settled the inevitable conflicts arising with one player or another, and organized the timing of his rehearsals superbly. In return, everything went extremely well. I never heard of any particular tensions in London; on the contrary, there are many good memories, ten years on!

Even before January 1971, Boulez was obviously invited to conduct his future orchestra. He also conducted the London Symphony Orchestra on tour: it was on one such occasion, in Vienna in June 1969, that I myself first met him. In December of the same year he conducted *Pelléas et Mélisande* at Covent Garden.

THE CONCEPTION OF *PELLEAS ET MELISANDE* (1969)

Boulez explained his conception of the work in various interviews, but mainly, and at some length, in the fine article which accompanies the 1970 recording,[21] and in which he again begins by playing devil's advocate:

What constitutes the profound originality of Debussy's aesthetic of the theatre has been for the most part slurred over, so that *Pelléas* has often appeared as a kind of disincarnate work, verging on what may be described as a 'poetic' tisane in the worst sense, a work in which the conflicts arise for no very apparent reason and can only seem incongruous, since they arise between characters who must never pronounce one word louder than another. A special 'tradition' has given the whole opera an elegant varnish, to which must of course be added the famous French clarity.

He emphasizes the sombre profundity of the drama, the violence which creeps in everywhere, the madness of Golaud, Mélisande and Pelléas's fear of discovering an erotic mystery – in short, what André Schaeffner refers to as this 'theatre of fear and cruelty' that the music breathes into Maeterlinck's problematic play. He then opts for an interpretation of passionate contrasts in which the orchestra's role is far from subsidiary – and in which the feline character of Debussy's music is exploited to good advantage.

The production had only a few performances and was not followed up by Boulez, who had neither the time nor the interest to become involved in any kind of theatrical routine. But the results are available to all, by means of a recording that is often superb – not only in the concentrated *élan* of the orchestral playing, but also in many dramatic exchanges like those of the scenes in the park. It also has its disappointments, in particular the shaky French pronunciation of almost all the cast. But once this defect is accepted, even interpreted as part of a detached anti-realism endemic to this particular work, Boulez's version of *Pelléas* has some fine moments – notwithstanding the contemptuous lip-pursing of most of the French critics.

Produced by Václav Kašlík and with a fine décor by Henri Svoboda, the London première took place on 4 December 1969.

---

21 See Discography. The article 'Reflections on *Pelléas et Mélisande*' has been reprinted in *Orientations*, pp. 306–17.

A 'NAIVE' WORK: *DOMAINES* (1968)

The first performance of *Domaines* for solo clarinet and six instrumental groups took place in Brussels on 20 December 1968, with Walter Boeykens as soloist. Two years later, on 10 November 1970, the work was given in Paris in a slightly revised version,[22] as part of a concert given by the ensemble Musique Vivante, again conducted by Boulez but with Michel Portal as soloist. Recorded shortly afterwards by the same players but this time conducted by Diego Masson under the supervision of the composer, *Domaines* quickly became a relatively popular work. This success was due to the innate attractiveness of this half hour of extraordinarily pleasing and varied virtuoso music. More fundamentally, *Domaines* benefits from the fact that, for once, its platform layout is self-explanatory, and helps to give the listener the feeling of being part of the work, rather than that its meaning in some way depends on its instrumental disposition.

The visual element here clarifies the listening process. At a time (1968) when the 'happening' made its appearance in concert halls, when it was no longer unusual to see one instrumentalist or another wandering about the platform during the course of a work, and when 'incident' tended to replace 'structure', the spectacle offered by *Domaines* seemed quite in line with the reconsideration of the traditional concert format postulated by fashionable debate.[23] To be sure, it was here developed within an eminently cautious framework, rather than 'with no holds barred'! Michel Portal, equally at home with all kinds of music, played a difficult work with seeming ease: echoed by one group of instrumentalists, the soloist meanwhile moves towards another group, plays in front of it, while it in turn responds to him, and so on – with six groups thus to be called upon, six 'domains' to be visited, in any order he chooses. Rather than being the 'operator' in the Mallarméan sense of the term, the soloist – according to the excellent description of F. and N. Bridgman[24] – is here the 'protagonist' of this quasi-theatrical display.

Once the soloist has completed his circuit, by visiting all six of the instrumental 'domains' offered to him, it is up to the conductor to organize the return (or 'miroir') circuit by determining the order in which the six groups are to play; after each group has had its say, the soloist

22 Notably as to the circular arrangement adopted today.
23 I intend a little self-criticism here: see the beginnings of the review *Musique en jeu*.
24 Text from the Harmonia Mundi recording.

replies with his own corresponding sequence. Thus he not only has the first word but also the last.

This re-evaluation of the role of the performer continued Boulez's involvement with the act of creative interpretation, seen in the Third Sonata, if not earlier. The work is thus 'semi-open' in the Boulezian sense: everything is notated, but the performer is allowed a certain freedom – not only as to the order of the sections themselves, but as to the details (nuances, types of sonority, expressive character) of their organization.

The work is equally attractive for its pleasing sonority, but it has become a cliché, at least since *Marteau*, to remark on Boulez's ability to select and to make good use of his instruments. I am not personally very keen on the sound of a trombone quartet, but I have to acknowledge its surprising elegance here; less surprising is the sheer aural delight offered by the pairing of marimba and double bass, or the trio of oboe, horn and guitar. *Domaines* is a work which will serve professors of sound and timbre identification as a better example to recommend to their students than the *Carnival of the Animals*!

This almost too successful work nevertheless leaves one with a slight feeling of unease – a feeling that may be openly admitted, since even the composer today declares his dissatisfaction with it. The idea for *Domaines* goes back to 1961, and a preliminary version for clarinet solo was premièred in Ulm three months before the Brussels version. According to Boulez, even the latter is 'too simple' in structure, and he goes on to say:

This symmetry of the group visits is too audible. Even if the soloist is for a time to be linked to one particular group, the sense of perspective might be increased by giving the other groups something to say. It is this which the present version lacks: at any given point one focuses only on the soloist and the group he is visiting, so that the other groups are left in the shade – almost in a state of non-existence.[25]

It could also be said that *Domaines* in some way represents the apotheosis, perhaps even the limit, of Boulez's two imagined ideals: namely, the permutability of sequences within a predetermined whole, and the oscillating play between two precisely stipulated propositions. Within a group of six elements there are 720 possible permutations: 720 possible versions of either the 'original' or the 'miroir' forms and so 720 x 720 possible ways of organizing the work as a whole. In terms of its form, *Domaines* drifts towards infinity. At the same time, the licence Boulez

25 *Conversations with Célestin Deliège*, p. 88.

allows his soloist is generally restricted to a binary system:[26] he must do this or else that, if he does this on the outward journey, he must do that on the return. A maximum number of possibilities is thus reduced to a minimum of probabilities.

The important, almost magical significance given to the figure 6 also helps to define the foreground procedures: there are six instrumental groups comprising between one and six players, six corresponding sequences and, within each of these, six structures to be played by the soloist – frequently polarized around six-note rhythmic groups.

Since 1974, Boulez has promised the imminent appearance of a reworked version, which will be more complex, less obviously sectional, and less contrived. Will this 'revision in progress' make *Domaines* less redolent of past or future works? It is impossible not to be reminded of *Marteau* in the marimba/double bass duo of sequence C, or of the end of *cummings ist der Dichter* in sequence E, when the loquacious oboe is supported by horn and guitar – or to find something of *Eclat/Multiples* in the string sextet of sequence B. And years later, during a demonstration by Boulez of the virtuoso abilities of the 4X machine at IRCAM, I was astonished to hear it achieve with terrifying perfection a 'mouvement perpétuel' closely resembling that played by the clarinet in sequence F! *Domaines* can be regarded as the crystallization of many experiments, its very limits attractive in themselves.

THE WORKS OF THE 1970s

It has become commonplace to evoke the picture of a composer stricken with sterility as he approached his fifties – although the more charitable hasten to add that this was a misfortune shared by colleagues of the 'Darmstadt generation' such as Stockhausen, Nono and Pousseur. But this is not born out by examination of the facts. On the contrary, Boulez appeared to be relatively prolific during these few years, but he deployed his creativity along channels of investigation rather than of realization, of research rather than production. The four works dating from this period are presently (1984) unfinished, and none can be placed on a par with their memorable predecessors, or with the finished perfection of future works like *Rituel* (1974) or *Messagesquisse* (1979), nor yet with the anticipated mastery of *Répons* (1981–4). They are studies, the experimental beginnings of works. Boulez was exploring, often successfully in terms

26 Cf. *Structures* Book 2.

of the micro-event, where certain passages have a felicitous ring. But on the larger canvas of a whole work the solution in its entirety was not noticeably forthcoming – and he himself made no secret of the fact. Let us briefly take a closer look at these scores.

Livre pour cordes (1968)

Aware that the incredible performance difficulties arising from his own inexperience resulted in an unconvincing 'sound product' that could only discourage potential performers, Boulez had for some years planned to revise his 1948 *Livre pour quatuor*. Apart from the Parrenin Quartet, there are after all few groups who have taken it into their repertoire. Accordingly, he withdrew it from his catalogue, advising against its performance except by those who had already rehearsed and played it, and prepared to re-cast it in terms of a string orchestra.

However, to date, only two sections have been rewritten (1a, *Variation*; and 1b, *Mouvement*); these were premièred in London on 1 December 1968, with a notable *succès d'estime*. The work sounded infinitely better than in the first version, not only because of an enhanced grasp of instrumental idioms on the composer's part, but also because the sound character, strangulated in the quartet, could blossom. There is, of course, the opposite view: compared with the extraordinary vigour, vehemence and alacrity of the quartet version, the more ponderous virtuosity of that for string orchestra suggests that the composer has gratuitously opted for a safer, though less exciting, solution.

This recomposition has for the present been abandoned.[27] The time that has passed since the incomplete London première is almost equal to that which elapsed between it and the quartet version. I am inclined to think that if Boulez had been completely convinced by his undertaking, he would have found a way to bring it to a successful conclusion. Could the answer to the very real problem posed therein lie in rewriting the quartet score itself, rather than in arranging it for a formation for which it was not originally intended? Such would appear to be the conviction of the members of the Alban Berg Quartet, and, as far as one can gather, of Boulez himself. One can only hope for the eventual emergence of a real masterpiece – for the benefit both of distinguished instrumentalists and of those listeners who already admire the work in its earlier version.

27 Movement 1a has since been reworked and was premièred, in a version that Boulez today (June 1989) declares to be definitive, at the Barbican Centre in London in January 1989. Movement 1b and the rest of the work remain to be rewritten for string orchestra.

cummings ist der Dichter (1970)

This work is in some respects one of Boulez's most attractive and accomplished scores. Boulez was introduced to the work of the American poet e.e. cummings (1894–1962) in 1952 by John Cage – and it was Cage whose advice he sought as to its interpretation. This poetry took a long time to digest. It was nearly thirty years later that he chose an initial text, setting it for mixed choir (sixteen voices), and small orchestra comprising flute, four oboes, bassoon, three horns, two trumpets, two trombones, violin, three violas, three cellos, double bass, and three harps. The work lasts about ten minutes.

<pre>
birds(
      here,inven
ting air
U
)sing

tw
iligH(
t's
   v
       va
           vas(
vast

ness. Be)look
now
      (come
soul;
&:and

Who
  s)e
      voi

c
es
(
are
  ar
  a
</pre>

The prophetic and almost infra-semantic statement of the text – with the jostling and colliding of its often dislocated syllables, together with the poetic meaning of such words as 'birds', 'twilight', 'soul' – finds no literal equivalent in Boulez's music but rather, a collaborative response that is both flexible, rhythmic, and evocative.

The two conductors required for the work do not necessarily beat at the same speed, neither are their functions and hierarchical relationships identical: the instrumental conductor has overall control even if the choral conductor sometimes takes the initiative. Incidentally, Boulez has never gone more deeply into the exploration of a vocal text. This exploration is begun by the poet in his idiosyncratic use of the words themselves, making it easier for the composer to distance himself from the literal meaning of the text – indispensable, at least these days, to poetic expression. Once again, as Ivanka Stoianova notes in a fairly detailed appraisal of the relationship between text and music in *cummings*, 'while the poem remains "central", it becomes "absent" by means of dissociation and interpenetration of the devices in play'.[28] Mallarmé's research into ways of arranging a text on a blank page is here extended to include the arrangement of syllables – so leading to an analogy with the way aural 'events' are inscribed on a texture of sustained chords. Traces of the aesthetic of the semi-open work make this work heir to the Third Sonata and – more directly – to *Eclat*.

The work was premièred in September 1970 in Ulm, by the Schola Cantorum of Stuttgart, conduced by Clytus Gottwald, and a group of instrumentalists under the direction of the composer. Its felicitous treatment and chamber music scoring place it within the composer's 'hedonistic vein', although Boulez never relinquishes his steadfastness of purpose. Although completely self-contained, it is a pity that this first 'panel' remains in splendid isolation (the whole work is destined to last about an hour).

The name arose from an amusing misunderstanding: a secretary from the radio telephoned Boulez to ask for the title of his new work in order to be able to print it in the programme. Boulez, whose German was then rudimentary, replied that he did not yet know – but that in any case, 'cummings is the poet'. The secretary understood this to be the name of

---

28 Ivanka Stoianova, writing about Boulez's *cummings ist der Dichter*, Berio's *O King* and Schnebel's *Für Stimmen . . . missa est* in an article entitled, 'Verbe et son; "Centre" et "Absence" ', *Musique en jeu*, No. 16, 1974.

the work – hence 'cummings ist der Dichter'. That sounded all right: fate, providence or the secretary had found the answer – and so the title stood.

Eclat/Multiples (1965–70)

I will here simply mention this still incomplete extension to *Eclat*, while referring the reader to the note devoted to the work on pp. 335 ff. It should however be noted that this is a work whose ambitious scope has not changed over the intervening years. To start with, it has an evolving programme, with the chamber music *Eclat* acting as rocket-carrier for the larger ensemble required for the section of *Multiples* so far completed – an ensemble that is, in turn, destined to be extended into a full orchestra. It seems that certain obstacles may stand in the way of this project: it is difficult to keep a large number of musicians on the platform with nothing to do for such a long time, and variable procedures – already mastered within the framework of a small ensemble – are fraught with dangers when the small group is increased to the size of a large orchestra. (But perhaps this calls into question the very purpose of the work.)

For the moment, the virtuoso *Multiples* section forms something of a solecism in relation to *Eclat*. The resolute rhythms dominating large sections of the orchestra are occasionally reminiscent of the lesser works of Stravinsky. However, one can hardly presume to judge *Multiples* from this half-way point.

'. . . explosante-fixe . . .' (1974)

This is an intermediate work, but it is important as an indication of Boulez's activities after 1973. Written on the occasion of Stravinsky's death in 1971, it will be discussed in a following chapter (pp. 176–7). It is included here only as evidence of a phase of 'research' that seems to define Boulez's output at the start of the 1970s – and which appears to show signs of a productive incubation rather than of any uncertainty.

CHAPTER TEN

Boulez the Conductor (II)

(1971–4)

The start of the 1970s marked a turning point in the decade (1963–73) that saw the 'explosion' of Boulez's conducting career. Until then, his successes as conductor had been brilliant, but sporadic; they were now to be made official. At the same time, orchestral conducting was only the outward manifestation of a less visible activity: directing the musical policy of an orchestra was essential to Boulez if he was to challenge the proliferation of compositional practices he considered unacceptable, particularly at the very time when his own creative vein seemed to be changing.

'OU EN EST-ON?'

On 13 May 1968 – a doubly symbolic date for the French – Boulez was invited by Maurice Fleuret to deliver a lecture in his old school at Saint-Etienne, in front of five hundred amazingly attentive pupils. Entitled 'Where are we now?', the lecture was fascinating for two reasons. To begin with, it was the first occasion for a long time that Boulez had expressed himself publicly in France on the subject of musical composition: secondly, he did so now in the midst of a period of cultural upheaval, at a time when rumour had it that he had more or less given up composing, and was escaping into the world of the great orchestras – a world which seemed to have scant connection with a revolutionary figure known to be ultra-critical of the generally accepted forms of musical communication.[1]

Where are we now? – At a crossroads; such was the general tenor of the

---

1 The lecture is published in *Orientations*, pp. 445–63.

lecture. Boulez begins by remarking that, at forty-three, he is no longer a 'young composer' and that, together with his interpretative functions, this fact enables him to occupy the position of intermediary between a work and its public. The text is extremely pedagogic, least boring when he begins by recalling the circumstances of the years 1945–6, when 'nothing was ready and everything remained to be done'. He goes on to say that it was then that he felt the need for 'the discovery of the grammar and the form necessary for the establishment of a solid and reliable language' and, 'after the precise codification of the language, we must once again concern ourselves with questions of aesthetics'. The diversity of approach adopted by individuals is held to be responsible for the lack of unity in musical thinking which is apparent today. This in turn is partly responsible for the 'discrepancy' which has arisen between the new music and the audience, 'between the creative artist and the mass of the concert-going public that interests itself in orchestral music and great artists'.

So one can seen that, for Boulez, compositional crisis is closely linked to the cultural problem of creating an audience; one might add that the diagnosis seems equally valid today.

As an up-to-date catalogue of the errors of the time, the lecture lists some of these problems in a less theoretically elaborate version than the subsequent 'Donc on remet en question' (1975, cf. pp. 170–2): the presentation of electro-acoustic music in funereal concerts; mixed media music, where the evidence of one's eyes is contradicted by the transmitted source of the sound; instrumental theatre, which attempts to transform instrumental players into actors – a role for which they have no natural aptitude; the conservative architecture of concert halls; the training of instrumentalists and (with regard to composition itself) the fashion for aleatoric music – the 'vague diagrams' given to the players and the self-conscious simplicity of its actual musical assertions. And he concludes: 'For this reason I consider it quite indispensable that our approach should be highly disciplined and quite ruthless about the possibilities of music, rejecting absolutely all the easy options represented by ready-made or purely superficial solutions.'

THE COMPOSER WITHOUT RESPONSIBILITY

Amidst all the turmoil of that incredible May of 1968, there began a phase that was to end only with the creation of IRCAM – an organization whose aspirations were to become increasingly entwined with the philosophy outlined above.[2] This was a phase during which Boulez was to reject the hegemonic practices invading musical life before proving worthy of his new engagements in London and/or New York.

Music was indeed ailing – for the reasons just mentioned, but more crucially, because a particular compositional doctrine was being challenged and destroyed by the new generation. Boulez did not express it in exactly these terms, but his conclusion is much the same. There is something about this pupil of the strict Montbrison Jesuits which makes him opposed to any abdication of creative responsibility, such as the introduction of chance into composition (Cage), forms that were 'open' to the point of negating the very idea of form (Brown), musical happenings, ('propositions') as substitutes for scores, graphic suggestions verging on affectation (Bussotti), improvised music, and music which seeks its salvation in a dubious orientalism. There was also the tinkering with electro-acoustics, individual or collective improvisation of a simplistic kind[3] which was largely dictated by players' own performance clichés, the fashion for instrumentalists walking clumsily around the platform, the aleatoric superposition of independent strands and the absurdly eccentric use of traditional instruments. He also objects to the devaluation of the idea of euphony, the glorification of all kinds of noise, ignorance of the most advantageous timbral combinations, derisory attempts at audience participation, and the opprobrium cast upon the bourgeois notion of 'a work'. For Boulez, this is no more than an unreliable type of frivolity, a joyless perversity – the sign of an amateurism that churns out empty witticisms clearly unlikely to lead to the formulation of a new aesthetic. Neither would the mediocrity of the 'works' thus produced result in attracting a public likely to be taken in by it. The musical institution thus becomes completely inward-looking, concentrating its attention upon the three hundred or so believers who rally to any aesthetic cause, but who constitute the entire population of the ghetto to which contemporary music is confined.

It looks very much as if this is the abdication of responsibility on the part of the composer, which was freely admitted by the interested parties themselves, and which is at the core of Boulez's contempt. He wholly

2 The main thread of the interviews of the period 1969–72, in particular of the most important one, published in L'Express (see Bibliography).
3 Around 1973, I sat next to Boulez at a presentation of collective improvisation by a specialist and talented group. I well remember my neighbour's exasperation at being so easily able to forecast the succession of events: warming up, explosion, deflation, stasis,

accepts the idea of feeling one's way, of trial and error, but he has not basically altered his 1954 view of the creator as one who attempts 'to forge his own pathway'.[4] As heir to a tradition of musical composition stretching from Bach to Webern, Boulez is convinced that the individual, inspired, and god-like creative act remains the basis of musical innovation.

MAKING GOOD USE OF CONTRADICTION

Since Boulez himself had contributed to this attack on Western compositional norms, his position appeared somewhat equivocal: as early as 1957, it was in fact he who had introduced the element of performer's choice into the concept of form. Once Boulez, as the representative of established serialism, had himself agreed to the subject of the open-form work being put on the agenda, quarrels over precedence with Stockhausen (or even Cage) made little sense. More insidiously, was it not he himself who had first launched the move to re-evaluate serialism – sharing the general view that it was only a stage in the definition of a language? An irreversible stage, to be sure, but one whose mannerisms inevitably led to all the academic imitations which leave music gasping for fresh air.[5] Was he really entitled to protest against new forms of concert-giving when one of his most famous German interviews was called 'The ritual of the concert must be changed'?[6] And having called for a bomb to fall upon the Opéra, its ceremonial and all its works,[7] should he be surprised to find some composers attempting to forge a path towards a new music theatre? Speaking more generally, how could a composer as notorious as Boulez for parting company with his predecessors after a whole series of (sometimes violent) disagreements be surprised to see the new generation reacting similarly against a generation that had occupied a virtually dominant position for the past twenty years?

Boulez counters all these questions – occasionally somewhat ironically posed by critics, colleagues, and observers – with replies that are sometimes facile, at other times more fundamental.

starting again to warm up towards . . . and so on – the diastolic–systolic system applied to music!

4 'The Composer as Critic', 1954, reprinted in *Orientations*, p. 108.

5 Cf. 'Recherches maintenant' (see this volume, p. 70).

6 'Das Ritual der Konzerte muss geändert werden', *Süddeutsche Zeitung*, 18–19 October 1969.

7 'Sprengt die Opernhäuser in die Luft!', *Der Spiegel*, No. 40, 1967. Cf. p. 140.

THE MANIFESTO 'TEL QUEL' (1968)

The fact that Boulez signed a manifesto published by the group Tel Quel (with which he was connected through the publication of *Relevés d'apprenti* two years previously) following the events of May 1968 and the split that gave rise to *Change*[8] should be seen as symptomatic, rather than as a positive action. After all, he was not a habitual manifesto signer, and the only precedent is probably the '121'[9] in 1960. It is significant to our discussion that the adoption of such a stance could, at the time, be viewed within the context of the first of several passing flirtations between the Tel Quel group and the French communist party – on the basis of their common renunciation of cultural and political leftism, and their endorsement (with no outcome on the PCF side) of formal research. The manifesto called for the emergence of a 'theory based on textual practice', if only 'to avoid the frequent stalemates of the debate already under way'.

Boulez is in no way averse to spontaneous criticism of the May 1968 kind; following the events closely but without much fellow feeling, for him the student movement came close to seeming as loosely structured as the work of aleatory composers.[10] He himself had always criticized those of his colleagues for whom 'artistic commitment' involved underlining a 'revolutionary' text with discreetly modernist music. That a fundamental re-questioning of language should bring about a true artistic and intellectual revolution is ultimately more or less commensurate with the view assigned to it in the history of music – if not history itself. The rest is mere frivolity. He is fond of saying that 'Governments have no fear of artists; they fear the real revolutionaries who may arise in their stead.' He regards the political pretension inherent in cultural leftism as 'farcical': 'I do not have the technique for changing society.'[11]

8 Quarterly review founded and directed by Jean-Pierre Faye as a break-away endeavour from *Tel Quel*, published by Le Seuil (1967); concerned with the theory of language based on the theoretical work of Noam Chomsky.
9 A manifesto signed in 1960 by 121 French artists, intellectuals, university personnel and writers in protest at the pursuit of the Algerian war: 'the cause of the Algerian people, which contributes decisively to the overthrow of the colonial system, is the cause of all free men'. Boulez was the only musician amongst the 121 early signatories (although Leibowitz later added his name).
10 The ambivalence of Boulez's feelings towards the events of May 1968 is revealed by the fact that, shortly afterwards, he envisaged composing a work based on the slogans and graffiti of the time. The plan (happily?) came to nothing. Incidentally, he resigned from his position as honorary president of the Paris Musicians' Union after the Confederation to which the Union belonged showed itself in favour of the more extreme elements in the student movement.
11 'Taking Leave of Predecessors', II (see Bibliography).

THE ONLY ANSWER: TO CHANGE MUSICAL LIFE

The technique he does have is a musical one – in this case an aptitude for direction, organization and communication. This was the ace hand that stood him in good stead as a means of overcoming the crisis rumoured to be threatening him. Accordingly, he changed the battle ground. Great orchestras are the focal point of city musical life: to be in charge of them is to have the means of influencing musical life in general, of changing it in depth, and above all, of narrowing the chasm separating the music-loving public from the creativity of its time – a chasm which the perverted trends of present-day practices attempts to hide without really reducing it.

So it was astonishing to find him periodically declaring himself 'a 300% Marxist–Leninist' – an extravagant claim that would have prevented him from gaining admission to just those bodies he wished – if not to destroy – at least to modify radically.

The period lent itself to numerous interviews during which the interviewer usually ventured a sacrilegious comment along the lines of 'you conduct so much because you compose so little'. Boulez was waiting to trap the impertinent, and able therefore to formulate the cautionary balance of his rejoinder. In such circumstances, he would lash out against the incredible 'diarrhoea of mediocrity'[12] which had taken hold of musical innovation, and remind one of his position as regards a task he was not prepared to surrender until it was at least partly achieved – and until he was convinced that his self-imposed mission to reform musical life (in the truly proselytizing sense of the word) had succeeded to a degree worthy of the time and energy devoted to it.

The time had come to move on to practical undertakings. The London experience has already been mentioned; a new opportunity now awaited Boulez on the other side of the Atlantic.

A FRENCHMAN IN NEW YORK

Following its foundation in 1842, the first three concerts given by the New York Philharmonic Orchestra consisted of Beethoven symphonies – as modern then as the music of the Second Viennese School in 1970. The problem was that since then this repertoire had become an established part of orchestral routine – the very exemplar of the preferred staple diet of the orchestra, its players, and its united audience. This was the first challenge that New York offered to Boulez. Doubtless no more conserva-

12 *L'Express*, 2–7 May 1972.

tive than the prevailing attitudes in Philadelphia, Detroit, Cleveland or Los Angeles,[13] the reactionary tendencies of the New York orchestra and its public nonetheless stood out as an unexpected shortcoming in a city permeated by modernity in other respects.

A second challenge lay in the fact that, unlike the BBC SO (with which Boulez was also involved at the time), the New York Philharmonic had to rely on its box-office. Without subsidies, it was financially at the mercy of its audience – a situation which may have been exciting for Boulez the artistic director, but which was a decidedly negative factor in respect of his missionary purpose: innovation was scarcely encouraged by the fact that policy could be justified only if it filled the hall. And finally (unlike London), New York has only one orchestra. This exclusive position may seem advantageous, but it also creates constraints: like public service radio, it has to cater to all tastes.

This then was the framework within which Boulez was to find himself working on his chosen mission. He arrived in New York to take up his appointment at the start of the 1971 season, preceded by the 'revolution-ary' (not to say 'iconoclastic') reputation which had surrounded his previous appearances as guest conductor. Now that he was really in charge of the orchestra, this reputation pandered to a journalistic penchant for shocking headlines, whilst alarming some of the orchestra, most of its audience, and even its president, Carlos Moseley – even though it was Moseley himself who had done everything to ensure Boulez's appointment, and who was to be his principle collaborator during the New York years.

THE LINCOLN CENTER CONCERTS

Everything began well. Boulez arrived in New York in a downpour, but found that the apartment booked for him by the orchestral management at the Navarra Hotel satisfied his immediate material needs: a large table and good lighting. From the *New York Times* he learnt that the first two weeks of the season were completely sold out:[14] it only remained for him to make his début in his new role. The first concert took place on 21 September 1971, in the presence of the city's mayor, John Lindsay, and of the upper crust of New York society. The programme consisted of Wagner's *Faust* Overture, two extracts from *Le Troyens*, Liszt's *Toten-*

13 The orchestras and audiences in Boston, and particularly in Chicago, were less conservative.
14 Peyser, op. cit., p. 197.

tanz (with Jorge Bolet as soloist), the *Prélude à l'après-midi d'un faune* and *The Rite of Spring*. During the interval, opinions were mixed, although enthusiasm for *The Rite* was unanimous.

The press reviews were good, as they generally were for Boulez during those years, with the influential (and excellent) Harold C. Schonberg giving significant support in the *New York Times*. Fulfilling his educational role, Boulez planned to have a double feature each season: Liszt and Berg the first year, Haydn and Stravinsky the second, pre- and post-romanticism in the third. His commitment to modernity also involved specialized conductors, seldom heard in New York before then. As early as October 1971 Michael Gielen came to conduct a programme of Strauss (*Metamorphosen*), Nono (*Canti di Vita e d'Amore*) and Berg (the *Lulu* Suite): it is said that the hall became progressively emptier as the concert proceeded, ostensibly indicating the line beyond which the public – and in particular, its generous subscribers – was not prepared to go. Year after year, the Boulez–Moseley policy was based on limiting the losses by means of a subtle balance in the repertoire, by rallying support from among the younger members of the public, and by arranging other kinds of sponsorship.

'PROSPECTIVE ENCOUNTERS': BOULEZ AND THE AMERICAN COMPOSERS

This was how Boulez came to organize the 'Prospective Encounters' in Greenwich Village; here, it was no longer a matter of attracting two thousand or so people with the great classics of the twentieth century, but of mobilizing a new, young and demanding audience, predisposed to contemporary music. These evenings took place about once a month in one of the theatres of the Shakespeare Festival Complex. The hall, in the round, was not unlike the Round House in London. The first year was entirely devoted to the music of American composers.

The history behind these concerts extends back over the previous two years. In the course of an interview somewhat rashly given on his first visit to New York as guest conductor, in the spring of 1969, Boulez had vigorously protested at the preposterous suggestion that he might take on the artistic direction of the orchestra. Nevertheless, he was not reticent in offering his opinion of the American contemporary music situation. In his view, there was no personality in America on a par even with Henze (!) in Europe; electronic music was a passing fashion – the next year they would probably discover the viola de gamba; music could not be modernized by playing Bach on a synthesizer; the celebrated review *Perspectives of New Music* reflected a book-keeping mentality; American avant-garde composers huddled closely together in their protective university ghettos, forming mutual admiration societies, and spending their time doing nothing in particular (those are not Boulez's exact words, but the spirit is the same).

These remarks caused quite a stir. As if it were not enough to have most of the older women against him at the Lincoln Center, the opposition clique was now reinforced by the cohorts of the avant-garde – especially since Boulez did not include any music by American composers amongst the nineteen new works he conducted at the Ojai Festival in California. This was too much. A joint letter was sent to the redoubtable Lawrence Morton – signed (amongst others) by Morton Feldman, Terry Riley, La Monte Young, and Frederic Rzewsky – accusing Boulez of displaying an intolerably nationalistic arrogance (the nation in this case being Europe) and furthermore, claiming that he courted easy success by conducting the modern classics, despite the fact that these were already widely played in the universities. In reply came Boulez's gleeful roar: 'Exactly, I just want to force them out of their university ghetto'. To the accusation of central-Europeanism, he chose to respond merely with a shrug of the shoulders.

And with a pragmatic gesture: in 1971, the season of Prospective Encounters opened with an exclusively American series, the two works making up the first evening being by Davidovsky and Wuorinen. These evenings usually took the form of a complete performance, sometimes repeated, with the instrumentalists naturally being drawn from amongst the members of the orchestra; following the performance, Boulez – together with the performer, the composer, or both – would talk about the work and give examples from it, ending with a public discussion.

This first year, the Encounters were attended by a small but attentive and enthusiastic crowd. However, it seems unlikely that these concerts were to give rise to Boulez's reconciliation with his American colleagues – who would in any case have preferred to have had their works played at the Lincoln Center, and who sometimes questioned the choice of programmes, and the preparation of the works themselves. The role played by Boulez himself was assessed in various ways: his goodwill was evident, as was the lucidity of his presentation, even his relative liberalism – since it was obvious that the works he presented (often under the heading of 'documents', as if regarding the score as some sort of laboratory specimen) could not please everyone. It was also pointed out on several occasions that while Boulez's explanations to the players under his direction were fascinating and convincing, they were much less so when addressed to the public. Peter Heyworth notes that 'Boulez is not at home in the role of compère', and another observer, John Rockwell, points to the uncertainty that often marks what he has to say in this respect: 'Boulez's explanations of a given piece sometimes fall uncomfortably between quasi-technical rigour and a well-meant vacuousness for the (non-existent, at least in this context) masses.'[15]

A PUNISHING SCHEDULE

Three months after taking up his appointment Boulez was invited to sign on again for a similar period, so giving him plenty of time to carry out his mandate – up to the end of the 1976–7 season.

He devoted about eighteen weeks a year to the orchestra and to the peripheral activities he had organized – not only the Prospective Encounters, but also a series of informal 'meet the composer' sessions. There were also a number of mini-festivals, like that devoted to Schubert and Ives in 1971–2, in which he included rare works unearthed in some music library or other. He also worked on modern scores with the students at the neighbouring Juilliard School. In addition, there were the 'Rug concerts' which began in 1974: with the seats removed from the hall at the Lincoln Center, young and old alike were invited to sit on cushions strewn around the carpet, and the players asked to dress informally.

Furthermore, there was the administrative work, especially the programme-planning sessions held with Moseley and the publicity director, Frank Milburn, in the course of which the subtle blend of concerts was adjusted in terms of the conductors and soloists who might or might not be invited. And then there were the numerous recordings that the orchestra made for CBS – amongst them flawless performances of the Stravinsky ballets (though *The Rite* was recorded with the Cleveland orchestra), some electrifying Bartók, some distinguished Ravel, and a Fifth Symphony famous for its slow tempos and its distinctly odd moments. (Boulez did not feel obliged to defend this interpretation for long but I personally continue to find it very interesting.)

In short, the four New York months – which sometimes included tours in the USA or abroad, notably to Paris in 1975 – were always periods of

15 John Rockwell, *Music and Musicians*, 1973, reprinted in *Le Monde*, 27 July 1973.

intense activity which Boulez managed, thanks to a strictly organized routine. He got up at 5.30 a.m. to work (composition); going without breakfast, he usually rehearsed from 10 a.m. till 12.30 p.m. After lunch, there would be a session with Moseley, and another rehearsal before he returned home, on foot if possible. (Boulez enjoyed living close to Central Park, within a stone's throw of the Lincoln Center.) He would have a short rest, then dine with Fischer-Dieskau, the French cultural attaché, or some American friends. Every day followed more or less the same pattern.

The New York period certainly represents a sort of culmination – not so much of Boulez's activity (the IRCAM years were to be comparable in this respect), but of his public integration into the institutional system governing musical life. Paradoxically, this enforced worldliness was in no way accompanied by changes in his attitude to daily life; he followed the same routine in New York as elsewhere, and it can be imagined that the average American observer, who was accustomed to the fashionable figure of Leonard Bernstein (currently the darling of the musical scene), saw Boulez as some kind of enigma.

The schedule itself was one of many contrasts, and created a perceptible upsurge of excitement in New York musical life. The wide range of events upheld Boulez's ideal that the music of our time should be ever present – which it certainly was.

In the second place, the Boulez era was to benefit the New York Philharmonic itself in terms of improving its sound, technique, style, and general level of musical culture – changes that caught the attention of many different commentators. He had cleansed the orchestra of its sedimentary layers of routine: 'Going to Boulez's concerts every week has restored for me the kind of freshness and excitement about orchestral concerts that I have not felt since I was an usher for the Boston Symphony too many years ago', wrote John Rockwell. Traditionally an orchestra of virtuoso individualists, the New York Philharmonic was in particular to learn to put virtuosity at the service of a technical homogeneity, and to develop an aesthetic and historical awareness. Its vision of the century was broadened, and an unmistakable elegance in the playing became the norm.

Less positively, it must be admitted that this stylistic rebirth of the orchestra was to be short-lived, owing to continual changes of conductor. Boulez's position in New York was not like that of Szell in Cleveland (ten years after the death of the great Hungarian conductor the decline in that orchestra can already be measured), or Karajan in Berlin. He was to be followed by Zubin Mehta; all value judgements apart, this was not the same thing, and Boulez was to regret that the work he had begun could not have been followed through along the same lines.

More generally speaking, had he succeeded in bringing New York up to date with the history of music as he saw it? Would the laboriously constructed bridge between the general public and the music of its own century be able to withstand his withdrawal? It seemed more likely that the situation would revert to what it had been: a major organization, predominantly conservative in outlook, resolutely opposed to a multiplicity of experiments and undertakings it regarded as alien but which nevertheless fell far short of Boulez's ideal in terms of programme planning and aesthetics.

Around 1968–70, Boulez was to insist that he was not interested in conducting *per se*, but in the opportunities it gave him to mastermind the creative organization of the musical life of a city; six years later, he was lamenting the bewildering weight of orchestral administration compared to the pleasure he got from conducting. He swore that in any event he would never take on such a job again.

THE TECHNIQUE AND AESTHETICS OF CONDUCTING

At what might be regarded as another turning-point, when the career – if not the work – of the conductor seems to have come to an end, it may be useful to examine the characteristics of Boulez the conductor. As we know, he shows great originality in this field – an originality that can be sensed and even seen, but which it would nevertheless be interesting to analyse.

Because the figure of Boulez the conductor is to all intents and purposes the only one known to the general public, journalistic comment has offered some gross simplifications: Boulez is precise, but cold; he dissects the most complicated scores, but with insufficient passion; he excels with the moderns, disappoints in the romantics; the sound he produces is refined and elegant, but it lacks strength and *Schwung*.[16] He conducts without a baton, but with the music, keeping scrupulously to the letter of the score; he is never clumsy, affected or theatrical: that just about sums it up.

This book essays a somewhat clearer analysis. Generally speaking, I would say that Boulez is first and foremost a practical composer who also conducts. I have observed him conducting concerts, attended dozens of

16 Almost onomatopoeic! To be translated as 'élan' or 'flight'.

rehearsals (particularly with the BBC orchestra) and questioned his players – in particular some of those from one of the major French orchestras. There is a general consensus of opinion that Boulez does not interpret a work, he quite literally presents it. For him, the score is the key to the whole work – far removed from the idea of a metaphysical dimension related to what we might call 'interpretation'. The score in its entirety is what counts: once intonation and rhythm are sorted out, the rest – emotion, for instance – will follow automatically. It was this particular selection of two fundamentals (corresponding to those which emerged during his compositional apprenticeship) which was to determine Boulez's conducting technique. The right hand, thumb and index finger tensed, indicates to the player the moment of an attack, the timing and duration of a pitch. Sometimes – with fingers closed together as if for a karate blow – the indication of a sharp-edged chord conveys information as to its placing and expressive colour. The left hand meanwhile acts as a potentiometer slide, measuring the transmission of dynamics in time; if it should for a moment remain still, the left arm seems to become disconnected from the body – as if retiring from the field of play to remain idle by his side. Michel Fano, a professional composer colleague, has this to say about him: 'The gesture is made in terms of the desired result; this is no choreography destined to create the music in front of its audience, but a collection of signs for the exclusive use of the players. The code, if one may so call it, depends on a lack of uniformity – with general, expressive (and in the end, purely superfluous) movements being replaced by a *collection of informatory gestures*[17] relating to attack, metre and dynamics, allowing the player concerned to "reverberate" in a manner and at a moment precisely specified.'[18]

This is another illustration of the principle that nature abhors a vacuum, or perhaps, that the end creates the means. Boulez received no training in orchestral conducting, and had little opportunity to see men like Rosbaud, Scherchen or Désormière at work. His job in the Marigny pit was less an apprenticeship in conducting than in making music and in dealing with players. It was therefore essential to find some means of filling the gap. In the event, he was to resolve the problem himself, by bringing his own specifically creative insights to the task of conducting. This explains the refreshingly iconoclastic impression one has of Boulez's conducting. He rejects the 'historicist' approach simply because his

17 The italics are mine (D.J.).
18 The article on Boulez in the 1982 edition of *Larousse de la musique*.

interpretation sets out to be almost a recomposition in the presence of an audience.

There is little more to add. It is obvious that Boulez would have found it absolutely impossible to conduct with a baton. His whimsical comment about the 'one-armed pirate-hook' in itself explains nothing – so if the players were unused to being conducted without it, and resented the fact, that was just too bad. They were nevertheless grateful to him for conducting from the score: they hate the exhibitionist posturing of the memorizers, who make them feel insecure. Boulez uses the music not because of a deficient memory, nor even because he is indifferent to the impression he makes on the audience, but because the score is the central objective, in the actual and the metaphysical sense, of his interpretative activity: its very existence brings it to life. One distinguished viola player told me that Boulez makes no distinction between rehearsal and concert; by this he meant that the actual performances produced none of that indefinable, transcendent quality which marked them out from the sessions of pure work at rehearsal: that would be anathema! Another player notes that he is one of the only conductors to persist in working on a passage involving an individual while a hundred others sit and wait; for Boulez, the inaccuracy of a single bar is an offence against the work itself – an offence that cannot be drowned out by the energy of the group. Here too, his analytical vision plays a part: a player from the New York Philharmonic described his legendary ear as being able to name the key in which a pin drops. Like those of the composer, the conductor's aural perceptions are developed to a remarkable degree.

In conclusion, it should perhaps be mentioned that Boulez's conducting is aesthetically intensely satisfying, and draws playing of great warmth from the orchestra.

CHAPTER ELEVEN

IRCAM

(1974–80)

As from 1 January 1976, Pierre Boulez will be in Paris –
a piece of news in itself sufficient to
symbolize the Beaubourg!
(*Robert Bordaz,*[1] *at the Press Conference held at the
Théâtre de la Ville on 7 March 1974, to herald
the launching of IRCAM*)

It is essential to establish a musical Centre in which
experimentation can take place on a permanent basis.
(*Pierre Boulez, Süddeutsche Zeitung, 18–19 October 1969*)

The idea of IRCAM seems to have originated as far back as 1966 or 1967,
when the above words formed part of a reflection on musical life in
general, during an interview given to the *Süddeutsche Zeitung*: entitled
'The ritual of the concert must be changed!'. This may well have been
the first time the idea had been publicly aired. In any case, the idea of a
centre for fundamental research set up specifically to rescue musical
composition from the stagnation (the 'tinkering', the 'diarrhoea of
mediocrity', the 'short-term solutions' . . .) into which it had settled was
to recur in various interviews. In 1970, in reply to questions from Michèle
Cotta and Sylvie de Nussac in *L'Express*, Boulez specified that 'A research
institute must be created, to be devoted to the necessary investigations . . . Present-day creativity involves a superabundance of tinkering . . . Take, for instance, the instrumental problem: instruments have

---

1 Member of the Council of State (born 1908); delegate, then president of the Pompidou
Centre from 1970–77.

scarcely changed over the past two or three centuries, and research in this field has become imperative.' The interviewers asked if he would be prepared to assume the directorship of such a centre, should the opportunity arise:

– Immediately, giving up conducting without regret.
– How much would you need to bring such a centre into being?
– Give me ten million dollars.

So the elements of a new chapter in the life of Boulez began to take shape. First, the dollars had to be converted into francs. Nevertheless, at the start of the 1970s, the idea of his return to Paris was not gaining much ground, even though a Boulezian claque chanted slogans for his return after each of his dazzling conducting appearances at the Salle Pleyel or the Palais de Chaillot. More was needed to bring this dream into effect. Boulez had had his fingers burnt[2] often enough by vague official offers, and was 'wary as a serpent', as he puts it. 1966 and 1968 were not that far off. Leaving aside the shadowy illusions occasionally dangled in front of his eyes by some member of the government or other, he had no lack of trophies – in the form of orchestras in New York, London, Bayreuth, or elsewhere. And then he had to compose, to record, and to write.

It was then that there came an intervention from on high: Louis XIV had constructed Versailles for his glory – Pompidou was to attach his name to the Beaubourg Centre. 'I would dearly love to see Paris possessed of a cultural centre that would be both museum and creative centre', he exclaimed in the course of a carefully planned impromptu speech in 1969. And so the idea was launched. The President of the Republic himself laid down its broad outlines: it was to include a Museum of Modern Art to replace the one in the avenue du President Wilson (which, through lack of space, could not even exhibit all it possessed), a public lending library, both to relieve the Bibliothèque Nationale and to allow every citizen access to the culture of his choice, and a centre for industrial creativity, besides serving various other functions.

To begin with, it seemed very much as if music had been forgotten. But no sooner was it thought of than the name of Boulez was immediately put forward – especially as Michel Guy was there to whisper it in the President's ear. Thus the most prestigious and internationally respected French musician – already known for his influence and enthusiasm, and

2 Not only in France. In 1966, the Max Planck Gesellschaft asked Boulez to draw up plans for a Max Planck Institute for musical research; the plan was discussed with both scientists and musicians, but fell through for economic reasons.

for his organizational talents – could at last return to his country by the front door, to take up a post commensurate with his abilities, putting behind him, once and for all, the insults suffered at the hands of the official musical establishment over many years. The Pompidou regime was to achieve what the Gaulliste government had merely contemplated. Boulez's nomination was effected in 1972.[3]

Just as the period from 1964–74 was the decade of Boulez the conductor, so the ten years of composition from 1974–84 (during which he wrote, *Eclat, Figures–Doubles–Prisms*, and *Domaines*) seem to me to present Boulez as Director of IRCAM. There were also personal compositional projects connected with the Institut, from '. . . *explosante-fixe* . . .' to *Répons* (not forgetting *Rituel*, though for other reasons).

At times, there were clearly conflicts of interest between the composer and his duties at IRCAM. There were always areas in which Boulez the director was of assistance to Boulez the composer. Beyond that, there was another area in which the creative artist was held back by the mass of administrative and representational tasks demanded by his function. Throughout his tenure at IRCAM, it became a matter of striking a balance between the two separate, yet overlapping functions of composition and musical administration.

In another respect, Boulez's beleaguered position within IRCAM rests on a succession of hypothetical statements he made at the start of the 1970s and which can only be verified in the long term:

In my compositional work I have myself met with fundamental obstacles [it was not a question of lack of time – orchestral conducting was the consequence and not the cause of the compositional silence]; on the other hand, these obstacles are not peculiar to me – similar obstacles face contemporary musical composition as a whole, so giving rise to a coincidence between my 'crisis' and that of music in general. The way out of this crisis will come from the reunion of previously dispersed creative forces, from meetings with scientists, and from the bias of the institution itself. IRCAM must be created as an institution which is to have musical research as its function, acoustics as its subject, and the computer as its instrument.

This intellectual interpretation was expounded in innumerable articles and interviews during the years between 1972 and 1979, when our communications specialist had plenty of time to elaborate his ideas with an abundance of apposite observations. Nevertheless, for a clearer definition of the purpose of the new Institut, we turn to a more

3 It seems that Georges Pompidou read an interview with Boulez published in *Le Monde* in early 1970, and that he then got in touch with him (Peyser, op. cit., p. 229).

theoretical text: the proposals of Boulez himself. 1975 saw the publication of *La Musique en projet* – a collection of contributions from those who would be responsible for IRCAM in the future, as well as from various sympathizers.[4] As a real intellectual charter of the Boulezian plan, two introductory articles by the composer are worth looking at in detail.

'DONC ON REMET EN QUESTION'
('*PRESENT AND FUTURE – A FUNDAMENTAL REQUESTIONING*')

This is the title of the first article. A master tactician, Boulez incorporates the view(s) of his opponent(s) – from which it may be guessed that he finds them wholly exasperating. Music is sick because it has been corrupted by the errors of our time. Boulez's tone is one of complete detachment towards the offenders, but his approach is singularly partisan in its defensiveness – and the text amazingly reminiscent of the 'Syllabus' of Pius IX (whose one hundred and tenth anniversary was then being celebrated).

In an introduction (1), Boulez points out the dichotomy, accepted by IRCAM, between research and communication – after which (2) he examines the extent to which various contemporary musical practices have broken with tradition, even recent tradition. Here he includes the decline of the concept of 'the work', of the usual forms of communication (the concert-giving crisis, for example), and the destruction of the fundamental balance between anarchy and order, freedom and discipline. He goes on to decry the search for instant glory at the expense of longer-lasting considerations – hence the 'denial of form' and of musical material, the 'torturing' of instruments, the impossibility of producing any common language because of the extreme individualization of notation, the priority given to ritual, to activity and to 'performance' (although he does not use the word) at the expense to the written work, and so on. He ends by asking whether all this is an indication of 'crisis' or merely of 'value transference'.

Boulez then moves on to the so-called solutions that some contemporary composers believe they have found. No names are mentioned, but it is easy to play the game of pointing a finger at the guilty: he cites the escape into time and space, the taste for allusion and quotation, and the use of parody. The transgressors are numerous enough to constitute a festival in

4 *La musique en projet*, Gallimard/IRCAM, 1975.

themselves,[5] since they include the neo-classical Stravinsky, Berio (in his *Sinfonia*), Bussotti, and Kagel, to name but a few. Then there is the recourse to extra-occidental – preferably oriental – inspiration, the 'exhausted inflexion of exoticism, even colonialism' (does he mean Stockhausen? Jean-Claude Eloy?), not to mention the American minimalists . . . A third blind-alley is represented by the recourse to science, or rather 'to scientism as the mysticism of substitution . . . In a more sophisticated, even perverse fashion, the connection between certain aspects of musical thought and the sciences is exaggerated in order to conceal the difficulties of aesthetic choice.' (From Babbitt to Xenakis, many may recognize themselves here.) Finally, he denounces the attitude which tries to make aesthetic validity depend on the 'goodness of the soul' – a form of musical politicizing. Other composers, including Nono, were dealt with just as summarily.

Boulez was not without sympathy for the dilemmas these composers had imperfectly resolved: 'is it surprising that all these choices occur at the same moment, in this condition of transference? They correspond to a real and fundamental need for truth, and if it may occasionally be irritating to find one idea exaggeratedly developed to the detriment of all the others, it should be recognized that the solutions adopted reflect a very real anguish, a genuine doubt.'

He then goes on to list the various practices resulting from these dilemmas: the formal 'opening up' of a work, group improvisation, a veritable regression towards 'an agglomeration of readily caricatured memories, referring more strongly than ever before to a set of emotive signals established through kinship with the works to which they owe their inception', in addition to all the anecdotal attempts to make instruments do things for which they are in no way endowed, by means of various devices.

One can well imagine the various remedies suggested: since (presumably) isolated individuals are no longer able to envisage generalized solutions, collective research must involve collaboration with scientists on two levels: the one mundane (where the scientist offers a solution to a problem posed by a composer), the other more ambitious, 'consisting – once the agreed terms of reference have been stripped of ambiguity – of giving new form and expression to theoretical considerations'. The article closes on a question as to the relationship to be established between basic theory and practical research.

5 Cf. SMIP 1973.

'Donc on remet en question' is a very important article, although when reading it, one is struck by conflicting feelings. First, one is irritated at the expression of such an intolerant and peremptory viewpoint: was he alone privileged with the truth? When the argument is considered more carefully, or outlined in simple terms, however, his criticism seems to make a great deal of sense. (At least, so it seems to me, though this is admittedly a subjective reaction.)

The fact remains that when Boulez is confronted with the underlying problems of musical composition in general – and his own in particular – both the thought and the manner of its expression are still most clearly revealed in the best articles of *Notes of an Apprenticeship*.

In just a few pages, this 'Syllabus' (as I have somewhat maliciously called it) begins to resemble what theologians describe as a summa. And, even if one has no liking for theology of a religious kind, one should still grasp the significance of the title of a fine work by the marxist Henri Lefebvre: 'La Somme et le reste' (1969). The sum of the present was revealed in 'Donce on remet en question'; the remainder – that is, the possibilities of the future – is to be the subject of the second article referred to above: 'Perspective-Prospective'.

'PERSPECTIVE-PROSPECTIVE'

An IRCAM session was held in public at the Théâtre d'Orsay in Paris from 19 to 23 October 1974, in the course of which the various department heads were given the chance to touch upon their intentions; by way of a final summing up, Boulez then set about giving a more specific outline of the collective undertaking. This short text – later published in *La Musique en projet* – is devoted in particular to the most pressing issue raised by IRCAM: the need for musicians to work with scientists.

Boulez was well aware of the objections emanating from the two groups: 'Music has nothing to gain from a collaboration with science: to refuse to acknowledge the essentially irrational element of creativity is to risk falling completely under the thumb of a fundamentally rational science – they are two irreducible entities.' There was the acknowledged reluctance of musicians, ill at ease in the presence of ideas and techniques for which their training had not prepared them – and the hesitancy of the scientists (and especially of the music lovers amongst them), faced with this musical invasion of their territory and their own scepticism about the successful outcome of such a project.

Boulez clearly defined the advance of each group into the realm of the other:

When studying orchestration, the composer does not have to study the mechanical system of an oboe, or to analyse the variations in its spectrum according to the most up-to-date means; he has only to know the technical possibilities of the instrument, its dynamic range, the extent of its register, its expressive flexibility, its mobility in relation to interval size, and its ability to blend or contrast with other instruments.

(An objection immediately comes to mind: how was it possible for Boulez to justify the need for scientific collaboration when he had a thousand times demonstrated his complete mastery of these fundamentals as the notable result of orchestral conducting?). On the other hand, the scientist

was obviously not required to learn the language of music up to and including the techniques of notation and composition; but he ought to be in a position to understand what it is that the composer or instrumentalist expects from him, to know something of present-day musical trends, and to direct his imagination accordingly.

Imagination is the key word here. It is this which musicians ought to abstract and absorb from scientific thought processes. 'Without this inner awareness the composer's imagination remains incomplete, a deficiency that can be related in present-day terms to the composer's very limited understanding of acoustics or sound synthesis.'

It seems to me that Boulez's ideas about a scientific contribution to music were largely intuitive in the early days of IRCAM, and that, if the truth be told, they were further limited by the fact that IRCAM experiments in this area were at the time strictly confined to the acoustic problem. This was to be the developmental phase of a field of research which was only later to come into effect: that of connecting the computer to the compositional problems themselves.

The article ends by justifying the need for an autonomous research centre – as opposed to the facilities offered by radio stations (which reduce their budgets at the first sign of financial difficulty), or universities (which absorb the energies of research workers in pedagogical tasks). In short, there had to be an IRCAM.

THE PRESS CONFERENCE AT THE THEATRE DE LA VILLE

Boulez had already reached this conclusion the previous spring when, one

March morning in 1974, he convened the whole of the musical world for the public launching of IRCAM.

It was an astonishing sight. All the supporters were there, amongst others. So that he could immediately outline the organizational policy which was one of his trump cards (and was to be one of his successes), Boulez had invited not only journalists and musicians but a larger number of representatives of communities and cultural groups that might be interested in the 'Petit-Beaubourg' (as it was then called, to distinguish it from the larger Beaubourg Centre).

After the customary short speech by Robert Bordaz, president of the Beaubourg Centre, the audience witnessed the unprecedented spectacle of a team of musicians ready and willing to work together. The musical world was accustomed to the idea of groups like 'Les Cinq' or 'Les Six' – in which individuals linked by friendship accepted some sort of blanket term for their largely disparate practices; but teams purporting to forego individual interests in favour of collective research and production were of a different order entirely. Putting aside for a moment their various contributions, the sight of the team actually assembled on the theatre stage was undoubtedly a shock for the whole musical community. It says much for Boulez's abilities that he could attract enthusiasm, and unite these strongly individual musicians more or less single-handed.

The 'gang of four' (soon of course to be five)[6] were there, calmly awaiting a sign from the conductor: Luciano Berio (electro-acoustics), Vinko Globokar (instruments and voice), Jean-Claude Risset (computer theory), and Gerald Bennett (the 'diagonal' department). The team had plenty of style, experience, and ideas. Boulez had played his trump card by selecting those particular musical personalities, and the least he could do was to allow them a broad autonomy. There was certainly no suggestion that Boulez was running a dictatorship; the very choice of personalities attested to a breadth of view and an open-mindedness which echoed the liberal *modus operandi* of the Domaine musical twenty years on. For instance, the presence of a musician like Globokar was in itself testimony to the fact that Boulez's personal tastes were not to influence his policy of engaging staff! Nor, for his part, was Luciano Berio a man to bow to someone else's direction: his own inventiveness ensured his independence. Michel Decoust was appointed head of a pedagogical department at IRCAM on the strength of reforms carried out at the Conservatoire de Pantin in the wake of the events of May 1968. Of the two other heads of

6 With the arrival of Michel Decoust as head of a 'pedagogical' department.

department, Jean-Claude Risset enjoyed the unequivocal esteem of the small number of musicians capable of keeping up with his work; the other, Gerald Bennett – whose strategic position was almost that of assistant director (co-ordinator of the various departments, artistic administrator of the projection space, controller of theoretical research) – was almost unknown: it was enough that he had caught the master's eye.

Boulez went on to describe the building rather than to elaborate on its function. The Petit-Beaubourg was, of course, to be part of the Centre, but geographically separate from it. Both for aesthetic reasons (to avoid obstructing the view of the beautiful domed roof of the Saint-Merri church) as well as for acoustic ones (an underground structure was thought to be more easily insulated against noise), the building was to be subterranean. As the *Sunday Times* remarked: 'Like modern Nibelungen, composers and technicians are hoping to forge new sounds for a cultural renaissance'.

The Wagnerian allusion is a happier choice than that of Lully or Versailles. It is in fact only the second time in recent history that a composer has succeeded in persuading the Prince to build him something altogether unprecedented in conception and uniquely capable of complying with his compositional plan – and Beaubourg has the same initial letter as Bayreuth.

Furthermore, this important event was well received, particularly by the foreign press: 'Major Step in Musical Rebirth of Paris' was the headline in the *Herald Tribune*, for example. But Boulez had not come back merely to don the white coat of the research worker. This may have accounted for a certain unease arising from the difficulty in reconciling the image of the composer of *Pli selon pli* with that of the Company Director inspecting his venture from a gantry on the building site. Rebelling against public misunderstanding, journalistic stupidity, and the inane behaviour of the French institutions towards himself, Boulez suddenly appeared in the guise of a modern manager, his speech riddled with anglicisms, and threatening to effect a take-over bid for the entire musical establishment.

While taking part in these proceedings, he feigned ignorance of the fact that a group like the GRM – for better or worse – had been working on the electro-acoustic question for thirty years. Similarly, in the field of ethnomusicology – which he seemed to want to include in the concerns of the Centre – he appeared oblivious to the fact that Gilbert Rouget[7] and his

7 Ethnologist (born 1916), director of the ethnomusicological department of the Musée de l'Homme since 1965.

team had carried out work in extremely difficult circumstances; and that, furthermore, the unremitting efforts of Emil Leipp[8] had enabled him – armed only with bits of string – to effect parallel work of the greatest interest in the field of acoustics. Psychologically speaking, Boulez's performance was unimpressive. The idea of a Promethean creator, driving his way through concert halls or editing rooms with insults on his lips, has a certain appeal, but faultless behaviour was expected of one who was inevitably going to play a political role in musical life. IRCAM was later to demonstrate the seriousness of his work, as well as an increasing tolerance towards the more significant members of the musical establishment; that morning he seemed unaware of the discoveries already made and arrogant towards the outside world.

The press reaction to the actual conference was coldly cautious; music critics were wise enough to report only the evidence. The daily press reviews comprised a tedious report of the morning. IRCAM's future detractors felt no need to reflect aloud on what the institute might represent in terms of fundamental alterations to the music of the future – there would be plenty of time for that when Boulez had been brought to his knees.

FROM '. . . EXPLOSANTE-FIXE . . .' TO RITUEL: A RETURN TO COMPOSITION

Let us for the moment leave IRCAM and return to Boulez the composer in the years 1972–4. Two works were added to his catalogue, both fine and interesting in themselves but entirely different from one another – though this difference is at least partly accounted for by the new duties of their creator.

'. . . explosante-fixe . . .' is a kind of absolution, pronounced on the occasion of Stravinsky's death in 1971. A brief musical text, published in the magazine Tempo, was intended by Boulez to provide material for proliferation of a wide range of different possible realizations. Boulez was naturally asked to produce his own version. The reference to Stravinsky is extremely oblique: a focal note, E flat, in German pronounced Es – like 'S' for Stravinsky; the stylistic connection between this work and the composer of The Rite of Spring is as tenuous as that between the

---

8 (1913–86) University lecturer, from 1963 head of research into musical acoustics at the University of Paris VI; author of La Machine à écouter (1977) and Acoustique et musique (1976).

Symphonies of Wind Instruments, written by Stravinsky in memory of Claude Debussy, and *Pelléas*.[9]

What is interesting here is to see how, even at the start of the 1970s, Boulez was writing a work of considerable duration in a decidedly 'pre-Ircamesque' vein. Indeed, '. . . *explosante-fixe* . . .' not only demonstrates a new concept of chamber music but brings a complicated piece of electro-acoustic equipment into play. This was the first time that Boulez had had recourse to artificial sound since *Poésie pour pouvoir* in 1958, and it was to inaugurate the practical collaboration of scientist with composer.

The scientist in question was Hans-Peter Haller, who worked at Fribourg, and had invented a machine called the halaphone. Its principle functions were twofold: to effect a degree of continuity between different instrumental timbres (one of the lines of research at IRCAM); and to make sounds 'travel' around a playing space. The work was premièred on 5 January 1973, in New York. This was followed by numerous other 'premières' in various places and with varying electro-acoustic success, since the halaphone is a somewhat temperamental machine. This fact was even to contribute to the definition of the work as open-form – a concept here rather peremptorily modified (though procedures of variable routes were involved) in order to apply to its realization. From the outset, the nature of '. . . *explosante-fixe* . . .' seemed particularly to suggest the work of a team (led by Haller, with his assistants, and instrumentalists) involved in an elaborate interaction of reflected images between composer and scientist, as well as stipulating a specific acoustic topology – the hall and its basic equipment. As a member of the audience at the Viennese première of the work in 1973, I received a clear impression of a new Boulez, an impression reinforced when Boulez began work in his new projection space at IRCAM, as future director there.

During the course of 1979, when IRCAM was already in full stride, Boulez announced a public revival of '. . . *explosante-fixe* . . .' with its procedures further computerized, but the operation proved extremely difficult to regulate and the performance had to be cancelled at the last moment. This was a pity because, apart from its 'research' interest, '. . . *explosante-fixe* . . .' happens to be a satisfying work in performance, serving as a reminder of what a formidable 'orchestrator' Boulez is. Its formal plan – of separate sequences progressively increasing in size until all the instrumental forces are in play, then decreasing again to the end – is

9 *Conversations with Célestin Deliège*, p. 106.

easily grasped by any listener able to appreciate *The Steppes of Central Asia*, a fact which contributes to making it a Boulezian classic.

Rituel in memoriam Maderna immediately struck one as another classic. In June 1973, rumours of Boulez's impending retirement from orchestral conducting became more insistent. This was the period of the various European performances of '. . . *explosante-fixe* . . .', and Boulez made it apparent that this was a practical involvement much closer to his own compositional preoccupations than the organization of orchestral schedules and the various delights of managerial office.

In December 1973, Bruno Maderna died. Apart from the fact that he had been a warm-hearted man with a relish for life, he was a composer of Boulez's own generation, of similarly exacting standards; even before Boulez, he was one of the rare conductors specializing in contemporary music, and Maderna was one of the musicians most esteemed by him. It is likely that his death brought an end to one of the most unclouded friendships Boulez had ever known: a short text of homage enabled him to express his affection for Maderna and the happy memories he associated with him.

Thus *Rituel in memoriam Maderna* is another kind of Boulezian absolution, a valediction composed at the time of an impending career decision. It is moreover an orchestral work of considerable length (more than twenty minutes), conceived and written by a composer–conductor, and with obvious audience appeal. It seemed to convey both a farewell to the orchestra and a desire to resume immediate, almost physical contact with the public, paradoxically at the very moment he had decided to some extent to break with it in order to devote his energies to a line of research he believed essential, regardless of the sense of isolation it may have entailed.

The audience appeal of *Rituel* results from the repetitive, throbbing, 'ritualistic' character of a work which, together with the second movement of *Marteau*, represents almost the only example of repetitive music in Boulez's output. He was, incidentally, to revise the score after the first performances in London on 2 April 1975, then in Brussels and Grenoble, where it was presented by IRCAM on 30 and 31 October the same year. This revision was to eliminate optional features originally offered to the players, a group of such size being unable to react to unforeseen requests with the same immediacy as a committed soloist. The ambiguity of open-form works manifestly remains intact.

FROM THE *RING* CYCLE AT BAYREUTH . . .

Even though he had resolved in principle to delay any decision concerning his conducting career, Boulez set out on another great adventure during this period.

From 1976–80, he spent two months each year in Germany – not exactly for touristic reasons, but in order to conduct the centenary performance of the *Ring* at Bayreuth at the invitation of Wolfgang Wagner. In the event this was a triple centenary, since it was in 1876 that the Bayreuth Festival was inaugurated, the Festspielhaus was completed, and that the cycle of *Der Ring des Nibelungen* was first performed. The task was therefore one of some importance and, surprisingly, Wolfgang Wagner asked a French team to take on the challenge (not to say the gamble) of 'reinventing' one of the most fascinating works in the musical repertoire, a hundred years after its first performance.

This 1976 production, which ran for five years and was recorded for television, can be regarded as a milestone in musical history. After an interregnum of ten years following Wieland Wagner's marvellous final production, the producer Patrice Chéreau managed to impose his vision of the work in collaboration with Boulez who was quite at home with his remarkable imagery.

This was to be yet another work in progress. At the outset, not only did Boulez not know Chéreau, but he had never seen any of his theatrical productions. Having considered various alternatives, including the director of the Berlin Schaubühne, Peter Stein,[10] Boulez was apparently persuaded by his sister Jeanne to propose the name of Chéreau (living in the locality, she made a point of knowing everything that went on at the TNP in Villeurbanne[11] where Chéreau worked).

The 'enfant terrible of the French theatre' had little experience of opera apart from a Rossini production in Milan and a remarkable *Contes d'Hoffmann* in Paris; he knew the German theatre very well, Wagner not at all and, to be frank, nothing much about music in general. So the odds

10 Who considered producing a 'digest' of the *Ring*; Wolfgang Wagner was against the idea.
11 A town in the Lyons district, site of a famous popular theatre, directed first by Roger Planchon, then by Patrice Chéreau, and of a famous music school, directed by Antoine Duhamel.

were stacked against Boulez, a fact which made his collaborative success all the more remarkable, particularly as it was sustained for so long. Originally for a three-year period, the contract was extended by one year, then another. Meanwhile the possibility had arisen not only of a recording but also of a film; from the audience point of view, the production could doubtless have been extended even up to the present.

Following that other encounter (established on a quite different basis) between Boulez and Wieland Wagner, the convergence of Boulez and Chéreau – both of whom were abundantly imaginative, quick-thinking, swift to respond, and specific in their conception – was all the more astonishing. The whole cycle, totalling more than fourteen hours, passed almost without a hitch.

The production represented a perpetual striving for perfection. Boulez has often explained that what he found at Bayreuth was not only an acoustically excellent theatrical premises, but also a 'studio' where it was possible to do real work, since it was empty for most of the year, apart from the period of the Wagner festival. Walking around the famous pit in the summer of 1980, he noted its exceptional acoustic, describing it (in IRCAM terminology) as 'a communicating machine' of rare effectiveness.

Thus the production of Patrice Chéreau, the décor of Richard Peduzzi, the costumes of Jacques Schmidt, and Boulez's musical direction, combined to approach the ideal of a shared inspiration. However great Wieland's production may have been in itself, from 1976 onwards Chéreau's extreme radicalism extended the boundaries much further. The intelligent connoisseurs in the audience were divided: some were frankly overwhelmed, others affected indifference, or made ironic comments on a particular aspect of the production. Musicians drew attention to the unevenness of Boulez's conducting, magnificent in *Rheingold* (at least in part), in Act I of *Walküre*, and at the end of *Götterdämmerung*; less effective at the end of *Walküre* and particularly in *Siegfried*. Even those closely involved in the production agreed that the staging misfired terribly: Peduzzi's décor, so evocative for the weir in *Rheingold* or for Hunding's hut, was less convincing for the forest in *Siegfried*, even less so for the famous Valkyries' rock, likened by some commentators to the Matterhorn, by others, more prosaically, to a heap of warm excrement!

These initial imperfections were progressively eradicated in a remarkable way. Boulez should certainly be given most of the credit here, since many improvements were implemented as a result of his persistent search for a homogeneous quality, first with the orchestra, later with the singers. This quest for perfection represents the most positive side of Boulez, demonstrating his ability to carry out a project, to persuade his collaborators to give of their utmost, and to organize the available time to best advantage: in short, to be the moving spirit behind the production. Because of this, however, he crossed swords with the Bayreuth orchestra, half of whom did not return the following year. Nevertheless, although they had not been especially brilliant in 1976, by the end of the production this body of players displayed a responsiveness, a flexibility and a degree of accuracy that was quite outstanding. (The recording, made in 1979 and 1980, attests to the prowess of the orchestra far better than the video film to that of the production.)

Thus each year between 1976 and 1980, Boulez buried himself in the Bayreuthian pit. Working in a short-sleeved red shirt that was both comfortable to wear, easily visible from the back of the pit and, most importantly, from the stage, Boulez conducted with a clarity and confidence I personally found very striking the year I was privileged to experience the production from the dubious vantage-point of the trombones and Wagner tubas. While Chéreau's beloved smoke machines partly obscured the half-sunken pit and the singers could scarcely be seen or heard, precise control and an excellent rapport between conductor and producer worked wonders.

The first year, some of the audience were predictably on the attack. The one-time detractors of Wieland could be observed in posthumous appeal to him, to prevent this 'mediterranean frivolity' from inflicting further damage on the work of the German master. Although they were referring to Chéreau rather than to Boulez, the latter affected to see no difference: a committed accomplice, he accepted responsibility for the whole production, defending and countering attack. It was a mistake to invoke Wieland Wagner before one who had known and worked with him. By the end of the year, the general attitude had largely changed, with admiration the order of the day. After the final performance of *Götterdämmerung* in 1980, Boulez and Chéreau had to withstand applause lasting an hour and a quarter.[12]

. . . TO *LULU* AT THE PARIS OPERA

It was wholly understandable that Boulez and Chéreau (together with Peduzzi and Schmidt) should agree to share in a second operatic

12 *Histoire d'un 'Ring'*, Bayreuth 1976–80, Laffont, 1980.

endeavour when, at the end of the *Ring*, Rolf Liebermann begged them to take on the newly completed version of Berg's three-act *Lulu*.

This is not the place to investigate the questions raised by the completion (the *Vollendung*) of Berg's work, nor even to give details of the episodes connected with its first actual performance on 24 February 1979, at the Paris Opéra. I will comment only on those aspects concerning the activity of Boulez himself.

Since he had, for some time, been in possession of a slightly pirated version of the material Berg left for the third act, Boulez was generally considered to be the musician best equipped to complete the scoring of the work. (Only the completed first two acts had hitherto been performed.) It appears that Boulez first hesitated, then declared himself unfit for the job – at which point Universal Edition turned to Friedrich Cerha, another of their house composers, who was also a conductor, and well acquainted with Berg's style.[13]

At the end of a somewhat colourful legal wrangle, the Cerha version was authorized for a series of performances 'by way of experiment', so fulfilling Rolf Liebermann's passionate and long-standing desire. The event was one of the most astonishingly fashionable affairs in the recent history of French musical life; nine performances were hardly enough to satisfy the appetite of the Parisian public.

I regard the phenomenal popular excitement generated by this production of *Lulu* as indicative of the status Boulez, rather than Berg, had achieved in France by that time. Until Boulez became the 'operator' of this new undertaking, virtually nobody in France knew of (or was interested in) *Lulu*. The work had never been given at the Paris Opéra even in its incomplete two-act version. Although it was regularly billed in many theatres in Germany, where I myself saw it a good half dozen times, it had been staged in France (and in French) only at the Opéra-Comique and in the provinces. The French music critics had ignored all these performances. Besides, Berg was still not really fashionable. However, the Bayreuth team was, and rightly so. A plan to mount the Bayreuth production of the *Ring* cycle at the Châtelet[14] had (fortunately for Chéreau!) come to nothing. The French public needed the services of the gang of four.

13 The French version of his account of the work was published by Jean-Claude Lattès as part of a two-volume set devoted to *Lulu* (coll. 'Musique et Musiciens', 1979).
14 A large theatre, seating more than 3,000 founded in Paris in 1862; in 1874 the popular programmes given there by the Concerts Colonne were to bring the name of Beethoven to the notice of the French.

At it happened, Boulez did not at first seem predestined either for *Lulu* or for Berg.[15] Admittedly, there was no one else in a position or with the ability to produce this new 'coup', but neither were there obvious intellectual affinities to link him with the work.

The rest of the story remains a matter of conjecture rather than hard fact: the production was not revived, and the existing film (pirated from a television repeat) is not available for general viewing. At the risk of appearing foolish, I feel I must protest – if only on my own account – at this unwarranted neglect, more especially since productions infinitely inferior to that of Chéreau have succeeded it in Zurich and elsewhere.

Moreover, what remains of the initial excitement has less to do with the salient features of a production that roused both the enthusiasm of the French press and much controversy, than with this first, eminently striking encounter between Pierre Boulez and the French musical establishment. It might be helpful to reflect at this point on the conditions surrounding this episode in the composer's affairs.

By the mid-1970s, Boulez was nearly fifty. He had experienced hatred, stupidity, and contradiction; opposed to 'anything, at home or abroad, to do with the official organization of music', he had exiled himself. He continued to be insulted from afar while so-called reforms in musical life were made without and against him. The Orchestre de Paris, which should have fallen to him after the death of Münch, was entrusted either to unskilled hands or to those already too busy elsewhere. His works were still hardly ever played.

Now, however, the wind seemed to have changed. Having once again proved that the prophet has no honour in his own country, Boulez at last found himself recommended in France for tasks befitting his talent: he was given IRCAM, the Ensemble InterContemporain and even the Orchestre de Paris – rather more often than he would have wished. Although not part of the same officialdom, a professorship at the Collège de France[16] was to complete his acceptance as a member of the musical establishment.

Until *Lulu* however, this was not accomplished without a gnashing of teeth: IRCAM had a network of controls imposed upon it, its budget was trimmed, and the Ensemble InterContemporain, the cause of much envy, had prescribed quotas of French players and involved Boulez in many

15 See 'Incidences actuelles de Berg', 1948, and the Berg entry in the Fasquelle encyclopaedia.
16 A teaching establishment of the highest order, founded by François I in 1530; independent of the University, it has the gift of fifty professorial chairs whose incumbents are co-opted by their future colleagues and named for life.

entrepreneurial tasks. Meanwhile, the radio remained solidly anti-Boulez. It was then that *Lulu* supervened.

The fact that Boulez conducted *Lulu* at the Paris Opéra was a musical event of more than merely aesthetic value. It was the outcome of a multiplicity of intentions from which (despite a few startling set-backs) a structure was to emerge. Together with its various protagonists, the bolted and barred institutional system was at last prepared to let in a little air.

Rolf Liebermann's tenure as director of the Paris Opéra was in need of a world-shattering event to bring it to a fitting climax. Despite much occasional trumpeting, there had been nothing to get excited about since Giorgio Strehler's production of *Le Nozze di Figaro*. Admittedly, there were some notable successes, even a renewed lustre, but no single *coup de théâtre* (the *Ring* of the Stein–Gruber team looked promising, but turned out to be a flop). The Paris Opéra really needed Berg's three-act *Lulu*.

The French state and its musical management needed a successful, cost-effective Boulez to offset the expenses he incurred at IRCAM; similarly, they needed a prestigious Opéra – even with an extravagant *succès de fou* – in order to cope with the ruinous costs of maintaining less exalted productions. It should not be forgotten that while Boulez was slightly annoyed by the criticism sometimes carried in the anti-IRCAM press, it was a salutary reminder of the curse hanging over the avant-garde musician; for obvious reasons, this criticism was much more disturbing to his backers.

The musical apparatus of radio, television, and the press needed a single object, easily recognizable and possessing absolute values, on which to focus its promotional faculties.[17] *Lulu* was to provide an ideal object, satisfying a general desire to colonize new territories (Mahler, Bruckner, and now Berg . . .) in a context of manufactured ephemera.

Finally, the public needed an undisputed success in order to restore confidence in its own judgement. Just as the circulation of capitalist culture dictates that supply must endlessly invent new products, so demand must be able to adapt to the new merchandise by sudden qualitative leaps which we call fashion. This attempt to re-evaluate and to recycle could not have lit upon anything better than *Lulu*.

The tools of the production, the financial sources, the promotional circuits, and lastly, the consumers were dependent upon a closed system, pronouncing upon its own success, and understandably deaf to all

17 I myself was to devote much time to it in broadcasts, lectures and articles.

criticism: this seemed to me like totalitarianism. It was however essential that the security of this system be guaranteed by someone whose recognized talent would place him beyond reproach and who, if necessary, would be able to affirm his support loud and clear: in other words, Pierre Boulez.

The meeting between Boulez and the musical establishment to which I referred earlier depended on this very understanding: on the one hand, that Boulez was the man for the job (notwithstanding his severe reservations about Berg and *Lulu* in the past, and his mildly insulting behaviour towards Liebermann); on the other, that he would fulfil the role expected of him (which he did, brilliantly).

There is always a certain amount of friction between men and institutions – particularly if the man in question is Boulez. Boulez is something of a self-made phenomenon, and a law unto himself. Hence we now find the former champion of enlightened and critical questioning, and every non-conformity, refusing to accept the least objection to the production, however courteous and well-reasoned. It was said that the orchestral ensemble was not always good and that the singers too often went their own way; that the production deliberately ignored the composer's most important indications (according to one connoisseur), lost its way in detail or effect, or was based on a misinterpretation of the principle role – all relatively minor issues. What was important was that, from Boulez's point of view, everything had to be perfect. And indeed it was: the casting, décor, orchestra and, of course, the production were all outstanding. Boulez's impeccable loyalty towards his colleagues, together with his pride, sometimes led him to interrupt his producer – who was engagingly ill at ease in the face of criticism – in order to reply on his behalf to a point raised by some impudent (or imprudent) adversary.[18] His authoritative knowledge of the score was his most powerful argumentative weapon. Upwind, the French press applauded,[19] just to cover themselves; downwind, they felt vindicated. Boulez understood not only how to control an orchestra but also a crowd, not only how to wield a (moral) baton but also a pen; any criticism would be used to confound the critic. Hence this exemplary conductor – whose reputation rested on his scrupulous and intelligent respect for the score – could begin an article

18 I here refer to the debate, or rather, to the ostentatious display in the production space at IRCAM in February 1979, following the Parisian première – an occasion when I allowed myself to make a few observations.
19 Both the German and the Anglo-Saxon press was much more reserved.

with the elegant opening words: 'the work is an axiom',[20] without fear of contradiction.

And so the *Lulu* episode drew to a close. This had obviously not brought out the most likeable side of Boulez. And yet, what a formidable task he had once again assumed – galvanizing an orchestra inexperienced in this kind of music, adapting himself to a production that was always demanding (whatever one may have thought of it), supporting, watching over, and guiding the singers. Boulez kept the spectacle at arm's length, mobilizing all the resources of his intelligence and energy, and finally presenting the public with this long-awaited performance of the complete *Lulu*.

The contract was fulfilled in other respects too. The Palais Garnier[21] gave the work nine times, with equal success: never had the partnership between an institution and the 'operator' of an event been so perfect. Boulez was hereafter to become part of the musical furniture, with the advantage that things were to be made easier for him in the position in which he now found himself.

Thanks to the ludicrous vagaries of the system, this much heralded production was to disappear completely from the billing without stirring the journalists to protest on anything like the scale of their previously lavish praise. Within the space of a single spring, one was able to observe how fashions come and go . . .

THE BEGINNINGS OF IRCAM

In considering the sustained success of Boulez's *Ring* cycle, and the sensational *Lulu* production, we have moved ahead by several years. To return to the fortunes of IRCAM: following the first press conference in the spring of 1974, this notable organization was on the verge of its future destiny.

Since the premises of the Institut were still under construction, IRCAM was for the time being located next to the building site, in some disused shower-baths – it was here that, for better or worse, the first large computer equipment had to be installed. And even while the internal procedures of the Institut were still being sorted out, IRCAM increased its work load – both in order to forge a sense of community within its confines, and to satisfy the lively curiosity of the outside musical world.

20 In 'Lulu', Lattès, 1979, p. 161.
21 Another name for the Paris Opéra, built by Charles Garnier at the time of Napoleon III.

Some of its work sessions were closed to all but professionals. As early as the summer of 1973, Boulez had gathered together twenty or so participants – scientists, composers, future heads of department – for an in-depth enquiry into music and technology. This session took place in the renovated abbey of Senanque – a reminder not only that IRCAM's ideal was of a monastic kind but that, in the Middle Ages, music in the universities had been taught alongside the sciences. Here they took stock of the principle electronic studies world-wide, discussed the teaching of *fortran* (the information language used to begin with), and talked about theoretical approaches and practical research. The American composer Milton Babbitt underlined the difficulties experienced by both musicians and scientists in their search for a common language: the reluctance of the former to accept a purely rational approach was equalled only by the latter's mistrust of musical claims on their world. Boulez concluded by drawing a parallel with the Bauhaus, which had renewed the artistic vision of its time by providing a meeting place for artists and scientists of all disciplines.

Another closed session was held at the start of July 1975 during the Anjou Festival; this again involved some twenty people, in addition to the IRCAM contingent, in a programme of discussion on the subject of musical and scientific research both in France and elsewhere. From a political point of view the topic was rather less significant than the event itself: IRCAM was putting out feelers towards the various sectors of musical research in France, including the Conservatoire, François Bayle[22] at the GRM, Giuseppe Englert at the University of Vincennes, various other universities that had made room for musical and/or electro-acoustic research (including Guy Maneveau in Pau, Georges Boeuf in Marseilles), Claude Lefebvre of the Centre for Acoustical Research in Metz, Christian Clozier of the Experimental Music group of Bourges, André Riotte of CEMAMu,[23] Alain Durel of French radio, and others I may well have forgotten. The management side was represented by the festival director, Jean Maheu.[24]

Such opportunities for meetings between musicians are rare enough in

22 Composer (born 1932) specializing in electro-acoustic music and one-time head of the Groupe de Recherches Musicales at French Radio.
23 Centre d'Etudes de Mathématiques et d'Automatique Musicales, founded by Xenakis in 1972.
24 Referendum adviser (born 1931) to the Cours des Comptes – an official body charged with overseeing the use of public funds; Director of Music at the Ministry of Cultural Affairs from 1974–9; president of the Pompidou Centre since 1983.

France to be remarked upon: attending the session as editor of the review *Musique en jeu*, I was well placed to appreciate both the value and the problems of this attempt at reducing the tension. While the actual results may not have been anything to write home about, at least people were learning more about each other. All the same, this meeting had no follow up, and relations between IRCAM and, for example, the university establishment, were never to be really satisfactory. In this respect the Nietzschean side of Boulez had always distrusted the 'university mind' and, more specifically, the organization of university music – an attitude with which one can sometimes sympathize. Besides, the French university system was to suffer a progressive decline throughout the 1970s, as the far-reaching repercussions of the events of 1968 found the authorities committed to attempt economic control of a troublesome milieu.

In December 1977, motivated by a wish to be involved on all fronts, and by a long-standing desire to enliven sluggish institutions, Boulez attempted to break into another professional scene – this time, the Conservatoire National Supérieur de Musique. The Conservatoire's instrumentalists were trained as soloists in a traditional repertoire: an initial session with Boulez, organized by Vinko Globokar, was intended to bring the players face to face with the need both to enlarge their repertoire, and to improve their playing techniques. A second session was then to be devoted to composition students, with Boulez conducting, commenting upon and criticizing the works of selected student composers.

This potentially useful, stimulating task proved to be something of a disappointment. There were probably faults on both sides, and with few exceptions (among them Olivier Messiaen) the Conservatoire teachers were reluctant to subject their protégés to the Boulezian baptism of fire. Boulez emerged from the experience a sadder man – but nevertheless bearing under his arm the score of a work soon to be publicly performed by the Ensemble InterContemporain: *Chant pour les abîmes*, by the young Jean-Bernard Dartigolles.

Some of the IRCAM sessions were private, and limited to professionals; others were public and 'amateur' in the best sense of the word. During these formative years, IRCAM travelled to spread the word: to Brussels and Grenoble in October 1974, to Angers (where they conducted a closed session devoted to questions of musical research) in July 1975, and in February 1976, to Metz – where, thanks to the excellent preliminary work done by the organizer, Claude Lefebvre, IRCAM's session was less than usually reminiscent of a visitation by a group of superior intellects from another planet.

These sessions were to demonstrate various aspects of IRCAM to a mixed but eager public: an audio-visual montage produced by Michel Decoust showed Boulez on a visit to the IRCAM building site, statutory helmet on head, whilst a computer played a synthesized version of Ravel's Trio in the background; it also outlined the plans for the concert halls and the future projection space. Music was performed and the composers heading the departments gave lecture–discussions.

Public response was both nonplussed and enthusiastic. IRCAM was by no means the first to attempt to make contemporary music widely available. All the same, one cannot overemphasize the fact that an operation like that of IRCAM – whose many experiments in bringing music before the public had already unearthed much talent and self-sacrifice – has an enormous capacity for mobilizing the enthusiasm of its potential audience, here for the first time confronted with a team clearly capable of doing justice to contemporary music. In another respect, IRCAM (in the person of Brigitte Marger) was also well aware of the formula for fruitful endeavour – of the need to prepare the ground in advance by preliminary demonstrations introducing its work, and to dispense its information clearly. Boulez was certainly directing an organization of the utmost professionalism.

THE FOUNDING OF THE ENSEMBLE INTERCONTEMPORAIN

It was then learnt that, not content with providing Boulez with an electronic plaything worth sixty million new francs, the powers that be had acceded to a further demand from their erstwhile spoilt child: he wanted an instrumental ensemble of his own. The news was not exactly music to their ears.

Even so, the need for this ensemble did not arouse any more misgivings than the extended activities of the enterprise, which had burgeoned owing to the very success of its early 'combinatorial' presentations.

Following a formula that was to cause some surprise, the regular arm of IRCAM was soon joined by a provisional one. According to Boulez's long-standing (and by now famous) precept that music exists only as a form of communication, the research institute – committed as it was to direct and practical instrumental confrontation with the public – had to have at its disposal a means of translating Boulez's projected history of twentieth-century music into sound. Furthermore, such an ensemble would devote itself to experiment and to public entrepreneurial tasks under the direct patronage of IRCAM.

However, it must be admitted that this new venture came about partly because of the circumstances in which similar groups found themselves around 1975. The Domaine musical had ceased its activities in September 1973. Taking over from Boulez in 1967, Gilbert Amy inherited working conditions that had become increasingly unfavourable. During the years in which there was a relative explosion of contemporary music, state subsidies (arrogantly turned down by Boulez in 1967) increasingly went to the specialized festivals – such as the Royan Festival, or the Semaines Musicales Internationales de Paris (later to become the Journées de Musique Contemporaine) which had achieved real success between 1968 and 1973 under Maurice Fleuret – rather than to the regular concert associations. Because a small number of specialized performers were constantly in demand, the increase in the number of contemporary musical events was, paradoxically, to create problems even for permanent ensembles of a more traditional kind. And finally, it can be imagined that the Domaine and all it represented had really had its day: after all, the years 1954–73 spanned a whole generation. It should also be noted that, having no taste for the role of *éminence grise*, Boulez had carefully refrained from any interference in the life of 'his' one-time association.

Once the Domaine had gone, what remained? There were certainly other groups, but Boulez felt no affinity with any of them apart from Diego Masson's thriving Musique Vivante, whose particular aesthetic requirements matched his own. It is true that another specialized ensemble – 2e2m – originated in 1973, but from the outset this was more or less confined to its home base in Champigny.

In any case, the ensemble Musique Vivante had been formed at another time and for already designated tasks; it no longer seemed to respond to the needs of the moment. It was, moreover, quite properly concerned with spreading the musical word in the provinces rather than in Paris – or so at least Boulez convinced himself, doubtless on the occasion of the concerts he conducted in Tours in July 1975. Paris needed a 'Sinfonietta' of international quality, capable of recording a twentieth-century repertoire in a manner to rival its London counterpart: this was to be the Ensemble InterContemporain.

Twenty-nine musicians (of whom eight were only part-timers) were recruited by process of election in the spring of 1975. The Ensemble comprises a chamber orchestra, with all instruments represented, though with a relatively small string section (none of the twentieth-century chamber orchestra repertoire demands many strings). The Ensemble's repertoire includes the twentieth-century classics (by the Second Viennese

School, Stravinsky, Varèse, and so on), works by the great names in contemporary music since the Second World War (such as Boulez, Stockhausen, Berio, and others), and 'experimental' music – particularly that resulting from the research conducted at IRCAM into the extended use of experimental methods, contact with electronics, etc. In fact, a statement issued by its promotors described the Ensemble as 'a musical group engaged in various activities, mainly outside the framework of the concert': it would bear the daunting responsibility of building its own audience, particularly outside Paris. 'The ensemble will have an educational part to play in giving the public a means of understanding the instrumental techniques and the kind of work involved in preparing the contemporary repertoire.' Instrumentalists are recruited on a three-year contract, and although they may accept other work, the Ensemble has the right to claim priority from its players within the carefully planned framework of their employment.

All this was taken for granted; both Boulez and Nicholas Snowman, the artistic director of the Ensemble, knew their business inside out. Furthermore, Boulez was to be president of the Ensemble, Michel Tabachnik – his one-time pupil and also a composer – its musical director. Its début took place at the end of 1976, first in the provinces and then in Paris during the concert series 'Passage du XXe siècle'.

'PASSAGE DU XXE SIECLE'

Beaubourg opened its doors in 1977; so did IRCAM, at least figuratively, for the plaster of the underground building was not yet dry. From his position as musical representative on the Adminstrative Council of the Pompidou Centre, Boulez insisted right away that the activity of the Institut should be incorporated within that of the 'Grand Beaubourg' and he set about planning a vast 'sound exhibition' of twentieth-century music, modelled on the great art exhibitions soon to be presented at the Centre. The IRCAM exhibition was in two parts: the first from January to July, the second from September to December. There were seventy events in all, – concerts, of course, but also workshops and various other presentations, including a Week of the Contemporary Soloist and an exhibition of electro-acoustic music planned by Luciano Berio. These concerts and other events were spread over many very different locations – the Théâtre de la Ville, the Opéra, the Théâtre des Champs-Elysées, the all-purpose hall at the Beaubourg, and so on. A large number of groups and soloists took part, many of them from abroad and often little known in France – like the John Alldis Choir or the soprano Phyllis Bryn-Julson. Well-known soloists performed taxing works which were relatively new to them: Pollini played the Schoenberg Piano Concerto, Yvonne Minton sang (and really sang) *Pierrot lunaire*. In short, Boulez was able to call upon the services of everyone who was anyone in music – in addition to French organizations like the Paris Opéra, the Orchestre de Paris, or the Conservatoire: after all, this was really why he had been brought back to France.

Rather than undertaking a critical examination of these events, it would be instructive to try to assess Boulez's musical view of the century in 1977 by examining the programming of 'Passage du XXe siècle', and in particular, to compare this view with that of the Domaine some twenty years earlier – even if there are many obvious structural differences between the two institutions. As Director of IRCAM, Boulez had been forced to open up his programming to a degree he had certainly not been obliged to do as director of a private association occupying a minority and polemical position. But just as he made unequivocal choices for the occasion, 'This is the Encyclopaedia according to Diderot, and not the Dictionnaire Littré,[25] which interests no one', so we are entitled to take note of what is favoured by recognition and what is excluded.

With regard to what was recognized, Boulez's view of the twentieth century had hardly changed at all: the three Second Viennese composers and Mahler, the Stravinsky of around 1910, Varèse, Debussy's *Jeux*, and a little Bartók (*Music for strings, percussion and celesta, Duke Blue-beard's Castle*). Under the heading of welcome extensions to the world of music is found the name of Ives – if somewhat resignedly. But no more than in 1954 could Boulez be persuaded that the musical landscape of the century was incomplete without the inclusion of composers like Proko-fiev, Poulenc, Janáček, Richard Strauss or Sibelius.

Curiously enough, while composers of the 1945 generation were certainly recognized, they were not exactly given a privileged position: Stockhausen, Berio, Nono, Messiaen, Maderna, and Pousseur seemed to have crept in by the back door. A copious programme of Boulez's own music was announced but never materialized. The great classics of the 1950s were sparingly represented – with notable omissions, like Stock-

25 The *Dictionnaire Littré* is a French language dictionary published between 1863 and 1872 by the philosopher–philologian Maximillian Littré (1801–81); the *Encyclopédie de Diderot* is a 17-volume dictionary giving reasoned explanations of the arts and sciences, published between 1751 and 1769 by the 'Lumières' philosophers and, in particular, by Diderot and d'Alambert.

hausen's *Mixtur* and *Gruppen,* Berio's *Differences* and *Epiphanie.* Regarded as too theatrical, Kagel was as good as ignored, even though a work like *Anagramma* (1957), dedicated to Boulez himself, had not been heard in Paris for five years. Xenakis was as always considered to be a necessary evil; Cage managed to sneak into a workshop or two, and Zimmermann was almost back in favour. On the other hand, under the heading of new arrivals, an important place was given to Ligeti – who, along with Elliott Carter, is one of the few contemporary composers about whom Boulez has nothing derogatory to say.

There were other composers, less generally well known, who fitted into this musical panorama: Carlos Alsina, Isang Yun, George Crumb, Toru Takemitsu, John Chowning (almost a house composer), Michel Phillippot, and many others. The selection was by no means a narrow one, and it revealed Boulez both as a musician unusually confident about his own choices and generous in his inclusion of almost everything worthy of note in the latter part of the century – even if some were rather condescendingly included as being of purely documentary interest.

Young composers were conspiciously present – not excessively so, but without flagrant omissions: Brian Ferneyhough, Giuseppi Sinopoli, Phillippe Manoury, Peter Eötvös, Rolf Gelhaar and Wolfgang Rihm represented the generation of the twenty-five to thirty-year-olds.

The exclusions were no surprise. There was a frontier in Boulez's mind between those composers whose existence he recognized (even if their work was little to his own taste) and those he refused to recognize, who were apparently alien to his concept of music. 'Passage du XXe siècle' ignored the tide of repetitive music by the Americans La Monte Young, Steve Reich or Philip Glass, the minimalist composers like Alvin Lucier or Robert Ashley, as well as electro-acoustic and 'concrete' music, and everything bordering on improvisation or music theatre. IRCAM was later to show more interest in the areas left uncharted on this occasion, but for the moment, the twentieth century was invited to proceed without them.

It all went very well. The events had a success in no way undermined by the rather disappointing début of the Ensemble InterContemporain, whose right it was to assume the formidable honour of opening the series. Their programme included a fair proportion of music by young composers (Manoury and Sinopoli), launched the new classic (Ligeti), offered a free platform to the future dissident (Xenakis) – and even managed to pay tribute to Boulez the composer.

This obviously diplomatic event was, however, only an extreme example within a series of other programmes all carefully planned and accompanied by first-rate written information. All too often neglected by concert-giving associations, these two details were certainly to play a positive part in the success achieved: from the outset, Boulez had imposed his concept of the concert as a didactic structure in which works were not hastily rehearsed, then juxtaposed at random and without further explanation.

The public sensed this quality immediately, and one of the main objectives of Boulez's return to France seemed close to being achieved – namely, the reconstitution of a contemporary music audience which his Parisian predecessors had let slip away, like sand between the fingers.

AN EXTRAORDINARY *RITE*

One of these events left an impression that was, quite simply, extraordinary. On 23 April 1977, Boulez conducted a programme of Bartók (*Music for strings, percussion and celesta*), Berg (Violin Concerto) and Stravinsky (*The Rite of Spring*), given at the Théâtre des Champs-Elysées.

It may seem that there was nothing special about this particular programme – not even the radiant presence of the remarkable violinist Itzhak Perlman. What made it stand out from the rest was the fact that most of the orchestral musicians were schoolchildren. The National Youth Orchestra of Great Britain is an amateur but officially constituted body of young people aged from twelve to nineteen who, while undergoing a normal education, meet in the school holidays for ten-day periods during which they work at an orchestral programme under the direction of a well-known conductor – such as Boulez.

In a work as symbolic as *The Rite*, it is impossible to compare the performance of this group with those of the great adult professional orchestras, but considered on the basis of their excellent ensemble playing and, above all, of their absolutely unique enthusiasm, the National Youth Orchestra gave a truly memorable interpretation of Stravinsky's work that particular evening.

Perhaps the commitment of the young players was in some way connected with the fact that they were performing in the same hall which had seen the scandalous première of the work more than sixty years earlier. But Boulez's conducting also had a lot to do with it. *The Rite* is a work with which he feels an astonishing empathy, developed over many years. These young people played with the relaxed seriousness characteristic of English musicians, plus a sort of youthful impetuosity – launching themselves almost recklessly into the most hazardous passages; in their company, the mixture of total awareness and inner intensity that Boulez can conjure up when he feels both strung up yet at ease in himself enabled him to construct a fascinating and exhilarating sound spectacle before our very eyes.

The success was immense and the applause long sustained. These boys and girls were delighted with the performance they had just given and obviously enchanted by Boulez; he himself was almost laughing with pleasure as he submitted to the beaming embrace of their manager Ivey Dickson. It seemed to me that, beyond the amazement this enthusiastic and knowledgeable audience experienced in the face of such a special concert, there may have been other more subliminal feelings: the music itself had produced a reaction far stronger than routine expressions of official admiration. Why do our own children lack this kind of opportunity? What was the mysterious alchemy which took place between the celebrated conductor and these very ordinary youngsters, evidently so transfigured by the experience? Centred around a particular score, this awakening of a mutual relationship between two separate generations can only have beneficial results for all concerned. In the face of this act of genuine paternity, it seemed to me that Boulez, already unreservedly admired, was seen that evening – perhaps for the first time – as a straightforwardly lovable figure.

THE TIME FOR HONOURS

These were years in which Boulez at last achieved widespread public and official recognition. Some of the honours conferred upon him were of little consequence. He received the Siemens prize in 1977, and expressed his thanks in a gracious and rather charming speech; two years later, he was awarded the 'Prix du meillieur ouvrier', and had to endure a long afternoon at the Sorbonne in order to receive his prize from Valerie Giscard d'Estaing – a man with little love for the Beaubourg. There were still other awards, scarcely worth mentioning.

Other nominations seem more like miscalculations. In June 1979, the local Parisian milieu were cynical about Boulez's nomination for the presidency of the Orchestre de Paris, especially as this unsolicited nomination was accompanied by a restrictive clause stating that the president was not allowed to conduct the orchestra: Claude Samuel noted that this was hardly an example of the best use of resources. And that was the end of the matter.

Boulez's dealings with the Orchestre de Paris could almost be the subject of a separate chapter in themselves. They were doomed from the start. Just as Gaeton Picon[26] once pointed out, the fact that the Orchestre de Paris was founded upon the ruins of the glorious Société National des Concerts du Conservatoire did not make the reconciliation between Boulez and this shining example of Parisian (and of French) musical life any easier, particularly since, compared with more experienced orchestras in London, New York, Cleveland, Boston or Bayreuth, the undeniable weaknesses of the orchestra invariably incurred his harshest criticisms.

Officially, the reconciliation took place on 5 January 1976, when Boulez conducted the Orchestre de Paris for the first time in a programme comprising Beethoven's Fifth Piano Concerto, with Daniel Barenboim as soloist, and the *The Firebird*. The fact that he had backed the nomination of Barenboim as chief conductor of the orchestra had helped prepare the ground. Thereafter, he conducted the orchestra from time to time but, it has to be admitted, without undue enthusiasm on either side.

It was nevertheless the Orchestre de Paris which commissioned *Notations* and which was to première four movements of the work on 18 June 1980. Scored for large orchestra, it is based on his own *Notations* for piano: written in 1948 and dedicated to Serge Nigg, these were premièred at La Triptyque[27] by Yvette Grimaud on 12 February that same year. Four orchestral *Notations* of the proposed twelve have so far been written and published. Meanwhile, the orchestral score includes the original piano versions before each movement, offering a useful comparison with the Boulez of the Conservatoire years.

The relationship between these few bars of piano music and the orchestral version is by no means obvious. The latter is almost like a set of orchestral studies that take the anonymity of the original material (in 1984, hardly recognizable as being by Boulez) as a basis for the extended development of a richly independent musical discourse. Remarkable for the composer's consummate command of orchestral timbre, these four contrasting *Notations* last a mere eight minutes in all. It will eventually be possible to perform any number of *Notations* between four and the complete twelve, and in an order of the conductor's choice; the order suggested by Boulez with regard to the four already written is 1-4-3-2.

26 Writer and literary critic (1915–76); friend of André Malraux and Director General of Arts and Letters from 1961–66. See also p. 139.
27 A concert society founded in Paris in 1934 by Pierre Darquennes, under the patronage of Ravel, Dukas, Roussel, Messiaen, Dutilleux, Sauget, and others; giving its concerts at the Ecole Normale de Musique, the association did much to promote young performers.

Since we are on the subject of occasional pieces, there are two other short works, written when Boulez was formulating his plans for IRCAM and offered to the public as 'mouth-watering titbits'. *Pour le Dr. K.* is a tiny piece, lasting less than three minutes, and written as part of a tribute to Alfred Kalmus – distinguished director of the London branch of Universal Edition. A number of other Universal composers took part in the tribute, and a privately issued disc of these includes miniatures by the likes of Stockhausen, Birtwistle, Boulez and Bedford.[28]

The other work is more ambitious. *Messagesquisse* for seven cellos was written for the La Rochelle cello competition in 1977, when Mstislav Rostropovich commissioned (though did not himself play) works from various composers, including Dutilleux. Boulez's piece also took the form of a musical tribute, this time addressed to Paul Sacher (a personal friend of Boulez and president of the IRCAM Foundation), and is based on the notes corresponding to the letters in its conductor–dedicatee's name. His beautifully judged score is ingenious, with a clearly perceptible design (of which an exemplary decription is given by Paul Mefano in the note accompanying his recent recording). Once again it is unfortunate that Boulez's large-scale works tend to eclipse these brief 'messages' from a musician whose creative energies were increasingly to be devoted to IRCAM.

LE COLLEGE DE FRANCE

Despite Boulez's apparent withdrawal from the active musical scene, his activities continue to embrace undertakings which may also be seen as distinctions conferred. In 1975, he was nominated to the Collège de France – an institution within which the demise of an incumbent professor means that his office ceases to exist. The death of Felix Lecoy – a specialist in medieval French language and literature – meant that a chair had fallen vacant and that a place had become available for the creation of another.

The idea of a chair in musical research was put forward at the suggestion of Michel Foucault,[29] Roland Barthes[30] and Emmanuel Le

---

28 Non-commercial disc produced by Universal Edition.
29 Philosopher (1926–84), author of *Eloge de la folie à l'âge classique* (1960), *Les Mots et les choses* (1966), and *Histoire de la sexualité*, volume I (1976); professor at the Collège de France, he was notable amongst those pressing for the establishment of a professorship in musical research, later conferred upon Boulez.
30 Critic and semiologist (1915–80), author of several essays on linguistics and of *Le Degré zéro de l'écriture* (1953).

Roy Ladurie.[31] Once the decision was taken, the choice became obvious: with Le Roy Ladurie as his sponsor, Boulez's election was secured in March 1975.

As far as Boulez the composer was concerned, this nomination had two very positive aspects. The first may have seemed unimportant at the time, but by putting him in a position of financial security, the Collège nomination (tenable for life) guaranteed his future independence. He could afford to break off relations with IRCAM, if at any time it seemed to be moving in a direction not to his liking; and finally, to envisage giving up conducting altogether.

The other aspect was more fundamental: because of the high standards it demands (without the constraints of syllabus or examination), and the total freedom it offers to all those interested in pursuing some kind of research, the Collège de France was to become the place for Boulez to collect his theoretical thoughts (once again in step with his progress as a composer), before embarking on new compositional projects.

Unfortunately, the Collège hall has no listening equipment, the subjects it deals with are extremely wide-ranging, and those who follow the courses are a strangely heterogeneous assortment of people. These unquestionable handicaps remain. Meanwhile, alongside the courses seminars were held at IRCAM itself – within an ambience where the teaching of Boulez is more obviously effective.

THE FRENCH MASTER OF MUSIC

Thus, at the end of the 1970s Boulez was increasingly regarded as the supreme master of music in France. This had the practical result that the media (increasingly his powerful allies) now proclaimed his cause, by making contemporary music available to a wide public, who are eager to understand, but will not tolerate specialist jargon.

Such tasks were entrusted to Boulez himself on numerous occasions, and he was never more relaxed than when he was able to work with musicians. I have witnessed this many times in recent years. Place him alone in front of a microphone to give an explanation and he is often disappointing, becoming deceptively clear as he discusses apparently abstract ideas with a virtuosity and a fondness for historical short cuts which are striking but simplistic. On the other hand, give him a score and

31 Historian (born 1929), professor at the Collège de France and one of the proposers for the creation of a chair in music.

put him in front of a group of players and he is sublimely in his element, able to expound subtle and even complex ideas with a penetrating clarity, and revelling in the affectionate empathy he enjoys with his players. (I am thinking in particular of the admirable explanatory sessions on *Eclat* held at the Théâtre d'Orsay with the Ensemble InterContemporain in 1979; doubtless benefiting greatly from the work done at Villeurbanne some years previously, these sessions were to provide material for Michel Fano's superb film, *Le Chef d'orchestre actuel*.)[32]

At the end of 1979, Boulez seemed effectively to be deploying every one of his many talents: as composer, conductor, editor, sought-after interviewee, computer operator, and IRCAM administrator. Then, in 1980, came the IRCAM crisis.

32 See Filmography: F2.

CHAPTER TWELVE

The Time of *Répons*

(1980–4)

It is difficult for the outside observer to speak about the 'IRCAM crisis' objectively, however sympathetic his attitude may be. The crisis arose in 1980, not through any specific blunder on the part of IRCAM, but through the exacerbation of a *malaise* destined by its very nature to be almost permanently present: a research institute does not possess limitless funds. In any case, 'crisis' was the very life-blood of IRCAM, almost its justification, and as long as crisis leads to progress it is certainly better than complacent routine. But outside observers could only see things in a somewhat clear-cut or polemical manner. Whilst I have little intention here of getting involved in the arguments that raged in the press as to the nature of the Institut, its products, and the personality of its director, it is important to try to grasp how, after five years, an institution that Boulez needed, and which he himself organized and directed, could have begun to malfunction – and how this affected the composer himself.

THE CRISIS

During the course of 1980, it was learnt that the five directors of the IRCAM departments (all appointed by Boulez himself) had left the Institut. They parted apparently on amicable terms – in Berio's case, to set up the Italian adjunct of 'an electro-acoustic antenna' in Florence – and Boulez seemed, on the face of things, to be relatively unconcerned, openly declaring these changes to be 'very healthy' (although he had previously claimed that they were merely 'provisional'). Nevertheless, the disbanding of a team formed six years previously can hardly be seen as a positive achievement, or one that had been anticipated.

In other respects there were wider ramifications to this crisis. IRCAM and its director had quite rightly sought contact with the public and engaged in confrontation with musical life in general: now Boulez found himself once more the centre of widespread controversy, although the public's grasp of the problems involved was only superficial, and the finer points of this political and financial wrangling passed them by. Nevertheless, it is an unfortunate fact that although legally, IRCAM is an association, it draws its main revenue in the form of public subsidy, and is therefore to some extent under public control.

It would here be useful to examine the more essential nature of the internal departmental research and organization at IRCAM.

Research at IRCAM (1974–80)

Within the compass of this study it is impossible to report on all the research conducted at IRCAM during these years: a review of the research undertaken in 1978 reveals no less than eighteen separate accounts of work conducted at the Institut in that year alone. I shall therefore consider the main axes of research concerning three of its sectors.

The first was the development of the *Music V* programme by Jean-Claude Risset's computer department; starting in 1969, this programme allowed for the provision of a numerical synthesizer such as the one perfected in successive versions by Giuseppe di Giugno.

The second sector, which was theoretically dependent on Luciano Berio's electro-acoustic department, was to be revealed as the most productive. As early as 1975, the engineer/data processor Giuseppe di Giugno had conceived a numerical synthesizer that could be used for concert-giving purposes. This machine, called 4A, was later to be perfected in its versions 4B, 4C, and finally, 4X: it is this last that Boulez was to use in *Répons* (1981–4).

The third sector related to the projection space. This was originally planned for the building at the side of the Beaubourg, to be connected to the centre by a tunnel, but it is now situated on the Saint-Merri side. This projection space gave rise to researches which at first were, obviously, to concern sound reverberation (since the design of its walls allowed for reverberation to be varied between 1.5 and 4.5 seconds); later, it came to have a direct bearing on the study of timbre – and in particular, on the definition of a new algorithm for calculating the computer simulation of room reverberation. In view of the reigning uncertainty as to the acoustic quality of a concert hall before it is played in (even though acoustics and architecture are, in principle, exact sciences), the practical importance of such a project can be appreciated.

These three principal research areas, all involving the computer, did not exclude other approaches. In 1978[1] the instrumental and voice department was occupied entirely with the construction of a new flute to facilitate production of multiphonics (that is, double or triple sounds), and another important sector, conducted by Xavier Rodet within Gerald Bennett's 'diagonal' department, was concerned with a project for word synthesis.

Alongside this actual research, the teaching sector organized educational sessions for explaining the new techniques to composers wishing to conduct personal research projects at IRCAM at a later stage. The first 'works' using these techniques were put to the test in concert performance: of the scores I heard, Tod Machover's *Light* seemed to me to be a successful blend of sensitivity and strictness.

The overall impression was that everyone working at IRCAM was on the move, that the results were considerable, and that Boulez's dominant position in no way stifled research that was definitely expanding. This impression of euphoria was almost certainly misleading.

The nature of the crisis

The contradictions within IRCAM were highlighted by the first seriously critical articles appearing in *Le Monde* under the name of Jacques Longchampt.[2] Referring to IRCAM's appearance at Metz in February 1976, he notes the discrepancy between a discussion prospectus which has still not succeeded in producing any practical results (and for good reason, at the time) and a much-needed organization, pledged to giving concerts and enlivening the musical landscape, which nevertheless reminded one of a museum. That this museum was a twentieth-century one did not alter the fact that it was peripheral to what was expected of a research institute.

Other problems arose from this ambiguity of role. IRCAM was both a laboratory for the future (the responsibility for which is perhaps solely in the hands of Boulez himself) and a body specially commissioned to promote contemporary music, while at the same time subject to administrative control. Speaking of this problem of control in relation to the Ensemble InterContemporain, Boulez is blunt about the committees responsible for distributing the manna of the state among the various

1 As instigated by Vinko Globokar and the flautist Pierre-Yves Arthaud.
2 *Le Monde*, 2 March 1975.

promotional organizations. In a recent interview he retorted testily and with some arrogance: 'At my age and in my position I refuse to be dependent on the kind of nonentities who join committees.' Within the framework of a Foundation presided over by Claude Pompidou,[3] IRCAM suddenly hit upon the formula successfully implemented by the Domaine musical: a system of private support to finance freedom of control. Setting this up involved time and energy, and stirred up resentment: these administrative duties left Boulez little time to compose.

Paradoxically, it was this atmosphere of relative material hardship that gave rise to the proceedings instigated by the jealous dissidents. I here refer to those composers and others who may have been struggling financially for years (sometimes, I might add, with good reason!), and who saw IRCAM and the InterContemporain as richly endowed rivals. Boulez could hardly claim that his events were highly competitive in terms of cost, or that IRCAM hardly had enough to survive or even that, in the ten years he had been away from France, nobody had attempted anything comparable. His enemies appeared to have a point.

In 1980, the political aspects of the controversy became still more insistent. While recognizing Boulez's stature as a composer, Harry Halbreich denounced him as the 'new Lully' of musical life, no sector of which escaped his influence. A close disciple of long standing, Jean-Claude Eloy voiced the criticism he had borne against IRCAM since 1978: questioning the data-processing strategy directed at IRCAM by Iannis Xenakis – who had been pandered to since the start of the Institut[4] and already had a project under way there – he came to the conclusion that IRCAM had always stood for something not far removed from evil incarnate.

At first it was only rumoured that the musicians associated with Boulez for the past seven years were no longer in agreement with him as to the aims of the Institut. But it was soon public knowledge that Gerald Bennett, Luciano Berio, Michel Decoust, Vinko Globokar and Jean-Claude Risset had parted company with IRCAM.

The departments in question

Although the departments concerned could not survive without leadership, there is evidence that there were already problems, and that the resignations had simply brought matters to a head. An early difficulty

---

3 Wife of Georges Pompidou (1911–74).
4 He was present on stage at the press conference held on 7 March 1974; frankly, his claims as to the possibility of a collaboration between CEMAMu and IRCAM convinced nobody.

concerned the relative standing of scientists and musicians. The status of the former was contradictory: their position was ideologically dominant but administratively subordinate. What Boulez had to say on the subject had made it clear that the scientists were equal partners of the composers; however, the latter, who had already established their reputations, insisted that they be given their head – hardly surprising, in view of the fact that Boulez had rightly chosen only those composers who were capable of asserting their own viewpoints. Obviously reorganization was imperative.

Another contradiction resulted from the ambiguity of a thesis, dating from 1974, that adopted the view that the classic electro-acoustic studio had had its day and that the moment had come for 'the use of data-processing techniques'. At the same time, an electro-acoustic department and a computer department were set up side by side, under the separate auspices of two first-rate musicians who respected one another but felt neither the desire nor the need for close co-operation. In effect, as we have seen, the most positive part of the IRCAM contribution came from Luciano Berio's department: it was he who had known where to look for Giuseppe di Giugno and who gave the computer a central place in his research, so reducing Jean-Claude Risset's computer department to the thankless and subordinate role of 'programme manufacturer' for the 4X machine.

There were also doubts concerning Vinko Globokar's instrumental and vocal department. Once again, there appeared to be a discrepancy between intention and action. Boulez had founded IRCAM partly as a result of his criticism of the kind of 'tinkering' with traditional instruments and playing techniques as a means of extending musical material, which was fashionable between 1960 and 1970. At the time, there was every reason to think that this was a criticism shared by Vinko Globokar. But to create such a department and to entrust it to an instrumentalist as practically inventive as Globokar inevitably led to a reinforcement of the very ills it claimed to eradicate.

The main problem with the 'diagonal' department was that it was ostensibly responsible for co-ordinating four virtually unstructured departments. Its other tasks included the management of the projection space (which had undergone long tests before eventually being opened in 1978) which, in effect, was already under the control of the engineers in charge of its functioning (notably the excellent sound engineer Ben Bernfeld), or of users pursuing their own research. And since Boulez did not then consider 'theoretical research' to be a priority, Gerald Bennett had to be content with a conscientious publishing of the various technical reports from the other departments.

Even the pedagogical department was not exempt from these difficulties. Again, it was to suffer because its function had been insufficiently defined at the outset. Was it to be a department of experimentation, committed to vital research into musical pedagogy, such as the personality, background and known preoccupations of its director, Michel Decoust, might have suggested? Or was it intended as a department for educating the public, with a view to binding it to IRCAM's ideals, and encouraging attendance at its events? (In practical terms, this is principally what it proved to be.) Or was it in the end to be a structure geared towards the education of composers invited to work at IRCAM, who needed to learn new techniques before they could understand the material and the technical procedures at their disposal? This third function – clearly favoured by Boulez – was well fulfilled by the foundation courses attended by both French and foreign composers, but not in the way anticipated either by Decoust or Boulez himself. Clearly, this was another area of IRCAM requiring attention.

The reorganization of IRCAM and the theory of the two sectors

As I have shown, the original departments all suffered from imprecise definition and too much autonomy. Returning to the central idea of 'an interaction between scientists and musicians', Boulez replaced the original departments with two large sectors, one musical, the other scientific. Between these was a pedagogical unit, run by the psycho-acoustician David Wessel in co-operation with tutors (Andrew Gerszo) and research co-ordinators (like Tod Machover), charged with the actual organization of this interaction.

We need a permanent scientific and technical team that will give us a strong structure in order to pursue long-term experiments and to fulfill programmes; on the other hand the artistic contribution must be continually varied so that the establishment does not stagnate ... However, the composers in charge of departments sometimes tended to become fixated on their own problems and to fail to show an interest in the students; so the departments were abolished, but these same composers are still free to come and work at IRCAM as and when they wish.[5]

5 Jacques Longchampt, *Le Monde*, 20 May 1980.

The question of whether the new organization was completely satisfactory remained to be put to Boulez in his next interview with the national press. There are, I think, three points to be borne in mind.

At first, a lot of work was done at IRCAM, as the 1983 disc 'A portrait of IRCAM' shows. In addition to a full report drawn up by Jean-Baptiste Barrière,[6] this comprised sound examples of the principle research being conducted there, including synthesis and sound simulation, psychoacoustics, composition with real sounds, the 'chant' programme,[7] and so on. The disc also presented extracts from specific works, such as *Répons*, and met with unexpected public success.

Later, the number of composers and groups either working at the Institut, or having works performed there increased dramatically. However, Boulez had acquired something of a sectarian image, reinforced by his famous riposte to Sylvie de Nussac and Michèle Cotta in *L'Express*, when he countered a question on this delicate topic by declaring: 'I am not somewhat sectarian, I am completely sectarian!' His own attitude was clearly at odds with the multi-directional opening up of IRCAM today; but Boulez is both realistic and pragmatic, and well aware of the fact that, in these straitened times, IRCAM will continue to receive financial support only if it proves to be of significant public service in terms of musical research.

Unquestionably, Boulez seems in the process of trying to disengage himself from his Institut. He knows only too well that its day to day functioning – and therefore its future survival – depends on his determined and exacting presence. But it no longer gives him any pleasure, and the success of the unfinished *Répons* has highlighted the advantages increasingly to be gained from directing the establishment from rather less close quarters.

THE TIME OF *REPONS*

Boulez had originally stopped conducting because of his wish to return to composition. But then he launched himself into IRCAM, causing much snide laughter among the sceptics: once a composer's creative vein is exhausted, what has he left? Even his most faithful followers were understandably anxious when confronted with works which seemed to lack real creative inspiration, notwithstanding their formal virtues.

6 Director (born 1958) of musical research at IRCAM.
7 The 'chant' programme: the name given to the research into word synthesis led by Xavier Rodet.

Furthermore, the image of the triumphant Company Director, involved in trivial duties and accruing honours, did not inspire confidence in his declared commitment to composition. In the face of such doubts, *Répons* stands as the vindication of Boulez the composer.

Towards the end of 1979, Boulez announced that he was reworking *Poésie pour pouvoir* – the piece for instruments and electro-acoustic apparatus which had remained a millstone around his neck since its 1959 première in Baden-Baden, and which certainly ought to benefit from IRCAM technology and in particular from the famous 4X. This news did nothing to lessen the scepticism: the machine was no substitute for imagination, if Boulez's creative talents were indeed failing. The musical world arrived in Donaueschingen beset with doubts.

They need not have worried. 18 October 1981 was an unqualified triumph. Although an element of suspense may have increased the tension, it was gripping from the first note of the introduction, even before the third page, with its seductive sea of trills followed by resounding trumpets. The entry of the soloists was miraculous; the interplay of human and mechanical elements was alternately free and apparently strict, the more 'detached' contribution of the machines providing a foil for the instrumentalists. The score was both elegant and eloquent. Boulez explained a number of things with great lucidity, and the work was repeated, to splendid effect.

The reception was unanimously favourable. The prevailing feeling seemed to be that, with *Répons*, Boulez had regained the heights of *Pli selon pli*. Two months later, the work was given again in the Paris area, making, if anything, an even more positive impression. It will be discussed in some detail in the final chapter of this book.

But while *Répons* was in some way grafted on to the problem period following the IRCAM crisis of 1980, its relationship with the Institut was to create problems. *Répons* was to make use of a considerable amount of equipment (in particular, that developed within the Institut itself), and to occupy a whole team of technicians and assistants, especially Andrew Gerszo. His importance as practical co-ordinator of the work, elaborator of its programmes, and servant of the machine during performance, made him almost its co-author. Because of all this, *Répons* ran the risk of being a demonstration work, and – had the invention been of lesser quality – of being no more than that.

Nonetheless, the relationship between Boulez and IRCAM was bound to reveal a demonstrable capacity for teamwork. During the whole period of its composition, Boulez worked without respite on the instrumental score of *Répons*, composing late at night and early in the morning in his Parisian belvedere before going to IRCAM to confer with the machine – to test his written sketches and to discuss technique with Gerszo and others. If *Répons* seems very much an IRCAM work, this is not only because of its evident deployment of technological resources, but also because its author had justified his 1970s hypothesis in the only way possible – by composing a masterpiece.

CHAPTER THIRTEEN

Pierre Boulez

(1984–6)

Since the publication of the first French edition of this book, Pierre Boulez has continued to fulfil his roles within IRCAM and with the Ensemble InterContemporain, as well as carrying out numerous other conducting engagements. Consequently, the time available for composition has inevitably been limited; nevertheless, he has revised a number of existing scores, and has completed two new works. In examining his latest achievements, it is worth considering whether they represent a new departure, or whether they should more properly be regarded as a continuation (or consolidation) of what has gone before.

THE RECENT EVOLUTION OF IRCAM

With regard to IRCAM, the most important change has been that of artistic director. Although still partly linked to IRCAM, Nicholas Snowman has been recalled to London for other tasks; his replacement, Laurent Bayle, who was chosen by Boulez himself, is known as a gifted administrator and, in particular, as the founder of Musica, the contemporary music festival held each September in Strasburg. There he had shown considerable adminstrative and entrepreneurial talents, and had succeeded in attracting an audience to contemporary music: coming at a time of crisis and budgetary reductions, his appointment to IRCAM clearly indicates a new commitment on the part of the Institut to fostering better relationships with the public.

At present, research is principally concentrated upon the uses and future extensions of the 4x machine; here, the experience of *Répons* is central, even if the success of the work has somewhat overshadowed other realizations also concerned with the 'production and transformation of sound in real time'. Together, such works seem to represent the current way of life at the Institut; the miniaturization of the 4X will eventually lead to its use within a configuration of individual computers.

In other words, the painful dichotomy – perhaps in itself not unfruitful – between research and production has continued to pose difficult questions of priority and 'identity', just as Boulez himself has come no nearer to finding a solution to his scarcely veiled desire to withdraw from administrative and directorial responsibilities.

THE ENSEMBLE INTERCONTEMPORAIN

The Ensemble had already made a considerable name for itself before 1984, and largely as the result of important foreign tours, it has now achieved top-level international standing rare among French orchestral groups.

Their success stems mainly from the unique relationship existing between Boulez and the players themselves: this relationship is one of total commitment and unequivocal obedience on the part of the players, even though they are afforded the freedom to discuss issues with him on equal terms. Respect without alienation, authority without authoritarianism, confidence without routine: the formula is an ideal one, and cannot practically be transferred to a large orchestra as its stands.

The striking result of all this has been publicly saluted – in particular by the American press during the Ensemble's 1986 tour of five American cities at the invitation of their respective orchestras: Los Angeles, San Francisco, Chicago, Boston and New York. The 'crack new music group' (as the *Time* critic called it) enchanted both general and specialist audiences unaccustomed either to such a level of performance or to such a degree of specialized expertise in the music of our time. While there were sometimes reservations about his conducting in general, and the reception of *Répons* was not exactly rapturous, in his role at the head of the Ensemble Boulez was unanimously acclaimed.

This success story has had its negative side, for Boulez's achievements with the Ensemble mean that he will be a very hard – if not impossible – act to follow. The following anecdote proves this point. In 1985, Philippe Seguin, mayor of the small Vosges town of Epinal, invited Boulez and the Ensemble for a concert to mark the composer's sixtieth birthday. Boulez himself was to conduct a performance of *Le Marteau sans maître* but, struck down by 'flu, had to withdraw at the last moment. His place was taken by the excellent Peter Eötvös, whose knowledge of the score and competence to rescue the concert was unquestioned. The public, however, disagreed. Half-myth, half-reality, the name of Boulez at the head of his Ensemble became indispensable for any prestigious concerts, or tours undertaken to enhance the image of the Ensemble. His presence became a decisive element in any promotion designed to attract public subsidy. Ironically, his success chains him to the rostrum, at the very time when he has made it abundantly clear that he would like to withdraw; there is something almost Wotan-like in this auto-destructive power:

'Das sind die Bande
die mich binden'[1]

THE BLOSSOMING OF THE CONDUCTOR

In discussing Boulez's conducting career during these two years, I will confine myself to a single concert I attended on 20 November 1984 which seems to sum up the present-day position of Boulez the conductor. The programme for this concert, given in the Barbican Hall in London by the London Symphony Orchestra, included Stravinsky's *Symphonies of Wind Instruments*, Berg's Violin Concerto, with Pinchas Zukerman as soloist, and the complete ballet *The Firebird*.

It is worth putting on record that Boulez's rehearsals with this first-rate English orchestra were as spellbinding as ever. The rapport between players and conductor was such that the few problems encountered seemed relatively trivial, and did not interfere with the extraordinary feeling of continuity between rehearsals.

The concert itself offered what might be described as 'vintage' Boulez interpretations. The reading of the *Symphonies* was impeccable – exactly what one has come to expect from a conductor who responds intuitively to an impassive, ritualistic kind of music. Likewise, his account of the Berg Concerto challenged the view – all too frequently endorsed – that Berg's music is over-refined, and that Boulez has little sympathy with what might be termed 'the Bergian rhetoric'.[2] His *Firebird* was no less stimulating: his broad yet precise gestures revealing an extraordinary talent for illuminating and clarifying the orchestral texture, for observing the finer points of

1 *Die Walküre*, Act II, scene 2: 'Such are the bonds that bind me . . .'
2 Something of this may be noticed in the recording of the occasion (see Discography). I myself have considered this point in more detail in a paper I presented at the International Alban Berg-Tage, in Luxemburg (13–24 December 1985).

balance, and for expressing himself by means of economical and communicative gesture. That evening, it seemed to me that Boulez's conducting had achieved a sort of classic perfection.

There have been many other opportunities, particularly during the American tours (of 1984, 1986, and 1987), to note Boulez's blossoming as a conductor. This development is undoubtedly linked to a personal serenity and sense of well-being that has been acquired with difficulty, but seems now to be firmly established.

SETBACKS

Despite this impression of security, Boulez has in fact suffered a number of setbacks. On a personal level, the death of his mother on 10 June 1985, at the age of eighty-eight, was followed by that of Jean Genet, who died aged seventy-six on 15 April 1986. In 1984, there had been the death of the philosopher Michel Foucault, who was instrumental in securing Boulez's nomination to the Collège de France, and one of the few men in France who measured up to Boulez intellectually. A still crueller blow came with the death, in September 1985, of the young flautist from the Ensemble InterContemporain, Laurence Beauregard. Boulez had liked and respected him greatly, and their close creative collaboration was evidenced by the projected new version of '. . . *explosante-fixe* . . .'

More generally, he has been involved with the concerns of a new opera house. In 1981, he was asked by the socialist authority to become associated with the creation of a centre for popular opera in the Place de la Bastille. At first, Boulez had reservations even as to the choice of site: he would have preferred it to be installed as part of the 'Cité de la musique' at La Villette, so that there could be a better structuring between the opera and the new Conservatoire being built there. Nevertheless, he allowed himself to be talked into giving this venture the benefit of his ideas and experience at a preliminary organizational stage. He has carried out this task with typical conscientiousness, while making it clear that he can in no way be counted upon to accept a position, once the Bastille Opéra is established. However, by summer 1986, political and economic pressures had persuaded the new government to axe the initial project. Rather than allow a project to which he had lent his name to sink without trace, Boulez launched himself into a crusade to see what could be salvaged, and – in alliance with the newly appointed Director, Maurice Fleuret – he collected many influential signatures, saw the Minister, fought in every possible way, and to some extent, succeeded. However, the time and energy spent pursuing this worthy cause has left little time for composition.

BOULEZ THE COMPOSER

Though Boulez has not composed a major work since 1984, he has spent time revising existing scores whose material and technique seem at variance with the compositional ideal on which they were based. To date, he has extended *Répons*, completed the definitive version of *Improvisation III*, revised *cummings ist der Dichter*, and composed two new works: *Dérive* (based on material from *Répons*), and *Dialogue de l'ombre double* (which is related to *Domaines*). In addition, he is completely rewriting *Le Visage nuptial*, and has so far completed two of the five movements.

The continuation of Répons

Répons 2 received its première in London, in 1982. In 1984, a new section was given in Turin, then in Basle, Metz, and Paris. Since then, the work has progressed no further.

Surprising for its restrained use of the 4X machine, the new material from *Répons 2* is interpolated between section G (the 'finale') and the coda. It thus forms an intermediary section, marked by the progressive disappearance of all computer treatment as the soloists fall silent, and linked to the ensuing coda almost without a break.

It is impracticable to discuss *Répons 3* further in its manifestly unfinished state; according to the composer himself, it is to be followed by a long slow movement which will in turn be linked to the displaced (and finally perfected) coda. The first performance of the complete work (which was to have lasted about an hour) had already been promised for October 1984, then again for the American tour in February–March 1986, but it has yet to take place. It is to be hoped that the future of the whole work will not be left in doubt indefinitely.

The definitive version of Improvisation III

Contrary to the view I expressed in 1984, that a definitive version of *Improvisation III* from *Pli selon pli* had been achieved, I must now confess that a further revision has attained still greater perfection. Dating from 1984–5, and first performed in London in February 1985 by the BBC Symphony Orchestra with Phyllis Bryn-Julson, this third version of *Improvisation III* is completely different from the two preceding ones:

(a) Supported by discreet instrumental contributions, the work begins with a considerably developed and extended vocal section, setting the whole of the Mallarmé poem in an almost monosyllabic style, with few embellishments. Only a brief instrumental interlude divides the second quatrain from the first tercet.

(b) Following the vocal introduction, there is a fairly long interlude featuring the xylophone.

(c) The soloist then repeats the first four lines of the poem (as in the second version of *Improvisation III*) in a style now embellished with 'tropes' and florid decorations, and with the lines separated by lengthy interludes (c 7'30" to c 17'30").

(d) The *Improvisation* ends with a postlude of about 1'30", so that the duration overall remains similar to that of the preceding versions.

This new version is extremely beautiful, it displays a natural facility, extraordinary clarity, and at the same time, much greater subtlety. Its radiance obliterates all memory of the truly tragic proposition of the text, or at least to contradict the poem's hypnotic fascination with creative impotence.

On a more intellectual level, it seems to me that Boulez's ideas are here finding a contemporary parallel to the aesthetic of the open-form work of the years after 1957 (as confirmed in *Dialogue de l'ombre double* – see below).

The idea of treating only the first quatrain as an embellished vocal line, after having given a simpler statement of the whole sonnet (as if it were an exposition of the material) is justified by Boulez in terms of duration: *Improvisation III* would have lasted too long if work on the text had continued with quatrain 2 and tercets 1 and 2. This may well be so. On the other hand, it does tend to imply that the composer – perhaps influenced by his data-processing experiences with *Répons* – has introduced the idea of some kind of pre-existing 'programme', established in advance of the vocal treatment, and which inflects the first quatrain without any real need to pursue its demonstration.

A revised version of cummings ist der Dichter

This dates from 1986. Rather than complying with his intention (announced in 1970) of continuing the work, Boulez has altered the orchestration – and consequently, the writing. The number of voices has doubled (to a maximum of forty-eight); the orchestra comprises two flutes, oboe, cor anglais, two clarinets, bass clarinet, two bassoons, two horns, two trumpets, two trombones, bass tuba, three harps, three violins, two violas, two cellos and double bass. Without interfering with its structure or its expression, he has intensified both its depth and its resonance.

Dérive

This piece, which lasts about six minutes, was written at the end of 1984 to mark the occasion of Sir William Glock's retirement from the direction of the Bath Festival. (It will be remembered that Glock played a major part in securing Boulez's first important foreign appointment.)[3] The work 'derives' from *Répons* and is scored for flute, clarinet, violin, cello, vibraphone, and piano; as in many chamber works, the piano is given a leading role. The elements characteristic of Boulez's writing can here be seen at close quarters – in particular, the rapid figuration which comes to rest on a long trill ending on a rising formula. The choice of tempos has an arch-like symmetry:

```
Fig.  0–27 :  Prelude
      27–36 :  ♩ = 40
      36–40 :  ♪ = 72
      41–42 :  ♪ = 60
      43    :  ♪ = 66
      44    :  ♪ = 69
      45    :  ♪ = 76
      46–54 :  ♩ = 40
```

Dérive was first performed on 31 January 1985 by the London Sinfonietta, under the direction of Oliver Knussen.

Dialogue de l'ombre double

Although the title of this work is taken from Claudel (*Le Soulier de satin*), it was written for the sixtieth birthday of Luciano Berio, and first performed in Florence in October 1985 by Alain Damien and the Ensemble InterContemporain. Dated 28 October 1985, the work bears the inscription:

'chemin et domaines . . .
. . . domaines et chemins'

The inscription also refers to Boulez's own *Domaines* (*Chemin* being one of Berio's titles) – a work he has for some time wanted to revise and

3 See pp. 142–3.

'complexify'. In *Dialogue*, Boulez has retained certain characteristics from his 1968 work; two devices relating to route, and a direct reference to the material.

There are two possible versions – according to whether the path followed is that of the Arabic or Roman numerals:

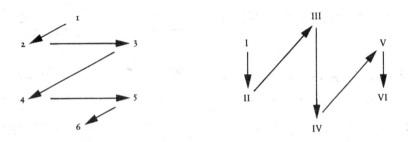

The piece (which can serve as a curtain-raiser to the present *Répons*) is a dialogue between the relayed sound of a clarinet, amplified and 'treated' by the 4X machine,[4] and a magnetic tape recorded by the player. The hall is plunged into almost total darkness as the work begins with the clarinettist's 'double' – an initial cipher in a 'hurried and mysterious whisper'. At the end of this first sequence, the light comes on, focusing on the soloist for his first entry – a series of trills, marked *assez vif, flexible, fluide*. He is answered by his 'double' and they continue to alternate – with various possibilities for longer or shorter dissolves from one to another. There are six pairings of this kind in all before the work ends with a final fast-moving cipher sequence for the 'double', marked *agité, mais murmuré*, and with the 'live' clarinet for the first time joining his taped partner on a sustained and uninterrupted soprano register C (a quotation from one of Berio's *Chemins*) – reinforcing his breath on the C intermittently attained by his taped double. The held note remains alone at the close, with sound and light fading concurrently as the instrumentalist leaves the platform.

Thus it can be seen that *Dialogue* is a somewhat theatrical piece – admittedly rather simple in its dramatization, but effective nonetheless. There is no stylistic difference between the writing of *Dialogue* and that of *Domaines*; only a minute portion of the material of the latter has been

4 As well as natural sound, the sound of the soloist is recorded through a microphone, then directed to a resonator sited behind him (in this case, an open piano). It is then re-recorded through another microphone, which conveys the sound to the 4X machine.

used in the new work – as if Boulez were here again putting forward the idea of a pre-existing programme whose partial unfolding leaves the potential for an entire piece of much greater dimensions (see *Improvisation III*/3, pp. 213–14 above).

There is little difference between the 'Roman' and 'Arabic' versions, although the different ordering of the sequences obviously changes the transitional cutting between the clarinettist and his 'double'. Listening to it, the work seems qualitatively worthy of its predecessor. It may not be the greatest Boulez, but it is certainly fine music, perhaps destined to open doors on the theatrical side, and in any case perfect for attracting an inexperienced yet exacting public.

Postscript

Notes for a portrait

Boulez has always been averse to the idea of any attempt at analysing his personality. It is not so much secretiveness on his part, but rather that he dislikes the thought of being circumscribed in this way. (This in itself would be one of the most salient features of any such attempt.)

In fact, he is remarkably prepared to accept criticism, and relishes disagreement. In situations where his opinions are challenged, he may jump to his feet to reply vehemently, ironically, even scornfully – but he does not reject the challenge. On the contrary, he seems to thrive on this sort of conflict. If, however, any more personally angled statement is made, or if anyone ventures comments upon his unconscious motivations, he regards this as completely unacceptable. He does not want his actions or pronouncements to be interpreted within a framework of explanations not formulated by him – in short, he resents any attempt to evaluate or (in Kantian terms) to judge him.

The intention here is simply, almost haphazardly, to note the recurring attitudes which have struck me during the writing of this book.

Parallels with Wagner

Boulez has written an impressive number of theoretical, aesthetic and polemical articles. He is in his element when giving interviews, airing his opinions in conversation, and making his position clear; his ability to encapsulate an idea within a formula is a godsend to journalists and historians.

The number of articles and other writings on Boulez the public figure far outweigh the relatively insignificant number on the composer, almost as if attention was deliberately being drawn away from the neglect of his music – an impression encouraged by the man himself.

He is proud, but not at all conceited, and has a wholly devoted circle of friends and relations. His knowledge of musical craftsmanship, of the work of performing musicians and of what an audience expects is profound. He is both patient and demanding towards performers. His instinct is to say nothing or to write what he cannot communicate more directly.

He is at home in the world of musical politics. He has shortcomings, enemies, and moments of unfairness; conversely he sometimes shows a misplaced confidence in others.

Lastly, through his (undiminished) output, his attitudes and his writings, he expresses the spirit of the age, and – like Wagner – an awareness of his own place in the history of music.

Feudalism

Boulez is at his best in his relationship with orchestral musicians – a relationship that has been described as a throw back to his student days.

Nevertheless, the same man who at one moment shows a boundless patience with players, is also capable of making highly provocative statements to journalists, declaring that orchestral musicians must be kept in their place, and not let loose for a single second, and saluting the Anglo-Saxon system which bristles with supervisory regulations . . .

It could be said in mitigation that Boulez differentiates between orchestral musicians in general – corporately ready to take advantage of any chance for relaxation – and the individual player who often shows a totally professional awareness, and even a dedication to Boulez reminiscent of the relationship between a devoted servant and his master.

Dictatorship

There is some truth in the claim that Boulez acts like a dictator. The institutions in which he takes an interest (the Domaine, various orchestras, IRCAM) all have to comply with the rules as laid down by him. He achieves results without recourse to extreme methods; nevertheless, at IRCAM for instance, he inspires a healthy respect. His relations with the personnel who work there are normally extremely cordial, though it must be admitted that the atmosphere is different when HE is there. It is not exactly that people feel intimidated (although everyone is anxious not to slip up). But there is a feeling of competitiveness, of (beneficial) tension and a sense of inspiration, stemming from Boulez's ability to arouse enthusiasm in those who work with him, and to provide the intellectual stimulus that makes people feel qualified for a task. The expression 'he brings out the best in you' is true, if trite: he has a natural aptitude for command. He also enables his acolytes to discover new potential within themselves. This may seem far-fetched, but has been experienced by those who work with him, and perhaps even by those whose encounters have been less direct, but who have become aware of the fascination Boulez can exert.

Freedom

Boulez gives his interpreters freedom, and except when conducting them, does not interfere with or judge their performances. To Yvette Grimaud, he wrote 'I have sent you the score of the Second Sonata. There are many superfluous indications – nuances, expression marks, etc. Once you have looked at them, don't trouble yourself further; they are only for the witless. *One should be able to play music almost without indications; do it just as you wish.*'[1]

This freedom sometimes enables his collaborators to take responsibility upon themselves. They are generally left in peace to carry out the task, even if eventually he may enquire as to the outcome. His reaction can then be harsh, at the very least, hasty – as the original team of IRCAM department heads undoubtedly found.

Anarchy

Boulez is both an orderly man and a revolutionary. He could also be called anarchic in the strictest sense of the word: that is, acknowledging only the discipline that comes from the inner self, without relying on others for the organization of one's purpose. Hence his inability to subscribe to any particular faction even while maintaining neighbourly relations with various successive authorities.

Because he is disciplined, he has a horror of disorder in the lives of others. Hence his rejection of the fashion for improvisation, for musical mixtures (free jazz), 'performance art', and even of 'happenings', all of which call into question the concept of the musical work itself, as also that of professionalism in composition or performance and ultimately, in the writing itself.

1 Personal correspondence; the phrase in italics was underlined by Boulez.

Tastes

Boulez's musical preferences are well known: the three Second Viennese composers, Stravinsky, Debussy, Wagner, some Bartók, and so on. When asked about his tastes he cites his discography. Should you then press him as to his tastes in non-orchestral music, the reply is equally predictable: Debussy's *Etudes*, Berg's Quartet, Op. 3, and numerous works of Webern. With regard to music of the past, the answer is more specific: the Art of Fugue, the St John Passion, the Missa Solemnis, the late Beethoven quartets, some Chopin, and so forth.

Sometimes he picks up a score that seems particularly relevant to his own work. He does not possess a record player, so presumably he does not play records.

Opera

While Boulez does not like opera as an institution he has a high regard for particular operas: *Pelléas*, *Lulu*, *Wozzeck*, some Wagner (from the *Ring* cycle onwards, and with a further weakness for *Meistersinger*, which he will never conduct), *Boris*, *Don Giovanni* and that is all. No Strauss, not even *Elektra*, not the Mozart of *Die Zauberflöte*, or the bitter-sweet comedies, nothing Italian, obviously nothing of the nineteenth-century French apart from Berlioz – and certainly not the would-be moderns of the twentieth century like Henze, Menotti, Zimmermann or others.

In fact he does not appear to like the operatic genre, the opera establishment, the opera audience or the operatic repertoire in general. He seems repelled by the second-hand emotions of this composite, debased, almost confused world where human tensions are both exacerbated and shallow, and where music has always to compromise with theatrical exigencies.

He had plans under way to write an 'opera' himself. Both the subject – an abstract consideration of treason – and the librettist (Jean Genet) were decided upon more than thirty years ago, but it now appears that the project has been put into abeyance.[2]

In black and white

Boulez's thinking is digital rather than analogical. Faced with the offer of a new reality, his reactions are immediate and decisive. He is at ease when confronted with opening-up processes as long as they have a practical application, and are approached successively as the need arises (like the

2 See p. 212.

reduction to binary selection, in performance, of a theoretical infinity of possibilities). Boulez thinks in terms of options rather than progressive evolution.[3]

Like most intellectuals, he is doubtless afflicted by uncertainty, self-questioning and irresolution, even if he hardly ever lets it appear so. He acts as he thinks – positively. Outwardly he gives an impression of resolution, mental alacrity, perseverance and self-justification – inwardly, one of evaluation, amendment, realism and self-criticism.

3 A distinction borrowed from a conversation with Andrew Gerszo.

PART TWO

COMMENTARIES

The second part of this book comprises twelve analytical introductions to Pierre Boulez's music. I have chosen works of which both the score and a commercial recording are readily available.[1] Of those obeying this criterion, I have however discarded works which were either undergoing revision (*Livre pour quatuor*, 1948), or were too incomplete (*cummings ist der Dichter*, 1970), or which seemed to me to be less decisive for a study of Boulez's development (*Structures* Book 2, 1962; *Messages-quisses*, 1977) than those selected. In any case, all these pieces, as well as those to be presented here, have been dealt with at some length in the first part of this book.

While the works chosen represent a range wide enough to include the essentials of Boulez's output, the purpose here is to present introductions rather than comprehensive analyses. I should say first that this under-taking is obviously based on my own study of the music and that judgements of a more general, aesthetic kind are expressed on this basis. The analytical background I describe does not claim to reveal the ultimate 'truth' of the works, but only to indicate the point at which I have arrived in my own understanding of them.

In my view, it is both necessary and rewarding to approach the composer's principle masterpieces by investigating them so as to get one's bearings from within, although this will involve some effort on the reader's part. The tables, diagrams and notes will require conscientious reading, sometimes a re-reading.

It seems to me that the main difficulty affecting the relationship between

[1] With the exception of the current *Répons*, which has not yet been recorded.

an audience, an individual and 'contemporary music' arises from a lack of awareness of musical timing. Sounds are heard without an awareness of how they relate to the musical narrative as a whole; the work seems impenetrable, and of indeterminate length; each event can be perceived only in relation to the one immediately preceding it, and one gains no impression of its overall form.

Because of this, I have generally sought to provide a visual counterpart to the aural experience of a work by means of a simplified diagram of events as they unfold, with reference to a scale of durations taken from a specific recording (there are, after all, not so many of them). These diagrams are in the nature of simplistic scores that may be followed even by the non-specialist music lover – if necessary with his stop-watch! I know that these diagrams are no substitute for the richness of the scores themselves, but at least they provide a means of focusing attention upon music which, by its very nature, tends to distract or mislead the listener. One might say that this is my own way of promoting audience participation in contemporary music!

I am aware, too, of writing for those anxious to get to know Boulez's scores more intimately. While some of my observations will strike more advanced students as elementary, the general reader will, I hope, find them an encouragement to further investigations.

In conclusion, I must again emphasize that this section is the result of my own study of the works, undertaken as carefully and as scrupulously as possible, with the help of my few predecessors in this field. Boulez himself has provided clarification on certain points, but the descriptions, as well as the judgements expressed, are my own. It is quite likely that his approach to these works, or that of other analysts, may be different from mine: there is no single correct view of so stimulating a subject.

Sonatine

FOR FLUTE AND PIANO

Composition: January 1946
First performance: Brussels, 1947; Jan van Boterdael (flute),
Marcelle Mercenier (piano)
Published: Amphion, 1954
Duration: *c* 13′–14′

Commissioned by the flautist Jean-Pierre Rampal (who never played it, finding the work incompatible with his own tastes), the *Sonatine* is the first complete work Boulez acknowledged as part of his catalogue. Following various student works (including the *Trois Psalmodies* for piano, 1945) and contemporary with the First Sonata and *Le Visage nuptial*, the *Sonatine* is a brilliant manifestation of a creative explosion which, shortly after the Second World War, was to mark Boulez out as the most important composer of his generation.

Along with the two other works just mentioned, the *Sonatine* completes the 'serial tryptich' of Boulez's output. Discovering Schoenbergian technique through the intermediary of René Leibowitz, he immediately seized upon it, while redefining it in his own terms. It was however on another level that the influence of Schoenberg was at first brought to bear.

AN ASSIMILATED FORM

In future years Boulez would seldom be heard to invoke the name of an important forebear, particularly in relation to form. Yet here, he cites both a composer and a particular work: the *Chamber Symphony* Op. 9 by Schoenberg. This acknowledged influence clearly has nothing to do with style: 'The *Chamber Symphony* is in a post-romantic idiom, and this aspect of it did not influence me at all.'[1]

Classical symphonic composers, above all the Viennese, had always cultivated a certain ambiguity in their instrumental music. The symphony or the sonata generally comprised four movements: an Allegro, a slow movement, a Scherzo (originally a Minuet), and a Finale. It happened that they concentrated most of their attention on the structure of the first movement. First-movement or sonata form structure follows a course which organizes two conflicting themes in relation to a certain number of harmonic constraints − [2] a formal design that itself comprises four clear stages: an exposition of the first and second themes and of the motifs connected with them, a modulatory development of these two themes, and finally a recapitulation of the whole of the thematic material according to the organization of the exposition. Hence one can see similarities between the way in which a whole sonata is divided into four movements, and the four-part division of a typical sonata-form structure.

Inevitably, both the larger and the smaller structures are characterized by their concern for coherence and unity − a cogent factor in any attempt to fuse them into one. Historically, a work like Beethoven's Sonata, Op. 110, had already moved in this direction, when the ideal of the classical sonata was still less than fifty years old. But it was Schubert's *Wanderer Fantasie* (1822), and later, Liszt's Sonata (1853) that were to point the way for a whole series of works seeking the unity of an instrumental discourse within the atmospheric diversity of a single, continuous movement.

The 'integrated form' of Boulez's *Sonatine* can be summed up as follows:

Introduction	the establishment of the series	1–31
Rapide	the exposition of the series and motif	32–96
Lent	paraphrase using trills	97–150
Tempo scherzando	with a trio in the form of cadenzas	151–341
Finale (rapide)	with introduction (cadenza)	342–495
Coda (lent)	symmetrical, harking back to the Introduction	495–510

---

1 *Conversations with Célestin Deliège*, p. 28.
2 See in particular Charles Rosen, *The Classical Style*, London, Faber, and New York, Norton, 1971.

THE MATERIAL: SERIES AND MOTIF

Before going ahead with a straightforward description of the *Sonatine*, it may be as well to mention the two fundamental elements governing its development: these are essentially a series of twelve notes and a three-note motif taken from it. This may give us some insight into the young composer's attitude to the series.

In the style of a declamatory recitative, the slow Introduction (bars 1–31) states these two types of basic material in a violent, non-functional manner. More precisely, the subject of the introduction is to establish the original series of the work (O) starting from the 'false statement' of the different series (FS) with which the work begins:[3]

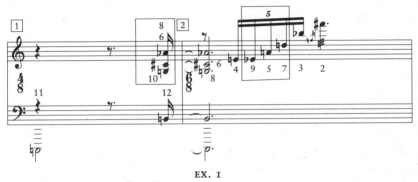

EX. I

The numbers given above the notes correspond to the pitches of the original or 'true' series, to be heard in its entirety only at the start of the first movement proper, as a theme on the flute:

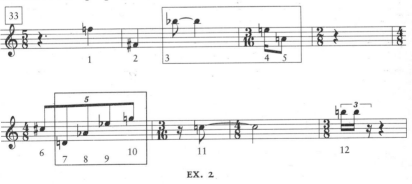

EX. 2

---

3 A similar procedure appears in the *Praeludium* from the Three Pieces for Orchestra, Op. 6, by Berg.

At the same time as announcing the initial 'false' series (FS), Boulez is already establishing a three-note motif consisting of a tritone (augmented fourth or diminished fifth), preceded or followed by an interval of a perfect fifth (or its inversion, a perfect fourth).

EX. 3A, 3B, 3C

Introducing his motif first as a chord (Ex. 3a), then as part of an anacrusis on the flute (Ex. 3b), the idea of later placing it at the start of the analogous answering motif (Ex. 3c) led him to discover the principle of a 'satisfactory succession': notes 3–7, preceded by 1 and 2, and followed naturally by 8 – all on the flute. Meanwhile, the piano will have completed the series with the missing notes 9–12, but still in a slightly 'erroneous' order (Ex. 3d). After the piano has repeated the elements of satisfactory succession (Ex. 3e) with the help of the same motif, it is left to the flute to complete the definitive series (Ex. 3f). We have thus moved from FS to O by means of a motif common to both, which will be used elsewhere in the *Sonatine*.

EX. 3D, 3E, 3F

THE DESIGN OF THE WORK

1. The slow Introduction (with chords, often arpeggiated, on the piano, and a free-style solo recitative on the flute) thus gradually establishes the original series with the aid of a motif drawn from it, and which forms the basis of the brief piano postlude.

2. The section marked *rapide* (bars 32–96) presents the serial theme of the work on the flute (Ex. 2). A twofold discourse for both instruments then unfolds, dense in style, and with an intensity that is harsh, even violent. The writing is reminiscent of the Three Pieces Op. 11, by Schoenberg, or sometimes (bars 85ff.) of Webern's *Variations* Op. 27 – using the piano as 'the very instrument of delirium', to use the composer's own expression.

3. The indication *très modéré, presque lent* signals the 'slow movement' of the *Sonatine* (or rather, a section of more relaxed character which in sonata form marks the second theme and its related motifs). This slow section is mainly concerned with a paraphrase built on the trill, at first for the piano (bars 97–115), then as a duo for both instruments (bars 116–40). This paraphrase is formed around a cantus firmus, with the notes of the trill successively adding up to the twelve notes of the original series transposed up a whole tone (G, G♯, C, F♯, B, D♯, E, B♭, F, A, D, C♯). This quasi-nocturnal section already emphasizes the composer's predilection for the middle-register sonority of the flute (cf. *Le Marteau sans maître*). Towards the end (bars 141–50), changes in the style of writing and the tempo prepare for the *scherzando* that follows.

4. The *tempo scherzando* (bars 151–341) is the most 'developed' section of the *Sonatine*. Interrupted half way through by a much freer succession of cadenzas for the two instruments, it is a kind of toccata based mainly on the exploitation of the motif shown in Ex. 1, which appears no less than fourteen times during the first part of the *scherzando* alone (bars 151–94). The flute line is astonishingly repetitive, emphasizing the interval of a third, and the writing for both instruments is extremely virtuosic, particularly in the third part of the *scherzando*. This is not only because of the difficulties inherent in the relationship between pitch and tempo, but also because of the continual changes in the level of tension affecting the scale of dynamics, which move constantly between *forte subito* and *piano subito*.

After this exhausting passage, the two instruments are allowed a brief respite at the centre of the *scherzando*, in the form of a short-lived relaxation of the tempo, followed by a pause. The *subito tempo scherzando* indicated in the score is only an illusion. For the time being, the *scherzando* tempo has given way to the succession of cadenzas already mentioned: flute cadenzas on a base of piano trills, a violent cadenza for the piano, and a dialogue between the two – ending with a reprise of the original series on the piano, written in octave-avoiding minor ninths:

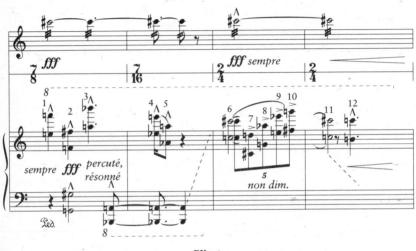

EX. 4

The toccata-like *tempo scherzando* resumes, carrying the two performers along in an atmosphere of even greater tension. There is a brief pause on a short flute cadenza (bars 294–5), before the section recommences, this time *legato* and *piano* rather than *staccato* and *forte*. The effect is striking: the music seems about to fade, before reasserting the wide-stretched intervals, the brilliance (but this time as *legato* as possible), and the powerful dynamics and accentuation which now leads the *scherzo* towards its apotheosis.

5. The finale of the work begins effectively in bar 341 and is reminiscent of the long cadenza for the two soloists at the start of the third movement of Berg's *Chamber Concerto*. The finale of the *Sonatine* also starts with a long and relatively restrained cadenza for the piano, later joined by the flute, before the music broadens out, and the finale proper begins abruptly in bar 379.

This is a *mouvement perpétuel* that starts precipitously with the indication (bar 340) *très progressivement de plus en plus rapide et tourbillant jusqu'à la mesure 474 (extrêmement rapide).* This spectacular section anticipates the keyboard writing of the Second Sonata, with a breadth and a tension that reaches a point of ultimate resistance when strongly accented chords on the piano make the flute almost inaudible.

6. The coda returns to the *andante* indication of the opening *très modéré, presque lent.* This section is in some ways even more of a summing up of what has gone before than the preceding one – even though the latter has a recapitulatory position: with its trills around a single B flat as a reminder of the cantus firmus from the slow movement, with the series harmonized in minor ninths (as in the *scherzando*), and with its piano chords finally restating the motif from Ex. 1, and with a closing gesture that echoes the beginning of the finale.

THE LESSONS OF THE *SONATINE*

It is reasonable to assume that a composer's first opus may well represent something of a bridge between inheritance and innovation. This is certainly true with regard to the *Sonatine.* We have already spoken of its antecedents; its innovative aspects are also clearly apparent. The aggressive sound of this duo came as a shock to those expecting a more traditionally pastoral, even elegiac work in this medium. Its astringent rhythmic atmosphere constitutes a radical reappraisal of conventional ideas about 'tempo'. The metre changes with every bar, so overriding any notion of regularity and making barlines superfluous except for reading or ensemble purposes. Serial technique is used only up to the point where it begins to conflict with imagination; Boulez was already thinking of the series more as a reservoir of intervals and of potential functions than as a straightforward succession of pitches. Finally, despite the difficulties involved, it reveals an instrumental affinity that has since become typical of the composer.

2

First Sonata for Piano

Composition: 1946
First performance: Paris (RTF), 1946; Yvette Grimaud
Published: Amphion, 1951
Duration: 4'25"+4'30" (as played by Klára Körmendi)

This work comprises two movements of similar length (*Lent*; *Assez large/ rapide*). While the first movement is generally evasive in character and restrained in dynamic range, its basically slow-moving background pulse admits figures that are faster, more headstrong, and often powerfully expressed. As these figures take on a greater continuity, the movement intermittently starts to resemble a toccata.

The second movement reverses these basic ideas. Leaving aside its introductory section for the moment, this movement is basically a toccata. Seemingly inspired by the toccata-like forays of the first movement, its progress is several times interrupted by figures that are again relaxed in tempo and dynamics but which show a marked melodic continuity (unlike those in the preceding movement).

This opposition, or apposition, of the two movements is characteristic of the whole Sonata. The fact that the Sonata has only two movements further emphasizes the duality which, since Beethoven (and particularly the Beethoven of the two-movement Op. 111) has constructed the sonata as an essentially 'combative' form. Here, the tension arising within as well as between movements (contrasted tempos, different types of writing) creates a similar sense of conflict.

THE SERIES, THE INTERVAL, AND MODES OF ATTACK
IN THE FIRST MOVEMENT

Even without going into a detailed analysis of an already complex work, we can still explore some of the devices characteristic of Boulez's writing. The start of the first movement comprises an initial proposition:

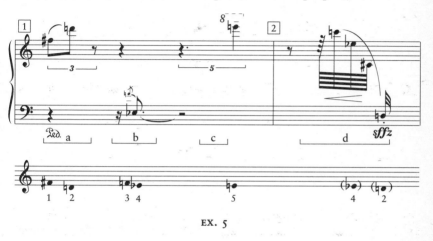

EX. 5

Four different gestures may be distinguished here:

a a melodic interval (in this case a sixth) expressed in equal note-lengths
b a grace-note up-beat preceding a held note
c an isolated note placed in a high register
d a rapid flurry ending in a sforzando

It will already be obvious that the first three almost static gestures contrast with the dynamism of the fourth. This microcosmic opposition mirrors that governing this movement, and also the macrocosm of the Sonata as a whole.

In a less obviously audible way, the first three gestures are also at variance with the fourth, in that they constitute the start of a series (the first five notes), while gesture *d* belongs to another structure[1] – so interrupting the series by repeating its third and fourth pitches. This second method of organization provides a new and continuing source of conflict between those elements in the First Sonata which comply with the Schoenbergian system of pitch serialization, and those which contest the

---

1 For clarification the reader should here refer to Charles Rosen's article, 'The Piano Music' in *Pierre Boulez: A Symposium*, London, Eulenburg, 1986, p. 85ff. (trans.).

system by means of a group of devices in which attacks, motifs, and the play of intervals take precedence.

As it happens, the series begun at the outset of the work is left stranded at the end of the first bar (Ex. 5), not to be completed until bars 15–16.

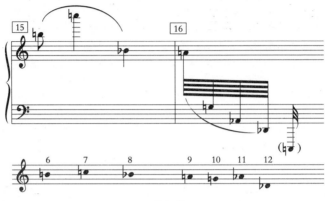

EX. 6

The dodecaphonic idea is thus seen to be broken up and separated by time. On the other hand, the succession *a-b-c-d* reappears *en bloc*, several times repeated, as in bars 69–70 (allocating different pitches to the four gestures in no way alters their character):

EX. 7

This is the start of the first movement's development section. In the same way, by allotting different registers to this succession of gestures, and by slightly varying the direction (ascending/descending) of its constituents, the start of the recapitulation is obtained:

EX. 8

Finally, the way in which Boulez reconciles the strictness of serial technique with the freer principles of motivic organization is illustrated by the coda to this first movement (bars 106–10: see Ex. 9).

Starting from the middle register downwards, then upwards, a huge arpeggiated chord brings the four elements *a-b-c-d* into play one last time (in the order *d-a-b-c*), with an alternative *b* consisting of a minor second sustained low in the bass. By thus announcing eleven of the twelve notes of the original series, the movement seems at an end.

But then, in a coda to the coda, the missing tenth note (G) is heard at the extreme top of the instrument, afterwards converted into a descending spiral reminiscent of *d*. Here the composer demands a *diminuendo*, without pedal, after which the performer must convey the succeeding silence.

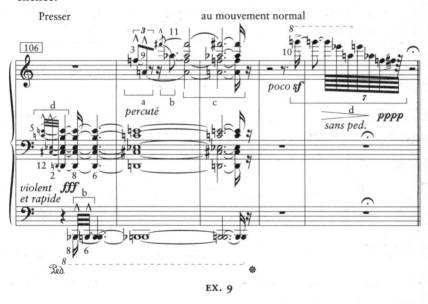

EX. 9

All these examples show how Boulez (at this time influenced by both Webern and Messiaen) reconstructed form by using intervals (the sixth and the third) dynamics (*piano*, *forte*, *sforzando*), durations and attacks (equal value notes, notes preceded by grace-notes, single notes, 'rocket-like' flurries). The opening succession *a-b-c-d*, with its possible variations, is a unifying factor throughout the movement.[2] The formal organization of the first movement is as follows:

2 Notably bars 1–12 or 101–3.

THE SECOND MOVEMENT

While the second movement may be composed with a bias towards strongly melodic interpolations, it can also be understood as a statement (bars 1–10) followed by its embellished commentary (from bar 11), rather like the second movement of the Second Sonata (see pp. 245 ff.). Written in a pointillistic style *à la* Webern (the *Symphony* Op. 21, in particular), the opening statement announces the series later to be commented upon.

This difficult toccata is played *staccato*, in a fast tempo, and within a wide range of dynamics that constantly change. While its contrapuntal character is clearly affirmed, passages of more relaxed writing introduce a succession of extremely elegant arabesques revealing an unsuspected lyricism.

Once past the opening measures, silence plays almost no part in the movement until the final page – notably in the last two bars, which act both as a reminder of the material of the first movement and a final homage to the crucial interval (the third or the sixth) of the Sonata:

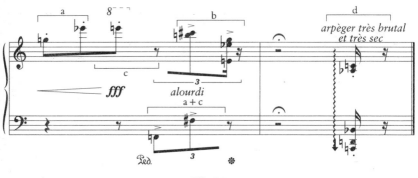

EX. 10

THE KEYBOARD WRITING

Boulez has openly admitted the direct influence on his keyboard writing in the Sonata of the Three Pieces, Op. 11, by Schoenberg, and especially the third – 'for the enormous density of its texture and the violence of its expression', he explains.[3] In fact, the affinity is more on the level of composition and of rhetoric than on that of traditionally pianistic expression. With Schoenberg, the heir of Brahms, one finds an accumulative style based on the octave and often filled out by chords; with Boulez, there is a much greater transparency, reminiscent of Webern.

On the other hand, what is striking about Boulez's score is the sheer number of different kinds of attack (*incisif, sec, très léger, très violent, très sec*, etc.), while the second movement constitutes an unremitting incitement to an acceleration of the tempo: *rapide, à peine moins rapide, accelerando, pressez, pressez un peu plus, plus vif* . . .

Thus the piano writing, even more than that of the *Sonatine*, suggests the feeling of 'instrumental delirium' described by the composer. At the same time, there are aspects of the Sonata as a whole which make it a pointer to the more lyrical works that were to follow.

3 *Conversations with Célestin Deliège*, p. 30.

Second Sonata for Piano

Composition: 1948
First performance: Paris, 29 April 1950; Yvette Grimaud
Published: Heugel, 1950
Duration: 32'00" (Boulez's score);
27'32" (Helffer, version 2); 29'15" (Pollini)

The following table gives a more detailed breakdown of the differences between the three timings listed above:

Movement	Boulez	Helffer	Pollini
1 *Extrêmement rapide*	7'30"	5'40"	5'57"
2 *Lent*	11'00"	10'15"	11'08"
3 *Modéré, presque vif*	2'30"	2'05"	2'10"
4 *Vif*	11'00"	9'22"	10'00"

An important early work by Boulez, the Second Sonata has already acquired the ambiguous status of a 'classic' as the result of numerous public performances and several recordings. But this does not make it any the less astonishing. In the first place, its half-hour duration is unusual in Boulez's chamber music (with the exception of *Le Marteau sans maître*), and puts it in the same category as the great sonatas of the repertoire, notably those of Beethoven.

It is also remarkably vehement. Apart from the second movement and the coda to the fourth, an eruptive violence pervades most of the Sonata. The piano writing is traditional as regards the techniques used to produce the notes. However, in terms of sheer virtuosity, the demands made by

Boulez upon his interpreter are formidable. The Second Sonata is a veritable touchstone for virtuosity – though few take on the challenge.

What is perhaps most striking about this work is its technical assurance. The Second Sonata is its composer's first truly post-serial work; rather than rejecting serialism out of hand, it brings the series into play on another organizational level: 'In the Second Sonata I simply broke with the "concept" of the Schoenbergian series. What then attracted me to the manipulation of the twelve notes was the idea of giving them a motivic and thematic sense in relation to some of the functions they are made to assume in this work.'[1] This will be further clarified by a more careful consideration of the score.

SERIALISM: FOR OR AGAINST SONATA FORM?

Outwardly, the design of the first movement resembles that of classical sonata form:

1 Exposition	1–159	theme A and its development	1–40
		theme B and its development	41–67
		reprise of A	69–127
		reprise of B	129–159

2 Development   161–167
3 Recapitulation 168ff

Though I have indicated these landmarks, their implications are inevitably seriously weakened, because although serial organization has its own logic, it obviously does not correspond precisely to the logic resulting from the play of tonality over the distance traditionally defined as sonata form. The above formal definitions are justified by certain characteristics and not at all by others.

At the start, an initial serial statement is launched in a strikingly peremptory manner – *extrêmement rapide*. This seems to conflict with Boulez's declaration that 'This sonata squarely renounces the dodecaphonic point of view and the formulations which ensue from it. No initial series is to be found here, either at the level of pitch or of rhythm'[2] (see Ex. 11). This initial series is repeated almost identically at the start of the third movement (see Ex. 12).

It is here worth noting the modification Boulez imposes on his series between the first and the third movement: the original series is broken up

1 *Conversations with Célestin Deliège*, p. 40.
2 Goléa, op. cit., pp. 82–3.

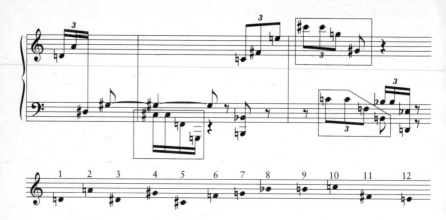

EX. II

EX. 12

into three groups, with additional pitch permutations within one of the permutated groups.

Variation plays a vital part in the serial (and, more generally, the musical) treatment of the Second Sonata, gradually transforming the original material into a succession of non-recognizable elements. Among the initially recognizable elements, three cells figure in particular:

(*a*) a cell of four equal-value notes, characterized by the repetition of the first note (boxed in Ex. 12). This cell can itself be varied (the final triplet in bar 3);

(*b*) the trill, which in this movement intervenes like a nervous tic, and which will later be seen as the pre-echo of a figure fundamental to the fourth movement;

(*c*) from the fourth bar onwards, a well-known cryptogram appears – an anagram of the letters B A C H, also to be found in the coda to the fourth movement. It appears at the same time as the first entry of the afore-mentioned trill:

EX. 13

These various small cells are at variance with the linear arrangement of the series from which they are derived, so allowing the composer to pursue his development by means of both melodic and rhythmic variation. By referring to the initial serial statement shown in Ex. 11, it can be seen that the series subdivides into groups of different notes in a succession that is, itself, 'serial':

One note: pitch 4
Two notes: pitches 8 and 9
Three notes: pitches 1, 2 and 3
Four notes: pitches five (repeated), 6 and 7

Then, once this arithmetical series has been expressed, the composer seizes upon one particular group – the three-note one – using it to complete his dodecaphonic series (10–11–12), before launching into a triplet variation of the same figure in bar 3. This simple example illustrates the strong connections between this music of necessity and an art based on freedom: a freedom in the use of the series is balanced by a necessity to observe – not so much a 'serial catechism' – but rather, the demands of serialism in compositional thought.

Finally, in relation to the musical curve, one cannot fail to be seduced by the violent elegance of this opening statement, with its two successive affirmations – the 'initial catastrophe' (bars 1–2) and the contrasting 'conquest of the keyboard' which follows (bars 2–3), and which seems like a variation on the first. However one describes it, the coherence of this first phrase evokes the balance and completeness of the opening phrase of Berg's Piano Sonata.

The first section closes with a long trill in the bass, a trill which is doubled and then tripled (bars 38–40). After this hallucinatory start, a moment's respite leads to a sequence of high-register chords in longer note-values which create a lull – even though the tempo marking is now *encore plus vif*.[3] According to Boulez himself, this is 'a kind of a second theme' – like Beethoven's use of a similar device in his *Waldstein* Sonata:

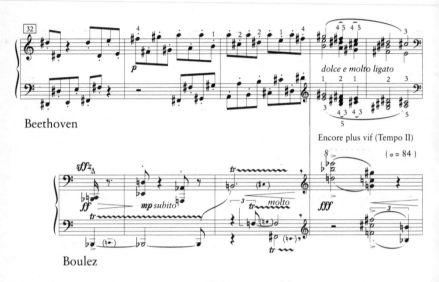

Beethoven

Boulez

EX. 14

Note the preponderance of octave-avoiding intervals (the major second and minor ninth), which should be interpreted as the subconscious result of his study of Webern, rather than a deliberate observance of one of the fundamental rules of serial composition.

The repeat of the opening material (bar 69) is indicated by an explicit return to *tempo 1*, with the recurring three-note groups becoming entangled with the groups of four (the motif with the initial note repeated) as the leading cell undergoes a subtle serial variation (see Ex.15).

The reprise of the second theme (bar 129) is more clearly marked than the first. The reprise as a whole is notably expansive in its violently exuberant character – with shapes and phrases derived from the original series sometimes locked into vehemently punctuating chords (as in bars 106ff. and in 121–2), often contracted into trills. This expanded reprise seems to act as an embellished variation of the exposition – a role

3 The beginning of the sixth movement of the *Lyric Suite* by Berg offers a similar example of cinematic illusion. See also *Don* from *Pli selon pli* (pp. 311–12).

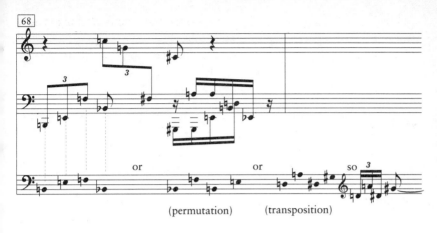

(permutation)   (transposition)

EX. 15

somewhat analogous to the second part of the slow movement in relation to its initial proposition (see p. 248).

The brief development (bars 161–7) is less the development of the preceding exposition than of a latent idea: the writing here is completely homogeneous and new. By contrast with the preceding small cells and violent chords, this is four-part polyphony; based on a simple isorhythm, it is played *piano* and very *legato* in the top register of the instrument, and lies very awkwardly for the hands. This silky, curiously unschematic passage is unique within the Sonata.

The recapitulation is marked by a return to *tempo 1* (bars 168ff.), reiterating the descending gesture which characterized the beginning of the Sonata but without taking up the original serial and motivic ideas. There is now only the merest trace of the second theme (bar 172). Moreover, this recapitulation is much shorter than the exposition, as if Boulez was deliberately applying the principle of progressive elision of recognizable contours to the form itself. The overall sense of balance and resolution becomes apparent only when the listener has familiarized himself with the movement.

THE SECOND MOVEMENT

This extremely fine movement contains much sumptuous writing for the instrument, with the composer's melodic gift much in evidence.

Standing as the '*andante*' of the Sonata, the second movement is built mainly from a proposition and its embellished commentary. It is worth analysing this eight-bar proposition in some detail, in order to understand the origins of Boulez's compositional technique. In it, he appears somewhat self-consciously to submit to classical values (though remember that the bar-lines are only a visual guide). With its Webernesque outlines, this eight-bar proposition follows a strict programme:

(*a*) a series of twelve notes which is to recur at the start of the fourth movement – like that of the first at the start of the third:

EX. 16

(*b*) two types of resonance: short, and sustained (although the notes with dots are never shorter than a semi-*staccato*);
(*c*) two types of configuration: an isolated note, and a group of two notes (heard either simultaneously or with one as an anacrusis to the other);
(*d*) a compound element of a dotted quaver tied to three dotted semiquavers; this is to be one of the elements of the fugue in the fourth movement. It appears twice as a symmetrically inverted configuration, shown clearly in superposition here:

EX. 17

Each of the two figures is the mirror version of the other, with an interval of a whole tone (or a minor ninth) at the centre and with avoided octaves (major ninths or minor seconds) on either side;
(*e*) three types of register band (narrow, broad, and medium) and three types of register (high, medium, and low).

This eight-bar proposition which divides into three fragments (of 3, 2½ and 2½ bars respectively) can then be reconstructed from these various, sometimes overlapping, parameters:

Section one

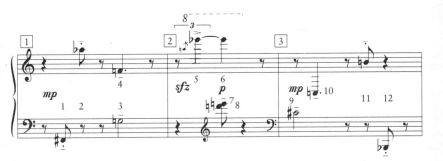

EX. 18

Pitches: the series, see Ex. 16
Attacks: 'points' (bars 1 and 3) versus 'blocks' (bar 2)
           mirror symmetries of detached notes (pitches 1 and 2, 12 and
           11) and sustained notes (pitches 3 and 4, 10 and 9)
Registers: medium (bar 1)
           high, in close position (bar 2)
           low, wide-spaced (bar 3)

Section two

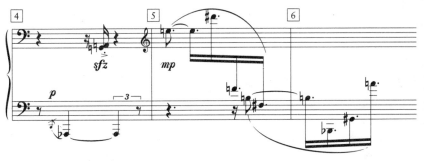

EX. 19

The differentiation of the preceding elements gives rise to a number of problems. On the serial level, these two-and-a-half bars introduce a new series, but one which maintains strict relations with the preceding one:

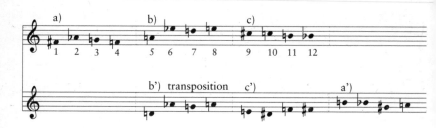

EX. 20

The new series is a plagiarized version of the first, with a permutation of its three fragments. The first four-note group of the new series is a simple transposition at the fifth of pitches 5–8 from the first series; the second group is a slightly permutated version of the chromatic cell which defined the third group (pitches 9–12) of the preceding series; the third group of the new series is a perceptible, but minimal, variation of the remaining cell from the first series (pitches 1–4). This is yet another indication of the process of dissolving and restructuring motifs which is fundamental to the composition of the Sonata as a whole.

On the level of attacks, the second section is at first (bar 4) characterized by an increase both in resonance and in the number of different configurations – both unaccented sustained notes and *staccato* blocks. The two dotted-semiquaver formulae already mentioned are now entwined and linked together, serving as prototypes for all the broadly developed melodic lines of the movement.

Finally, there are two types of register configuration:

(*a*) a narrow bass register (bar 4);
(*b*) a broad register centred around a medium tessitura (bar 5 and the beginning of 6).

Section three

EX. 21

The third section of the initial proposition accentuates the difference in register that had already marked the second in relation to the first, forming a fine close to the phrase.

From the serial point of view, this section proffers a third series which continues increasingly to distance itself from the first:

EX. 22

This includes notes (in brackets) which are repeated at the octave (a crime of lèse-Schoenberg!). One has to concentrate on the idea of intervallic variations and permutations if one is to maintain the image of a recognizable series, although the chromatic cell remains clearly present.

Meanwhile, there is a reprise of the attacks and increased resonances – the detached or *tenuto* notes of bar 6, and the sustained notes preceded by an appoggiatura of bar 8. Between these two is a *legato* melodic complex which is evidently a reminder of the phrase from bar 5: the variation process is already under way even within the initial proposition.

Another feature is Boulez's use of contrasting registers: the broad register band of bar 6 is set against the narrow register band of bar 7 (although both exploit the whole width) and, as the sound dies away, the eventual outcome of bar 8 draws attention towards the medium register with which the phrase began.

I have dwelt on this opening proposition at some length, without attempting a level of analysis more properly left to the composer. While what I have given here is little more than a description, this preliminary study shows that the initial proposition contains in embryo the whole syntax to be developed in the greatly embellished variation that follows. It also emphasizes the simplicity of the means used by Boulez, as well as providing the theoretical and descriptive material from which the reader can satisfy his or her curiosity by analysing the whole movement. This huge, free variation – by turn exploiting the assembled material and inserting unrelated embellishing elements – seems to me to result from the tension of the creative act itself, through the dialectical conflict between necessity and freedom that it maintains with the initial proposition. With Boulez, variation is not merely a matter of skilled procedures used to modify the appearance of initial material; it is much more an invitation to exploration, adventure and discovery – in other words, to creation. This movement is a quest for the unknown, an initiatory process, a mystical – even erotic – experience.

Sometimes a parenthesis temporarily interrupts the flow of sound, and another type of organization takes over. Then the parenthesis is closed and the thread of the discourse resumed as if with new vigour, together with its original tempo, register, and expressive character:

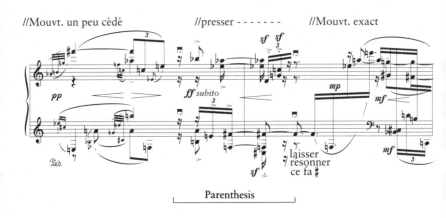

EX. 23

Such parentheses, already present in the Boulez of 1948, are to become part of the theoretical structure for the aleatory works of which the Third Sonata (1957) is the archetype.

There are other significant landmarks in this movement. At the end of the first variation (bars 9–28) there is a kind of reprise (bars 29–44), interrupted by a number of pauses, which makes way for exactly the kind of parenthesis just mentioned. This is followed by a central section (bars 45–67) that presents a succession of mirror procedures – that is, comparable elements symmetrically placed on either side of a vertical axis – stretched over a wide register and built entirely on the avoided octave (bars 59ff.). A long *crescendo* reaches a climax that Boulez marks *très sonore*. In the second part of the movement (bars 68–97), the melodic cells multiply by diminution, imparting a restlessness to the whole passage. Then the pauses reappear, breaking up the vehemence of the discourse to return to the calmer lyricism of the first part. A cadenza in a faster tempo makes one last attempt to draw together the threads of the debate but the mood remains eloquently relaxed. An eight-bar coda arrives almost imperceptibly to restate the separate elements of the initial proposition in reverse.

THE THIRD MOVEMENT

'The third movement is much more conventional. Here I tried to combine variation and scherzo form. This was one of the last remnants of classicism with which I felt able to experiment in the world of form'[4] Boulez's laconic summing up of this three minute movement renders prolonged comment superfluous.

Nevertheless, this brief interlude serves ideally to reaffirm the overall argument of the Sonata between the comparative relaxation of the second movement and the somewhat spasmodic introduction to the last. What is striking is the conflict between its formal development in space (four scherzo sections, alternating with three trios) and the way in which it is constricted in time.

This arrangement of four scherzos and three trios is reminiscent of the tavern scene in the second act of *Wozzeck* (even though that scene is the most developed of the whole opera). Boulez's movement contrasts a very lively sequence of detached notes or chords with sequences that are *légèrement au dessous*, that is, slightly slower than the main tempo as well as being legato and in longer values. This imparts to the three trios a more pronounced melodic character, as may be seen from the score.

I have already mentioned that the series as used in the scherzo sections

4 *Conversations with Célestin Deliège*, p. 41.

reverts mainly to that of the first movement (Ex. 12); the serial plan of the movement as a whole is as follows:

A1 Scherzo 1 original series
B   Trio 1
A2 Scherzo 2 retrograde inversion of the series
C   Trio 2
A3 Scherzo 3 different series, identical rhythm
D   Trio 4
A4 Scherzo 4 retrograde of original series, transposed
                        upwards by a semitone

It seems that this 'divertimento' was composed earlier than the rest of the Sonata, then incorporated into it. This is underlined by the movement's occasionally Bartókian character (noted by Claude Helffer).

THE FOURTH MOVEMENT

This imposing movement is intellectually demanding, but nonetheless stimulating for those prepared to make the effort to come to terms with it. As to its ground plan, it is made up as follows:

Introduction 1–33
Fugue   34–67, stretto at bar 59ff.
Rondo   68–221
Coda   222–235

Its original serial material is derived from the initial series of the second movement – like that of the third from the first:

Très librement, avec de brusques oppositions de mouvement et de nuances

EX. 24

Again, it will be seen that, in this Sonata, the Boulezian series is not an imperative order of succession, but rather a reservoir of intervals and microstructures made to evolve freely, both horizontally and vertically.

Most importantly, it is really the rhythmic organization that sets up the 'introductory' content of the introduction in relation to the fugue. This is not in fact a thematic fugue, but a rhythmic one, based on five motifs: These form the subject of the rhythmic fugue:

Motif	Rhythm		Ex. from introduction	Possible variants	Ex. from Fugue subject
a		up-beat to single note	bar 3		
b		four equal quavers	bars 9-10		
c		incomplete triplet	bar 1		
d		crotchet, three unequal notes	bar 30		
e		triplet, two equal notes	bar 26		

EX. 25

Sans timbre, sans nuances, très lié

EX. 26

In the tradition of Stravinsky and Messiaen, these 'rhythmic characters' are thus to have their own existence in the fugue, and to 'energize' the entire counterpoint independently of the pitches that embody them.

Motif *a* has been present since the second movement of the Sonata (see p. 247). Other stylistic gestures, such as the trill that pervades the introduction, or the dry, percussive semiquaver counterpoints, have also become almost familiar figures; these contribute to the tense dynamism of the piece to such an extent that the beginning of the fugue creates an effect of relaxation – or at least of contemplation: the intensity has decreased and *legato* prevails. A simple summary of the expressive indications in the fugue is as good as any description:

Bar 1	Introduction	*Tempo I (Vif,* ♩ = 104*). Très librement, avec de brusques oppositions de mouvements et de nuances*
Bar 34	Fugue	*Tempo II (Très modéré, mais sans traîner,* ♪ = 104*). Sans timbre, sans nuances, très lié.*
Bar 36		(♪ = 126). *Articuler le plus nettement possible la construction, malgré les registres étendus*
Bar 47		*Tempo III (Modéré – plus vite que très modéré,* ♪ = 152*).*
Bar 59	(stretto)	*Tempo IV (Modéré, très allant,* ♪ = 176*), des nuances très fines, dans une grisaille sonore.*
Bar 68	Rondo Theme	

Much in the manner of the second movement, the rondo section of the fourth is presented as a proposition (bars 68–83) and its extended commentary (84–221). The proposition is simple, linear, monodic, and set within the dynamic range of an 'exacerbated' *forte* – continuing the extravagant demands of the preceding stretto. While the commentary quickly reinstates the contrapuntal play, it nevertheless begins less dynamically than the previous section: *très léger, pas d'attaques profondes, à peu près sans pedale.*

The course of the rondo is marked by a progressive and relentless increase in both dynamics and speed, culminating in the widely distended register range marking the climax of the movement (bars 212–15) – where the indication to 'pulverize the sound' is self-explanatory.

Thus, a classical form is seized by an almost expressionistic frenzy, and with a violence that forces submission. The composer here asks for the utmost force, without nuance – demanding a degree of commitment from performer and audience alike, which stretches their respective capacities to the very limit.

At the indication *sans élargir* the discourse breaks off abruptly, and the Coda begins. This final page of total calm serves not only as Coda to the movement but to the Sonata as a whole. The tempo moves from slow to very slow, with minor fluctuations; the dynamic stays between *mezzo-piano* and *pianissimo*, with only the briefest increase to *mezzo-forte*. Two structures are superimposed: the first is formed from an echo of the first four cells from the Fugue, again in a linear succession (bar 1), the second from the omnipresent B A C H figure (which returns no less than six times on this page, up to and including the final cadence) that punctuates the polyphonic apotheosis represented by this Sonata and by serial thinking in general (Ex. 27).

It seems relatively insignificant that the four rhythmic motifs announced here constitute a series of twelve notes, since it has no connection with the other series of the Sonata – although the B A C H motif can be traced to the chromatic fragments that form part of each of the series from the second movement. In this encounter between structure and coded narrative we find something akin to the mysterious combination of means that enabled Berg – in his Concerto 'To the memory of an angel' – to introduce the component notes of Bach's chorale 'Es ist genug' alongside the original series of his own work. It would be impossible to imagine a more eloquent conclusion.

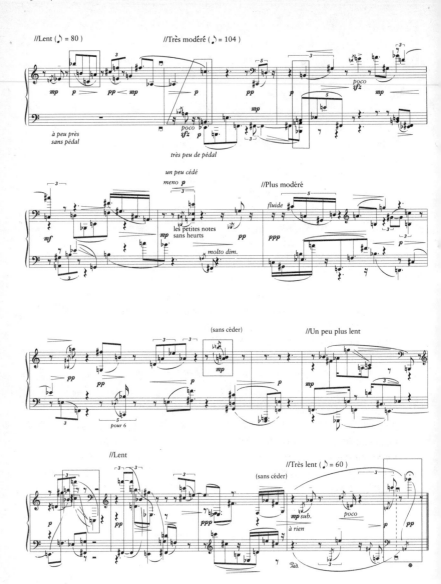

EX. 27

4

Le Soleil des eaux

Based on settings of words by René Char,[1] this work underwent four successive stages:

> *Le Soleil des eaux* 1: incidental music for the radio programme of the same name. Workshop for creative radio (RTF); broadcast April 1948.
> *Le Soleil des eaux* 2: cantata formed from a revision of the above, with the addition of a second movement (*La Sorgue*). For three vocal soloists (S.T.B.) and chamber orchestra; first performance: 18 July 1950, at the Théâtre des Champs-Elysées, under Désormière.
> *Le Soleil des eaux* 3: as version 2, with the addition of mixed (S.T.B.) chorus, and full symphony orchestra; first performance: Darmstadt, 1958, under Ernest Bour. Published: Heugel, 1968.
> *Le Soleil des eaux* 4: for soprano soloist, mixed (S.A.T.B.) chorus, and orchestra; first performance: Berlin, October 1965, Berlin Philharmonic Orchestra, Philharmonia Chorus, Catherine Gayer, under Boulez. Published: Heugel, 1968. Duration: *c* 8'00"

As details of the first three versions are given in the first part of this book, I shall deal here exclusively with the fourth – which the composer calls the definitive version.

As it now stands, *Le Soleil des eaux* has two movements: *Complainte du lézard amoureux* and *La Sorgue*.

---

1 Copyright: Editions Gallimard.

COMPLAINTE DU LEZARD AMOUREUX

Char's poem is mostly sung by the soloist as an unaccompanied monody, following the overall plan given below. There are seven stanzas (quatrains), of which Boulez reverses the order of stanzas 5 and 6.

> *N'égraine pas le tournesol,*
> *Tes cyprès auraient de la peine,*
> *Chardonneret, reprends ton vol*
> *Et reviens à ton nid de laine.*
>
> *Tu n'es pas un caillou du ciel*
> *Pour que le vent te tienne quitte,*
> *Oiseau rural; l'arc-en-ciel*
> *S'unifie dans la marguerite.*
>
> *L'homme fusille, cache-toi;*
> *Le tournesol est son complice.*
> *Seules les herbes sont pour toi,*
> *Les herbes des champs qui se plissent.*
>
> *Le serpent ne te connaît pas,*
> *Et la sauterelle est bougonne;*
> *La taupe, elle, n'y voit pas;*
> *Le papillon ne hait personne.*
>
> *Il est midi, chardonneret,*
> *Le séneçon est là qui brille.*
> *Attarde-toi, va, sans danger:*
> *L'homme est rentré dans sa famille!*
>
> *L'écho de ce pays est sûr.*
> *J'observe, je suis bon prophète;*
> *Je vois tout de mon petit mur,*
> *Même tituber la chouette*
>
> *Qui, mieux qu'un lézard amoureux,*
> *Peut dire les secrets terrestres?*
> *O léger gentil roi des cieux,*
> *Que n'as-tu ton nid dans ma pierre!*

Opposite is a diagram of the whole of the first movement. As I see it, this movement exploits a kind of antiphony between voice and orchestra, the latter supporting the former only for the second stanza and part of the seventh; from time to time there are other short overlaps which my graphic design could indicate only at the cost of a serious distortion of the time scale.

Soloist	1 2 3	4 5 6	7
Orchestra	▬ ▬ ▬	▬ ▬	▬
Figures	2 3 6	8 11	15
Timing	0′ 1′	2′ 2′25″ 3′	3′50″
Tempo	A rall.	BA BA	
Dynamics	*mp*...... *ff*>*pp* *pp*	*ff*>*mp* *p* <*f*>*p* *pp*	

Two main tempos, or rather, two overall tempo scales are at work here: a moderate tempo (A) which may be slightly slowed down or speeded up, and a brief fast tempo (B). These tempos apply only to the orchestra, since the voice is asked to sing 'not in strict time' or 'as if improvised' – with the exception of the short phrase where it overlaps with the orchestra.

The moderate basic tempo is matched by a medium dynamic (*mezzo-piano*) which has only two main variations in the form of two orchestral *fortissimos* between figures 3 and 8 in the score. During the orchestral interlude separating the soloist's stanzas 6 and 7, there is a perceptible *crescendo* followed almost immediately by a *diminuendo*.

Apart from the antiphony already indicated, the overall plan of this movement seems to be that of a diptych formed from the first three stanzas on the one hand, the next three on the other – with the orchestra forming an intermittent background to the figures represented by the vocal interventions[2] and with the seventh and last stanza appearing as a final coda.

The orchestra

The orchestra used for *Complainte* is imposing: two flutes, oboe, cor anglais, clarinet, bass clarinet; three horns, two trumpets, two trombones, tuba; a group of resonant instruments comprising xylophone, vibraphone, celesta and two harps; a large percussion section; and lastly the strings (22–8–8–6).

But this is not an orchestra used for mass effect. As I have said, its medium dynamic seldom rises above *mezzo-piano*, and its peaks of

2 In terms of the psychology of form, the intermittence of the background is not an obstacle to its perception as such, at least within a certain time span. Boulez intuitively respects the rule in this movement, and it may be thought to explain the presence of the orchestra during the second stanza.

intensity are short-lived, violent, and eruptive. The extreme differentiation of the groups in the orchestral interludes separating stanzas 3 and
4, and 6 and 7, poses problems of balance and clarity that make this
movement difficult to play.

The voice

The vocal part is articulated in a number of different ways: *quasi parlando*
('Oiseaux rural'); *Sprechgesang* ('Tu n'est pas un caillou du ciel');
monosyllabic song; finally multi-syllabic, with melismas on certain words
('laine', 'famille', 'ô [léger . . .]'). The word-setting is supple and very
malleable, with the rhythmic values matching the sense ('cache-toi') in a
generally unmeasured, quasi-improvised way. Not surprisingly, this vocal
part poses severe intonation problems, while giving considerable opportunity for what might be called atonal *bel canto*.

The serial organization

Le Soleil des eaux is one of Boulez's most carefully considered pieces as
regards its serial writing, which is largely of a splintered, quasi-secretive,
and very personal kind. What follows is a mere outline analysis of the
movement.

   Complainte is based on three successive series, quoted in full in the first
stanza sung by the soloist.

EX. 28

The three statements do not exactly coincide with the cadences of the text. Without their expressive connotations, an arithmetical analysis of the pitches gives a poor indication of the elegance of this opening phrase.

These three series are clearly connected, since the first six notes of series II correspond to the first six notes of series I, transposed up a semitone. The relationship between series III and series I is less obvious:

Series I

Series 1 reversed

transposed a minor third

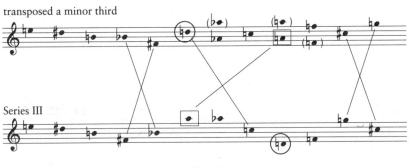

Series III

EX. 29

Because the relationship between them is more tenuous, this one example shows something of Boulez's serial approach in the early years: starting with the series, he then organizes and develops its constituents, concealing more and more of its thematic aspect through a proliferation of cells, motifs and intervals.

From the series to the motif

Thus the original four-note cell from series I (Ex. 29) constitutes a motif in itself – almost like a symbolic design – which forms the basis of the whole of the first long orchestral sequence following the third stanza. This motif resembles an inverted 'N' with the stems displaced (notably on the bass clarinet, second bassoon, violins and the first harp), and its suggestive melodic shape, which itself embodies a kind of canon, effectively generates a rhythmic canon within a dense passage describing the jungle of grass and sprouting leaves in which the lizard urges the goldfinch to hide:

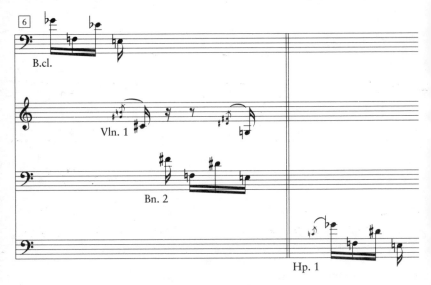

EX. 30

In the same way, the serial material allotted to the soloist is first used to construct the opening section forming a prelude to the movement. Series I is stated in its entirety by the two flutes, but here with the second half of the series in counterpoint with the first:

EX. 31

In addition, series I spreads across the whole first section, beginning with the most resonant instruments and continuing on the brass. Meanwhile, a defective form of series II, with several pitch variations, is stated by the oboe. Series III is likewise foreshadowed on the violins in a succession of micro-groups, split up and inverted:

EX. 32

The fragmented organization of the serial material described here is typical of the whole piece, though in a way that is obviously not always audible.

The sequential succession

The work opens with an instrumental prelude whose dynamic shading ranges between *piano* and *mezzo-piano*; it is transparently scored, within a moderate tempo. As I have indicated, the future serial material is stated on the first page, while the second prolongs certain pitches by means of trills. The prelude ends with a pause on a scaled-down dynamic.

As mentioned earlier, the first stanza, sung unaccompanied, states the three basic series. Boulez resists the temptation to interpret the words in a literal or superficial sense, making the voice descend on 'reprends ton vol', before allowing it to take flight on 'Et reviens à ton nid . . .'. A beautiful melisma on the final word is underlined by the entry of the orchestra.

The second stanza is supported by the orchestra only on the sung words; at this point, Boulez's recitative accompaniment takes the form of chords or harmonic blocks of arpeggiated notes. It is this stanza which asks for *parlando* and *Sprechgesang*. Note the rhythmic shimmer on the orchestra at the word 'arc-en-ciel'.

The third stanza is again unaccompanied. Like the first, it begins with a calm, even line that becomes increasingly agitated. The vocal writing is extremely fine: the intonation may be difficult, but the singer's range is always respected (a low note being justified by the indication *Sprechgesang*).

Based on the aforementioned motif shown in Example 30, the following orchestral section comprises a vast polyphony of twenty-seven separate contrapuntal lines. It is followed by the fourth and fifth stanzas, which are linked by the unaccompanied voice, and represent a peak of tension and vocal agitation: the note values contract, there are frequent changes of register, and many kinds of attack. This increased tension clearly explains the need to avoid interrupting the text between the two stanzas, and to raise the tension still further following the final words of the line 'tituber la chouette'.

The next orchestral sequence is abrupt, fast-moving, and *staccato e marcato* – a sort of astringent *scherzo*, 'staggering' like the screech-owl in the poem, and ending with *fortissimo* trills on the violins and piccolo.

The sixth stanza reverts to the previous medium range of tempo and dynamics, while the rhythm – at first agitated – becomes more relaxed and uniform towards the end.

The relatively long orchestral sequence wends its way back to the more transparent type of writing of the prelude. Expressively, it is organized according to a scheme of *crescendo/decrescendo*, coupled with an *accelerando*, but without the ensuing *rallentando*.

It is the seventh stanza which begins with a sudden return to the moderate tempo and *mezzo-piano* dynamic of the opening. By posing a question to which there is no possible answer, the admirable text draws to a close, by surrendering to the noise of the world (the orchestra). The poem's last two lines represent the crude recognition of a hopeless desire: with a final *pianissimo* phrase on the voice, the external world is banished to an unknown destination.

So ends this strangely beautiful piece in which Boulez's design matches the 'cultural' point of departure of the one who seeks to revive the role of troubadour, story-teller or familiar poet by making poems that sound like music.

LA SORGUE

The second movement of *Le Soleil des eaux* is totally different from the first. After complaint, incantation; after contemplation – action; after lyricism – drama; after seduction – violence. Somewhat cryptically connected to one another (transposed down a semitone, the first six notes of series I from the first piece are found again at the beginning of the second, divided between celesta and vibraphone), the two movements comprise a diptych of violently contrasted colours.

At first hearing, *La Sorgue* seems a simple piece. A variably constituted chorus hums, speaks (though avoiding *Sprechgesang*) and finally sings. The soprano soloist intervenes only twice, and belatedly, in Verses 5 and 9;[3] the orchestra operates in large blocks sometimes reminiscent of Stravinsky. Yet the piece seems to me to be defined by the conflict between the apparent simplicity of the structure and the extreme sophistication of the choral writing (and to a lesser degree, that of the orchestra).

The eleven verses

La Sorgue is a psalm-like poem (a characteristic that Boulez was to underline) of eleven verses; the composer follows these step by step, more or less separating them from one another and adding a prelude and a postlude to the whole.

> *Rivière trop tôt partie, d'une traite, sans compagnon,*
> *Donne aux enfants de mon pays le visage de ta passion.*
>
> *Rivière où l'éclair finit et où commence ma maison,*
> *Qui roule aux marches d'oubli la rocaille de ma raison.*
>
> *Rivière, en toi terre est frisson, soleil anxiété.*
> *Que chaque pauvre dans sa nuit fasse son pain de ta moisson.*
>
> *Rivière souvent punie, rivière à l'abandon.*
>
> *Rivière des apprentis à la calleuse condition,*
> *Il n'est vent qui ne fléchisse à la crête de tes sillons.*
>
> *Rivière de l'âme vide, de la guenille et du soupçon,*
> *Du vieux malheur qui se dévide, de l'ormeau, de la compassion.*
>
> *Rivière des farfelus, des fiévreux, des équarrisseurs,*
> *Du soleil lâchant sa charrue pour s'acoquiner au menteur.*
>
> *Rivière des meilleurs que soi, rivière des brouillards éclos,*
> *De la lampe qui désaltère l'angoisse autour de son chapeau.*
>
> *Rivière des égards au songe, rivière qui rouille le fer,*
> *Où les étoiles ont cette ombre qu'elles refusent à la mer.*
>
> *Rivière des pouvoirs transmis et du cri embouquant les eaux,*
> *De l'ouragan qui mord la vigne et annonce le vin nouveau.*
>
> *Rivière au cœur jamais détruit dans ce monde fou de prison.*
> *Garde-nous violent et ami des abeilles de l'horizon.*

---

3 She also intervenes, somewhat surreptitiously, in order to sing 'de ma raison' with the sopranos of the chorus at the end of the second verse – in much the same way as the soloist in a concerto warms up by playing a few bars of the *tutti* preceding his first entry.

The prelude (figures 1 and 2) immediately introduces the group of sopranos; at first they hum (in three parts), then hum with mouths half open (in two parts), and finally with mouths scarcely open, then almost open (in four parts). The extremely supple orchestral accompaniment remains for the most part at a *piano* level, with the strings already divided, and with particular emphasis being given to notes sustained by trills or pulsations.

Verse 1 (figures 3 and 4) is performed by the men alone, at first 'spoken, almost shouted', then 'without breath' on the words 'trop tôt partie, d'une traite, sans compagnon', ending with a heavy accent, *tutti* and *fortissimo* (with the hammering orchestra being transmuted into song for the last word of the verse). The text is here articulated in unison. In contrast, Verse 2 (figure 5) is polyphonic. The chorus is now divided into nine parts, with the meaning of the shared text becoming almost indiscernible. The following diagram gives an idea how the text is distributed between the various voices:

Solo				de ma rai-son
S 1			de ma	rai - son ———
2			de ma	rai - son ⌢
A 1			de ma	rai - son ———
2			de ma	rai - son ———
T 1		qui roule aux marches d'oubli		de ma rai- son ⌢
2		qui roule aux marches ( )		de ( ) rai- ( )
B 1	Où l'éclaire			
2		finit et où commence ma maison	la rocaille	de ma rai son ⸝
3			la rocaille	ma rai ( )son

It is interesting to note that this sharing of the text gives rise to texts of a different kind if certain voices are read horizontally without regard for the true shape of the poem; this produces a poetic ambiguity which the composer – soon to be seduced by Mallarmé's *Livre* – could hardly have overlooked. In any case, he underlines it here.

Verse 3 (figures 6 and 7) returns to the vehement scansion of Verse 1, with the writing for the chorus reverting to a more homophonic organization. The change from song to speech is abrupt. The ravishing second phrase of the verse is sung by the female voices (humming with mouths half open) within an extremely economical and exceptionally transparent orchestral sonority.

Verse 4 (figure 8) is an extraordinarily impressionistic section, based partly on the multiple sub-division of both voices (22 parts) and orchestra (31 separate parts), and partly on oscillations around pivot-notes. The overlapping entries of the words are grafted onto this complex web of sound. The texture at the end of the verse is more homophonic.

Verse 5 (figures 9, 10 and 11) marks the first real entry of the soprano soloist, restoring the chorus – now more unified, even 'harmonic' – to its more traditional supportive function.

The one phrase allotted to the soprano is a beautiful arabesque:

EX. 33

At the end of this verse, *divisi* strings revert to the oscillating trills with which Verse 4 began.

In a lively tempo, the homophonic choral writing of Verse 6 (figures 12 and 13) underlines the two rhymes ('soupçon', 'compassion'), as song gives way to speech. The orchestral writing, too, is particularly striking here: the *divisi* strings form large blocks of harmonics, fading from *mezzo-forte* to *mezzo-piano*, which underpin the pointillist flecks of sound from the rest of the orchestra.

In Verse 7 (figures 14 and 15) women's speaking voices contrast with the singing voices of the men. This choral homophony is supported by the orchestra, in particular by the rich polyphony of the lower strings.

Verse 8 (figures 16 and 17) adds further groups of wind to the string polyphony, while the *divisi* chorus splits into different groups: one of the groups of basses voices a syllable which continues as a hummed resonance while another takes over. In the same way, the sopranos speak, while altos and tenors sing the text – then the roles are reversed, within a perceptible shimmer of orchestral sound.

Verse 9 (figures 18 and 19) is a huge *tutti* for orchestra, chorus, and the soloist – whose part has a striking *bel canto* lyricism as the chorus resumes its supporting role:

Ri - - viè - re des_____ é- gards au son - - - ge

où____ les__étoi - les ont__ cet- te om - bre____

____ qu'el- les re - - - fu - - - sent à la mer____

EX. 34

Acting as a brief moment of calm before the finale, Verse 10 (figures 20 and 21) comprises a homogeneous five-part song; it opens out into a huge *crescendo* leading directly to the start of Verse 11 (figures 22, 23 and the spectacular 24). Blocks of sound seem to triumph here as the chorus makes its entry between four massive *tutti* chords. After a rapid disintegration of the orchestral texture, the second part of the verse leads to a chorale for *divisi* voices, with sopranos and altos speaking, the tenors singing, and the basses first humming, then singing. The soloist takes over the last word ('Horizon') as in a cinematic dissolve. The postlude consists of a vocalise for the soloist on the first vowel of her word, as the orchestral sound quickly dies away, until only the *bisbigliando* of the first harp remains to fade into silence.

5

Structures Book 1

FOR TWO PIANOS

Composition: 1951 (*1a*) and 1952
First performance: (*1a* only), Paris, 4 May 1952;
Olivier Messiaen and Pierre Boulez; (complete), Cologne,
13 November 1953; Yvette Grimaud and Yvonne Loriod
Published: Universal Edition (UE 12267), 1955
Duration: *Structure 1a, 3'25"*
Structure 1b, 8'30"
Structure 1c, 2'10"

What follows is a preliminary description of *Structure 1a*: model and matrix for the whole of Book 1, this is the piece in which Boulez applied total serialization in order to effect a combined organization of pitch, duration, dynamics and attack. Before going further, it will be useful to determine the series relating to these four criteria, then to look at the ways they are distributed and organized within the piece as a whole.

THE PITCH SERIES

I explained earlier (p. 51) that Boulez chose as his basic series a row taken from Messiaen's *Mode de valeurs et d'intensités*, by way of confirming that the rift between the two composers had healed. This reconciliation was publicly acknowledged through Messiaen's participation in the first performance. Boulez's use of 'borrowed' material also had the practical advantage of eliminating any subjective or personal factors from his experiment at the outset.

EX. 35

This is the original order of the series (O); reading the notes from right to left gives the retrograde (OR):

EX. 36

If the intervals of the original series are inverted, this will give the inversion of the original (I):

EX. 37

Finally, reading the notes of the inversion from right to left will give the retrograde inversion of the series (RI):

EX. 38

These four forms of the pitch series can be applied to any of the twelve degrees of the chromatic scale, so that there are forty-eight (12×4) possible statements of an original row. The first few are given below (the arrow ← indicates the retrograde versions). The twelve possible statements of the series – one for each degree of the chromatic scale – are numbered from 0 to 11 (the original and 11 semitone transpositions):

EX. 39

. . . and so on, back to the D♮ (E♭) of the starting point.

THE DURATION SERIES

The duration scale is based on twelve units of increasing value, starting with the demi-semiquaver:

EX. 40

The numbers indicate the number of demi-semiquavers in each duration; thus the succession given below can be numbered:

EX. 41

Matching the pitch series from Ex. 35 above with the duration series from Ex. 41 will give (in close position) the opening of the first piano part from *Structure 1a* (bars 1–7):

P.	1	2	3	4	5	6	7	8	9	10	11	12
D.	12	11	9	10	3	6	7	1	2	8	4	5

EX. 42

Obviously, the duration series from the above example can undergo all the transformations of a pitch series: it can be read as a retrograde, an inversion (according to the convention which gives each duration an 'inversion' in that the sum of each pair of numbers adds up to thirteen), and so a retrograde inversion. Moreover, by successively moving the first duration to the end of the series, each of these four forms can be 'transposed', as follows:

$$12 \quad 11 \quad 9 \quad 10 \quad 3 \quad 6 \quad 7 \quad 1 \quad 2 \quad 8 \quad 4 \quad 5$$
$$11 \quad 9 \quad 10 \quad 3 \quad 6 \quad 7 \quad 1 \quad 2 \quad 8 \quad 4 \quad 5 \quad 12$$
$$9 \quad 10 \quad 3 \quad 6 \quad \text{etc.}$$

Thus, like the pitch series, the duration series has forty-eight possibilities (12×4). Combined with the forty-eight possible versions of the pitch series, this will give 2304 options for any chosen version of either series (in terms of combinatory analysis, the number of possible permutations of a finite group of twelve objects is about 480 million). Practically speaking, one must choose from this almost infinite number of possibilities to determine the organization of a work – whether that choice be the result of chance (as advocated by Cage) or of the composer's will. Predictably, Boulez was to make the latter choice. The problems posed are evidently not dissimilar to those of the 'open-plan work' (see pp. 300 ff.).

THE DYNAMIC SERIES

Boulez defines a series of twelve dynamics, also theoretically forming a 'regularly' increasing scale:

pppp   *ppp*   *pp*   *p quasi p*   *mp*   *mf*   *quasi mf*   *f*   *ff*   *fff*   *ffff*

1   2   3   4   5   6   7   8   9   10   11   12

It is theoretically possible to imagine transpositions of dynamics on the same pattern as the transpositions of pitch and duration, and to construct a table analogous to the foregoing. It is also possible in theory to formulate retrograde and inverted forms of the series. In practice, it is probably more useful to direct the reader to the first page of *Structure 1a* itself, where he can see that Boulez's dynamic field keeps to just two strongly contrasted dynamics (numbers 5 and 12 above).

THE SERIES OF ATTACKS

The various ways of striking the keys of a piano can supposedly produce a range of different timbres. I list below the twelve envisaged 'attacks' in Boulez's series,[1] which correspond to those used by Messiaen in his *Mode de valeurs et d'intensités*. Once a numbered succession is established, it is here again theoretically possible to deduce *n* different versions:

1	˃	Accent	7	˃	*Staccato* accent
2	.	Detached	8	‒	Detached *tenuto*
3	.	*Staccato*	9	⌢	Detached but slurred
4	‒	*Tenuto*	10	*f* / ∧	Sudden attack
5	⌢	Legato	11	*sfz*	*Sforzando*
6	˃	Detached accent	12	∧	Normal

Nevertheless, when all the particulars of pitch, register, placing, tempo and dynamics are already specified, to define specific kinds of attack seems superfluous.

THE OVERALL ORGANIZATION OF *STRUCTURE 1a*

Structure 1a is divided into eleven separate sections or 'texts', each with its own tempo. Three tempos, A, B and C, are arranged as follows:

1 In his letter to John Cage (1952) – published in *Orientations*, p. 129 – Boulez indicates that they come from *Mode de valeurs et d'intensités*.

TEXT	BARS	TEMPOS		DURATION
1	1–7	*Très modéré:*	$\flat = 120$	*c* 10″
2	8–31	*Modéré, presque vif:*	$\flat = 144$	*c* 30″
3	32–39	*Lent:*	$\flat = 120$	*c* 20″
4	40–56	*Modéré, presque vif*		*c* 20″
5	57–64	*Très modéré*		*c* 10″
6	65–72	*Lent*		*c* 40″
7	73–81	*Modéré, presque vif*		*c* 10″
8	82–89	*Très modéré*		*c* 10″
9	90–97	*Modéré, presque vif*		*c* 15″
10	98–105	*Lent*		*c* 25″
11	106–115	*Très modéré*		*c* 15″
			Total	3″ 25″

These may be viewed as two partly overlapping symmetrical cycles centred around section 5 (which in fact represents a crucial moment in *Structure 1a*):

```
A   B   C   B   A
        A   C   B   A   B   C   A
1   2   3   4   5   6   7   8   9   10  11
```

We must now go into what might be called the poetics of the work, remembering what Boulez said to Célestin Deliège about the relationship between the material and the self – a relationship that is progressively reversed in the course of Book 1. Even if *Structure 1a* was written during a single night by means of the simple development of a strict serial programme designed to eliminate subjectivity, it remains only one of the millions of possibilities at his disposal: Boulez has made a choice – whether consciously or unconsciously. It is important to understand the nature of these choices, in order if possible to derive an aesthetic for these three-and-a-half minutes of music.

PROGRAMME AND ORGANIZATION IN *STRUCTURE 1a*

In order to show the ways in which an organizational will may be exercised on a given (borrowed) series of pitches, a fixed dynamic order, an initial series of durations, and three available tempos, I shall enlist the help of a few figurative diagrams – which are not to be taken as research tools in themselves, but rather as a means of illustration.

Pitch density

Each of the eleven sections of *Structure 1a* brings into play one or more of the several serial formulations derived from the original series. Each of these represents one voice in the polyphony, so that the forty-eight possible ways of stating the series are all employed here, each of them once only. The following diagram shows the distribution of the forty-eight forms across the eleven sections:

DISTRIBUTION OF THE TEXTS WITHIN THE SERIAL GRID OF PITCHES

Transpositions		Original	Retrograde	Inversion	Retrograde inv.
0	(E flat)	T1 PI	T11 PII RH1	T1 PII	T11 PI RH2
1	(E natural)	T2 (a) PI LH	T 8 PII RH	T3 PII LH2	T11 PI LH
2	(F)	T3 PI LH	T 6 PII LH	T4 (b) PII RH	T 8 PI LH
3	(F sharp)	T4 (a) PI	T 9 PII LH	T3 PII LH1	T 7 PI
4	(G)	T5 (a) PI solo	T 9 PII RH	T2 (c) PII solo	T 6 PI RH
5	(G sharp)	T4 (b) PI RH	T10 PII	T2 (b) PII	T 6 PI LH1
6	(A)	T2 (a) PI LH	T11 PII LH	T2 (a) PII LH	T11 PI RH1
7	(B flat)	T2 (b) PI RH	T 7 PII LH	T4 (b) PII LH2	T10 PI
8	(B)	T2 (b) PI LH	T 6 PII RH	T4 (b) PII LH	T 9 PI LH
9	(C)	T3 PI RH2	T 7 PII RH	T4 (a) PII	T 9 PI RH
10	(C sharp)	T4 (b) PI LH	T 8 PII LH	T3 PII RH	T 8 PI LH2
11	(D)	T3 PI RH1	T11 PII RH1	T2 (a) PII RH	T 8 PI RH

Abbreviations: T (1–11) the 11 texts of *Structure 1a*
            P1, P2 piano 1, piano 2
            RH, LH right hand, left hand
                      Texts 2 and 4 are subdivided (T2a, T2b, T2c, T4a, T4b)
                      The right and left hands may also be divided between
                      two separate series (RH1, RH2, LH1, LH2)

It will be seen that certain sections comprise few serial statements (one only in T5, two in T1), while others encompass several – the maximum being attained in T3 and T11 which comprise six each. These are clearly distributed between the two pianos and the two hands of each pianist: hence the notion of pitch density, which varies from 1 to 6 and which appears to proceed irregularly from a lesser to a greater degree of density. Diagram 1 below is a simple representation of the way in which the *Structure* is heard in terms of these variable densities, with sections 2 and 4 subdivided into three and two parts respectively – as defined by the introduction of a new series:

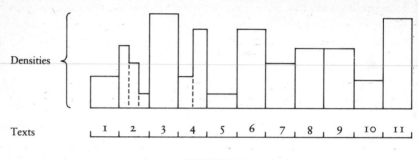

Densities

Texts

$$I \quad 2 \quad 3 \quad 4 \quad 5 \quad 6 \quad 7 \quad 8 \quad 9 \quad 10 \quad 11$$

DIAGRAM I

Diagram 2 follows roughly the same device, but in a somewhat refined form. The densities are distributed on either side of the central sectional axis, corresponding to the part played by each of the two pianists: since this difference is not perceptible to the ear, Diagram 2 is an analytical rather than an aural representation. I have shown the inversions (whether retrograde or not) in black, leaving the originals blank; arrows separate the original from the retrograde forms:

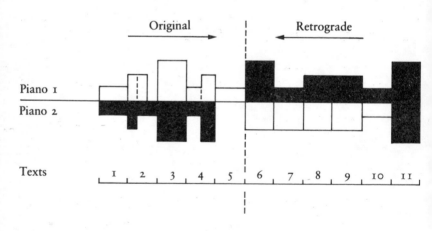

DIAGRAM 2

Diagram 2 is instructive in several ways. Firstly, it gives visual confirmation of a particular 'event' at the beginning of the sixth section: here, all the forms employed become retrograde, while the distribution of original and retrograde forms between the two pianists is inverted. One could perhaps say that *Structure 1a* is divided into two parts, an Antiphon (sections 1–5) and a Response (sections 6–11) – with the Response being marked by a general increase in density, as already shown in Diagram 1.

The relationship between density and dynamics

Diagram 3 takes up the ideas of Diagram 2 as to the distribution of densities between the two pianists, but additionally indicates the dynamics from 1 (pppp) to 12 (ffff). Within an acoustic approximation that takes account of the approximate nature of a 'series' of dynamics, simple addition of the numbers gives a dynamic index for each section (noted on a line beneath the diagram).

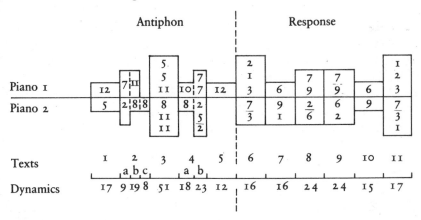

DIAGRAM 3

Diagram 3 reveals a certain dynamic agitation in the Antiphon where, despite the peak represented by section 3, dynamic intensity is less sustained than in the Response. The function of section 5 is now clear: with its minimum density (its powerful dynamic sustained by one performer), it forms a transition to the following section without effecting any break in continuity.

Diagram 4 represents the curve obtained from the dynamic index. Here, I have departed from the system of allegedly equal sections in order to make the line indicating the sections into a real time-axis (the approximate duration of each section, taken from the recording by the Kontarsky brothers, is indicated on p. 274; the almost negligible silences between the sections are incorporated into these timings, with the numbers rounded off to the nearest second).

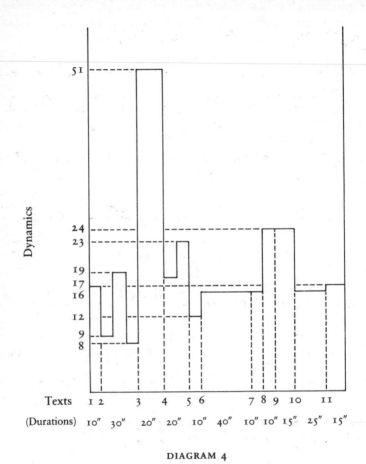

DIAGRAM 4

Diagram 4 again confirms that *Structure 1a* is divided into two parts of analogous (if not equal) duration, with the changeable dynamics of a comparatively agitated Antiphon set against those of a more stable Response. It seems to me that the stabilizing element within each half is different, since the noticeable dynamic increase in section 3 makes it the organizational axis of the Antiphon, while the long section 6, with its medium dynamic intensity, favours the axis of duration above the other determining factors. It could also be said that the two dynamic peaks are symmetrically placed at the centre of each half.

What one can infer from a particular diagram is necessarily limited, since it concerns itself only with a single set of ideas. This leads me to the idea of a synthesizing table, which would give a clearer impression of durations.

The durations: the emergence of a cantus firmus

One may imagine that there are to be forty-eight duration series corresponding to the forty-eight serial statements which are the fibres of the pitch space in *Structure 1a*. However, although Boulez begins with a first section comprising two series of pitches and one of durations, he divides the first part of the second section into three sub-sections, using, (a) four series of pitches and two series of durations, (b), three series of pitches and one of durations, and (c) one of each. The third main section comprises six pitch series but only one of duration. For the forty-eight pitch series there are a mere twenty-six corresponding duration series.

Two questions then arise: why is there such a difference between the two, and how are the polyphonic lines organized in terms of their rhythm? As the self-made prisoner of a programme that requires the serial treatment of keyboard 'attacks', it seems that Boulez soon became aware of the contradiction between the serial organization of duration (with the notes sustained for a longer or shorter time) and that of attacks (which involves notes being sustained in different ways and often not sustained at all). He had thus adopted a twofold durational world: on the one hand, with certain strands depending on serially organized duration; on the other, with serial pitch statements whose notes are always, and sometimes violently, detached. These latter surround the former with embellishing elements, in the manner of tropes on either side of a cantus firmus.

In passing, it is worth pointing out the novelty of this idea of a cantus firmus defined by a differentiated durational organization, rather than a melodic line. The following is an unusually simple example of such a superposition. It is taken from section 10, which comprises only two statements of the pitch series: the rhythmic cantus firmus is on the second piano, while the rhythmic counterpoint of the first piano is not part of a rhythmic series:

EX. 43

There does not appear to be any mechanical law dictating either the occurrence or the disposition of such a cantus firmus, since each section adheres to its own formula. Some sections merely comprise a counterpoint of pitch and duration series (sections 1, 2 and 8); in others, a cantus firmus stands isolated from the surrounding procedures; a fine counterpoint between two cantus firmi forms the basis of the 'sextet' of section 11 (see Diagram 3 above).

TOTAL SERIALIZATION IN ACTION

Diagram 5 summarises the points made by these fragmentary observations:

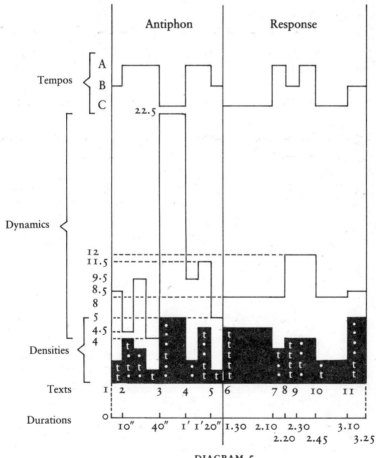

DIAGRAM 5

(a) The bottom line represents a time-axis akin to the one already established in Diagram 4; this gives an approximate idea of the relative lengths of the eleven sections of *Structure 1a*. The long section 6 is shown both to centre the movement as a whole and to inaugurate the Response of its second half.

(b) The densities summarized in Diagram 1 correspond to an aural perception of the movement. In Diagram 5, I have used a small 't' to mark the serial strands (matched by serial durations) that serve as cantus firmus; other procedures are marked by a single dot to represent the detached attack of each note. There again, section 6 seems to stand apart; slow, and of a medium dynamic intensity, its five strands (all serially organized as to their durations) form a superb polyphonic quintet.

(c) The dynamics from Diagram 3[2] are given again here; with their curve logically following that of the densities, the dramatic peak of section 3 arises from the superposition of six strands at a high dynamic level. Note that the movement ends on the same dynamic level with which it began, and that the dynamics of the second half are less variable than those of the first.

(d) Since each section is defined by its tempo, the top of the diagram represents a single tempo curve. The medium tempo, A – with which the piece begins and ends, and which reappears twice during the the course of the movement – flanks a slightly faster tempo, B, and an obviously slower one, C. The two symmetries already noticed run parallel to the dynamic curve, so confirming the chosen position of section 6: dense, slow, and restrained in tone, both initiating the Response and serving as an acoustic hollow, this section is the expressive centre of the movement as a whole, and can clearly be heard as such.

CONCLUSIONS ON *STRUCTURE 1a*:
PROGRAMME, CHOICE, POETIC EXPRESSION

My various diagrams do not purport to give a complete – still less a scientific – account of the famous and little understood *Structure 1a*. Their job is at best only to try to define the areas of 'choice' and of 'programme'. By indicating the parameters selected by Boulez to serve as his basic material, they define the field of the possible within which he has made his

---

2 Both for graphic reasons and because it is the dynamic relationships and not the absolute values that are important here, I have halved the values in Diagram 4.

choice. At a first hearing, these three-and-a-half minutes of music appear somewhat undifferentiated – a matter merely of 'blackboard' music; my efforts will be justified if they facilitate listening, and reveal the almost involuntary beauty of Boulez's chosen approach.

THE TWO OTHER *STRUCTURES* OF BOOK I

It is not my intention to discuss *Structures 1b* and *1c* in as much detail: these two movements are progressively less 'programmed', and Boulez professes to have disguised his procedures.

Structure 1b: a rondo defined by its tempos

Formally reminiscent of the slow movement of the Second Sonata, *Structure 1b* comprises ten sections:

T 1 bars	1–17	Très rapide	♩ = 180
2	18–40	Lent	♪ = 100–138
3	41–59	Très modéré	♩ = 80
4	60–70	Lent	
5	71–115	Moins lent	♪ = 138–160
6	116–132	Rapide	♪ = 152
7	133–250	Très lent	♩ = 80–100
8	250–286	Modéré, preque vif	♪ = 96
9	287–324	Lent	
10	325–341	Assez rapide	♩ = 120

However, these indications should only be regarded as guidelines, since, unlike the first movement, there are frequent tempo variations within each of the ten texts which create a more 'fluid' effect overall. Also, tempo indications do not take into consideration the level of agitation of any given passage. A section like the seventh is so densely written that it sounds fast, and it is around this section that the whole movement is organized, alternating passages of lesser density (sections 1, 3, 6, 8 and 10) with those that are much more hectic (sections 2, 4, 5, 7 and 9).

An example taken from the beginning of *Structure 1b* will show the more covert nature of its material, as shown by the pitch series of text 1:

EX. 44

As may be seen by comparing the above with Ex. 39 on p. 271, the second piano merely repeats the eleventh transposition of the first movement's original series – but the first piano juxtaposes the first five notes of the retrograde of the fourth transposition with the remaining seven notes of the original of the same transposition (although with minute permutations). This may fancifully be interpreted as 'the composer striking back at his material'.

Structure 1c: a fast, quiet mouvement perpétuel

The third *Structure* of Book 1 is the shortest of the three. It is played without a break, despite the fact that it comprises three successive variations, all in a fast tempo (*assez rapide*, bars 1–48; *très rapide*, bars 49–104; and *rapide*, bars 105–50). But while the first section is constantly speeded up by the indication *précipité*, a note-by-note style triumphs in the second, and a more busy type of writing in the third. The works ends *très ralenti*, with a brief solo for the second piano.

6

Le Marteau sans maître

FOR VOICE AND SIX
INSTRUMENTS

Composition: 1953–5
First performance: Baden-Baden, 18 June 1955;
a section of the Südwestfunk Orchestra of Baden-Baden,
with Sybilla Plate (mezzo-soprano), under Hans Rosbaud;
first performance in France: 25 April 1956; soloists
of the Domaine musical, with Marie-Thérèse Cahn
(mezzo-soprano), under Boulez
Published: Universal Edition (UE 12652), 1954, rev. 1957
Duration: *c* 35′00″

THE ORGANIZATION OF THE WORK AND ITS
INSTRUMENTAL DISPOSITION

The way in which the three poems of René Char chosen by Boulez were shared between three interwoven cycles has already been discussed (p. 77). These cycles comprise nine movements in all. Each of these is differently scored, according to a subtle instrumental organization partly dependent on an acoustic continuity defined by Boulez: the voice and the flute both use breath; the flute and the viola are both monodic instruments; the viola and the guitar both have strings that may be plucked; the guitar and the vibraphone are both instruments with resonating bodies; and the vibraphone and the xylorimba are of a construction that involves the striking of resonant plates. Boulez shows a characteristic preference for middle register instruments, such as alto flute, viola and guitar, as well as for the alto voice.

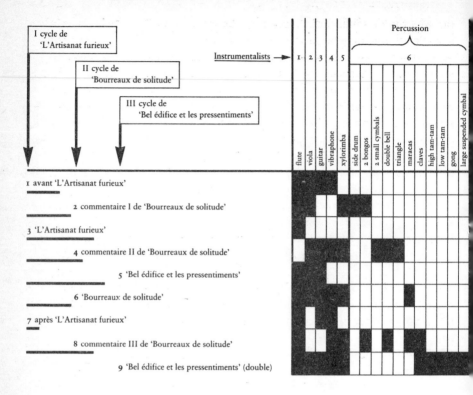

The unpitched percussion is particularly important: like the piano in *Pierrot lunaire*, it functions as a continuum in seven of the nine movements. It is never used for shock effect, but rather for the exotic colour it imparts to the work. It should be noted that the instruments are in no way 'tortured': they play within their tessitura and at a natural dynamic level, with conventional articulation. Boulez has never subscribed to the view that an outrageous misuse of instruments could help to resolve the problems of traditional instrumental design in relation to compositional evolution; these were matters to be examined much later, under the auspices of IRCAM.

THE TREATMENT OF THE VOICE AND THE RELATIONSHIP BETWEEN TEXT AND MUSIC

The five different forms of vocal articulation that the score requires are similarly restrained, though widely contrasted. These are:

(a) Melismatic song, characterized by a supple continuity of line in which a single syllable may be sustained through several notes. The twelve-note series that supports the article 'du' in the phrase 'du clou' (movement 3, see Ex. 45) is a particularly dramatic example of melisma. In general, the whole of this third movement is melismatic, since the text is relatively brief compared with its musical setting. The vocal writing becomes less melismatic when a lengthy text is distributed only within certain sequences of a movement like the first version of 'Bel édifice . . .' (movement 5).

(b) Syllabic song, where each syllable is assigned one note. This happens in 'Bourreaux de solitude' (movement 6), where a short text is distributed over short sequences, interspersed with instrumental passages.

(c) Schoenbergian *Sprechgesang*, which is half-way between syllabic song and *parlando*, occurs only in movement 9, the 'double' of 'Bel édifice . . .'. Here the phrase 'Enfant la jetée promenade sauvage' is set first in *Sprechgesang* ('Enfant la'), then *parlando* ('jetée promenade sauvage'), in a low tessitura, since the speaking voice is normally lower than the singing one. This is one of the observations on which Boulez bases his questions (1962) or his convictions (1977) as to the right way of executing *Sprechgesang*.[1]

(d) An overtly declamatory *parlando* here fulfils its traditionally dramatic role.

(e) Finally Boulez requires humming, (*bouche fermée*) in the 'double' of 'Bel édifice . . .'.

L'ARTISANAT FURIEUX
La roulotte rouge au bord du clou
Et cadavre dans le panier
Et chevaux de labour dans le fer à cheval
Je rêve sur la pointe de mon couteau le Pérou.

BOURREAUX DE SOLITUDE
Le pas s'est éloigné le marcheur s'est tu
Sur le cadran de l'Imitation
Le Balancier lance sa charge de granit reflexe.

BEL EDIFICE ET LES PRESSENTIMENTS
J'écoute marcher dans mes jambes
La mer morte vagues par-dessus tête
Enfant la jetée-promenade sauvage
Homme l'illusion imitée
Des yeux purs dans les bois
Cherchent en pleurant la tête habitable.

© Editions José Corti

1 See a note on *Sprechgesang*, from the sleeve note to the record of *Pierrot lunaire*, 1962. Also the discussion with Dominique Jameux on the subject of *Pierrot lunaire* – from a flexible disc included with the 1977 recording.

THE SERIAL ORGANIZATION AND THE ORDER OF THE MOVEMENTS

The cycle of 'L'Artisanat furieux'

Since the encircling instrumental movements (1 and 7 for 'L'Artisanat'; 2, 4 and 6 for 'Bourreaux'; 9 for 'Bel édifice . . .') are serially dependent on the main vocal movements, I shall only comment on the serial organization of the latter.[2] 'L'Artisanat furieux' (3) is a serial triptych whose particular form echoes that of the whole cycle. Written for voice and flute, it is a direct instrumental reference to the seventh movement of *Pierrot lunaire* ('Der kranke Mond').

After a brilliant, two-bar flute introduction centred around the note B♭ , the voice begins the first verse unaccompanied, rejoined by the flute on the word 'bord'. Flutter-tonguing, the flute then plays a broad serial melody, in turn joined by the voice on the words 'du clou' — set within a similarly supple melody which is simply the retrograde of the first, with a slight re-ordering of the last four notes:

EX. 45

2 For further explanation see the analysis by R. Piencikowsky (details in Bibliography).

The dialogue between the two proceeds by developing cells extracted from the preceding series, and by imitative play between voice and flute. It ends with a duet that repeats the series transposed up an augmented fourth, together with its slightly altered retrograde. This tripartite structure returns in the central fifth movement.

The cycle of 'Bourreaux de solitude'

In his initial statement, Boulez uses not only a pitch series, but also a series of durations (which takes precedence over the former):

EX. 46

Excluding the unpitched percussion, Ex. 46 shows the first bar of 'Bourreaux de solitude' (the flute sounding as written). The twelve notes it comprises constitute a series of pitches, which are in fact a chromatic scale, starting from D♮ . However, this is no arbitrary arrangement, since the notes succeed one another according to a series of progressive durations, with the D♮ the smallest value (a semiquaver), the second note, E♮ , twice as long, the third, E♭ , three times the value, and so on – until the twelfth note, C♯ , is worth the full twelve semiquavers of a minim tied to a crotchet. This strict organization obviously leaves room for variation during the course of the movement; it also provides the organizing principle for the commentaries. While Boulez could have adopted a more complex series of rhythmicized pitches, he has started from the simplest possible succession of the chromatic scale.

The cycle of 'Bel édifice et les pressentiments'

The serial statement of 'Bel édifice . . .' is specific to this movement, and is heard on the viola at the outset:

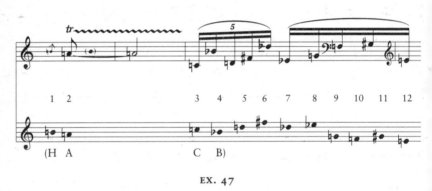

EX. 47

Once stated on the viola, the initial series immediately makes way for various transformations; thus it seems that serial development is of lesser significance in a movement which appears to depend on different points of departure, other stabilizing factors.

THE DEVELOPMENT OF THE WORK: THE UNITY OF THE CYCLES

Any description of *Marteau* ought to take into account the ambivalence of its form. I would seriously suggest that the reader who wishes to understand this work from a compositional point of view would benefit from listening to the work cycle by cycle: that is, movements 1, 3 and 7 (the cycle of 'L'Artisanat furieux'), followed by movements 2, 4, 6 and 8 (the cycle of 'Bourreaux de solitude'), and finally, movements 5 and 9 (the cycle of 'Bel édifice et les pressentiments').

The cycle of 'L'Artisanat furieux'

This is the shortest cycle of the triptych. Framed at a distance by a prelude and a postlude, equally brief and rapid in character, its central panel has a brief text and a restrained instrumentation:[3]

	1 Avant 'L'Artisanat furieux'	3 'L'Artisanat furieux'	7 Après 'L'Artisanat furieux'
Duration	1'45"	2'25"	1'0"
Timbre	flute vibraphone guitar viola	voice + flute	flute vibraphone guitar
Tempo	rapide	modéré, sans rigueur	rapide
Form	5 homogeneous statements, separated by pauses	supple counter-point, contrasting registers	the same as 1

The obvious similarities of timbre, tempo and figuration between movements 1 and 7 emphasize the extreme simplicity of this three-part structure. The agility of the whole gives an impression of lightness, transparency, even alacrity, with the brevity of the movements well suited to the epithet of the title. The flute's sonority colours the entire cycle.

The cycle of 'Bourreaux de solitude'

With two instrumental commentaries preceding and one following the sung movement, this cycle is both more articulated and more complex than 'L'Artisanat furieux'. The fact that the movements of the cycle comprise all the even-numbered ones reinforces the impression of internal

3 The durations are taken from the recording with Yvonne Minton, directed by the composer (see Discography).

regularity within the cycle itself, the regularity of the balance within the work as a whole (see below), and the sense of monotony, stemming from the title.

	2 *Commentaire* I	4 *Commentaire* II	6 *Bourreaux*	8 *Commentaire* III
Duration	4′00″	4′35″	4′13″	5′48″
Timbre			voice +	
	flute		flute	flute
	side drum	small cymbals	maracas	various percussion,
	xylorimba	xylorimba	xylorimba	xylorimba
		vibraphone	vibraphone	vibraphone
	viola	viola	viola	
		guitar	guitar	
	(central section: flute tacet + modifications in percussion)	(modifications in percussion throughout)		
Tempo	modéré–vif–modéré	assez rapide → tres variable	assez lent → plus lent → accel.	assez lent with variations
Form	3 processes: melody percussion counterpoint central section: percussive trio	no melody	melody flute/voice	as II
		Silence as a structural element		

The whole cycle is characterized by features which provide a sense of continuity, alongside others which emphasize discontinuity. The element of continuity derives mainly from the presence of an irregular metrical 'scansion' on the percussion (heard more or less continuously), which acts as a frieze to the four movements, and also from the abrupt silences that repeatedly interrupt the discourse. The instrumentation is also relatively homogeneous, with the xylorimba in all four movements (which are each of similar length).

The main disruptive feature derives from a radical evolution of the opening material, which is reconstituted at the end of the cycle. This erosion of an initially clear structure was already a characteristic of the Second Sonata (see p. 242).

The design of the first movement of the cycle is particularly clear, falling into three unequal sections. The first is polyphonic: in counterpoint with xylorimba and viola, seven successive flute statements of a melodic line are placed over an irregular, though continuous, percussive background. This first section ends with a flute trill. The central section (from bar 54) is a lively trio, without the flute, and with two bongos taking over from the preceding drum. Pauses play an important part here. The flute then returns (bar 103) for an abbreviated repeat of the first section (like that of a scherzo following a trio) – a rare example of 'repetitive' music in Boulez's output. The movement ends with an isolated note on the flute.

The second movement of the cycle takes up the preceding device of percussive 'wallpaper' music (as it will be described in *Répons*), with *staccato* counterpoints on the other instruments: without the flute this movement gives the impression that an essential element (melody) is missing. The disruptive gesture of abrupt and repeated silences is intensified: this is an accompaniment with nothing to accompany – a device turned in upon itself in a merciless isolation.

The third movement of the cycle includes the voice. It maintains a threefold arrangement of melody, counterpoint, and percussive background. The melody is shared between voice and flute; the comparative length of the movement in relation to that of the text has the effect of submerging the poem and enhancing the expressive quality of the flute, which provides a passionate echo of the textual images ('charge de granit').

The beginning of the fourth movement still keeps to the melody/ counterpoint/percussion instrumental deployment, but appears less formally stable owing to the introduction of continual changes of tempo in addition to the pauses. The various percussion instruments alternate in succession, and the end of the piece reverts to a simplified statement of the material that has undergone development.

The cycle of 'Bel édifice et les pressentiments'

This is the central movement of the work, both by virtue of its position and because of its 'double' – the term 'double' applying to duration as well as to the fact that it repeats the same text. (A third meaning of the word will be revealed later.)

	5 'Bel édifice' (first version)	9 'Bel édifice' (double)
Duration	3'50"	8'03"
Timbre	voice flute xylorimba vibraphone guitar viola	voice flute xylorimba vibraphone percussion guitar viola
Tempo	*assez vif* *'tempo et nuances trés* *instables'*	free, variable, within overall *modéré*
Form	voice very sustained within *tutti*	a) singing voice very sustained within *tutti*; b) humming voice; flute and percussion cadenzas.

The first movement comprises four asymmetrically placed statements. After a relatively long introduction (bars 1–14), the words 'J'écoute marcher dans mes jambes la mer morte vagues par-dessus tête' are announced in a single statement; this is followed by expansion or contraction of figures belonging to pairs of words which are connected by meaning ('écoute/tête', 'marcher/jambes', 'mer/vagues'):

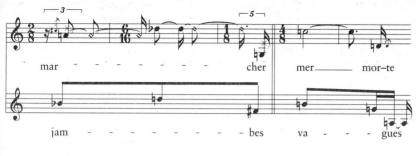

EX. 48

Neither is a suggestion of word-painting excluded, when flute, guitar and viola appear to wander off as if on tiptoe (bars 19 and 20).

After a second interlude (bars 30–62), the comparatively long second vocal statement of '(Enfant) la jetée promenade (sauvage)' is homophonically accompanied; with the word 'sauvage', the writing changes to become an explosive recitative, set amidst flute trills and chords on viola and guitar. The line which follows 'homme l'illusion imitée' is delayed, and the last (and syntactically, the only meaningful) phrase comes still later, and is extended in time. The voice ends alone, having sketched out a dialogue between itself and the flute which is further explored in the last movement.

Movement 9 can also be regarded as a 'double' because it is divided into two sections: the first with the sung text, the second with the voice humming as part of the instrumental ensemble.

Because this movement (which was composed after the rest) is the finale to the whole work, it is not surprising that all the instrumental resources are called upon (as in *Pierrot lunaire*). In section A (with the sung text), changes of tempo provide an element of flexibility and accommodate the necessary pauses. Two pairs of instruments are contrasted here – the resonant percussive sounds of the vibraphone and xylorimba, with the drier, more focused timbres of the viola and guitar (both capable of greater melodic continuity). The instruments remain paired in this way throughout, apart from two dialogues between flute and percussion. The percussion features very little in section B (where the voice hums), until the melodic exchange between voice and flute gives final victory to the latter; then, *in extremis*, the flute is rejoined by the percussion for two cadenzas which echo the central movement of the 'Artisanat furieux' cycle. The second of these cadenzas ends the movement and the work on a final flute trill, fading into the prolonged oscillation of a large suspended cymbal.

THE OVERALL ORGANIZATION

The way in which the three cycles are intertwined could obviously have risked sounding like an arbitrary succession of nine movements, since the characteristics common to each movement – which include an extended use of serialism, a supple vocal style, a homogeneous and 'exotic' instrumental colour, and the predominance of the flute as a 'go-between' – could not alone guarantee the unity of the work as a whole. The three cycles were therefore organized in such a way as to compose a fourth: the ultimate succession of nine movements.

The succession and the continuity between one piece and the next

1. The connection between the first and second movements is a somewhat abstract one: movement 2 is a smaller-scale version of the threefold organization of the 'Artisanat furieux' cycle begun in movement 1.

2. Movement 2 pushes the flute into the foreground; this flattering promotion prepares for its dominant role in movement 3 – summoned by the signal-like top register G, the final note of 2.

3. On the other hand, there is no real link between movement 3 and movement 4: having fulfilled its function right to the last solo notes, the flute has completed its task, and is silent throughout movement 4.

4. The flute is replaced in movement 4 by viola and guitar, already paired in movement 1. They had separated in movement 2, were omitted in 3, but now return to take over the function of melodic continuity hitherto assumed by the flute.

5. It is also the viola that opens the central movement of the work with a definitive serial statement (see p. 290). The flute returns, but since it has lost its privileged position, its exploits (virtuoso passage-work and trills) are immediately copied by the viola.

6. Having ended movement 5 unaccompanied, the voice has only a few bars in which to draw breath, before linking movement 5 with movement 6. Here, the pairing of xylorimba and vibraphone provides a marked opposition to the viola/guitar pair in a double counterpoint between the two melodic duos, and between the reciprocal (and even hybrid) characteristics of the two pairs themselves: the less focused continuity of the viola/guitar and the resonant percussiveness of the vibraphone/xylorimba.

7. This short *scherzo* for three players relates to the size of the previous movement like that of a delegation to a general assembly: it is scored for a

single melodic instrument (the flute), and one from each of the two preceding pairs (vibraphone and guitar).

8. With an overlapping effect, the xylorimba and vibraphone weave around the main melody. The movement ends in an instrumentally scattered manner.

9. The voice enters right at the start of the fully scored ninth movement. The relationship of this finale to the preceding movement is one of exclusion and antagonism. Moreover, as a kind of summation of what has gone before, this movement includes quotations from all three of the previous vocal movements, and 'doubles' them, at least in part.

IN CONCLUSION

Le Marteau sans maître is a work that is much admired, and that invites critical appraisal from all quarters. However, I think it is important to draw attention to a fact that seems to have escaped even the most perceptive commentators: this work of Boulez suggests the possibility of variable interpretation within an unchanging whole.

While the score leaves the performers hardly any freedom, except for short phrases where the tempo is indicated as *libre* (movement 9) or *modéré sans rigueur* (movement 3), it nevertheless offers a fascinating formal organization which forces the listener to view each movement in two ways: as part of a cycle with its own coherence, and as part of a numerical succession, preceded and followed by another movement from another cycle.

The richly ambivalent nature of the work demands a mental capacity for substitution on the part of the listener. At the same time, it seems to me that the active listening required here is a good deal less puzzling than the many attempts being made elsewhere to modify the allegedly passive attitude of the listener to 'serious' music. *Le Marteau*'s twofold nature has both a provenance and a purpose. The Wagnerian leitmotif shares a similar ambivalence, since it is recognizable both as the reflection of a dramatic reality already encountered, and because it is attached – in *Götterdämmerung* undergoing constant modification – to the narrative thread as soon as it is heard. But it is the 'sonata' from Berg's *Lulu*, its two sections comprising two scenes divided by various episodes, that best represents this essential duality in the act of listening – because it reflects the dramatic reality of characters who exist at different moments in the work.

Boulez's purpose is the active participation required of his audience, and he achieves this by attracting the listener's attention towards the meaning of his titles. Just as the listener to *Répons* should be able to find his bearings within the various kinds of responses, so (on a level much closer to *Marteau*), he should realize that the form of *Improvisation I* (*Pli selon pli*, see pp. 316–17) arises from an interpretative understanding.

How Boulez derives and varies the 'double' of movement 5:
the final words of the poem

EX. 49

7

Third Sonata for Piano

The five movements (or *formants*) comprise:

1 *Antiphonie* c 4'00"
2 *Trope* c 8'00"
published by Universal Edition (UE 13292), 1961
3 *Constellation–Miroir* c 10'00"
published by Universal Edition (UE 13293b), 1963
4 *Strophe* c 1'00"
5 *Séquence* c 1'00"

Total duration: c 24'00"

(This rather approximate timing corresponds to that of the first performance of the complete work given by Boulez himself at Darmstadt in September 1967. However, to date, only movements 2 and 3 are published, and accordingly played and recorded; of the remainder, *Antiphonie* has been completed but awaits revision, while the other two movements are to be both extended and completely reworked.)

The reader should refer to chapter 6 of the present book for details of the various first performances of the Third Sonata, and in particular, for the overall meaning of the work with regard to its 'open' form, its literary antecedents, and the conditions influencing its musical evolution. What follows is only a rather summary description of the two published movements.

The Third Sonata should eventually comprise five movements that Boulez calls *formants*, each of which is planned to give rise to subsequent developments (trope-like variations of the initial *formants* which the composer calls 'developings'). Only two *formants* are published, and it seems as if no 'developing' has yet been completed – in addition to the published material there are only a few sketches

Present-day performances of the Third Sonata are therefore destined to be incomplete – a 'defect' that nevertheless makes each performance like a separate version of the whole, providing a minimum number of rules are observed. In practice, there are currently four possible versions:

1   *Constellation* alone
2   *Constellation–Miroir* alone (the *Miroir* is the *Constellation* movement played backwards)
3   *Trope*, followed by *Constellation*
4   *Constellation–Miroir*, followed by *Trope*

When the work is complete, there will be eight possible ways of linking the five formants – as in the following diagram, which specifies the central position of *Constellation* (or its *Miroir*):

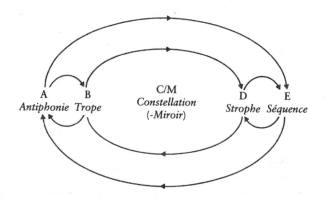

A   B   C/M   D   E
Antiphonie Trope   *Constellation*   *Strophe Séquence*
                     (-Miroir)

The eight possibilities offered are:

ABCDE   EDCBA   BACDE   DECBA
ABCED   EDCAB   BACED   DECAB

When taking the retrograde route, the *Miroir* version of *Constellation* must be played in the case of successions beginning with D or E, and this remains the formal rule – although today this rule is sometimes disregarded, with *Trope* being followed by *Constellation–Miroir*.

Clearly then, the Third Sonata is a work of circular organization and of an optional nature. These two concepts are to recur within the *formants* themselves.

TROPE

The designation 'trope' comes from medieval music and is generally taken to mean 'secondary embellishment' in relation to given material. Boulez specifies[1] the three ways in which the trope may be present in relation to the main text: it may be rhythmically integrated into the text, grafted on to it, or interpolated within it. In the first two instances the embellishments are obligatory; in the third, their inclusion is optional.

Trope comprises four sections whose titles are also borrowed from medieval scholasticism: *Texte*, *Glose*, *Commentaire* and *Parenthèse*. These four sections are graphically reproduced within a spiral binding so that they may be turned around without altering the printed order of succession.

Since *Trope* may start with any one of the four sections, there are four possible ways of linking them. But in addition, the performer is given the option of playing *Glose* before or after the neighbouring *Commentaire*, so that there are eight possibilities in all:

1. beginning with *Parenthèse*   PGCT or PCGT
2. beginning with *Commentaire* CTPG or CGTP
3. beginning with *Glose*   GCTP or GTPC
4. beginning with *Texte*   TPGC or TPCG

It will be seen that the eight possible successions available here make *Trope* a reflection of the overall structure of the Sonata, with its eight possible ways of linking the *formants*, and its intermittently circular organization.

The four sections of *Trope* are sufficiently different in kind for the transition from one section to another to be audible, they are played without interruption, with 'contact zones' provided by Boulez.

Texte

Texte is a comparatively monodic section, with a serial cantus firmus:

---

1 'Sonate, que me veux-tu?', *Orientations*, pp. 143–54.

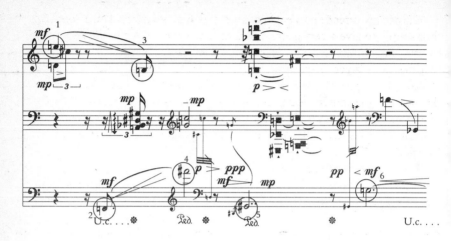

EX. 50

The composer divides the series into four groups of notes *a*, *b*, *c*, and *d*:[2]

EX. 51

2 *Boulez on Music Today*, p. 74.

It is not my intention to engage in a serial analysis of the Third Sonata,[3] but simply to give a very general idea of the way in which Boulez not only writes but 'thinks' serially. Here, the series can be perceived by the ear because it is given a quasi-melodic outline, but it also creates its own resonances where the law of non-repetition (never of much concern to Boulez) is obviously flouted. Later on, the series is reduced to its component fragments and returns to what it was – a reservoir of functions and of intervals (as in Boulez's own earlier works) rather than an ersatz theme.

Texte includes a second series, again positioned as a cantus firmus, and this forms the basis of the second and third systems (starting from *Accélérer assez peu*). This is the same series as the previous one, transposed up a diminished fifth:

EX. 52

The linear nature of the piece makes it easy to follow. From the point of view of tempo, it combines the opposites of constraint and freedom which pervade the whole Sonata by means of the rondo-like alternation of a basic tempo and sections which oscillate around this tempo in the following order:

1 Tempo (*presque lent*; ♩ = 50)
　2 *Retenu*
3 Tempo
　4 *Accélérer assez peu*
5 Tempo
　6 *Retenu*
7 Tempo, ending with *presser légèrement* (or *sans presser* if the movement is not to end with *Texte*)

3 This has already been done by Manfred Stahnke, 'Struktur und Ästhetik bei Boulez', *Hamburger Beiträge zur Musikwissenschaft*, XXI, Hamburg, 1979.

Parenthèse

As its title indicates, this is a section (again in a slow tempo) whose main 'text' is interrupted by five parentheses which are optional in performance. There is a rhythmic contrast between the strict tempo of the main text, and the freer tempo of the parentheses.

The serial material of *Parenthèse* is the same as that of *Texte*. The series from Ex. 51 is split up into its four groups *a*, *b*, *c* and *d* – the three groups *b*, *c* and *d* being heard at the start of the piece, the fourth, *a*, after the first parenthesis. Three residual notes (G, A, A♭) belong to fragment *d* of the series from Ex. 51c above. Ex. 53 shows how the series is distributed at the start of *Parenthèse*: the first parenthesis occurs at the end of the first bar, preceded and followed by a pause (see Ex. 53).

The example opposite gives a clear instance of one of the ways in which text and parentheses are linked by amplified development. The three 'gestures' outlined in the text recur in the parenthesis: the sustained note *b* becomes a huge chord in *b1*; the simple intervallic pattern *c* expands into a vast skein of notes in *c1*; the three-note motif *d* is echoed complete in *d1* which, once the parenthesis is closed, to some extent prepares for the resumption of the main text with the notes of group *a* from the original series.

These parentheses function like the implied ones already encountered in the slow movement of the Second Sonata, where they were an integral part of the musical text. But here, the fact that once they are over, the main text returns to the register, tempo, attacks and dynamics from before the interruption allows these parentheses to be omitted.

This section is calm and meditative, of variable length, and very flexible.

Glose

Glose is another slow section, but one which undergoes frequent accelerations. It is based on sonorities sometimes reminiscent of Messiaen; its characteristic trills, clusters and wide-stretched registers make it a relatively colourful section.

Commentaire

This section has a more lively tempo and a dense texture which again includes a number of optional sequences. It is more harmonic, based on the interplay of chords, and finishes with a remarkable rumbling of low trills which can make one of the most effective endings to the *formant* as a

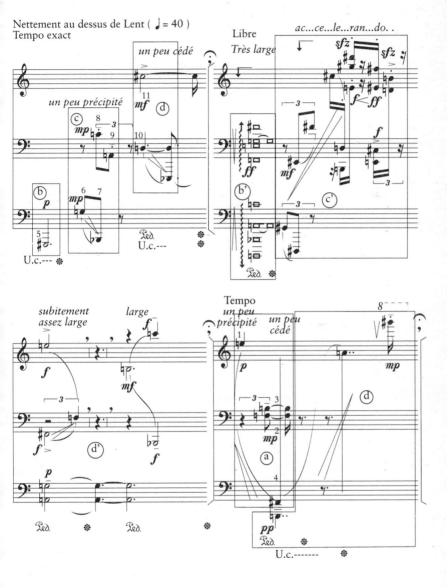

EX. 53

whole. Logically, it seems best to separate the two sections with options; one could then begin with *Texte*, the most linear section, and end with *Commentaire*. This is the order (TPGC) adopted by Charles Rosen (who recorded the work under Boulez's supervision) and by Claude Helffer in his second recording. But there is no accounting for taste: the pianist Klára Körmendi plays TPCG.

The keyboard writing of the four sections of *Trope* is in no way melodic; it comprises isolated detached notes, of varying lengths, chords hurled violently across the whole keyboard, an almost continual use of grace-notes, fast-changing alternations of arpeggiated and incisive chords, meticulous writing for both pedals, great dynamic variety and abrupt tempo changes. Even more than in the Second Sonata, a whole new vocabulary is created here – which was to prompt Boulez into experimenting still further with form.

CONSTELLATION (–MIROIR)

First a word of clarification on the instructions for performance. When I say that *Constellation–Miroir* is the 'retrograde' of *Constellation*, the term means something other than a serial retrogradation (where the notes are played from 12 to 1 instead of from 1 to 12). It even implies something different from the retrograde routes which with Berg, for example (in the *Chamber Concerto*, the *Lyric Suite*, *Der Wein*, *Lulu*), presents whole sections of the musical text in reverse, read as if from right to left.

The structural fragments of *Constellation*, to be called respectively A, B and C, are played in the order C, B and A in *Constellation–Miroir*, but within these structural fragments the chronology and direction of events remains unchanged, and is still read from left to right. The 'reading of pages from right to left' cited by Ivanka Stoianova[4] as one of the most important structural ideas of Mallarmé's *Livre* is here adopted in exactly the same way: simply by reversing the sequence of events. However, it should be borne in mind that written language can only be understood if read in one direction, while music is by nature more ambivalent.

Constellation (or its *Miroir*) is printed on nine large and separate sheets (reminiscent of the *Livre*), headed A to I, on which five main structures are set out: three are structures of 'points', printed in green, and two are structures of 'blocks', printed in red. Points and blocks are perceptibly

---

4 Ivanka Stoianova, 'Pli selon pli. Un portrait de Mallarmé', *Musique en jeu*, No. 11, 1973.

different in style: 'The antiphony of the two formal structures is impressive, with its contrast between the pointillist, discontinuous and transparent working of the "points", and the dense, compact and concentrated style of the vertical groupings and melodic curves in the "blocks".'[5]

The five main structures are played alternately, beginning and ending with a structure of points. They are preceded (*Constellation*) or followed (*Constellation–Miroir*) by a brief sixth structure called *mélange*, comprising three sequences of points and three of blocks (with colours reversed): this 'microcosm of the whole constellation' (Boulez) is like an antechamber, coming from or leading to *Trope*.

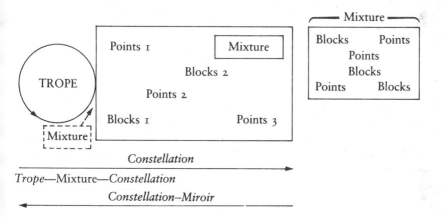

Within these five main structures the performer can to a certain extent choose his route, or at least, the means of linking the various fragmentary structures available within the large blocks or points. This is a supervised freedom, obeying a 'highway code' that suggests certain sequences, ordains some, forbids others. Boulez directs that everything has to be played, and each sub-structure is entirely written out.

Finally, certain optional possibilities within the sub-structures are left to the performer's discretion, as in the following example,[6] where he can either play or omit the lower system:

5 Ibid., p. 25.
6 This was the subject of a demonstration given by Boulez in the film that Michel Fano made about him in 1966 (see the Filmography at the end of this book) and which provides a brief opportunity to see Boulez playing his own work.

EX. 54

THE OTHER FORMANTS: *ANTIPHONIE* (1), *STROPHE* (4) AND *SEQUENCE* (5)

The following is no more than a summary of the few brief indications given by Boulez in 'Sonate, que me veux-tu?'. In their original order (*Antiphonie, Trope, Constellation, Strophe* and *Séquence*) the five *form-ants* represent an increasing number of possibilities with regard to the 'opening up' of form.

Antiphonie is the most 'fixed' movement, allowing no variation other than of its overall design. Two different structures, A and B, form an antiphony written on two separate pages. One of these comprises two fragments, the other three (cf. *Constellation*). The structure itself is written on the right-hand page, its variation on the left; this means that there can be four overall forms for *Antiphonie*:

1. all the structures from the right-hand page;
2. structure A from the left-hand page, structure B from the right;
3. all the structures from the left-hand page;
4. structure A from the right-hand page, structure B from the left.

The form of *Strophe* is built from Mallarmé's notion of the 'density' of the *Livre* as a 'formal landmark'.[7] Four stanzas (cf. *Trope*) of different

---

7 Mallarmé's notion of the 'thickness' of a book fascinated Boulez. Instead of a simple juxtaposition, his theory was that each succeeding part of a work should be enriched by the preceding ones.

duration are connected by the similarity of their material and linked according to contact zones analogous to acoustic nodes.

Finally, *Séquence* confronts a technical problem that the composer acknowledges to be as yet unresolved: the determination of variable pitches. This *formant* remains the least worked out of all.

8

Pli selon pli

The work comprises five movements:

Don, for large orchestra
Published: Universal Edition (UE 13614), 1967
Duration: 15'00"

Improvisation I sur Mallarmé, for voice and instrumental ensemble
('Le vierge, le vivace, et le bel aujourd'hui')
Published: Universal Edition (UE 12855, small version), 1958
(UE 16641, large version), 1977
Duration: 6'00"

Improvisation II sur Mallarmé, for voice and instrumental ensemble
('Une dentelle s'abolit')
Published: Universal Edition (UE 12857, single small version), 1958
Duration: 12'00"

Improvisation III sur Mallarmé, for voice and instrumental ensemble
('A la nue accablante tu')
In preparation (separate large version)
Duration: 19'00"

Tombeau, for large orchestra
Published: Universal Edition (UE 13616), 1971

(For the history of the various stages of *Pli selon pli*, see chapter 7, and
for a detailed discussion of the Mallarmé texts, see Appendix.)

When the work is given in its entirety, the large version of *Improvisation I*
should be performed in place of the small. However, it is possible to
perform *Improvisations I* and *II* alone, in which case it is the small version

of the first that should be given. My study of *Improvisation I* is based on the small version. I list only the differences in instrumentation between it and the large version, since the form remains the same.

DON

The first movement of *Pli selon pli* calls for large forces: four flutes (including alto flute), cor anglais, three clarinets, bassoon, four horns, three trumpets, two trombones, three harps, piano, celesta, mandolin, guitar, two vibraphones, timpani, bells, glockenspiel, and a full percussion section requiring seven players, in addition to the sixteen strings (4–4–5–3). The soprano voice has a small but decisive role.

Don begins with a resounding shock: a *tutti* chord which sets the scene for the whole work, before dying away rapidly. Singing or speaking (most performers choose to sing), the soprano announces the initial alexandrine of 'Don du poème' over an orchestral murmur: the phrase 'Je t'apporte l'enfant d'une nuit d'Idumée' comprises six notes centred around B♭ , a half series for the first half line of the verse and a 'sterile' repetition of the same notes for the second – with an obvious reference to the image of sterility inscribed in the text (see Appendix, pp. 400–402).

After this 'flyleaf' the first movement may be divided conveniently into four distinct phases:

1. Pages 2–17 of the score: from 0' to *c* 6'15".[1] The orchestra is split into three groups, musically constituted (but not spatially separated, which poses problems for the conductor) so as to allow for different characteristics to emerge during the course of the section:

a flutes, clarinet in B♭ , horns, violins, violas, glockenspiel
b vibraphone, harps, mandolin, guitar, piano, celesta and tubular bells
c timpani, bass drum, harp, bass clarinet, bassoon, trombones, cellos and double basses

The three groups do not play simultaneously. Group *b*, based on long resonances, plays unconducted within the time allowed. Groups *a* and *c* are directed by the right and left hands of the conductor (which thus have to be held on different levels – one high, the other low). The mainly low-pitched group *c* echoes the resonance of *b*, while the high-pitched *a* operates in a more detached and agitated manner. An opening section of

1 Boulez's second recording.

'smooth' time leads to a section of more 'striated' time (page 5 of the score, around 1'35"), *moins hésitant et moins lent*. Here, the groups are still heterophonically related, even when group *b* is subdivided, group *c* becomes more exuberant, and instruments begin to move from one group to another (as when the horn from group *a* joins group *c*). The piano, previously part of group *b*, becomes independent (page 7, *c* 2'30") – introducing its discreet punctuations to the *pianissimo* accompaniment of a low cymbal.

Like the following sections, this whole opening paragraph comprises an exposition of the material for the cycle, and for *Improvisation III* in particular: the celesta and guitar figures on page 8 (2'50"), the cello solo on page 9 (3'20"), the cadenza for vibraphone and xylophone on pages 11 and 12 (4'10"), the harp solos on pages 12 and 13 (4'30") – even the entry of the brass on a sustained C on page 10 (3'40"), which foreshadows an analogous entry at the beginning of *Tombeau*.

The first section ends on a general pause (page 17).

2. Pages 17–21 of the score; from *c* 6'15" to *c* 7'40". This is a section of forcefully marked time, of increasing intensity, and with the whole orchestra (still divided into more mobile groups) now being conducted. The indication *agité* is used several times for what remains of group *b*, which is no longer characterized by its lingering, elusive resonances. The orchestral colouring includes hints of *Petrushka* (the wind writing on page 20), or of Messiaen (the vibraphones on the same page). In other respects, the whole section is centred around the tritone F$\sharp$ – C, which acts like a signature, right from the opening bars.

3. Pages 22–8 of the score; from *c* 7'40" to *c* 12'10". This central section focuses on the voice in a series of 'prior reminiscences' (Boulez) of the following sonnet. It starts with a violent orchestral introduction, which ignores the original instrumental groupings, and is controlled by a single beat. The writing loses all linear implications as trilled chords explode into short, violent attacks with sharply contrasted dynamics. Then the voice enters with a condensed version of the three sonnets, in reverse order:

i. Over long sustained notes on the strings and *pianissimo* cymbals, the voice (sometimes in quarter tones) pronounces key words from *Improvisation III*: 'basalte', 'écho', 'écume', 'laves', 'éparves'. Inserts which are sometimes obligatory, sometimes optional (though generally included by the singer), mix in syllables taken from other words.

ii. Following the device that allows for notes to be sustained for as long as the singer's breath will permit (see *Improvisation II, Senza tempo*), three verbal structures anticipate 'Une dentelle s'abolit': 'selon nul ventre', 'enfui' and 'blême'. The scoring is transparent and small-scale, with only keyboards, harps and a few touches of mandolin or guitar in the first two, and still fewer instruments in the third. The three structures, which are linked by an accompaniment of strings, cymbals and maracas, may be taken in any order, provided the first is not followed by the third.

iii. Finally, as an introductory approach to *Improvisation I*, the singer is offered seven statements from the first sonnet:

a d'autrefois se souvient	*a1* vibre
b resplendit	*b1* c'est lui
c pour n'avoir pas	*c1* qui sans espoir
d hiver	

Certain of these statements may be omitted, and their succession obeys semi-optional rules. Perhaps encouraged by the conductor, the singer in the two existing recordings chooses the order a–c1–b–a1–d. Here again, the accompaniment of strings and percussion is lightweight, and does not distract the listener's attention from the words.

4. Pages 28 to the end of the score; from *c* 12'10" to *c* 15'15". After the preceding section ends in a haze of resonant trills, the huge coda to the first movement begins. This time, the forces are divided into two groups, the first comprising woodwind, horns, harps, xylophones, bells and cymbals, and the second, brass, strings, piano, vibraphones and gongs. The two groups alternate a musical text according to one of the six procedures offered by the composer. Here again, it seems that in the two recorded versions, Boulez deemed it unnecessary to change the first (evidently satisfactory) succession. At the start, everything is *agité et instable*, and all six versions end in the same way – with a violent *tutti* that finally explodes onto an incisive chord in which the A (the middle note of the tritone F$\sharp$ – C) predominates.

In conclusion, this is what Ivanka Stoianova has to say:

A description of the material used in *Don* is proof of the fact that the musical structuring of the movement is dictated by its place in the cycle – Boulez would hardly have been able to justify an autonomous piece of such relatively disparate textual content. *Don* is not a piece fenced in by remote organizatory connections, although the development and interaction of remote material is also used as a structuring principle. *Don* is thought of as a special kind of 'open form' – an anticipatory programme of the materials and procedures of the whole extended cycle. The movement is structured like the '*Page*' with which the '*Livre*' begins – as the open microcosm of an 'expanding universe' which, 'fold upon fold', is to produce the portrait of Mallarmé.[2]

Nevertheless, a distance exists between this programme and the reality of the versions played and recorded – the distance that separates every conceptual project from its professional realization. Without dwelling on details, the range of different possibilities essential to its purpose seems much reduced. What is important is that *Don* remains like a magnificent and imposing gateway through which one gains access to the work.

IMPROVISATION I: 'LE VIERGE, LE VIVACE, ET LE BEL AUJOURD'HUI'

The overall organization of the Improvisation

As if echoing Mallarmé's pessimistic enquiry into the flight of creativity, Boulez has treated the sonnet in an almost mechanical manner. He sets the text of two quatrains and two tercets for the voice, placing three instrumental interludes in the spaces between the stanzas and punctuating the whole with a reflexive instrumental coda:

Quatrain 1	'Le vierge . . .'	voice and instruments	Score: o
(space)		instruments	A
Quatrain 2	'Un cygne . . .'	voice and instruments	B
(space)		instruments	C
Tercet 1	'Tout son col . . .'	voice and instruments	D
(space)		instruments	E
Tercet 2	'Fantôme . . .'	voice and instruments	F
(end)		instruments	G

Two kinds of organizational logic may be discerned here. The one follows the structure of the poem by contrasting the two 'sails'[3] of its quatrains and tercets; the eight sections of the score then divide into 4+4 – as indicated by the tempo organization:

> O and D: *pas trop lent*
> A and E: *modéré*
> B and F: respectively *très modéré* and *pas trop lent*
> C and G: *très lent*

2 Ivanka Stoianova, op. cit., p. 94.
3 The term chosen by Ivanka Stoianova, who has made an extensive study of *Pli selon pli* (1973, see Bibliography) – from which I have in part drawn my inspiration.

The other may for the moment be represented as a sort of arch form, of which the interlude C is to be the corner stone, section G the outer coda.

The instrumental organization

The chamber version is scored for soprano voice, vibraphone, bells, harp and four percussion players: the first has two metal blocks, two tam-tams and a bass drum, the second a pair of high-pitched crotales and two high-pitched side drums, the third has the same instruments but pitched lower, the fourth three suspended cymbals and three gongs of different tessituras.

It is particularly interesting to trace the use of some of these instruments. The harp is employed in three ways. At the very beginning, there is a single instance of a *sforzando* and *staccato* chord produced together with the vibraphone; the harp is not heard again in this first section, so I tend to regard this example as peripheral. Then, at the start of sections A and E, an ascending figure occurs, based on an arpeggiated chord. Finally, in sections C and G, the harp intervenes with resonant chords – or, exceptionally, *sforzando* and *staccato*, as at the beginning of the movement.

The vibraphone plays in all sections, but in two different ways. In the vocal sections O, B and D, it is accompanied by metal blocks as it supports the voice with resonant chords or notes sustained by vibrato; in the instrumental sections A and E, it has a more melodic function. This division of roles is by no means entirely predictable, since the vibraphone is used resonantly in the instrumental section C, and forms a duo in counterpoint with the voice in section E.

The *bel canto* vocal part is supple, sympathetically placed throughout its tessitura, and flexible in relation to the given metre (which changes with almost every bar). The four vocal passages are differentiated from each other both by a syllabic/melismatic opposition that will be explained later, and by their rejection of serialization.

We can now observe the patterns of instrumentation at work in *Improvisation I*. The first is an instrumental quartet composed of crotales, gongs, vibraphone and metal blocks. This supports the vocal line in sections O and E. Slightly modified, this instrumental pattern is still based on the pairing of vibraphone and metal blocks but in section B substitutes cymbals for gongs, and in section D adds cymbals to the first group, thereby increasing its resonant effect.

For the wholly instrumental sections a second combination is established by the pairing of vibraphone and harp in section A, and its resonance is extended by the gongs in section E.

With the exception of the metal blocks – made redundant by the tam-tam and bass drum – an instrumental *tutti* is finally convened for section G (foreshadowed without the gongs in section O).

Timed from the first recording conducted by the composer, the duration of the various sections reveals an appreciable difference between the overall timing indicated in the score (6′00″) and that actually realized in performance (4′55″). The internal timings indicate three durational units: the short sections A and E are about 15″, the medium-length sections O, B, D, F and G (that is to say, all the vocal sections and the 'finale', G) last about half a minute each, and the long section C (after the quatrains) about 1′20″.

This information is collated in the following table:

SECTIONS:	O	A	B	C	D	E	F	G
Text	Q1	space	Q2	space	T1	space	T2	silence
Music	vocal	instr.	vocal	instr.	vocal	instr.	vocal	instr.
Duration (5′)	40″	17″	33″	1′20″	40″	15″	35″	35″
Tempo	pas trop lent	modéré	très modéré	très lent	(a)	(b)	(a)	(d)
	(a)	(b)	(c)	(d)				
Voice part	syllabic		slightly melismatic		melismatic		syllabic	
Instruments	+harp at the outset		+ cymbals – gongs – crotales	– gongs	+ cymbals	+ gongs		
Repetitive organization								
Symmetrical organization								Finale
(reminder)	O	A	B	C	D	E	F	G

The two organizational logics: repetition and symmetry

While it is no more than a graphic summary of the preceding information, this table clearly shows that two organizational logics are simultaneously at work in *Improvisation I* – a remarkable phenomenon which means that there are two different ways of listening to this short, approachable work. This duality is also inherent in the type of mobility that Boulez envisaged at the time: a fully notated material open to various interpretations. The meeting with Mallarmé takes place here on the interior level of perceptive decision. Incidentally, this device (already encountered in *Le Marteau sans maître*) obviously calls for more active participation on the part of the listener than many of the gimmicky courses of action offered by sensation-seeking composers of the seventies.

Thus *Improvisation I* seems to include the possibility of a twofold organization. The first would seem to be dictated by the structure of the poem (see p. 402). This organization is corroborated by a tempo structure which offers more or less the same succession in sections D, E, F, and G as in O, A, and B (a repetitional logic that was soon to be tempered). Finally, the durations of the last four sections correspond almost exactly to those of the first. *Improvisation I* will therefore be heard as a form of the verse/response kind, with the response shortened to fit the smaller dimensions of the tercets in relation to the quatrains. It can be seen that the instrumentation seems likewise to observe a succession of pairs uniting similar patterns: the first group for O and D, the second for A and E, the third for C and G.

However, this instrumentation can also be understood in a way that involves a reinterpretation of the previous data. Provided that section G is regarded as a true 'finale', as suggested by its tutti scoring (like the conclusion of *Le Marteau sans maître*), a symmetrical organization can be discerned, in which the outer vocal sections O and F correspond, as do the neighbouring instrumental sections A and E; the two other vocal sections B and D symmetrically enclose the long instrumental section C.

The other data can of course be understood as similarly ambiguous: durations, arranged symmetrically from O to F around the long section C, and tempos – of which the *pas trop lent* of section F is authorized by the symmetrical hypothesis alone. The instrumentation clearly reinforces this emerging arch form, which offers the additional advantage of the judicious isolation of section C – a section which corresponds to the role played by the silence separating the quatrains from the tercets in a sonnet.

The sectional succession of Improvisation I

EX. 55

In the first quatrain (O), the start of the sung verse rests on a chord played by the vibraphone and the harp, delicately underpinned by percussion (see Ex. 55). The first phrase, which lies within the constantly reaffirmed range of an eleventh (D–G1), does not announce a series, as its syllabic character might suggest. Instead, it settles on certain focal notes, principally the C, G, non-accented in bar 1, accented on 'bel' in bar 2 and D, alpha and omega of the line progressively rising in intensity from the simple article 'le' in bar 1, to the non-accented syllable 'vi' in the same bar, to the accented article 'le' in bar 2, finally landing on the tonic accent 'hui' in bar 3. This encompasses the whole dynamic shape of the line.

This first line is significant in that it shows a kind of melodic writing alert to the text, progressing by successive rebounds onto focal notes, and apparently rejecting any serial obligations (only ten of the twelve notes are sounded, omitting the E♮ and the B♭).

The first interlude (A) 'corrects' the defective series by entrusting the vibraphone with the melodic role of the absent voice:

EX. 56

While the vocal writing had seemed to attempt flight from its chosen surroundings, the commentary seems to speak of the futility of such a hope by pinning the melody down within the discipline of an inflexible series.

In the second quatrain (B) the melismatic writing for the voice suggests a euphoric relaxation: this is the time of happy memories ('une cygne d'autrefois se souvient . . .'). Here, 'autrefois' applies to 'cygne', symbolizing the flight of time. The instrumental accompaniment becomes unobtrusive, with the vibraphone reduced to a delicate *tremolando* scarcely fluctuating in intensity, and the percussion remaining *pianissimo*. The melodic line is almost effusive here, with the basic unit now the semiquaver (absent from O) and with the pitch range reduced. The repeated notes on '(ré)gion où vivre' and '(en)nui' evidently serve a purpose.

After the rhetorical optimism of the first quatrain and the exorcism of sterility in the second, the second interlude (C) brings us to the centre of the piece. It is a moment to pause, to reflect, and to review the available forces. This is a long, slow and harmonically filled-out section: sustained chords set low on the harp and in the middle register of the vibraphone are extended by medium-range bells played with felt mallets. After a punctuating bar of resonant and non-resonant percussion (bass drum, side drum and cymbals) that breaks off on a pause, the section ends with a seven-note chord.

In the first tercet (D) the illusory optimism of the text draws the voice into an intensified melisma more striking for the broadening of its rhythmic values than for the extension of single syllables within the vocal line itself. This is the most lyrically sustained section of the *Improvisation*, supported by vibraphone and a homogeneous rhythmic pattern on the percussion. Particular emphasis is placed on the word 'espace', positioned mid-phrase as the highest note, the longest value (a dotted crotchet), and with the maximum intensity (*quasi forte*).

The third interlude (E) is very brief. It presents a melodic commentary on the vibraphone, in principle analogous to section A, even though it is now non-serial. This is a wide-ranging melody (from low G to the C$\sharp$ in the third octave above) which underlines the optimistic aspirations of the preceding tercet. The gongs form an accompaniment to the vibraphone, which has what amounts to a virtuoso cadenza at the end of the section. We are here in the realm of 'bravura'.

The second tercet (F) banishes irrational hope. More spoken than sung, 'fantôme' refers as much to the image of the 'cygne d'autrefois' as to the image of flight. This section conveys the sense of a tragic immobility, with the melody again syllabic, again favouring certain widely separated notes, as in the first quatrain. The tessitura of the melody lies between the middle E$\flat$ and the soprano A$\flat$ which is repeated six times, each time strategically placed so as to outline an increase in dynamic intensity that reaches a triple *forte* at the word 'inutile' – the very epitome of failure:

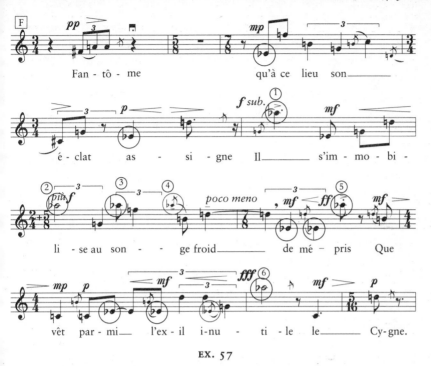

EX. 57

This crisis point of the text – 'ex-*il i*-nu-ti-le' – is underlined by the repeated Ds of the vocal line. A seven-note vibraphone counterpoints the voice, together with an inflexible and seemingly neutral pattern on the percussion.

The finale (G) then sums up the content of the whole sonnet: all the instruments are assembled, but their elusive resonances and quasi-mechanical *sostenuto* impart an air of futility. The three identical percussive gestures with which the movement ends resound like the three blows of fate.

IMPROVISATION II: 'UNE DENTELLE S'ABOLIT'

Scored for soprano voice and nine instruments, *Improvisation II* contrasts five very resonant instruments with the percussion placed between them – as in the following diagram:

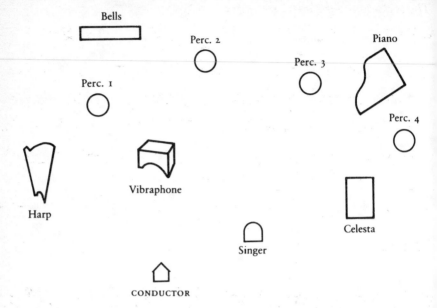

This choice of instruments places those of fixed pitch (the five listed above) alongside others (the percussion) which border on noise. In certain circumstances, it is possible for the former to approach the latter; Boulez explains[4] the acoustic reasons for this disposition:

I arrange the platform so as to mix the three different categories of sound: determinate pitch, non-determinate pitch, and noise. This produces a kind of stereophony of instrumental characteristics. The celesta is not particularly resonant, so it is placed in front – close to the conductor's rostrum on the right. The harp is more resonant, but its sound may be covered by that of the piano if they are too close together, so I put it in front on the left. The vibraphone is of medium dynamic strength, so it occupies the middle of the platform in front of the conductor. Because of its dynamic power, the piano goes at the back on the right, with the most resonant instrument (the bells) on the left and the unpitched percussion forming a group in the centre.

This idea of distributing the percussion between the other instruments was, of course, inaugurated in *Doubles* and revived in *Rituel*, while instrumental spacing in general is a notion dear to Boulez – and the initiating principle for '. . . *explosante-fixe*. . .'.

4 'Construire une improvisation', from the Strasburg conference of 1961, published in *Orientations*, pp. 155–73 (p. 157).

The evolution of the poem I: the two types of vocal writing

	A : instrumental	0′00″	0′30″
Q₁	B : vocal + instrumental	0′30″	1′20″
	'une dentelle s'abolit'		
	C₁: instrumental	1′50″	0′50″
Q₂	D : vocal + instrumental	2′40″	4′15″
	'cet unanime blanc confit'		
	C₂: instrumental	6′55″	0′10″
T₁	E : vocal + instrumental	7′05″	2′00″
	'mais chez qui du reve'		
	C₃ instrumental	9′05″	0′10″
T₂	F : vocal + instrumental	9′15″	2′15″
	'telle que vers quelque fenêtre'		
	G : instrumental	11′30″	0′35″
		Duration	12′05″

Outwardly, *Improvisation II* treats Mallarmé's text as in the preceding *Improvisation*: as two cycles of quatrains and tercets separated by interludes and enclosed by a prelude and a postlude. The position and duration of section D seems to make it the centre and the pivot of the musical poem – an impression reinforced by its basic material.

As in *Improvisation I*, the interweaving of the various sections is organized according to a network of correspondences (concerning either the tempos, or the vocal gestures, or the instrumentation), but now in a less obvious manner.

Boulez himself[5] tells us that the whole piece is built on the initial opposition of two types of vocal writing, *a* and *b*. The first (*a*) is ornamental, 'and here the melody consists chiefly of melismas and ornaments. In these circumstances syllabic declamation is impossible . . . This results, of course, in a certain unintelligibility but this is deliberate.' The first entry of the voice makes the point:

EX. 58

5 *Orientations*, p. 169.

This ornamental structure *a* governs the whole of the first quatrain, while the second is ruled by the syllabic structure *b*. Here, the improvisatory character of the piece is affirmed, since the tempo of this section is entirely determined by the soloist, who must sing her phrase in a single breath – leaving the conductor to distribute the instrumental text in relation to the progress of the vocal line. The *senza tempo* is a clear indication of the spontaneous, even improvised, character of this arrangement.

The piece thus concerns the relationship between these two modes of writing, which are initially exclusive, then combined, and finally re-asserted separately. Structure *a* returns during the course of the second quatrain (page 32 of the score), where it is combined with structure *b* on the words 'plus qu'il n'ensevelit'. It then returns for the first tercet, at the end of which it makes way for structure *b* in the manner of the preceding stanza ('aux creux néant musicien'). In the second tercet, *a* is again interrupted by *b* on 'selon nul ventre', while the end of the line combines both forms. The final line of the poem ('Filial on aurait pu naître') is built entirely upon structure *a*.

The basic tempos and their instrumentation

The tempos of different sections of the piece constitute a network of sectional connections. The *andante alla breve* of the introduction (A) later alternates regularly with other tempos during the instrumental statements in sections D (the second quatrain) and E (the first tercet). The *lent et flexible* tempo belongs to B (the first quatrain) and the essentially similar E (the first tercet) – and, together with the preceding, to F.

The *senza tempo* belongs to the vocal statements D and E, where the voice adopts structure *b*, and again, to F.

To these three tempos of the vocal sections a fourth is added for the interludes, moving between *assez vif* and *vif*.

The instrumentation is sometimes resonant, without percussion (A); sometimes it has a more diversified but subordinate role: supporting, echoing, adding resonance, or imitating (B). Elsewhere it freely accompanies the *senza tempo* with brief (and occasionally more incisive) interjections – as when the harp is treated almost like a guitar in bar 55.

Just as the interludes C1, C2 and C3 have their own tempo, so they offer a strikingly individual instrumental detail: the dominating sound of the maracas gives the interludes the character of real 'refrains', as Ivanka Stoianova has observed.

The evolution of the poem II: the word engulfed in sound

The most logical way of studying *Improvisation II*, is to look at the piece as a succession of events. The introduction (A) is a short and uncomplicated section, with frequent stopping points, scored for the five resonant instruments alone. In the first quatrain (B), sense is not yet contradicted by the ornamentation of vocal structure *a*. It opens with a rapidly unfolding arpeggiated gesture on the piano; the vocal line then begins a series but does not pursue it: using the C and E♭ as pivots (cf. Ex. 58), the phrase is repetitive in effect. The interlude C1 sets clusters on vibraphone and bells and one incisive harp chord against a wave-like succession of *crescendo–accelerando* on the maracas. Both the maracas and the basic tempo (*assez vif / vif*) are interrupted by a short segment marked *large, plus calme*.

Section D, the second quatrain, is the most developed. As we have seen, this is ruled by the second type of vocal structure *b*, with its monosyllables set within long note values. It is here that the improvisation proper begins, guided by a succession of notes at first corresponding to the arrangement of the lines, then progressively dislocating them – as in the following diagram:

Senza tempo	cet unanime blanc conflit	syllabic (8 syllables)
Andante–alla breve	(instrumental)	
Senza tempo	d'une guirlande	syllabic (4 syllables)
Andante–alla breve	avec la même	syllabic (4 syllables)
Senza tempo	enfui/contre la vitre/blême	syllabic (2 + 5 + 1)
	flotte	syllabic/ornamental
Andante–alla breve	plus qu'il	
Senza tempo	(qu'il)	
Andante–alla breve	n'en	
Senza tempo	(n'en)	ornamental
Andante–alla breve	-se-	
Senza tempo	-ve-	
Andante–alla breve		
Senza tempo	-lit.	

Starting from 'plus qu'il n'ensevelit', the sung word is fragmented and finally buried, as the two types of vocal structure interpenetrate one another. The instrumental writing either supports the voice with a resonance often produced by harmonics, or offers a commentary on the words through the five main instruments, underpinned by suspended cymbals.

It is worth noting the virtuoso brilliance of the celesta in bar 65, the damping of the harp in bar 66, and the chameleon-like behaviour of the other instruments in the same bar.

The interlude C2 is extremely brief. It is followed by section E (the first tercet), which starts out in the melismatic manner of section B. It then integrates both the syllabic style of *b* – 'au creux néant' – and the elements employed in the interlude, including the maracas. This is a composite section, somewhere between the strict definition of the preceding quatrains and the finale-like character of the following section F. This last vocal section is provided with its own prelude (bars 109–12). All the various tempos found throughout the piece recur here, each affected with its own inaugural style:

(a) bar 113 *Lent, flexible*	melismatic voice ('tel que vers quelque fenêtre'); instrumental *tutti*
(b) bar 117 *Andante – alla breve*	instruments and a little percussion, then maracas
(c) bar 120 *Senza tempo*	syllabic voice ('selon nul ventre'), resonant punctuations
(d) bar 121 *Alla breve – poco più lento*	extended resonances
(e) bar 124 *Senza tempo*	continuation of (c) ('que'); *staccato* punctuations
(f) bar 126 *Alla breve – adagio*	continuation of (d)
(g) bar 127 *Senza tempo*	continuation and end of (c) and (e) ('le')
(h) bar 128 *Alla breve–più adagio*	continuation and end of (d) and (f)
(i) bar 129 *Senza tempo*	syllabic voice on one syllable ('sien'), with instrumental support of the interlude type
(j) bar 130 *Ad libitum*	five instrumental gestures in imitation of the five syllables of (c)
(k) bar 131 *Lent, retenu*	return to melisma ('filial on aurait pu naître'); instrumentation close to that of (b)
(l) bar 134 *Alla breve – andante*	postlude: piano, then maracas

It will be seen that the sequence is interrupted between bars 120 and 128 with a system of parentheses later to be used in the Third Sonata. The overall movement here is really that of a confrontation of opposing forces, the hypothesis of their productivity, and an abrupt return to the point of departure: an almost direct reflection of the interpretation of Mallarmé's poem.

IMPROVISATION III: 'A LA NUE ACCABLANTE TU'

Improvisation III confronts the analyst with a twofold and considerable difficulty. On the one hand, unlike the two preceding pieces, Boulez sets only the first few lines of the Mallarmé sonnet to music. Giving them an extended articulation that tends to obscure the literal sense, he then places them in a particularly sumptuous orchestral setting that suppresses the idea of a subordinate (or even merely commentating) relationship between orchestra and soloist.

However, after recording *Pli selon pli* in London for the second time in November 1981, using a still unpublished score and orchestral material, Boulez decided to make some rather far-reaching alterations to *Improvisation III*. We are thus faced with somewhat disparate material:

(a) the manuscript conducting score (in a copyist's hand) used at the recording
(b) a first recording (with Lukomska) made from this score
(c) a second recording (with Bryn-Julson), made from this score, but with the addition of changes made during rehearsal
(d) a manuscript score (in Boulez's hand) still in course of publication at the end of 1983

To sum up: the work to be heard on a recent disc corresponds only in part with the work as presented today. One hopes – perhaps over-optimistically, given the present climate with regard to the recording of contemporary music – that the revised version will eventually be available in a third complete recording.

Meanwhile, it would be useful to discover what the recorded and written versions have in common, as well as the differences between the two, and to examine the direction and the significance of the changes.

The permanence of the poem

The most spectacular change between the two versions is the addition of the fourth line of the sonnet to the three already set. But that does not alter Boulez's intention to immerse parts of the literary text within the music, so that the poem should influence the music from within – in a manner all the more effective for its subtlety. The poem is therefore implicit in a way more reminiscent of parts of *Le Marteau sans maître* (notably 'Bourreaux de solitude', and the 'double' of 'Bel édifice . . .') than of the two preceding *Improvisations*.

In another respect, the prominence given to the wordless voice makes it serve as a transition between the voice singing the text and the instrumental ensemble itself. The dislocation of syllables has a similar function. In addition, the use of quarter-tone writing for the voice and harps also establishes a vocal and instrumental continuity.

The form of the piece is firmly controlled, articulated as in the preceding *Improvisations* by the repetition at a distance of structural fragments relating to the organization of timbre and tempos, as well as of melodic and harmonic material. For example, four *Indicatifs* (heard at the beginning, in the middle at around 7', and at the end – about 16'30") serve to scan and to mark out the piece: harp, voice, guitar–mandolin–percussion, and xylophones, then as brief reminders, xylophones, harps, celesta–bells, mandolin–guitar; other separated correspondences may be found.

But it goes without saying that Boulez's approach to the treatment of the text involves abandoning the straightforward alternation of instrumental and vocal sequences used to govern the organization of the two preceding *Improvisations*. Like the caesura separating the quatrains from the tercets in the sonnet, the central *Indicatifs* divide *Improvisation III* into two parts; yet this comparison is obviously vulnerable when confronted by the identity and the placing of the sung texts. All in all, it is better to retain the idea of *Improvisation III* as a form whose articulation is in some way camouflaged.

The evolution of the form, both central and absent

What follows is an indication of the main differences between the two versions (the timings are taken from the second recording, the rehearsal figures from the score presently being published):

RECORDING (1981)	SCORE (1983)
(A)	*Fig.*
0'00" Harps	1 + sustained tenor trombone
0'10" Wordless voice, unaccompanied	2 Modified vocal line; accompaniment (flutes/others/flutes) abolished
1'40" Guitar, mandolin, percussion	Abolished
1'57" Xylophones	8 Xylophones
(B)	
2'12" Harps, with other instruments	9 Harps + sustained tenor trombone
	10 Harps tacet; other instruments
	11 Harps resume
2'25" Wordless voice (as in A) + instruments (mandolin, guitar, percussion)	12 The same vocal line with flutes and harps
(C)	
4'25" Xylophones	15 As before
	20 Intermediate section, numerous instruments
(D)	
6'10" Voice and orchestra: 'A la nue . . .'	21 As before
(E)	
7'05" Xylophones	22 Xylophones (as before)
	23 Interlude
7'20" Harps	24 As before
7'30" Celesta, bells (punctuating chords)	26 Orchestral interlude with trills on celesta, bells and:
8'00" Mandolin, guitar	27 Mandolin, guitar
(F), (G) – optional voice	
8'15" Orchestra	

8′55″ Voice and orchestra: 'Basse de basalte et de laves'	27 As before
Orchestra	28 Orchestra, with:
(H)	30 Vocalise (+ orchestra) until
	31
12′00″ Celesta solo	34 As before
12′15″ Orchestra, with solo cello	35 As before
	37 With hummed vocalise
14′40″ Voice and orchestra: 'A même les échos esclaves'	41 As before
16′10″ Celesta solo	46 Voice + orchestra: 'par une trompe sans vertu'
16′35″ *Indicatifs*' ending in succession	48 *Indicatifs*' ending intertwined
18′25″ End	

1. The opening vocalise, previously unaccompanied, is given instrumental support.

2. The section for harps preceding the second entry of the voice (*c* 2′12″) is interrupted by a sequence for trombones at figure 10, resuming at figure 11.

3. The orchestral interlude at figure 26 has incorporated the orchestral section previously occurring *c* 8′15″, together with the preceding mandolin–guitar sequence.

4. An accompanied vocalise occurs at figure 30 as a somewhat distant echo of the sung line heard earlier (*c* 8′55″).

5. Similarly, the humming voice appears with the orchestra between figures 37 and 38, preceding the third line (the last in the recorded version) of the sonnet.

6. Most importantly, there is the addition of a fourth line of the sonnet (the last of the first quatrain) at figure 46: 'par une trompe sans vertu'.

7. The final *Indicatifs*, which were successive (at 16′30″), now combine in a cinematic dissolve:

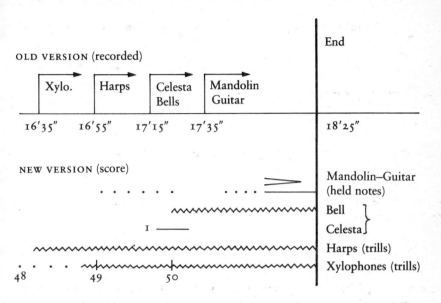

The direction and significance of the changes

These differences paradoxically make for a greater complexity and at the same time a greater clarity and decipherability within the now more closely woven texture. Wordless vocal techniques, such as vocalises and humming, occur more often, and these interpolations subtly underline the transitions. The extra fourth line gives the voice a greater presence in the second half than in the first. There is another more general difference: the disappearance of any elements of variability. The few variables that there were mainly concerned the last two statements of the poem ('basse de basalte et de laves' and 'A même les échos esclaves') which could each be superimposed upon the supporting orchestra at two different points. In the second recording, Bryn-Julson places the first as early as possible, while delaying the second. Many details (of minor importance in themselves, but together comprising a positive gesture) were endowed with a degree of freedom in performance that makes *Improvisation III* the closest to the traditional concept of 'improvisation'.

All these have disappeared in the new version. The more subtle, if not more sophisticated, musical text eliminates all traces of variability stemming from the period in which *Improvisation III* was written and first performed. We are now faced with a new work, which perfectly reflects Boulez's heightened awareness of the impossibility of making subtlety compatible with variability, at least not with large forces. A form which is obscured as soon as it is varied clearly indicates the necessity for a fixed route in order to avoid the surreptitious reintroduction of inadvertent chance leading merely to a defective realization. Boulez's thinking (notably via Wagner, Berg and Proust) was increasingly directed towards complex forms which hide their procedural methods and encourage those who are interested to make new discoveries every time they examine them. It was therefore logical that *Improvisation III*, the penultimate evolutionary point of *Pli selon pli*, should acquire this specific dimension. Far from alienating the imagination, this potential complexity fires it with a vision of all the possibles.

TOMBEAU

This is the last piece of the cycle and the one which gives the work as a whole its ultimate poetic meaning. It is scored for large orchestra: two flutes, cor anglais, three clarinets and bassoon; horn, two trumpets and three trombones; two harps, piano, celesta, guitar, an important percussion section, and strings (4–4–2–2).

Like the tombstone of its title, this is a block-like piece that cannot be grasped through the detail of a particular articulation, but essentially as three stages:

1 The first phase, which occupies almost half the movement (pages 1–38 of the score, figures 0–260, from 0'00" to 7'15"), represents a progressive consolidation of the discourse, from the initial two-note chord on the piano to the eventual bringing into play of the whole orchestra. Written as a series of sustained chords punctuated by rapid *staccato* motifs, the number of players increases, notwithstanding the generally quiet dynamic level. The time organization is relatively flexible, notably as the result of pauses over rests, where the orchestra is silent apart from one or two instruments that sustain the sound over a duration left to the conductor's discretion.

2 The second phase (pages 39–76 of the score, figures 260–520, 7'15" to 13'15") is a little more compressed than the previous one, but it adopts a similar scheme: an opening virtuoso cadenza for the piano (over sustained string trills and resonating notes on bells and harps) is followed by the progressive addition of all the other instruments, building into a spirited discourse for the whole ensemble.

3 The last phase begins after a sudden interruption. Here, the orchestra is split into resonant groups, separated by pauses, and alternating with a series of five regularly spaced chords:

harps–celesta=vibraphone–guitar, then piano echoing	five chords	2″
brass	resonance	5″
xylophones, bells, gongs, tam-tam,	five chords	2″
woodwind	resonance	8″
group I	five chords	2″
strings	resonance	6″
piano	five chords	2″

The durations are those indicated in the score; the various episodes are linked by a sustained note on the horn, foreshadowing its important role in what follows.

This is a sung coda in which the voice states the last line of 'Tombeau de Verlaine' – a poem that indicates the precise nature of poetic creativity. 'Un peu profond ruisseau calomnié la mort' begins as an extremely supple vocal line in counterpoint with the horn, and surrounded by remarkable writing for the guitar, against a background of trills on strings and wind. The vocal part fades away until the singer reaches the end of her breath on the word 'mort'. The splitting up of the main body of the orchestra in the preceding bars (see above) thus leads to the last word of the poem and of the whole work. The violent final chord, *tutti* and *fortissimo* closes the work as it began: the extremities of both *Don* and *Tombeau* suggest an infinite renewal of the organization of poetic expression.[6]

I end with three general remarks on *Tombeau*. Firstly, unlike the preceding pieces (*Don, Improvisations II* and *III* – and in particular the first version of the latter), *Tombeau* does not include the principle of variability beyond the normal interpretative decisions taken by the conductor; such a principle would have been inappropriate in relation to the poetic image suggested by the title. The completely traditional aspect of the work's development contributes to the reinstatement of the 'work as object' – a status forcibly reaffirmed by Boulez at the time.

6 In order to reinforce the character of 'eternal return' displayed by this ending which is also a beginning, it has often been said that the final chord of *Tombeau* is identical to the first chord of *Don*. The gesture is certainly the same, but the assertion is naïve in respect of the actual notes: the chromatic content is total in both cases but, when it comes to timbre, the forces used are much larger in *Tombeau*.

Secondly, the increasing consolidation of the discourse takes place in two successive waves that depend on a perceptive illusion: while the tempos indicated get slower and slower, the impression is that of an acceleration – since an increase in the number of sound events occurring within successive sequences additionally entails a natural dynamic augmentation. This type of gesture has a famous precedent in the beginning of the last movement of Berg's *Lyric Suite*.

Finally, one of the structural procedures at work in *Tombeau* is its organization around a number of focal notes. The first section gives a privileged position to the progressively more assertive C (the violin trills at 60, the flutter-tongued trumpet at 155, the violin solo at 175, the lidless piano at 180, violins and flutes at 190, 205, and so on – up to 255–7). In the second half this reference is abandoned, so clarifying the division between the two parts. It then seems (though more conjecturally) that the work is centred on the A: specifically, the voice at 520 enters on a D♯ which in a chromatic scale beginning on A represents a least a median degree, and the final chord gives a privileged position to the A through the registration of its formalized chromatic totality.

9

Eclat
Eclat / Multiples

Eclat, for fifteen instruments

Composition: 1964–5
First performance: at the Monday Evening Concerts,
University of California, Los Angeles, 26 March 1965,
under Boulez; first performance in France: at the
Domaine musical, 1966, under Boulez
Published: Universal Edition (UE 14283, photocopy of MS), 1965
(UE 17746, fair copy of score), 1983
Duration: 8′00″–10′00″

Eclat/Multiples, for twenty-five instruments
(as *Eclat*, plus basset-horn and nine violas)

Composition: 1971–
First performance: (partial), London, March 1974
a section of the BBC SO, under Boulez
Published: Universal Edition (UE 14283 1w; fair copy
of *Eclat*, and a photocopy of the MS of Eclat/Multiples[1] –
conducting score only)
Duration: 26′43″ (1974–83)

The work is presented as a three-stage 'rocket', with the small *Eclat* which is divided into two unequal parts as the initial vector. The second stage consists of a new development, *Eclat/Multiples*, in theory destined to

[1] As it stands at present, the manuscript score of *Multiples* ends at letter O in figure 86 on page 130; the CBS recording (26′45″) stops at figure 83 on page 116.

acquire the dimensions of a large orchestra. But because of the problems involved in having a large part of the orchestra sitting in silence for more than half an hour (while first fifteen and then twenty-five players take part in *Eclat* and the first part of *Eclat/Multiples*), it seems that this idea may be abandoned.[2]

It may be helpful to refer to what was said earlier (pp. 132–3) on the aesthetics and psychology of the work, before looking at the successive stages of the two connected sections of this 'work in progress'.

ECLAT

The instrumental forces

The instrumental ensemble is divided into two groups: those whose resonance dies unless sustained by trills; and those whose sound is maintained by breath or by some movement on the part of the player, and which may also be inflected by trills. The basic sound of *Eclat* depends on this twofold division. The second group functions as an acoustic background onto which the soloistic figures emanating from the first group are grafted and inscribed.

The fifteen instruments comprise piano, celesta, harp, glockenspiel, vibraphone, mandolin, guitar, cimbalom and tubular bells (in the first group), and alto flute, cor anglais, trumpet, trombone, viola and cello (in the second). (See opposite.)

The development of the work

The work opens with a piano cadenza, from the beginning of figure 3 (*c* 1′25″).[3] This was developed from a piece for piano solo, which exists only in an embryonic manuscript embellished with features for development and 'proliferation' in several coloured inks. After this brilliant exordium (marked *librement*), the 'background' sustaining instruments enter with a chord superimposed on the piano resonance – a chord which starts to alter in intensity as soon as the keyboard resonance has faded. This is the only appearance of these non-resonant instruments for some time to come. Once the chord has died away, the piano resumes the expressive thread of its cadenza, at first spasmodically, but gradually settling into a *mouvement perpétuel*. At the end of this section the resonance again fades to the

2 A typical case of a work whose medium should (and could) be exclusively that of video.
3 Timings taken from the version on disc, conducted by Boulez.

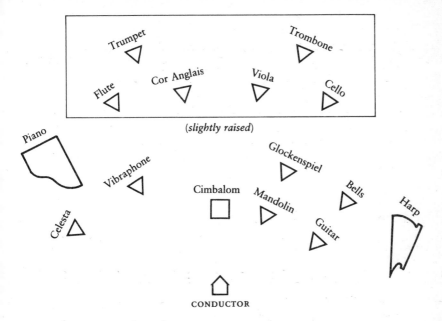

(slightly raised)

CONDUCTOR

limits of perception, and the work proper begins. This is a finely judged opening, in which virtuosity, sheer love of sound, gestural balance and comprehensibility are all successfully combined.

The main section of *Eclat*, from figure 3 to figure 14 (*c* 1′15″ to *c* 4′45″), is more 'unpredictable'. Here, a whole range of resonances is introduced (although only the first group of solo instruments play in this and the following section). More specifically, this is the section which establishes the relationship between the written text, and the inserts – whose arrangement is to result from a last-minute decision on the part of the conductor.

These inserts are of several kinds. For instance, at the start of the passage at figure 3 (see Ex. 59, p. 338), a regularly-spaced group of eight notes on the harp is played independently of the other instruments – like 'a little musical clock', according to Boulez.

The player begins the succession with any note he chooses (apart from two, which are not permitted), following through to complete the circle back to the point of departure – but without repeating the initial note. Meanwhile, four other instruments (piano, celesta, mandolin and vibraphone) have the option of playing a succession of brief motifs comprising

EX. 59

one to three notes. There are four successive entries, and here the conductor uses his right hand to indicate which of the four should start the sequence. He then completes the cycle (for example, in the order III, followed by IV, I and II). This may be summarized as follows:

CHORDS	I	II	III	IV
Piano	4 notes	o	o	o
Celesta	3 notes	o	o	o
Mandolin	1 note	1	1	1
Vibraphone	2 notes	o	2	2
Harp	8 notes equally distributed			

This insert can thus be played twenty-four different ways (four possible successions of the chordal entries multiplied by six possible successions of the harp figure), although pitches, dynamics and tempos are entirely predetermined.

In this section there are eight inserts in all, of which two are of this 'optional' type. Others depend on the conductor giving a last-minute indication to the players. A given number of instruments are divided into sub-groups (for instance, a group of five may be subdivided into three and two); within the sub-groups the conductor starts the players in any order he chooses, the overall effect being extremely fast, fleeting and nimble.[4] These are the 'instantaneous' inserts, of which there are four in the section under discussion.

There is a third type of insert, which occurs twice; here each of the given instruments has a precise motif to play, and their succession is pro-grammed in the score; however, the placing of these motifs again depends on a last-minute decision by the conductor. In such instances, the conductor uses the players rather like a pianist uses his fingers, so this type of insert will be called the 'controlled' insert.

Whether they be optional, instantaneous or controlled, these inserts give rise to a tension between conductor and players which contributes to the sparkle and mercurial brilliance of the work. Nevertheless, there is no evidence that this plan of action liberates the performer – who has never been more dependent on the good-will of the conductor.

Between these inserts, the musical text continues. Based on various kinds of resonance, on trills and spread chords, it illustrates the idea of the

4 In his 'Leçon de musique' devoted to *Eclat* (see Filmography F2) Michel Fano accompanied this lively sequence with underwater pictures of a darting fish.

'contemplation of sound' – a concept that has for some time fascinated Boulez, who sees it as the one lesson that Western music has learnt from the East.[5]

Flexible time operates between figure 14 and figure 25 (from *c* 4′45″ to *c* 8′45″). The scoring still includes only the resonant instruments of the first group, but the writing changes at this point, becoming more pointillistic in the ongoing text, while the inserts readily take on the character of solo cadenzas for one or more instruments.

This whole section is defined by its free tempo. Without any pre-established rhythmic pulse, it depends on the combination of large units of duration indicated by the left hand of the conductor, and subordinate units indicated by the right. He indicates the dynamics according to the position of his hand: open for *forte*, closed for *piano*.

The listener gets a clear impression of a more compressed discourse than in the preceding passage, because here the tempo seems tighter (even if unpredictable), and also because of the increasing instrumental density. The development becomes progressively tauter, abandoning the nervous nonchalance of the opening, and arriving at a sort of acoustical and psychological hiatus, before the sudden contrast of the following section.

This brief, interrogative section extends from figure 25 to figure 27 (*c* 20″). The sustaining instruments from the 'background' group make their oblique entry by means of a *mouvement perpétuel* shared between them, accompanied only by the piano from the opposing group. At figure 26 the *mouvement perpétuel*, by then on the viola, is brusquely interrupted by an arpeggio on the piano – as if wishing to resume its resonant role. But the game is over.

A coda in the form of a connecting passage, from figure 27 to figure 30 (*c* 8′40″ to *c* 9′15″ concludes *Eclat*. It comprises an instrumental *tutti* directly foreshadowing *Multiples*. The solo instruments from the first group now occupy the middle ground, in a subsidiary and punctuating role, while the foreground is allotted to the second group. These now make up for their long silence by playing with vehement and concerted energy. The first group joins in, and *Eclat* closes with a brilliant *fortissimo* chord for the whole ensemble.

---

5 In the Radio France/IRCAM cassette devoted to *Eclat* (see recordings), Boulez speaks of the overall conception of the work and, with the aid of examples, gives a clear explanation of the disposition of these inserts.

MULTIPLES

It is obviously not possible to talk of *Multiples* in the same terms as *Eclat*: the latter is a work that was completed some time ago, as a clearly articulated, self-contained form. *Multiples* is still unfinished (1984) and cannot make total sense until its completion. Its purpose so far seems to be to build an entirely new section based on the same motivic material as *Eclat*.

The instrumentation has been enlarged to include nine violas and a basset horn. The violas introduce a darker colour and a 'virulence' of purpose (as the composer said recently at rehearsal) which completely changes the crystalline and almost bell-like quality of *Eclat*. The basset horn has a special role. As alto clarinet it acts as mediator between the alto strings (the violas) and the solo instruments of the first group. Again according to Boulez himself, it becomes something of a 'hostage' to the violas. For this reason, it is 'allowed' a solo, readily identifiable as in the style of *Eclat*. This exemplifies Boulez's long-standing predilection for the medium tessitura of alto instruments (cf. *Le Marteau sans maître*).

The layout of the instrumental ensemble is here the same as for *Eclat* (see p. 337) with the addition of the group of nine violas seated in a semicircle at the front of the orchestra; the basset horn is positioned within the group of sustaining instruments and a second piano is placed alongside the first.

Multiples already reveals various phases. To begin with, there is a rhythmic phase, starting from the last section of *Eclat* (figures 30 to 35), which is immediately taken up and 'multiplied' with an almost Stravinskyan vigour. A fluctuating cadenza for the violas (figure 35 to 36) leads to the aforementioned basset horn solo (figure 36 to 37). From here begins a long sequence in which the *tutti* violas conduct a rapid and energetic development, again reminiscent of Stravinsky, while the rest of the orchestra is relegated to an auxiliary role. This section effects a uniform sound block, of considerable duration, in complete contrast to the extreme transparency of *Eclat*. There, Boulez underlined the restricted range of both density and duration; here he fills things out, making use of the whole sound spectrum. It could not exactly be said that the sound is more concentrated, but rather that it is more 'activated'. I would describe this type of movement as showing the 'durational effect'.

This section (which lasts until figure 62, *c* 7′00″) will only be heard in its proper aesthetic context – as a splash of sound colour within the equilibrium of the whole work – when *Eclat/Multiples* is completed.

From figure 62 the sustained development shows signs of running out of breath, as the orchestral texture starts to lighten. Here – as indeed from the beginning of *Multiples* – there are no more enclosed sequences, performance options or 'unpredictable' areas (or for that matter, any pauses). It is like finding oneself at the end of a tunnel, about to re-emerge on a more cheerful landscape. The tempo too has slowed down, before picking up a little. With a vast undulation of trills on all the instruments, this important work provisionally comes to an end.

10

Domaines

Domaines I, for clarinet solo

Composition: 1961–8
First performance: Ulm, 20 September 1968, Hans Deinzer

Domaines II, for clarinet solo and six instrumental groups

Composition: 1961–8
First performance: Brussels, 20 December 1968, Walter Boekyens
and the symphony orchestra of Radio Belgium, under Boulez;
first performance of revised version: Paris, 10 November 1970,
Michel Portal and the ensemble Musique Vivante, under Boulez
Published: Universal Edition (UE 14503 1w), 1970;
to date (1983) this only includes the solo parts
for *Domaines II*, but the same material can
also serve as the score for *Domaines I*

The following observations relate only to *Domaines II*

THE PLAYING ARRANGEMENTS

In addition to the conductor and the soloist, the work involves six instrumental groups:

A a trombone quartet (one alto, two tenors and a bass)
B a string sextet (two violins, two violas and two cellos)
C a marimba/double bass duo
D a mixed quintet (flute, trumpet, saxophone, bassoon and harp)
E a trio of oboe, horn and guitar
F a bass clarinet

The work comprises an outward or *Original* route and a return or *Miroir* version, each lasting about quarter of an hour.

The soloist has at his disposal six double sheets marked A, B, C, D, E and F. In the *Original* he plays them in any order he chooses, placing himself in front of the corresponding instrumental group; the latter respond immediately, while the soloist makes his way to the next group, and so on, until all six sheets have been played.

In the *Miroir* the procedure is reversed, with the conductor now determining the order of succession of the six instrumental groups, one of which begins the return route. The soloist intervenes after each, playing the corresponding *Miroir* sheet. Like that for the soloist, the score for each of the instrumental groups comprises twelve sections, paired two by two for the *Original* and the *Miroir*.

THE VERSION ON DISC

Since the number of possible permutations within a group of six units is 720, there are $720 \times 720 = 518,400$ possible successions for *Domaines II* – without including the many secondary variants provided for on the level of tempo, dynamics and phrase succession. It is left to the interpreter to find the most satisfactory form. I give here the version chosen for the recording supervised by the composer, together with an indication of the timings for the start of each section so as to allow the listener to keep track of the events on disc:

Original	Soloist A	0″→Instrumental			
		entity		A	0′35
	B	1′40		D	2′45
	C	4′		C	4′45
	B	5′30		B	6′45
	E	8′45		E	9′45
	F	11′25		F	13′30
					(End at 15′30)
Mirror	Group D	0″→Soloist		D	1
	C	2		C	2′40
	E	3′20		E	4′30
	A	5′15		A	6′50
	B	7′30		B	9′50
	F	11′35		F	12′20
					(End at 14′30)

The fact that the work here begins with sequence A and in both cases ends with sequence F is purely coincidental, but it allows the work to close with the splendid dialogue between bass clarinet and the soloist. The durations range between a maximum (the string sextet B) and a minimum (the duo for marimba and double bass C) – and this applies to the soloist as much as to his instrumental partners.

The route of the work may also be understood in a spatial sense, since the soloist changes his position in relation to the circle of instrumental groups. 'The trajectory he describes is in effect the trajectory of the music itself . . . There is no better way of visualizing a structure than to make it a visible part of the performer's route.'[1]

The diagram below shows one possibility of this spatial arrangement:

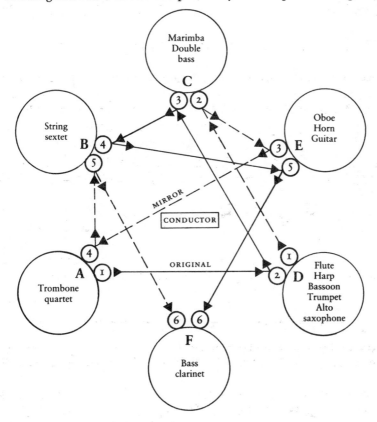

Diagram of the recording, designed by F. and N. Brigman (record sleeve HM).

1 *Conversations with Célestin Deliège*, p. 87.

THE DEVELOPMENT AND THE CONTENT OF THE SOLO SEQUENCES

By virtue of the way it is written – on mobile and permutatable sheets, with performing alternatives within each page – *Domaines* represents the final stage of the hypothesis of interpretation set out after Boulez's work on Mallarmé's *Livre* (a hypothesis pushed towards extremes of didactic schematicism during the 1960s).

Each solo sheet itself comprises six structures symmetrically arranged on the page as, for example, on sheet D:

```
        x           x
              x
              x
        x           x
```

Bearing in mind that Western reading material obeys two directional axes – from left to right and from top to bottom – there will be two possible ways of linking the six structures of the sequence below, according to the axis chosen:

```
    1       2              1       5
        3           or         3
        4                      4
    5       6              2       6
```

For the outward or *Original* route the soloist may choose either one of the above successions, but must then take the other for the return or *Miroir*.[2]

Each of the structures in the *Original* has its corresponding one in the *Miroir* – an exact retrograde as to the pitch of the notes, tempo, dynamics and expression. The simplest example can again be found on sheet D:

Original D/3   Mirror D/4

EX. 60

2 Whether without thinking, from a sense of mischief, or from a desire to add his own cryptic signature, Michel Portal makes a 'mistake' in the order of two of the structures on sheets C (*Original*) and A (*Miroir*).

Clearly, the two corresponding structures cannot occupy the same place on the page. Other changes may affect the manner in which they are played: dynamic variations, tapping the keys, trills, or flutter-tonguing. The use of retrograde would seem like one of the last (and certainly the most obvious) indications[3] of a serial system which has been completely rethought, but which still makes use of the dramatic force deriving from repetition and from circling around focal pitches (in this case, B♮):

EX. 61

or again, around the E♮ and F♯ :

EX. 62

The arrangement described above concerns the overall form of the work as much as the detailed linking of particular structures. While this is obviously fundamental to *Domaines*, it is not the work's most crucial feature, nor is the listener generally aware of it. Nevertheless, the concept of 'response' between instrumental groups and soloist has a particular significance – as a means of supporting and justifying the very purpose of the work – although it is a difficult idea to grasp from the recording alone.

The Original

The following notes are naturally only fully applicable to the version chosen for the one existing recording of *Domaines*:

3 As always, in formulae which admit certain pitch variations, the durations remain as written.

1. The initial clarinet sequence (A) is mainly pitched in a low register. The last structure played (6) is a long-held *fortissimo* on the middle F♯, followed by a silence and then by a flutter-tongued low G which reverts to *fortissimo* before stopping abruptly. The trombones then take up this idea in long notes, sharply accented – a device which is later modified to give prominence to the long notes, around which violently incisive *staccato* notes circle at speed.

2. Overlapping with the end of the trombone sequence (A), the clarinet sequence (D) becomes more voluble as it moves into a higher register, in contrast with what went before, and in preparation for what is to follow. The wind and harp quintet develops a transparent texture, seizing upon the trill formula characterizing the last clarinet structure to add a resonant glow to the whole sequence.

3. Again linked to the end of the preceding quintet, the clarinet sequence (C) presents an extremely restricted musical text: six brief structures, interspersed with many silences.[4] The last structure (two successive semiquaver triplets, one slurred, the other *staccato*) acts as a percussive anticipation of the following duo for marimba and double bass – which is as restrained and as hard-edged as the preceding solo.

4. The clarinet sequence (B) initially maintains the atmosphere of the preceding sequence. Then it gradually becomes more animated until the silences disappear completely from structures 4 and 5 – while the delicate structure 6 foreshadows the agility of the string sextet to come. This contrasts in imitative polyphony with *tutti* chromatic passages almost in the manner of Gesualdo (!) – the whole section is effusive, yet with an expressive understatement that suggests elision and abbreviation.

5. Influenced by the chattering strings at the start, the clarinet sequence (E) forms a bridge with the equally loquacious response from the oboe – here sustained by horn and punctuated by guitar in a trio which acts as a charming interlude within the piece as a whole. A more sharply-etched episode for all three instruments is heard in the middle of the sequence.

6. The clarinet solo (F) is one of the most developed sections of *Domaines*, very varied in style both in the *Original* and the *Miroir*. Isolated notes in contrasting registers and with different kinds of attack predominate in structure 1; structure 2 comprises a *mouvement perpétuel*

4 Michel Portal plays structure 4 before structure 3.

with grace-notes; in structure 3 there is a whirling succession reminiscent of electronic music; micro-motifs and silences feature in 4; 5 offers a contrasting melodic continuity;[5] whilst structure 6 is an extended recitative. The bass clarinet generally imitates the soloist (especially in structure 2) in an agile version that eschews the lower register. The choice of clarinet as solo instrument here allows for subtle colour relationships, since the clarinet is really more of an alto than a soprano instrument.

The Miroir

The material for the soloist is the same as in the *Original*: the structures are merely given in a retrograde form, without altering their rhythmic shape, dynamics or attacks – and obviously not their tempos, since it is these which define the structures within each sequence, whether original or retrograde. On the other hand, the sections for the instrumental groups are somewhat different from those of the *Original*:

1. This time the clarinet soloist takes the trill of structure 1 from the flute of the quintet (D). The instrumental group is both more effusive and more detached in style than on its previous appearance.

2. The marimba/double bass duo (C) develops *sotto voce*, with a fine sense of colour, and with a restraint that yields only to silences – a recurring characteristic of the following solo, whose textual brevity was noted in the *Original*.

3. In the trio (E), the oboe and guitar are now in counterpoint over sustained notes on the horn. After this, the horn embarks on a solo cadenza, followed by the guitar, with the oboe now less dominant than in the *Original*. A relatively long overlap leads to a particularly spectacular and daring solo sequence – full of wide leaps, virtuoso trills and brilliant passage work.

4. The trombone quartet (A) is much less massively homophonic here than in the *Original*. After bursting at full strength into a series of rapid and percussive exclamations, everything gradually comes together in a homophonic, chattering *mouvement perpétuel*. The relationship between this version of (A) and the soloist is here one of contrast: there is a sense of

---

5 The solo structure 5 in F (*Original*) returns in the score as identical, not in its retrograde form, in the homologous F 4 (*Miroir*). In the recording, Michel Portal leaves out the first version, substituting an improvisation of similar character; he then plays F4 (*Miroir*) as written.

continuity in structure 1; there are trills in structure 2; structure 3 has a transitory nature;[6] structure 4 is slow and resonant; 5 is *legato*; and structure 6 serves as a kind of final punctuation.

5. Sequence (B) for the strings moves towards one of the full-textured alto register *tuttis* of which Boulez is so fond. The overlap with the soloist is relatively long.[7]

6. The two solo sequences for clarinet and for bass clarinet seem here to occupy a position more characteristic of a postlude than of a final piece, since the tone-colours of the two instruments are almost identical. The work ends with the isolated notes of structure 6 – widely contrasted as to pitch, dynamics and attacks – which offers three possibilities for the final solo, all of medium intensity.[8]

6 Michel Portal plays 3 before 2.
7 The soloist accepts the invitation to permutational play offered in structure 5.
8 Michel Portal chooses the loudest.

11

Rituel

IN MEMORIAM MADERNA

Composition: 1974
First performance: London, 2 April 1975; BBC SO, under Boulez
Published: Universal Edition (UE 15941; original
and revised versions),[1] 1975
Duration: *c* 25'00"

PIERRE BOULEZ: THE INTRODUCTORY DEDICATION TO
RITUEL

Perpetual alternation:

A sort of verse and response for an
imaginary ceremony.

A ceremony of remembrance – whence these
numerous returns to the same
formulae, while changing profile
and perspective.

Ceremony of extinction, the ritual
of disappearance and survival:
in this way are images imprinted on
the musical memory –
present/absent, imprinted on uncertainty.

---

1 They bear the same copyright date; the first version is in manuscript, the revised version is
printed.

The reader is referred to p. 178 in the first part of this book for information concerning the dedication to Boulez's friend Bruno Maderna.

As a work with immediate audience appeal, *Rituel* is relatively simple. Its simplicity is twofold: it stems both from the systematic character of its development, and from the limited number of linguistic elements brought into play in relation to its length. The obsessive nature of this simplicity is clearly connected to the emotional purpose of the work.

THE INSTRUMENTAL FORCES

Rituel is written for an orchestra divided into eight instrumental groups plus an important array of percussion. Each percussion player is attached to one of the instrumental groups, with the eighth and last group requiring two percussionists; in addition, these last two players have a quite specific role in relation to the other percussionists.

The eight groups are of increasing size:

     I oboe solo
     II two clarinets in B♭
     III three flutes
     IV four violins
     V wind quintet (oboe, clarinet, saxophone and two bassoons)
     VI string sextet
     VII wind septet (alto flute, oboe, cor anglais, E♭ clarinet, bass clarinet and two bassoons)
     VIII brass ensemble (four trumpets in C, six horns in F and four trombones)

There is an unusual amount of percussion:

1. tabla, small Japanese bell, small Japanese wood block (mokubio), small maracas, small guiro, tambourine (on a horizontal stand), sizzle cymbal
2. wood block, medium cowbell, high side-drum without snares, suspended Turkish cymbal, two guiros (large and small), small tube maracas
3. bongo, medium claves, medium tube maracas, Chinese cymbal, suspended Turkish cymbal, sizzle cymbal, large triangle
4. fixed drum, largish cowbell, two large maracas, two small maracas, two tube maracas (large and small), castanets

5. temple block, small nipple gong, side-drum with snares, two cowbells (medium and slightly larger), large triangle, small Japanese bell
6. medium tom-tom, log drum, temple block, wood block, castanets, claves, small Japanese wood block
7. conga, side drum with snares, high side-drum without snares, tom-tom, fixed drum, bongo, tabla
8. seven nipple gongs and seven tam-tams, the gongs in decreasing order of size from the lowest (1) to the highest (7), the tam-tams increasing in size from the highest (1) to the lowest (7); each gong to be placed above the corresponding tam-tam, and the pairs of instruments to be arranged in a semi-circle
9. as 8

The orchestra as a whole is then laid out as follows:

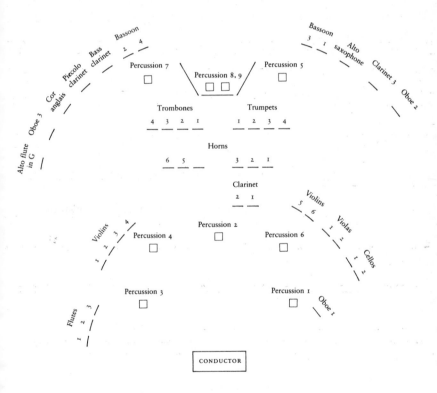

THE ORGANIZATION OF THE WORK

Rituel comprises fifteen sections of unequal duration, with the fifteenth (which is itself subdivided into seven sections, designated A to G) occupying more than a third of the work.

The odd-numbered sections are organized differently from the even-numbered ones, and function as responses, forming conducted refrains. Since group VIII is present throughout, so too are percussionists 8 and 9 – who play independently of the other instrumental groups once their starting point has been indicated by the conductor. In this way they constitute a regular background against which the conductor places the chords of the instrumental ensemble concerned.

The even-numbered sections act as the couplets in a strophe and are not conducted: the conductor indicates the starting point, in relation to the length of the different sequences played by the various groups. The order in which these groups enter may vary, apart from the placing of the first – which always has the longest part. 'Each group, strictly synchronized within itself, is led by a player (generally the first listed) designated as leader, while the tempo is maintained by the percussionist associated with the group.' (From the preface to the score.)

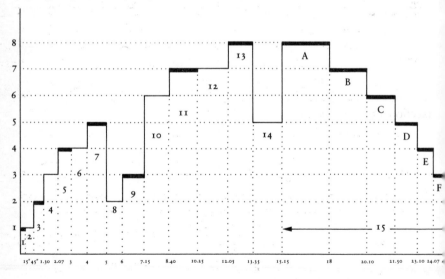

The horizontal line shows the timings (according to Boulez).
The left-hand vertical line gives the number of groups used.
The heavy lines indicate the uneven-numbered sections in which group VIII (brass and percussion) figures.

Each section then brings one or more groups into play, the overall form resulting from the cumulative effect of this procedure – from section 1 for group VIII (the brass ensemble) alone, to the *tutti* sections 13 and 15. Then, within the different subdivisions of the long section 15, the groups are eclipsed one by one, beginning with the smallest (the solo oboe), so that eventually the ever-present group VIII is left with the wind septet for the final *diminuendo* on the last chord.

Using the diagram opposite, it is possible to follow the whole progress of the work. As can be seen, each section in the first part of the work (section 1 to 14, from 0′00″ to *c* 15′15″) runs for about one minute, apart from the first two, which are shorter. It will be seen too that the even-numbered 'verses' are immediately filled out by group VIII for the odd-numbered 'responses' which follow, and that the progression from 1 to 14 is not an absolutely straightforward one, since it takes a backwards step in 8 and 14.

From the start of section 15, a retrograde and symmetrical process of instrumental paring down takes place: this makes *Rituel* into an arch whose descending slope resounds like a slow death struggle. Unfortunately the diagram omits an essential part of this curve – that of a dynamic evolution which is not necessarily parallel with the size of the forces brought into play. I will merely point out that the work begins and ends *pianissimo*, that a general increase in intensity takes place from section 3, and that this increase is endorsed by the following sections (including the lightly-scored section 8). It then undergoes moments of withdrawal (the beginning and end of section 9), of stasis (section 10, despite the relative density of its texture), and of apparent instability (section 13); meanwhile sections 11 and 12 have resumed their dynamic progress. The reduction of instrumental forces in section 14 coincides with a lowering of the dynamic level to a point that suggests that a second *tutti* – section 15 – will inevitably lead to a climactic outburst. However, at the culmination of the piece, Boulez keeps his ensemble within limits appropriate to the 'interior' nature of the ritual; despite its length, section 15 represents a slow *decrescendo* towards final extinction.

THE MUSICAL AND HARMONIC MATERIAL

The simplicity of the material itself matches that of the procedures. *Rituel* is derived entirely from one chord – or rather, one mode comprising seven degrees of the chromatic scale within the range of a twelfth. This mode contains three tritones and a seventh note:

EX. 63

The chord can obviously be transposed, just as certain of its notes can be elided. The following example, which I have borrowed from the book by Paul Griffiths[2], is an extract from section 5 (groups VIII, I, II and III, which Griffiths transcribes in short score to make it easier to read):

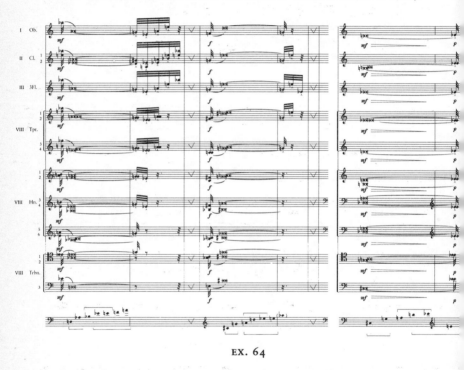

EX. 64

The even and odd numbered sections are heard as clearly contrasted. The latter are based on sustained chords, sometimes preceded by an anacrusis of one or several notes, and ended either with a sharp accent or an after-beat – again of one or several notes. These chords are synchronized within each instrumental group but the groups themselves do not necessarily begin simultaneously (at least, in the versions

2 See Bibliography.

subsequent to 1977; in earlier versions they had to, and were notated thus in the original score).

The even-numbered sections are much freer and more mobile, most often consisting of a succession of relatively long notes connected by ornamental successions: these long notes belong to the 'chord modes' mentioned earlier. Again, the various strands in the even-numbered sections were originally notated simultaneously but made to enter successively, in an order determined by a last-minute decision on the part of the conductor; the contingencies of performance led Boulez to mark the order of the entries in the published score – even though this means programming a variability clause that would seem unlikely to be abused either by the composer himself, or by his colleagues.

12

Répons

FOR INSTRUMENTAL ENSEMBLE, SOLOISTS, AND ELECTRO-ACOUSTIC EQUIPMENT

Composition: 1981
First performance: *Répons 1*, Donaueschingen,
18 October 1981, under Boulez[1]
Répons 2, London, Royal Agricultural Hall,
6 September 1982, under Boulez
Répons 3, Turin, then Basle, September 1984;
Metz and Paris, October 1984
Duration: *Répons 1, c 19'30"*
Répons 2, c 32'15"
Répons 3, c 45'00"

The following commentary concerns *Répons 2*.

PERFORMERS, MATERIAL, SPACE

In general, musical works envisage these three entities as separate; however, *Répons* is concerned with the spatial presentation of a performance material that is both instrumental and electro-acoustic.

In this instance the playing space cannot be a traditional concert hall. *Répons* reflects the composer's reservations concerning the relationship between audience and loudspeaker – something he has tried to come to terms with ever since *Poésie pour pouvoir*. The audience for *Répons* is placed within a hall of sufficient size to accommodate it, the musicians, and the encircling loudspeakers – allowing for the fact that Boulez also

---

1 It was *Répons 1* that the concert-going public of the Paris region heard on 15–17 December 1981, at the Seine-Saint-Denis Bobigny Cultural Centre as part of the Autumn Festival.

intends there to be a clear spatial separation of his soloists (reflecting an already long-term concern noted in '. . . explosante-fixe . . .', *Doubles*, and *Rituel*). Thus, performances of *Répons* have, up to the present time, taken place in fairly large, 'neutral' spaces, either square or rectangular in shape (the projection space at IRCAM would be ideal for the purpose if its capacity were not so limited). It is hardly necessary to emphasize that the search for a suitable space, particularly for one with the right acoustic, poses a problem each time a performance of the work is planned.

There are three categories of performing personnel: an instrumental ensemble, a group of soloists, and a technical team. Directed by the conductor, the instrumental ensemble is installed on a central rostrum. This ensemble comprises twenty-four players: two flutes, two oboes, two clarinets, bass clarinet, two bassoons, two horns, two trumpets, two trombones, tuba, three violins, two violas, two cellos and double bass. They play without either amplification or electro-acoustic transformation.

Also seated on rostrums, the six soloists are placed symmetrically in the six 'corners' of the hall – each playing a principle instrument and, in theory, one or more secondary instruments.[2] The solo instruments comprise piano 1, piano 2 (doubling organ), harp, cimbalom, xylophone (doubling glockenspiel), and vibraphone. This group, which represents almost a digest of Boulez's instrumental preferences, is characterized by its resonance, and its capacity to respond to electro-acoustic treatment.

Each soloist is also equipped with a tape-recorder which (beginning at a particular moment in the score) plays a tape of sounds synthesized by the 4X machine. This tape comprises what Boulez calls continuous 'wallpaper music' which only becomes audible when the corresponding soloist exceeds a certain dynamic. The tape is relayed over a small loudspeaker placed above each soloist and reserved for this purpose. A second relay system comprises six large loudspeakers placed above and between the six soloists. At the outset, each soloist is linked with the speaker immediately to his right. But the eventual purpose of *Répons* is to disseminate the music of the soloists – the only 'treated' sound – throughout the whole loudspeaker system.

2 I have indicated the only two alternatives at work in *Répons 1* and *2*. Originally (and perhaps in the final version) there were to have been many more of these subsidiary instruments; only a few weeks before *Répons 1*, Boulez was certainly indicating at least the following doublings: piano 1 (+ celesta), piano 2 (+ organ), harp (+ two other, differently tuned harps), cimbalon (+ percussion). The performance difficulties of the already complex *Répons 1* and *2* have modified the composer's ambitions – at least for the time being.

Finally, at the foot of the central instrumental podium, two important pieces of apparatus are in the hands of the production assistant:[3] the 4X machine, (coupled with a less powerful computer, the PDP 11/55), and the halaphone. The 4X machine was invented at IRCAM by the engineer Giuseppe di Giugno and his team; it is an extremely versatile and powerful computer, with a huge programming and storage capacity, which can function at 200 million operations per second. This is a signal treatment computer – a term covering both its traditional functions of synthesis and transformation (modulation, delay, detection of events) and its ability to treat data and 'real time' sounds, particularly those produced by the soloists.

The PDP 11/55 is to the 4X what the commercial vehicle is to the racing car: it executes the simpler functions and gives the orders to the 4X – a task that the latter is not capable of undertaking itself. Perhaps the PDP 11/55 could be described as the 'conductor' of the 'orchestra' represented by the 4X.

The halaphone's inventor, Hans-Peter Haller, was an engineer at the experimental studio of the Heinrich Strobel Stiftung at Freiburg in Breisgau, and also worked for the firm LAWO which constructed the apparatus. The halaphone had already been used by Boulez in '. . . explosante-fixe . . .', and for a similar purpose: to 'spatialize' the sound (that is, to control the diffusion over one or more loudspeakers of the sounds produced by the soloists or the 4X). It is an 'interconnectional matrix', a sort of 'circulatory agent' which distributes the sound material in space in such a way as to produce results of maximum richness and minimum interference.

IRCAM has now perfected an apparatus capable of fulfilling the same functions as the halaphone, but which is only an eighth of its size. Clearly, the halaphone is destined to be superseded in future presentations of *Répons*.

THE TRANSFORMATIONS

The electro-acoustic transformations used in *Répons* may be reduced to three main categories, two of which relate to the emission of sound, and the third to its reception:

1 The modulation of a solo instrument by a synthetic sound. This traditional ring modulation process involves treating an instrumental

3 Andrew Gerszo.

sound with a sinusoidal one, resulting in the production of two sounds whose frequencies are respectively the sum and the difference of the frequencies particular to the two initial sounds. This gives an appreciable enrichment of the initial signal, all the more so because the process of a twofold speed reduction is also applied to the harmonics of the initial signal – with a natural decrease in intensity. But even without taking this into account, the enrichment of the spectrum is considerable.

Here is an example, taken from figure 34 in the score:

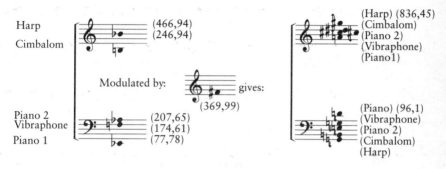

EX. 65

The figures in brackets indicate the frequencies per second (A=440). In the resulting chord, the instrumental indications are given merely to show the origin of the modulation, since the sounds themselves are not recognizable in terms of their timbre. For the sake of clarity, I have included only the results of the harp modulation. It will be noted that the chord produced by modulating this sound gives a result that is both homogeneous and symmetrical in its registration (bearing in mind that a negative frequency – the result of subtracting one frequency from another, smaller one – is heard as a positive frequency of the same size).

2 Methods of delay and phase displacement aimed at creating rhythmically complex motifs. In *Répons*, the term 'delay system' is used to describe the process whereby a sound played by one of the soloists is projected as a repetition in space – like a multiple echo – according to a distribution within time which can be regular or irregular. The delay system is heard on numerous occasions, but notably at full volume on the entry of the soloists or in the coda (see below).

This 'delay' is itself a form of 'response' made to an initial sound. The phenomenon of response is also imitated on the instruments of the central ensemble (the trumpets, for instance) in the form of *staccato* repetitions of the same note: ♪♪♪ ♪♪♪ etc.

Delay is a form of response in time; another responsorial form, this time in frequency space, is effected by an apparatus included within the 4x machine – the frequency shifter, which itself accomplishes the transpositions of an initial signal. Ex. 66 (a) represents the seven notes of a chord heard on piano 1 at the entry of the soloists (one bar after figure 21). The frequency of each of these seven notes is reduced by frequency shifting, so giving rise to several other notes – selected by the composer – which are of the same pitch class as the notes of the initial signal, but which together considerably enrich it. Given below are the reductions (b) and (c) relating to the first two notes of the initial chord (a).

EX. 66

3 The regulation of sound placement over the loudspeaker network. This is a matter of distribution, not of production and, as previously mentioned, it is a function carried out by the halaphone. The amplified sounds of the soloists can come from one loudspeaker (not necessarily the one assigned to each soloist at the start), or from several in turn, according to a programmed itinerary. The transfer of sounds over the different loudspeakers happens at a speed sufficient to erase all aural perception of successive destinations. This cryptic form of delay and response from one loudspeaker to another therefore gives the impression of a continuum. Of course, the spatial displacement of a note, a chord, or of any other signal is a quality lacking on disc.

The following shows the spatial orbits of the soloists on their entry at figure 21 (this passage figures on the IRCAM disc 0001):

The seating arrangements and the disposition of the sounds in *Répons*

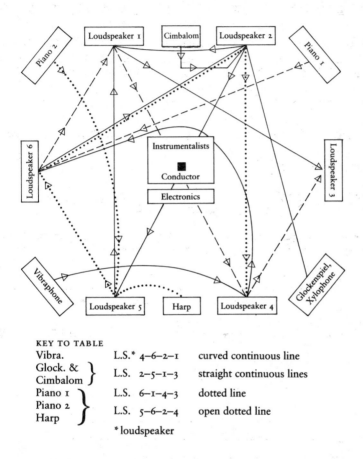

KEY TO TABLE

Vibra.	L.S.* 4–6–2–1	curved continuous line
Glock. & Cimbalom }	L.S. 2–5–1–3	straight continuous lines
Piano 1, Piano 2, Harp }	L.S. 6–1–4–3	dotted line
	L.S. 5–6–2–4	open dotted line
	* loudspeaker	

To summarize: the sounds emitted by the soloists are despatched to the various loudspeakers through the medium of the halaphone (an electronic unit), and not directly – as the diagram, representing the listener's perception, might suggest; the audience is placed between the instrumental group and the soloists and loudspeakers; both the instrumental group and the soloists are placed on podiums; the six large loudspeakers are symmetrically positioned above the players.

THE DEVELOPMENT OF THE WORK

Before looking at the various stages of the work's development, two points should be made. Firstly the work I am describing is still (1984) unfinished. *Répons 2* is equal to about half the projected length of the complete work – which will doubtless see the light of day long after the completion and publication of the present volume: this is the general rule for a composer still at full stretch and who has long accustomed us to the charms of the 'work in progress'! This incompleteness (which, I repeat, refers to the duration of the work, rather than to the state of the writing itself) necessarily distorts perspective. *Répons 2* – with its present 'coda' perfectly balancing the purely instrumental introduction and its two huge 'durational effects' – therefore presents a formal achievement which is in fact an illusion. It is nonetheless a provisional completion, since Boulez here succeeds in giving a 'proper' finish to a partial preview of the work, while providing for its uninterrupted continuation. (To a lesser extent, he had already achieved this with *Répons 1*.)

Secondly, *Répons* is a work which rests entirely on the 'responsorial' relationship between instrumental sounds and their electro-acoustic transformation – a relationship that is, moreover, extraordinarily complex and problematic as to its production. But like the methods applied to the instrumental writing, the transformations themselves are very simply defined, sharply contrasted, and almost transparently clear. (During this period, Boulez applied the same mastery to the considerable clarification of *Improvisation III*.) My attempts to define the successive stages of the present work rest upon this relative structural clarity.

A The instrumental introduction, from the beginning to figure 21 (0′00″ to *c* 6′50″) is marked *rapide, énergique*. It begins in a fragmented, *staccato* style, with a degree of homophony between the three groups of wood-wind, brass, and strings. At 25″, the atmosphere changes abruptly: a string trill, preceded by up-beats, provides a background to the rise and fall of woodwind figures. The whole passage is sharply punctuated by the brass. At 3′30″, the mood is modified by a spasmodic figure on the unison brass – their own kind of 'delay'. This 'morse code' sequence continues and is developed into a cumulative *tutti* which then accelerates (*c* 6′30″) in order to reach a somewhat abrupt halt.

B The entry of the soloists and the first phase of their drama, from figure 21 to figure 27 (*c* 6′50″ to *c* 10′15″), is a veritable acoustic miracle, and produces a striking psychological effect. The sight of the silent soloists creates a tension that is suddenly released by their intervention in the form of six huge arpeggiated chords (merely amplified, without transformation) that rend the sound-space apart. From the next bar onwards, these unsynchronized chords are treated by delay and transposition (frequency shifting), alternating with simple amplification. In the latter instance, the sounds are moved around the loudspeaker system. This gives the following series of responses:

1 amplification alone	2 amplification + delay + frequency shifting
sound transfer	no sound transfer
forceful instrumental participation	weak instrumental participation

C Antiphony between the soloists and the instrumental group is particularly spectacular during a section from figure 27 to figure 32 (*c* 10′15″ to *c* 12′20″), in which the soloists are placed under the regime of the delay system, but this time used irregularly and without transformations. These irregular delays are contrasted by motifs composed of equal values (played by the instrumental group) like the one first given to the strings. A total of five such motivic entries alternate with the material of the soloists, which is distributed over the loudspeaker system, first as a straightforward relay, then with displacement.

D The 'Balinese section', from figure 32 to figure 42 (*c* 12′20″ to *c* 14′05″), was so named by Boulez and Andrew Gerzso because of its similarity to the fast, percussive style of the gamelan. This is a *mouvement perpétuel* for the *tutti* instrumental ensemble, which serves as background for the eight long-resounding arpeggiated chords of the soloists. After an initial up-beat, these chords resolve onto single-note trills modulated by a synthetic sound (following the example cited above, p. 361, in relation to the first of these chords). The fundamental contrast of the work, in terms of its 'Répons' (responses), is here dependent on the crisply articulated development pursued by the ensemble in support of the resonant solo writing. The modulated chords, with displacements, are later distributed over the loudspeaker network.

This section is very uniform and even repetitive in style – a typical example of what I call the 'durational effect', even though its actual duration is fairly short. More will be said about this concept with reference to the following section.

E The 'funeral march', from figure 42 to figure 47 (*c* 14′15″ to *c* 19′35″), also called the 'Scriabin section', was the final section of *Répons 1*. This is a long sequence, giving another instance of the durational effect, but this time of a real kind. This expression was used in relation to the *Multiples* section of *Eclat* (p. 341) to describe a sequence of uniform, even undifferentiated writing which in theory contrasts with the more distinctive, soloistic, elusive and a-rhythmic sequences that precede or follow it. Such durational effects are used to place a block of sound at a particular moment in the musical argument, so as to give the impression of an extended period of time – in the same way that a 'blot' on a picture by Klee or Miró can sometimes occupy a large share of the space, providing contrast, and functioning as a fixed point in relation to the teeming events all around it.

Here, the durational effect is borne along by a huge *crescendo* which includes the first intervention of the pre-recorded tape – according to the rules of play given above. The *tutti crescendo* is built mainly from the extension of a formula based on ascending and descending chromatic scales; these are intentionally undifferentiated, and gradually fill the whole sound-space, setting it alight in the manner of certain works of Scriabin (like *Prometheus: the Poem of Fire*). At the end of this section, the dynamic sonority decreases, finally breaking up and settling on to a held note on the muted horn, which acts as a transition to the following section.

F I call the passage from figure 47 to figure 53 (*c* 19′35″ to *c* 22′40″) the 'rain music' section, because it is reminiscent of the music that floods the final scene of Berg's *Lulu*: long trills on the instrumental ensemble are interrupted only by unequal-length sequences of pulsating chords. Meanwhile, the soloists have been divided into two dissimilar rhythmic networks whose units of time change as they progress. As this section evolves, there is increasing confluence of the soloists, among each other and with the strings of the instrumental ensemble (which here also includes quiet, sustained brass chords).

G The 'finale', from figure 53 to figure 70 (*c* 22′40″ to *c* 29′00″), is not designated as such by Boulez, and is in any event only a provisional ending. However, with the work in its present state, this huge and somewhat uniform *crescendo*, within a gradually evolving *tutti* (another durational effect), clearly gives the impression of fulfilling this function.

The most important figures are those of the repeated notes on the solo instruments, together with the chromatic scales previously encountered (all in a very fast tempo). This *mouvement perpétuel* (which begins at figure 54) is preceded by a sort of latent period, during which the soloists at first seem somewhat aimlessly dispersed, while the strings and brass finish their own exhausting gestures. Then a brilliant, mercurial motif appears on the woodwind, hesitates, picks up again, rallies the brass – and suddenly launches into the *mouvement perpétuel*.

The soloists function variously as a concerted group, or in canon, on occasion integrating the contrasting chromatic scale gesture. In this section their sound is not transformed, merely amplified and distributed over the loudspeakers, with few displacements.

H The present 'coda', from figure 69 to figure 80 (*c* 29′00″ to *c* 32′15″), is as provisional as the preceding 'finale' (and for the same reasons), even though its coda-like character is fairly clear. Once again, the argument is entrusted to the soloists alone, in 'response' to the section for the ensemble alone at the start of the work. The writing again comprises arpeggiated chords, treated by the whole arsenal of transformation: delay, frequency shifting, and modulation. The slow tempo of this section makes the phenomena of delay, transposition and timbral modification more clearly perceptible. Surrounded by ever-increasing areas of silence, the piano and the harp conclude the present version of *Répons* in splendid isolation.

These basic facts are summarized in the following table:[4]

4 My thanks to Andrew Gerszo for his help with the checking of this chapter from the technical point of view.

	A	B	C	D	E	F	G	H	
Score		2 1	2 7	3 2	4 2	4 7	5 3	6 9	80
Sections	(A)	(B)	(C)	(D)	(E)	(F)	(G)	(H)	
Timing	0	6.50	10.15	12.20	14.20	19.30	22.40	29	32.15
Version						R1 →		R2 →	
Title	Introduction			'Bali'	'Scriabine'	'Lulu'	'Finale'	'Coda'	
Tempo	vif. lent, vif	varié	rapide	vif	lent, mais de plus en plus chargé	lent			
Ensemble	+	+	+	+	+	+	+	−	
Soloists	−	+	+	+	+	+	+	+	
Tape	−	−	−	−	+	−	−	−	
Delay	−	+	+	−	−	+ (networks)	+	+	
Frequency-shifting	−	+	−	−	− (amplification alone)	−	−	+	
Modulation	−	−	−	+	−	+	+	+	
Transference of sound within the hall	−	+	−/+	(+)	+ (piano I) / − (others)	−	(+)	−	

− absence
+ presence

Catalogue of Works

SOURCES

Paul Griffiths: *Boulez*, Oxford Studies of Composers, London, 1978
G. W. Hopkins: *Grove's Dictionary of Music and Musicians*, London, 1980
Wilfred Brennecke: *Die Musik in Geschichte und Gegenwart*, 1973
Information privately obtained

1 *Prelude, Psalmodie, Toccata, Scherzo, Nocturne*, for piano, 1944–5 (withdrawn)

2 *Thème et variations*, for piano left hand, 1945 (withdrawn)

3 *Trois Psalmodies*, for piano, 1945 (withdrawn); radio recording INA

4 12 *Notations*, for piano, 1945 (originally withdrawn from catalogue, but now published by Universal, 1985); radio recording INA

5 Quartet, for four ondes martenot 1945–6 (withdrawn); two of the three movements recomposed as Sonata for two pianos, 1948 (withdrawn)

6 *Sonatine*, for flute and piano, 1946 (Amphion, 1954)

7 Piano Sonata No. 1, 1946 (Amphion, 1951)

8a *Le Visage nuptial* (René Char), for soprano, contralto, two ondes martenot, piano and percussion, 1946–7 (unpublished)

8b *Le Visage nuptial*, for soprano, contralto, female chorus and large orchestra, 1951–2 (Heugel, 1959)

8c *Le Visage nuptial* for soprano, contralto, female chorus and large orchestra, 1989 (unpublished)

9 *Symphonie concertante*, for piano and orchestra, 1947 (lost 1954)

10 Sonata for two pianos (*Passacaille–Variations* + two movements from Quartet for ondes martenot), 1948 (unpublished)

11a *Le Soleil des eaux* (René Char), for voice and orchestra, incidental music for radio, 1948

11b *Le Soleil des eaux*, for soprano, tenor, bass, and chamber orchestra, 1948 (version withdrawn)

11c *Le Soleil des eaux*, for soprano, tenor, bass, STB chorus and orchestra, 1958 (Heugel, 1959)

11d *Le Soleil des eaux*, for soprano, SATB chorus and orchestra, 1965 (Heugel, 1968)

12 Piano Sonata No. 2, 1948 (Heugel, 1950)

13a *Livre pour quatuor*, for string quartet, 1948–9 (Heugel, 1960, without IV)

13b *Livre pour cordes*, orchestration of 1a and 1b from *Livre pour quatuor*, 1968 (unpublished)

13c *Livre pour cordes*, new version of 1a and 1b, 1989 (unpublished)

14 *Un Coup de dés*, for chorus and orchestra, 1950 (project)

15 3 *Essais*, for percussion, 1950 (withdrawn)

16 *Polyphonie X*, for eighteen instruments, 1950–51, part of projected *Polyphonie* for 49 instruments (unpublished)

17 2 *Etudes*, single-track tape, 1951–2 (*Etude sur un son* and *Etude sur un accord de sept sons*)

18 *Structures*, Book 1, for two pianos, 1951–2 (Universal, 1955)

19 *Oubli signal lapidé* (Armand Gatti), for twelve voices, 1952 (unpublished)

20 *Le Marteau sans maître* (René Char), for contralto, alto flute, guitar, viola, vibraphone, xylophone, and percussion, 1953–5 (Universal 1954, revised version 1957)

21 *L'Orestie* (Aeschylus/Obey), for voice and instrumental ensemble, incidental music for theatre, 1948

22 *La Symphonie mécanique*, music for the Jean Mitry film (single-track tape), 1955

23 Piano Sonata No. 3, 1956–7 (Universal: *Trope*, 1961, and *Constellation/Constellation–Miroir*, 1963; a fragment from *Antiphonie* was published under the title of *Sigle*, 1968, then withdrawn)

24 *Le Crépuscule de Yang Koueï-Feï* (Louise Fauré), incidental music for radio, 1967

25 *Strophes*, for flute, 1957 (incomplete, unpublished)

26 *Pli selon pli* (Stéphane Mallarmé), 1957–62:

26/1a *Don*, for soprano and piano, 1960 (unpublished)
26/1b *Don*, for soprano and orchestra, 1962 (Universal, 1967)

26/2a *Improvisation I*, for soprano and small percussion ensemble, 1957 (Universal, 1958)

26/2b *Improvisation I*, for soprano and orchestra, 1962 (Universal, 1977)

26/3 *Improvisation II*, for soprano and small ensemble, 1957 (Universal, 1958)

26/4a *Improvisation III*, for soprano and orchestra, 1959 (unpublished)
26/4b *Improvisation III*, for soprano and orchestra, revised 1983–4 (Universal, in preparation)
26/4c *Improvisation III*, for soprano and orchestra, definitive version, 1984–5 (Universal)

26/5 *Tombeau*, for large orchestra, 1959–62 (Universal, 1971)

27a *Doubles*, for large orchestra, 1957–8

27b *Figures–Doubles–Prismes*, for large orchestra, 1963

27c *Figures–Doubles–Prismes*, for large orchestra, 1968 (Universal, MS)

28 *Poésie pour pouvoir* (Henri Michaux), for orchestra and five-track tape (unpublished)

29 *Structures*, Book 2, for two pianos, 1956–61 (Universal, 1972)

30 *Marges*, for percussion ensemble, 1962–4 (sketches only)

31a *Eclat*, for fifteen instruments, 1965 (Universal, in preparation)

31b *Eclat/Multiples*, for twenty-seven instruments, 1965– (Universal, in preparation)

32a *Domaines*, for clarinet solo, 1961–8

32b *Domaines*, for clarinet and six instrumental groups, 1961–8 (Universal, 1970)

33 *For Dr. Kalmus* (contribution to *A Garland for Dr. K.*), for flute, clarinet, viola, cello and piano, 1969 (unpublished)

34a *cummings ist der Dichter* (e.e. cummings), for small choir and chamber orchestra, 1970 (Universal, 1976)

34b *cummings ist der Dichter*, revised version, for medium-sized choir and chamber orchestra, 1986 (Universal)

35a '. . . *explosante-fixe* . . .', for variable ensemble, 1971 (*Tempo* magazine)

35b '. . . *explosante-fixe* . . .', for flute, clarinet, trumpet, harp, vibraphone, violin, viola, cello and electro-acoustic equipment, 1972– (unpublished)

35c '. . . *explosante-fixe* . . .', for flute and electronic equipment, 1989 (unpublished)

36 *Rituel in memoriam Maderna*, for eight orchestral groups, 1974–5 (Universal, 1975)

37 *Ainsi parla Zarathoustra* (Nietzsche/Barrault), incidental music for voice and instrumental ensemble, 1974

38 *Messagesquisse*, for cello solo and six cellos, 1976 (Universal)

39 *Notations*, for large orchestra, 1977–8 (Universal, 1984, Nos. 1–4)

40 *Répons*, for six instrumental soloists, instrumental ensemble, and electro-acoustic equipment, 1981– (Universal, MS)

41 *Dérive*, for flute, clarinet, violin, cello, vibraphone, and piano, 1984 (Universal)

42 *Dialogue de l'ombre double*, for clarinet and electro-acoustic equipment, 1985 (Universal)

43 *Mémoriale* ('. . . *explosante-fixe* . . .' *originel*), for flute and solo and eight instruments, 1985 (Universal, 1985)

Discography

I

(Listed in chronological order of composition)

Sonatine, for flute and piano

S. Gazzelloni and D. Tudor (with works by Berio, Messiaen and Stockhausen)	Vega
W. Bennett and S. Bradshaw (with works by Berio, Haubenstock-Ramati, Messiaen, R. R. Bennett)	Delta
S. Gazzelloni and F. Rzewski (with works by Haubenstock-Ramati and Maderna)	RCA
J. Castagner and P. Méfano (with works by Berio, Messiaen, Prokofiev and Sari)	Adès
M. Debost and C. Ivaldi (with works by Webern and Schoenberg)	VSM
A. Nicolet and J. Wyttenbach	Wergo
K. Zöller and A. Kontarsky	EMI
I. Matuz and Z. Benko	Hungaroton

Sonatas for piano (1, 1946; 2, 1948; 3, 1957)

C. Helffer 1, 2 and 3	Astrée

1 and 3 (with works by Berio and Webern)	Guilde
2 (with Berg)	DG
C. Rosen 1 and 3	CBS
A. Marks 1	CRI
H. Henck 1, 2 and 3	Wergo
K. Körmendi 1 and 3 (*Trope* only) (with works by Berio, Holliger and Messiaen)	Hungaroton
Y. Loriod 2 (excluding finale) (with works by Berg and Webern)	Vega
D. Burge 1 (with works by Berio, Dallapiccola, Stockhausen and Krenek)	Candide
M. Pollini 2 (with Webern)	DG
Biret 1 2	Finnadar/ Atlantic

Le Soleil des eaux (1958 version) J. Nendick, B. McDaniel, L. Devos, BBC Chorus and Symphony Orchestra, P. Boulez (with works by Koechlin and Messiaen, cond. A. Dorati)	VSM/Argo

Livre pour quatuor (extracts)	
Parrenin Quartet (I, III, V)	ERA
Parrenin Quartet (I, II) and Hamann Quartet (V)	Mainstream

Etude No. 2	Barclay

Structures for two pianos (Book I 1952; Book II, 1962)

Alfons and Aloys Kontarsky

Books I and II	Mace
Books I and II	Wergo
Book I (with works by Kagel, Pousseur and Stockhausen)	Vega

Le Marteau sans maître

M.-Th. Cahn, the soloists of the Domaine musical, P. Boulez	Vega
M. McKay, an instrumental ensemble, R. Craft (with Stockhausen)	PHI
J. Deroubaix, Domaine musical ensemble, P. Boulez	Adès
Y. Minton, Musique Vivante ensemble, P. Boulez (with *Livre pour cordes*)	CBS
M.-Th. Cahn, the soloists of the Domaine musical, P. Boulez – extracts only (with works by Nono, Stockhausen and Webern)	Vega (25 cm)

Pli selon pli

H. Lukomska, BBC SO, P. Boulez	CBS
B. Bryn-Julson, BBC SO, P. Boulez	ERA

Improvisation I, II

E. Sziklay, Budapest Chamber Orchestra, A. Mihaly (with works by Schoenberg and Webern)	Hungaroton
V. Lamores, Philadelphia Forum Ensemble, J. Thome (with works by Dallapiccola and Pousseur)	Candide

Livre pour cordes   CBS

New Philharmonia Orchestra, P. Boulez
 (with *Le Marteau sans maître*)

Eclat

Orchestra of our Time, J. Thome (with works by Crumb, Dlugoszewski, Berio and Weill)	Candide

Domaines

M. Portal, Musique Vivante, D. Masson   HM

cummings ist der Dichter

ORF Symphony Orchestra of Vienna, B. Maderna   Telefunken
(with works by Lutoslawski, Messiaen and Stravinsky)

Eclat/Multiples

Ensemble InterContemporain, P. Boulez   CBS
(with *Rituel*)

Rituel

BBC SO, P. Boulez   CBS
(with *Eclat/Multiples*)

Messagesquisses

Ensemble 2e2m, P. Mefano   CDM
(with Lefebvre and Mefano)

Specially issued recordings
IRCAM, a portrait
Répons (extract, 5′30″)   IRCAM

Ensemble InterContemporain, P. Boulez
(This recording also comprises examples of sounds and
extracts from works by J. Chowning, J.-C. Risset,
J. Harvey, T. Machover, M. Maiguashca, Y. Höller and
M. Subotnik)

For Dr. Kalmus

This work figures on a disc of homage to Alfred Kalmus,   UE
founder of Universal Edition, London, on the occasion of
his 80th birthday. The other contributors were:
D. Bedford, H. Wood, R. R. Bennett, L. Berio,
C. Halffter, R. Haubenstock-Ramati, H. Birtwistle,
K. Stockhausen, B. Rands and H. Pousseur

Interview with Pierre Boulez

Nous avions vingt ans en 1945   HDS (17 cm)

II
BOULEZ THE CONDUCTOR

(The dates indicated are those of the recordings, when they figure on the discs)

BACH, Carl Philipp Emanuel

Concerto in D minor, for flute	HM
Concerto in A major, for cello	
J.-P. Rampal, R. Bex, H. Dreyfus, the Paris Opéra Chamber Orchestra	

BARTÓK, Bela

Duke Bluebeard's Castle	CBS (1976)
T. Troyanos, S. Nimsgern, BBC SO	
Concerto for orchestra	CBS
NY PO	
Concertos 1 and 3, for piano	HMV
D. Barenboim, NPO	
The Miraculous Mandarin (Dance Suite)	CBS
NY PO, Schola Cantorum	
Music for strings, percussion and celesta	CBS
BBC SO	
(with Stravinsky)	
The Wooden Prince	CBS (1977)
NY PO	
Rhapsodies Nos. 1 and 2, for violin and orchestra	VSM
Y. Menuhin, BBC SO	
(with Berg)	

BEETHOVEN, Ludwig van

Symphony No. 5	CBS
(with Cantata, Op. 11)	
John Alldis Choir, NPO	

BERG, Alban

Chamber Concerto; Pieces for Clarinet and Piano, Op. 5;	DG (1977)
Sonata for Piano, Op. 1)	
P. Zukerman, D. Barenboim, Ensemble	
InterContemporain	

Chamber Concerto; Three Orchestral Pieces, Op. 6;   CBS
Altenberg Lieder, Op. 4
S. Gavrilov, D. Barenboim, H. Lukomska, BBC SO

Lulu   DG
T. Stratas, Y. Minton, H. Schwarz, F. Mazura, K. Riegel,
T. Blankenheim, R. Tear, Paris Opéra Orchestra

Lulu Suite; *Der Wein*   CBS
J. Blegen, J. Norman, NY PO

Seven Early Songs   CBS
H. Harper, BBC SO
(with Wozzeck, Act 3 of the recording below)

Lyric Suite (string orchestra version)   CBS
NY PO
(with Schoenberg's *Verklärte Nacht*)

Violin Concerto   VSM
Y. Menhuin, BBC SO
(with Bartók)

Violin Concerto   CBS
Three Orchestral Pieces, Op. 6
P. Zukerman, LSO

Wozzeck   CBS
W. Berry, I. Strauss, F. Uhl, K. Donch, Chorus and
Orchestra of the Paris Opéra

BERIO, Luciano

Alleluja II   RCA
BBC SO
(with *Nones* and Concerto for Two Pianos, conducted by
Berio himself)

See also Anthology 4

Sinfonia   ERA
Eindrücke
New Swingle Singers, Orchestre National de France

BERLIOZ Hector

Nuits d'été; *La Mort de Cléopâtra*   CBS
Y. Minton, S. Burrows, BBC SO

Symphonie Fantastique; *Lélio*   CBS
J.-L. Barrault, J. Mitchinson, J. Shirley-Quirk, John
Alldis Choir, LSO

Les Troyens (extracts); overtures: *Béatrice et Bénédict*   CBS
(plus the *entr'acte*); *Benvenuto Cellini*; *Le Carnaval
romain*
NY PO

BIRTWISTLE, Harrison

See under Anthology 2

CARTER, Elliott

Symphony of Three Orchestras   CBS (1981)
NY PO
(with *A Mirror on Which to Dwell*, conducted by
R. Fitz)

DEBUSSY, Claude

Images; *Danses*, for harp and orchestra   CBS
A. Chalifonx, Cleveland Orchestra

La Mer; *Prélude à l'après midi d'un faune*; *Jeux*   CBS
NPO

Nocturnes; *Rhapsodie*, for clarinet and orchestra;   CBS
Printemps
John Alldis Choir, NPO

Pelléas et Mélisande   CBS (1970)
D. McIntyre, E. Söderstrom, Y. Minton, D. Ward,
G. Shirley, Chorus and Orchestra of the Royal Opera
House, Covent Garden

DUFOURT, Hugues
See under Anthology 3

DUKAS, Paul

La Péri   CBS
NY PO
(with Roussel)

ELOY, Jean-Claude
See under Anthology 1

FALLA, Manuel de
The Three-cornered Hat (complete); Harpsichord   CBS
Concerto
J. de Gaetani, I. Kipnis, NY PO

FERNEYHOUGH, Brian   ERATO
Funérailles I and II
(with Höller – see below)
Ensemble InterContemporain

GRISEY, Gérard
See under Anthology 3

HANDEL, George Frideric
Water Music (complete)   Guilde
Residentie Orchestra of The Hague

Water Music (extracts); *Royal Fireworks Music*   CBS
NY PO

Royal Fireworks Music; *Berenice*: Overture;   CBS
Concerto a due cori in F
NY PO

HARVEY, Jonathan
See under Anthology 3

HÖLLER, York   ERATO
Arcus
(with Ferneyhough – see above)
Ensemble InterContemporain

KAGEL, Mauricio
String Sextet (conducted)   Vega
Members of the Domaine musical ensemble
(with works by Boulez, Pousseur and Stockhausen,
unconducted)

KURTAG, György

See under Anthology 2

LENOT, Jacques

Allegories d'exil IV   HM
Ensemble InterContemporain
(with other works of Lenot, various performers)

LIGETI, György

Aventures; Chamber Concerto; Ramifications   DG
M. Thomas, J. Manning, W. Pearson, Ensemble
InterContemporain

MAHLER, Gustav

Das klagende Lied; Symphony No. 10 (Adagio)   CBS
E. Söderström, E. Lear, G. Hoffman, E. Haefliger, LSO

Rückert Lieder   CBS
Y. Minton, LSO
(with Wagner)

MESSIAEN, Olivier

Et exspecto resurrectionem mortuorum; Couleurs de la   ERA
cité céleste
Y. Loriod, Percussions de Strasbourg, Domaine musical
ensemble

Poèmes pour Mi   CBS
F. Palmer, BBC SO
(with Tippett, conducted by D. Atherton)
See also under Anthology 1

MILHAUD, Darius

Christophe Colomb   Decca
(incidental music for the Renaud-Barrault company)

MOZART, Wolfgang Amadeus

Piano Concertos, K.37, 39, 40 and 41   Vega
Y. Loriod, Domaine musical ensemble (a series of
recordings made in response to Yvonne Loriod's

performances of the complete Mozart Piano Concertos, given in the hall of the old Conservatoire in the 1960s, and conducted alternately by Pierre Boulez and Bruno Maderna)

NONO, Luigi

See under Anthology 6

POUSSEUR, Henri

See under Anthology 1

RAVEL, Maurice

Concerto for Piano Left Hand   CBS
P. Entremont, Cleveland Orchestra
(with Concerto in G conducted by E. Ormandy)

Schéhérazade; *Trois poèmes de Stéphane Mallarmé*;   CBS
Chansons Madécasses; *Don Quichotte à Dulcinée*; *Cinq
mélodies populaires Grecques*
H. Harper, J. Gomez, J. Norman, J. van Dam, Ensemble
InterContemporain, BBC SO

Daphnis et Chloé: suite No. 2; *Rapsodie espagnole*;   CBS
Pavane pour une infante défunte; *Alborado del gracioso*
Cleveland Orchestra and Chorus

Une Barque sur l'océan; *Valses nobles et sentimentales*;   CBS
Le Tombeau de Couperin
NY PO

La Valse; *Menuet antique*; *Ma Mère l'oye*   CBS
NY PO

Daphnis et Chloé   CBS
NY PO, Camerata Singers

Complete orchestral works, including 4 discs above plus   CBS
Fanfare pour l'éventail de Jeanne; *Schéhérazade*:
Overture; *Boléro*

ROUSSEL, Albert

Symphony No. 3   CBS
NY PO
(with Dukas)

SCHAT, Peter   CBS

Entelechie 1   Donemus
Concertgebouw

SCHOENBERG, Arnold

Gurrelieder   CBS
M. Napier, Y. Minton, J. Thomas, S. Nimsgern, BBC SO

Verklärte Nacht (version for string orchestra)   CBS
NY PO
(with Berg's *Lyric Suite*)

Moses und Aron   CBS
G. Reich, R. Cassilly, BBC Singers, BBC SO

Pierrot lunaire   Adès
H. Pilarczyk, soloists of the Domaine musical

Chamber Symphony No. 1; *3 Little Pieces for Chamber*   Adès
Orchestra
Domaine Musical

Violin Concerto; Piano Concerto   CBS
P. Amroyal; P. Serkin

Pierrot lunaire   CBS
Y. Minton, P. Zukerman, L. Harrell, M. Debost, A. Pay,
D. Barenboim
(recording accompanied by an interview between Pierre
Boulez and Dominique Jameux)

Serenade; *Gurrelieder*; *Song of the Wood Dove*; *Ode to*   CBS
Napoleon
J. Norman, J. Shirley-Quirk, D. Wilson-Johnson,
Ensemble InterContemporain

Suite   Adès (1959,
Domaine musical ensemble   reissued 1984)

Suite; *Verklärte Nacht*   CBS
Ensemble InterContemporain

Serenade   Adès
Domaine musical ensemble

Five Pieces for Orchestra; *A Survivor from Warsaw*;   CBS
Accompaniment to a Film Scene; *Variations for Orchestra*
G. Reich, BBC SO

Various works included in a boxed set of four discs: CBS
Die glückliche Hand, S. Nimsgern, BBC SO and chorus;
Lieder Op. 22, Y. Minton, BBC SO; *Chamber
Symphonies* Nos. 1 and 2, Ensemble InterContemporain;
Three Pieces for Orchestra (1910), Ensemble
InterContemporain; *Erwartung*, J. Martin, BBC SO; *Die
Jakobsleiter*, S. Nimsgern, M. Mespie, O. Wenkel
Hudson, I. Partridge, J. Shirley-Quirk, BBC SO

STOCKHAUSEN, Karlheinz

See Anthologies 4 and 5

(A recording of *Gruppen* for three orchestras was made
by the WDR of Cologne, with the Cologne Radio
Symphony Orchestra, under the direction of Pierre
Boulez, Bruno Maderna and Karlheinz Stockhausen, then
issued in the Collection Zeitgenössische Musik in der
Bundesrepublik Deutschland No. 4, distributed by
Harmonia Mundi)

STRAVINSKY, Igor

L'Histoire du soldat   ERA (1980)
R. Planchon, P. Chéreau, A. Vitez, Ensemble
InterContemporain

Les Noces; *Pribaoutki*; *Berceuses du chat*; *Four Russian*   Festival Guilde
Songs; *Four Russian Peasant Songs*
D. Scharley, J. Brumaire and others, with the Chorus and
Orchestra of the Paris Opéra

Ballets (complete versions):   3 CBS
The Firebird; *Petrushka*
NY PO
The Rite of Spring
Cleveland Orchestra

Firebird Suite   CBS
BBC SO
(with Bartók)

Pulcinella; Concertino for 12 Instruments   ERA (1980)
Ensemble InterContemporain

Pulcinella Suite; *Scherzo fantastique*; *Symphonies of Wind*   CBS (1978)
Instruments
NY PO

The Rite of Spring	Festival Guilde

National Orchestra of the RTF
(with *Quatre Etudes*)

Recordings comprising various works:

Renard; Concertino for 12 Instruments; Three Pieces	Adès

for String Quartet; Three Pieces for Clarinet; *Symphonies of Wind Instruments*
Domaine musical, Parrenin Quartet, G. Deplus,
J. Giraudeau, L. Devos, J.-J. Rondeleux, X. Depraz

Song of the Nightingale; *Four Russian Peasant Songs*;	ERA (1981)

Quatre Etudes; Three Pieces for String Quartet, Study
for Pianola
Radio France Choir, Orchestre National de France

Concertino for String Quartet; Double Canon for	DG (1980)

String Quartet; *Dumbarton Oaks*; *Ebony Concerto*;
Elegy for Viola; *Epitaphium*; *Eight Instrumental
Miniatures*; Three Pieces for Clarinet
G. Causse, M. Arrignon, M. Damiens, Ensemble
InterContemporain

Pastorale; Verlaine Songs; Bal'mont Songs;
Three Japanese Lyrics; *Trois petites chansons*;
Pribaoutki; Cat's Cradle Song; Four Songs; *Tilimbom*;
Chanson de Paracha; Shakespeare Songs; *In memoriam
Dylan Thomas*; *Elegy for J.F.K.*
P. Bryn-Julson, A. Murray, R. Tear, J. Shirley-Quirk,
Ensemble InterContemporain

VARESE, Edgard

Amériques; *Arcana*; *Ionisation*	CBS

NY PO

Density 21.5, *Déserts*, *Equatorial*, *Hyperprism*,	CBS

Intégrales, *Octandre*, *Offrandre*
Choeurs de Radio-France, Ensemble InterContemporain,
R. Yakar, L. Beauregard

Hyperprism; *Octandre*; *Intégrales*	Adès

Domaine musical
(with Schoenberg)

WAGNER, Richard

Das Liebesmahl der Apostel   CBS
Siegfried Idyll (original version)
Westminster Chorus, NY PO

Der Ring: Das Rheingold; Die Walküre; Siegfried;   PHI
Götterdämmerung
Bayreuth Festival Chorus and Orchestra, 1979
(*Götterdämmerung*), and 1980 (the three others),
G. Jones, P. Hofmann, D. McIntyre, H. Schwarz,
M. Salminen, M. Jung, H. Zednik, O. Wenkel,
H. Pampuch, S. Egel, F. Mazura, J. Altmeyer, etc.

Faust Overture, overtures to *Die Meistersinger;*   CBS
Tannhäuser; Tristan und Isolde: Prelude and Liebestod
NY PO

Parsifal   DG
J. King, G. Jones, F. Crass, T. Stewart, D. McIntyre,
Bayreuth Festival Chorus and Orchestra, 1970

Wesendonck Lieder   CBS
Y. Minton, LSO
(with Mahler)

WEBERN, Anton

Complete works: a boxed set of four discs, recorded   CBS
prior to 1971, comprising all Webern's published works,
and including his own recording of his orchestration of
Schubert's German Dances – together with his version
of Bach's Six-Part *Ricercar*, this time conducted by
Boulez, who also put his stamp on the unconducted
works There is a plan to record a second set (of three
discs) containing Webern's unpublished works

Cantatas 1 and 2   Vega
I. Steingruber, X. Depraz, the E. Brasseur Chorale and
the Domaine musical
(with Stravinsky's *Canticum sacrum*, conducted by
R. Craft)

See also Anthology 6

ZAPPA, Frank

The Perfect Stranger   EMI
Ensemble InterContemporain, The Barking Pumpkin
Digital Gratification Consort

Anthologies

1 ELOY, J.-C., *Equivalences*   Adès
   MESSIAEN, O., *Sept Haïkaï*
   POUSSEUR, H., *Madrigal III*
   Percussions de Strasbourg, Y. Loriod, G. Deplus,
   G. Jarry, M. Tournus, D. Masson, J.-C. François,
   F. Boury, soloists of the Domaine musical

2 KURTAG, G., *Messages of the late Miss R. K.*   ERA (1983)
   Troussova
   A. Csengery, M. Fabian
   BIRTWISTLE, H., . . . agm . . .
   Ensemble InterContemporain, John Alldis Choir

3 DUFORT, H., *Antiphisis* (1982)   ERA
   HARVEY, J., *Mortuos plango, vivos voco*
   GRISEY, G., *Modulations* (1983)
   I. Matuz, Ensemble InterContemporain

4 BERIO, L., *Serenata I*   Vega
   STOCKHAUSEN, K., *Zeitmasze*
   Soloists of the Domaine Musicale (with Boulez's
   Sonatine, S. Gazzelloni/D. Tudor, and Messiaen
   Cantéyodjayâ, Y. Loriod)

5 NONO, L., *Incontri*   Vega
   STOCKHAUSEN, K., *Kontrapunkte*
   WEBERN, A., Songs, Op. 8 and Op. 13; Symphony,
   Op. 21
   J. Héricard, Domaine musical
   (with Boulez's *Le Marteau sans maître*, extracts)

6 SCHOENBERG, A., *Maiden's Song*   Vega
   WEBERN, A., *Cantata 2* (extracts)
   NONO, L., *Incontri* (recording of public concert)
   C. Herzog, X. Depraz, P. Jacobs, A. Goléa, Domaine
   musical ensemble

A document: Boulez, as pianist, accompanies Jean   Decca
Giraudeau in works by Mussorgsky (*Songs and Dances
of Death*) and Stravinsky; as conductor, he directs the
musicians of the Renaud-Barrault company in other
pieces of chamber music by Stravinsky

A curiosity: an introduction to serial music, the text   Vega
spoken by Antoine Goléa, musical excerpts played by
Paul Jacobs and sung by Colette Herzog and Xavier
Depraz, with the Domaine musical ensemble under the
direction of Pierre Boulez (excerpts from works by
Boulez, Bach, Webern, Schoenberg and Nono, taken from
concerts given by the Domaine)

Boulez on Cassette

AN IRCAM/RADIO FRANCE COLLABORATION

SERIES I: *Musical Time*

Cassette 1 BOULEZ, P., *Éclat* (1964)
Ensemble InterContemporain, Pierre Boulez
Cassette 2 LIGETI, G., *Chamber Concerto* (1969–70)
Ensemble InterContemporain, Pierre Boulez
Cassette 3 MESSIAEN, O., *Mode de valeurs et d'intensités* (1949)
Pierre-Laurent Aimard
CARTER, E., *A Mirror on Which to Dwell* (1976), extracts
Deborah Cook, Ensemble InterContemporain, Pierre Boulez
Cassette 4 An Introduction to the History of Musical Time from Guillaume de
Machaut to the Present
Ensemble InterContemporain

SERIES II: *Musical material and invention*

Cassette 1 DEBUSSY, C., *Etude pour les quartes* (1915)
Alain Neveux
VARESE, E., *Intégrales* (1926), extracts
Ensemble InterContemporain, Peter Eötvös
Cassette 2 WEBERN, A., *Six Bagatelles*, Op. 9 (1913)
Quartet InterContemporain
Cantata 1, Op. 29 (1939), movements 1 and 3
Groupe vocal de France, Ensemble InterContemporain,
Pierre Boulez
Cassette 3 CHOWNING, J., *Stria* (1977), extracts
STOCKHAUSEN, K., *Kontakte* (1960), extracts
Pierre-Laurent Aimard, piano, Michel Cerutti, percussion
HÖLLER, Y., *Arcus* (1978), extracts
Ensemble InterContemporain, Peter Eötvös

SERIES I: *Eye and ear*

Cassette 1 BERG, A., *Chamber Concerto* (1923–1925), extracts
Miriam Fried, Elisabeth Leonskaia, Ensemble InterContemporain,
Pierre Boulez
BERIO, L., *Sinfonia* (1968), extracts
Swingle II, Ward Swingle, Orchestre National de France,
Pierre Boulez

Cassette 2 WEBERN, A., Concerto, Op. 24 (1934), Symphony, Op. 21
(1928), extracts
Ensemble InterContemporain, Pierre Boulez
MESSIAEN, O., *Livre d'orgue* (1951), extracts
Almut Rössler

Cassette 3 BARTOK, B., *Music for strings, percussion and celesta* (1936),
extracts
Orchestre National de France, Pierre Boulez
FERNEYHOUGH, B., *Funérailles I* and *II* (1969–77, 1980),
extracts
Ensemble InterContemporain, Pierre Boulez

Producer: Jean-Pierre Derrien; production assistant: Marianne Manesse

Filmography

I. *In France*[1]

F 1 *Pierre Boulez*, by Michel Fano, 1966.

F 2 *Le Chef d'orchestre actuel*, by Pierre Boulez: a 52′ film produced by Michel Fano, transmitted 10 April 1977, within the framework of Mildred Clary's series, 'La Leçon de musique', on TF 1. The film of a series of rehearsal sessions for *Eclat*.

F 3 *Naissance d'un orchestre*: a 52′ film, transmitted on 25 June 1978 as part of the same series as above, featuring an orchestra of young people from the Orchestre de Paris. In the second programme Boulez comments on a session concerning the interpretation of a Haydn symphony under his direction.

F 4 *Introduction à la musique contemporaine*: two series of seven programmes by Michel Fano and Dominique Jameux in which Boulez is presented as conductor (Ligeti's *Chamber Concerto*, Stockhausen's *Kreuzspiel* and *Kontrapunkte*, Varèse's *Octandre* and *Intégrales*); as composer (Third Sonata, played by Kate Wittlich and Claude Helffer); and as commentator, notably in Film 1, (*Musique et modernité*), and Film 5, (*Materiau*). Series produced by Seuil-Audiovisuel for Antenne 2. Broadcast in March and April 1982; copyright Unitel.

F 5 *Ecoutez votre siècle*: an IRCAM video magazine, issued monthly in 1983–4, in which Boulez makes a number of appearances. Broadcast on FR 3; various producers.

II. *In England*

Boulez has taken part in a large number of films for BBC television – in particular,

---

1 There are many French TV productions in which Boulez makes guest appearances. I single out in particular *Le Volontaire du futur – un portrait de Pierre Boulez*: a 52′ colour film broadcast by TF 1 on 7 April 1982.

several films directed by Barrie Gavin with an educational approach both fresh and serious that is a model of its kind:[2]

F 6 *Portrait, Analysis, Performance* (1966): a 35mm black and white film lasting 59', in which Boulez speaks about his life and about music, and conducts *Improvisation II* (with Halina Lukomska); an animated version of the music appears on the screen as it is being sung.

F 7 *The New Language of Music* (1968): a 60' film with animated music examples, freeze frames, and divided screen, with Halina Lukomska, BBC Chorus and Symphony Orchestra, in the first of Berg's Three Orchestral Pieces, Op. 5; *Farben*, from Schoenberg's Five Orchestral Pieces, Op. 16, and Webern's *Cantata*, Op. 31. Berg is here compared to the architect Gaudi, Webern to Klee.

F 8 *Telemarteau* (1968): co-production with the SWF of Baden-Baden, a 67' colour film devoted to *Le Marteau sans maître* (with Yvonne Minton, Aurèle Nicolet, Serge Collot, Jean Batigne, Claude Ricou and Georges von Gucht). In eighteen quasi-independent sections, the film may be shown in any order.

F 9 *The New Rhythm of Music* (1969): Boulez on Stravinsky and Bartók. A 16mm colour film lasting 50', in which he conducts excerpts from *Music for strings, percussion and celesta* and *The Rite of Spring*. Animated examples of polyphonic lines illustrate successive entries, while a visual mixing of the various groups indicates the superpositions; Boulez speaks of Ezra Pound and of Joyce.

F 10 *The Outsiders* (1970): a 59' colour film on Varèse and Ives. Ives is compared with Braque and Schwitters: the technique of collage and the *objet trouvé*. Parallels are drawn with Mahler. 'When I have to conduct this music (Ives) with two different speeds, I conduct one speed with one arm, the other with the other arm' (he demonstrates). Unlike Ives, Varèse is shown as a rootless composer belonging to no one country.

F 11 *Alban Berg* (1972): a 16mm colour film lasting 60'25", with Helene Berg, Jascha Horenstein, Alfred Kalmus, Willi Reich, Jean-Rodolphe Kars and the Delmé string quartet.

F 12 *Vision and Revolution* (1973): a 16mm 55' colour film on Olivier Messiaen. It evokes Moreau and Redon, artists who were both religious and erotic, and Messiaen is filmed notating birdsong in a wood. Excerpts from *Chronochromie* and *Poèmes pour Mi*.

F 13 *Bogeyman–Prophet–Guardian* (1974): a 16mm colour film on Schoenberg, in two parts, lasting 80' and 76'; Boulez conducts the end of *Verklärte Nacht* with eyes closed. It includes interviews with Alexander Goehr, Georg Eisler and Rudolph Kolisch, and Schoenberg's spoken declaration that: 'I had fallen into a billowing sea without knowing how to swim and with the tide against me – but I never gave up'.

F 14 *A Different Beauty* (1977): a 16mm colour film on Webern, lasting 76'. A

2 Sincere thanks are due to Carolyn Johnson (BBC, Music and Arts Department), Barrie Gavin's assistant and collaborator, for her invaluable help in compiling this part of the book.

co-production by the BBC and RM Productions, with Boulez conducting orchestral and vocal excerpts and Peter Stadlen playing (very slowly, with *rubato*!) and talking about the *Variations*, Op. 27.

F 15 *Boulez Now* (1983): a 16mm colour film lasting 59′20″. Boulez rehearsing *Répons*, plus a retrospective of his career so far. Quotations from preceding films.

F 16 *Hommage à Pierre Boulez* (SWF, directed by Barrie Gavin): 60th birthday concert in Baden-Baden: *Rituel, cummings ist der Dichter, Improvisation sur Mallarmé III, Le Soleil des eaux, Notations.*

There are many other films with Boulez as conductor or commentator – such as the filmed report on the travels of the BBC SO on tour in Czechoslovakia and the USSR with Boulez, sporting a cap, being attacked in the press for his 'modernism' – 'I was strong enough to withstand it!'. He conducts *Eclat*, also Debussy and Webern; *Eclat* was also performed in Warsaw. The other conductor on the tour was Sir John Barbirolli. 1967, black and white; directed by Anthony Wilkinson.

III. *Other countries*

F 16 In a RAI series organized by Luciano Berio, a film on Boulez the conductor (1963, in Italian, double-track) shows him giving a lesson to an English pupil on the Prelude to *Parsifal*.

Films were made of two concerts while Boulez was director of the NY PO, and it seems that these still exist in the USA:

F 17 Schoenberg: *Variations*, Op. 31
Schumann: Symphony No. 4 (last movement)
Haydn: Symphony No. 49
RM Production (Unitel), 16mm, 1973.

F 18 Boulez: *Eclat*
Berg: Three Orchestral Pieces, Op. 5
Japanese koto music and improvised waltz rhythms
Co-production PBS/WNET Channel 13.

Bibliography

I

BOOKS BY OR IN COLLABORATION WITH PIERRE BOULEZ

PIERRE BOULEZ, *Penser la musique aujourd'hui*, Paris, Gonthier, 1964. The original copyright belongs to Schott, Mainz, 1963. Published in English as *Boulez on Music Today*, London, Faber, and Harvard University Press, Cambridge, Massachusetts, 1971.

PIERRE BOULEZ, *Relevés d'apprenti*: selected articles chosen and presented by Paule Thévenin, Paris, Le Seuil, Coll. 'Tel Quel', 1966. Published in English as *Notes of an Apprenticeship*, New York, Knopf, 1968.

PIERRE BOULEZ, *Points de repère*: selected articles and other writings collected and introduced by Jean-Jacques Nattiez, Paris, Christian Bourgois, Coll. Musique/passé/présent, 1981. Published in English under the title of *Orientations*, London, Faber, and Harvard University Press, Cambridge, Massachusetts, 1986.

ANTOINE GOLEA, *Recontres avec Pierre Boulez*, Paris Juilliard, 1958, re-issued by Slatkine, with an introduction by Martine Cadieu, 1982.

PIERRE BOULEZ, *Par volonté et par hasard: entretiens avec Célestin Deliège*, Paris, Le Seuil, 'Tel Quel', 1975. Published in English as *Pierre Boulez: Conversations with Célestin Deliège*, London, Eulenburg, 1976.

Important articles by Pierre Boulez

(N = Notes of an Apprenticeship; O = Orientations)

1948	Present-day encounters with Berg	N
	Proposals	N
1949	Trajectories: Ravel, Stravinsky, Schoenberg	N
1951	A time for Johann Sebastian Bach	N
	Stravinsky remains	N
1952	Eventually	N
	Schoenberg is dead	N

1954	The composer as critic	O
	Today's searchings	N
	'. . . Auprès et au loin'	N
1955	'. . . To the farthest reach of the fertile country'	N
1956	Corruption in the censers	N
1957	Aléa	N
	Directions in recent music	N
1958	Sound and word	N
1961	The teacher's task[1]	O
1963	Speaking, playing, singing (on *Pierrot Lunaire* and *Le Marteau sans maître*)	O
	Ten years on (an assessment of the Domaine musical)	O
1964	'Sonate, que me veux-tu?' (Sonata 3)	O
	Putting the phantoms to flight	O
	Taste: 'The spectacles worn by reason'	O
1966	Wieland Wagner: 'Here space becomes time'	O
1968	'Where are we now?'	O
1969	Reflections on *Pelléas* and *Mélisande*	O
1970	Approaches to *Parsifal*	O
1975	Present and future – a fundamental requestioning Perspective-Prospectives[2]	

II
BOOKS ON PIERRE BOULEZ

PAUL GRIFFITHS, *Boulez*, London, Oxford University Press, 1978.
JOAN PEYSER, *Boulez: Composer, Conductor, Enigma*, New York, Macmillan, 1976.
WILLIAM GLOCK (ed.), *Pierre Boulez: a Symposium*, London, Eulenburg, 1986.
THEO HIRSCHBRUNNER, *Pierre Boulez und sein Werk*, Laaber, Laaber Verlag, 1985.

III
COLLECTIONS OF DOCUMENTS ABOUT PIERRE BOULEZ

'Dossier: Pierre Boulez', edited by Jean-Pierre Derrien, *Musique en jeu*, No. 1, Editions du Seuil, 1970.
'Plaquette Boulez', for the Autumn Festival, 1981 (text by Célestin Deliège, notes on the works by Dominque Jameux), Editions de l'Avant-scène, Paris, 1981. The booklet was reprinted as a supplement to No. 36 of *l'Avant-scène opéra*, devoted to *Wozzeck* by Alban Berg (September–October 1981).

1 Originally published under the apocryphal title of 'Down with disciples!'
2 Boulez's contribution to the IRCAM manifesto booklet, *La Musique en projet*, Paris Gallimard, 1975.

'Dossier: Pierre Boulez', articles by György Ligeti, Ivanka Stoianova; interviews with Claude Helffer, Michel Tabachnik and Pierre Boulez. *Musique en jeu*, No. 16, Editions du Seuil, 1974.
Pierre Boulez. Eine Festschrift zum 60 Geburtstag am 26 Marz 1985. Contributions from E. Carter, E. Fleischmann, W. Glock, C. Gottwald, P. Griffiths, J. Hausler, D. Jameux, H. Mayer, L. Morton, R. Piencikowski, H. Oesch, P. Sacher, M. Stahnke, W. Wagner – assembled by J. Hausler in connection with the events organised by the SWF, Baden-Baden, in March–April 1985; Vienna, Universal Edition, 1985.

IV

STUDIES ON PIERRE BOULEZ

SUSAN BRADSHAW/RICHARD RODNEY BENNETT, 'In Search of Boulez', parts 1 and 2, *Music and Musicians*, January and August 1963.
MICHAEL FINK, Pierre Boulez: a Selective Bibliography, *Current Musicology*, No. 13, 1972. This Bibliography is a mainly Anglo-Saxon one: there are chapters on Boulez's writings, on his contributions to collected writings, on books discussing Boulez together with other composers, and on studies of successive works by him.
MICHEL FOUCAULT, 'Pierre Boulez ou l'écran traversé', *Nouvel Observateur*, 2 October 1982. A fine article on Boulez's creativity.
PETER HEYWORTH, 'Taking Leave of Predecessors', parts 1 and 2, *New Yorker*, New York, 24 and 31 March 1973. A clear and well-documented study.
DOMINIQUE JAMEUX, 'Sur Pierre Boulez: esquisses et notations', Paris, art press 51, September 1981.
DOMINIQUE JAMEUX, 'L'experience Mallarmé' ('Die Erfahrung Mallarmé'), *Festchrift Pierre Boulez* (see above), German translation by J. Hausler.
DOMINIQUE JAMEUX, 'Berg et Boulez', *Internationale Berg-Tage*, Luxemburg, 13–14 December 1985; unpublished.
DOMINIQUE JAMEUX, 'Gustav Mahler, Pierre Boulez. Parallelismes/Divergences', *Colloque international Gustav Mahler*, Paris, 25–7 January 1985; Paris, Association Gustav Mahler, 1986.
DOMINIQUE JAMEUX, 'Mallarmé, Debussy, Boulez', paper presented by the *Convegno internazional su Claude Debussy*, Milan, La Scala, 2–4 June 1986; *Silences*, 1986.
DOMINIQUE JAMEUX, 'Pierre Boulez, l'oeuvre singuliere', *Programme du Festival international des musiques d'aujourd'hui*, Musica, Strasburg, September 1986.
BAYAN NORTHCOTT, 'Boulez's Theory of Composition', *Music and Musicians*, December 1971.
ROBERT PIENCIKOWSKY, 'René Char et Pierre Boulez, an analytical study of *Le Marteau sans maître*', *Schweizer Bieträge zur Musikwissenschaft*, Verlag Paul Paupt, Bern and Stuttgart, 1980 (in French).

IVANKA STOIANOVA, *Geste–texte–musique*, Union générale d'édition, 1978. This book reprints and complements articles on Boulez (on *Pli selon pli, Rituel*, the Third Sonata, *cummings ist der Dichter*, etc.) which had previously appeared, mainly in the review *Musique en jeu*.

V

SELECTED INTERVIEWS

'Sprengt die Opernhäuser in die Luft', *Der Spiegel*, No. 40, 1967. Boulez's attitude towards the operatic institutions at the end of the 1960s.

'Boulez, l'exilé de la musique française, s'explique', *Lectures pour tous*, July 1969. In a non-specialized publication, an in-depth interview on Boulez's attitudes at the time.

'Das Ritual der Konzerte muss geändert werden', *Süddeutsche Zeitung*, 18–19 October 1969.

'L'Express va plus loin avec . . . Pierre Boulez', conversation with Michèle Cotta and Sylvie de Nussac, *L'Express*, No. 979, 13 April 1970.

'L'Organisation de la musique en France: une absence totale d'idées . . .', *Le Monde*, September 1970 (from an interview with Louis Dandrel).

'Pierre Boulez and Michel Fano: a conversation', *Oktober*, New York, 1982. A fruitful conversation on the subject of modernity.

Appendix

MALLARME: FROM HERMETICISM TO INTERPRETATION

My interpretation of the sonnets drawn upon by Boulez in *Pli selon pli* has been guided by various commentators.[1] The following six poems will be considered in some detail, in an attempt to convey something of the elusive, evocative nature of Mallarmé's writing that Boulez found so attractive:[2]

BOULEZ	MALLARME
Pli selon pli	'Remémoration d'amis belges'
	(*L'Art Littéraire*, 1893)
Don	Don du poème
	(for *Le Parnasse contemporaine*, 1865)
Improvisation I	'Le vierge, le vivace, et le bel aujourd'hui'
	(*La Revue indépendante*, 1885)
Improvisation II	'Une dentelle s'abolit'
	(*La Revue indépendante*, 1887)
Improvisation III	'A la nue accablante tu'
	(Pan Berlin, 1985)
Tombeau	'Tombeau' (de Verlaine)
	(*La Revue blanche*, January 1897)

1 My reading of the sonnets has been guided by the interpretations of various authors. I refer here to such classic works as Guy Michaud's *Mallarmé*, Paris, Hatier, 1953 (re-issued 1971); *L'Univers imaginaire de Mallarmé* by Jean-Pierre Richard, Paris, Le Seuil, 1961; and above all to Emilie Noulet's *Vingt poèmes de Stéphane Mallarmé*, Paris, Geneva, Librairies Minard et Droz, 1947 (re-issued 1972). The Mallarmé editions used are the *Oeuvres complètes* as collected by Henri Mondor in *Pléiade* (Paris, Gallimard, 1945, re-issued 1979) and *Poésies* (also published by Gallimard, 1969). The English translations are by Michael Purser (MS, author's copyright, 1986).
2 The references given here are those of the first published versions; the texts I have opted for may contain slight modifications and variants which do not affect the general sense of the poems.

Pli selon pli

> A des heures et sans que tel souffle l'émeuve
> Toute la vétusté presque couleur encens
> Comme furtive d'elle et visible je sens
> Que se dévêt pli selon pli la pierre veuve
>
> Flotte ou semble par soi n'apporter une preuve
> Sinon d'épandre pour baume antique le temps
> Nous immémoriaux quelques-uns si contents
> Sur la soudaineté de notre amitié neuve.
>
> O très chers rencontrés en le jamais banal
> Bruges multipliant l'aube au défunt canal
> Avec la promenade éparse de maint cynge
>
> Quand solennellement cette cité m'apprit
> Lesquels entre ses fils un autre vol désigne
> A prompte irradier ainsi qu'aile l'esprit.
>
> This city, even when the air is still,
> drifts, at times, as if into a decay,
> incense-coloured, a furtive lifting away,
> I sense, of mournful surfaces, until
>
> it hovers, with nothing significant in view,
> unless to conjure the moment of meeting
> of us immemorial ones at that first greeting
> of friends discovered so suddenly new.
>
> In the momentous and never banal
> Bruges, with images of dawn in a still canal,
> of swans scattered swimming, and those sons
>
> of the city I met, who now return
> to quicken my mind, spirits that discern
> in life a radiance – O my dear ones!

Some of the difficulties in understanding the poem arise from its lack of punctuation. When the poem is recited, its alliteration may require a caesura, or the indication of a comma after 'antique' and before 'esprit', without it being necessary to write it in. The line transfer of 'Bruges' gives a similar structure to line 10: this is an early instance of an underlying logic, the more significant because it escapes superficial interpretation.

More broadly speaking, it is the grammatical and logical functions vested within the poem as a whole which gradually reveal the significance of the text. Lines 3 and 4 are in parentheses, line 7 is an ablative without preposition ('par nous immémoriaux . . .'), and the first two quatrains are thus understood in an elusive, even elliptical manner: 'toute la vétusté . . . flotte ou semble par soi n'apporter une preuve sinon d'épandre pour baume antique le temps sur la soudaineté de notre amitié neuve'. A poetic structure becomes apparent through a process of 'unfolding' – in the same way that a logical sequence of events may be perceived intuitively in a piece of music, without recourse to intrusive markings.

This parallel approach also involves a semantic ambivalence. For the performer, choice is the very principle of his interpretation; here, too, the reader should reject the single meaning of the word 'aube', in order also to see it as the image of whiteness ('albus') of the neighbouring 'cygne' – despite the fact that the colour of dawn is also tinged with white. The phrase 'couleur encens' in line 2 can likewise only refer to burning incense – such as would fill the air at a ceremony 'solennellement' (line 12) offered (figuratively speaking) to the memory of a great poet. Furthermore, in the successive occurrence of words linked by the same image ('vol', 'cygne', 'aile'), one can see a parallel between the idea of the poet taking flight on wings of glory, and the burgeoning of a new friendship.

'Don du poème'

'Don du poème' was written in 1865 and today appears as the conclusion to the series of sonnets which were grouped together in 1866 as Le Parnasse contemporain. However, it was not until 1883 that Mallarmé entrusted it to Paul Verlaine for inclusion in an anthology which the latter was preparing under the title of Poètes maudits.

> Je t'apporte l'enfant d'une nuit d'Idumée!
> Noire, à l'aile saignante et pâle, déplumée,
> Par le verre brûlé d'aromates et d'or,
> Par les carreaux glacés, hélas! mornes encor,
> L'aurore se jeta sur la lampe angélique.
> Palmes! et quand elle a montré cette relique
> A ce père essayant un sourire ennemi,
> La solitude bleue et stérile a frémi.
> O la berceuse, avec ta fille et l'innocence
> De vos pieds froids, accueille une horrible naissance:
> Et ta voix rappelant viole et clavecin,
> Avec le doigt fané presseras-tu le sein
> Par qui coule en blancheur sibylline la femme
> Pour les lèvres que l'air du vierge azur affame?

> I've brought you this child of a night in Idumea!
> Bleeding, plucked and pale, the wings of the morning,
> drawn through glass burned to spice and gold,
> through frozen panes, dull still, and sad,

crashed on the lamp I work by, the light of palms
and angels. Then revealed this relic to the giver.
When he tried an unpaternal grin, a shiver
sprang up in the blue and sterile solitude.
The cradle there, our daughter at your breast,
your cold bare feet, your voice like music of viol
and harpsichord – such innocence to receive
so foul a birth! And will your work-worn hand press
the milk of a Sybilline wisdom into lips gone dry
with a craving for the azure of a virgin sky?

The poem is not a sonnet, although it comprises fourteen lines. Perhaps Mallarmé wished to avoid a form inconsistent with the two-part arrangment of a poem in which an initial invocation is answered by two propositions[3] – the second being interrogative or, more precisely, imperative ('accueille'), then interrogative ('presseras-tu'). 'Noir' is an epithet somewhat distanced from 'aurore'. Lines 3 and 4 are anticipatory ablatives to the first independent proposition 'se jeta', while in the second proposition (with the principal clause 'a frémi') the subject of the subordinate clause 'a montré, elle' refers to 'aurore' and not to 'solitude'.

This is one of Mallarmé's most accessible poems – certainly the least obscure of those used by Boulez in *Pli selon pli*. In addition, its meaning is considerably clarified by a letter Mallarmé wrote in 1886, in which he explains to Madame de Josne (a friend of Baudelaire) that the text evokes 'the sadness of the poet faced with his child of night', the poem of an evening's inspiration; when the miserable dawn shows it to be sombre and lifeless, he brings it to the one who will revitalize it'. Guy Michaud paraphrases: 'At dawn, after a night spent desperately toiling away by the light of a lamp, the poet discovers his work in its true light. Although he now judges it harshly, he nonetheless brings it to his wife, who "nourishes" the new-born poem, whilst rocking their little daughter Geneviève'.[4]

Charles Mauron stresses the likelihood that the 'poem' of which the text under discussion is the 'gift' was 'Hérodiade', a large-scale contemporary work that occupied Mallarmé over a period of several years, costing him all the obsessional anguish of creative impotence. It is the first line of 'Don du poème' which is essentially of interest here, since it was the only one of the whole poem to be used by Boulez: placed as a foreword to his opening movement, it serves to link the poem referred to – also set in Idumea – with 'Don du poème' in a parable of poetic difficulty. Does this refer to Idumea or Edom? According to Jewish tradition, Edom was a country where God placed a monstrous form of humanity that reproduced itself without women. In the same way, the poet creates his poem alone, without female aid: a monstrous birth that produces an accursed child, loathed in advance by the world into which it is born and encountering no more than a 'sourire ennemi' even from its own father.

3 It would be better to speak of the response of the two double propositions (each comprising two subsidiary propositions).
4 Guý Michaud, *Mallarmé*, Paris, Hatier, 1953 (re-issued 1971), p. 50.

Again to quote Charles Mauron,[5] 'Don du poème' is nevertheless an uncharacteristically 'optimistic poem' compared with the 'depressive poems' like 'Une dentelle s'abolit' and 'A la nue accablante tu' (to mention only those used by Boulez) of the Parisian period to follow. Difficult and disappointing as it was, this birth nevertheless took place, out of the flames of the external light of 'l'aube', and the internal illumination of the 'lampe angélique': a blaze that arouses the enthusiasm of the admiring interjection, 'Palmes!'. Were these the symbols of victory promised to the poet – or merely a vegetable form representing 'the evolutionary curve of a successful emergence?'[6] The enthusiasm of the begetter evaporates rapidly when confronted with a dawn that cruelly reveals the still-born relic of a poem that will only be brought to life by the milk of human kindness. Mallarmé's vocabulary speaks of iciness and sterility, of cold whiteness and virgin blue – so composing a symphonic environment that casts strong doubts on the future of his creation.

'Le vierge, le vivace et le bel aujourd'hui' (Improvisation I)

This is a famous sonnet published in 1885 and abundantly annotated.[7] In the first line, the imagery of nocturnal genesis of the previous poem is extended to embrace the idea of a new day, full of promise.

> Le vierge, le vivace et le bel aujourd'hui
> Va-t-il nous déchirer avec un coup d'aile ivre
> Ce lac dur oublié que hante sous le givre
> Le transparent glacier des vols qui n'ont pas fui!
>
> Un cygne d'autrefois se souvient que c'est lui
> Magnifique mais qui sans espoir se délivre
> Pour n'avoir pas chanté la région où vivre
> Quand du stérile hiver a resplendi l'ennui.
>
> Tout son col secouera cette blanche agonie
> Par l'espace infligé à l'oiseau qui le nie,
> Mais non l'horreur du sol où son plumage est pris.
>
> Fantôme qu'à ce lieu son pur éclat assigne
> Il s'immobilise au songe froid du mépris
> Que vêt parmi l'exil inutile le Cygne.

---

5 Des Métaphores obsédantes au mythe personnel, 1964, p. 51.

6 Jean-Pierre Richard, L'Univers e imaginaire de Mallarmé, p. 236. On p. 500, the author notes the importance of the lamp to 'Mallarmé's mythological furniture'. What if he had visited the house in Baden-Baden!

7 By the following: Emilie Noulet, Guy Michaud, Jean-Pierre Richard, Charles Mauron and others, notably Albert Thibaudet (1913), ? Vivier, ? Duchesne-Guillemin, etc.

The virgin day, live and lovely, will it show
the flash of an impulsive wing, and break
this hard, clear ice, enclosing far below
the unflown flights that haunt the forlorn lake.

Remember, long ago, he was the swan
who bravely strives to free himself in vain,
not having sung of the country still to gain
when sterile winter's glittering boredom shone.

That white anguish of the freezing sky brought
on the proud bird, his thrusting neck will thwart,
but not the mire in which the plumes are caught.

Spirit, that is to this pure brightness born,
here the swan swathes himself in the cold thought
of an absurd exile he bears with scorn.

First, a few peripheral notes. It is, for instance, the third time we have met the word 'aile' ('Remémoration' line 14, 'Don' line 2) as the image of poetic inspiration: 'Ses ailes de géant l'empêchent de marcher . . .' (from Baudelaire's 'l'Albatros'), or simply 'les ailes de l'inspiration'. It is the second time we have come across 'le cygne', here twice over, as a white, now flightless bird, resigned to a cold climate, an ambiguous creature whose plumage is trapped in the ice of a wintry lake. As a symbol for the poet fallen prey to sterility, it merits one of Mallarmé's rare capital letters – the last word of the sonnet.

The whole sonnet thus conveys a sense of movement. With the alliterative 'v' 'strengthened by the "b" ' (Noulet), the first line launches a quatrain whose question sounds optimistic: will this still-promising day bring an end to the writer's inability to write, to this coldness of the spirit, these poems which fail to take wing? The age-old swan ('autrefois' relates to 'cygne' and not to 'se souvient' – there are no pleonasms in Mallarmé) becomes aware that it has not succeeded in creating an atmosphere suitable for writing, a region whence to escape the 'sterile hiver' (here understood in the dual sense of a season which the non-migratory bird cannot escape, and as an image of old age and Saturnian impotence). Again, he can only contemplate the derisory possibility of allowing himself to shake off the superficial cold, which is only a form of death – underlining how much the subject is denied its very essence: a bird without space, the creator without creation. In its apparently definitive immobility, the final tercet responds sadly to the optimistic suggestion of the first quatrain.

The permanence of a powerless beauty is emphasized by the monochromatic reiteration of sounds throughout the sonnet, intensified in the assurance of the last line:

Que vêt permi l'exil inutile le Cygne.

The vocabulary employed is no less coherent:

'Remémoration'	'Don'	'Le vierge . . .'
dawn (meaning 1)	virgin (blue), innocence, dawn	virgin
		today
wing (prompt)	wing (bleeding, pale)	wing (intoxicated)
canal	leakage, window panes, glass, frozen glass, barren	lake, hoar-frost, haunt, transparent, glacier flocks which have not fled
swan, decrepitude, time immemorial antique balm	relic, recalling viol and harpsichord, drooping fingers	a swan from the past remembered
Bruges deceased, widow	Palms solitude (sterile) dejected, to mourn	Magnificent unable to sing agony
dawn (meaning 2)	whiteness, horrible	white, horror
furtively		Phantom
radiant	blue and barren	pure white, assign, immobilize, taken
	the child of a night	dream
	cold	cold
	dejected, wounded	boredom, useless

Such an inventory is not given in order to evade the narrative sense of the verse, but to draw attention to the network of expressive images common to all three texts. A vocabulary hinging on creative uncertainty, even impotence, is progressively drawn up: virgin, white, harsh, transparent and cold on the one hand, immobility, the past, and death on the other. At the end of his first *Improvisation*, Boulez found himself confronted with a scene, or rather a *mise-en-scène* representative of sterility: the text of 'Le vierge . . .' feigns escape from sterility in the first quatrain, only to become still more trapped by it in the final tercet.

'Une dentelle s'abolit' (Improvisation II)

Published in 1887 together with three other poems,[8] 'Une dentelle s'abolit' has a vocabulary, a colour and a tortuous precision with which we are becoming familiar. At the extreme limit of comprehensibility, it pursues the same theme of the plausibility of the poetic object itself:

> Une dentelle s'abolit
> Dans le doute du Jeu suprême
> A n'entr'ouvrir comme un blasphème,
> Qu'absence éternelle de lit.
>
> Cet unanime blanc conflit
> D'une guirlande avec la même,
> Enfui contre la vitre blême
> Flotte plus qu'il n'ensevelit.
>
> Mais, chez qui du rêve se dore
> Tristement dort une mandore
> au creux néant musicien
>
> Telle que vers quelque fenêtre
> Selon nul ventre que le sien
> Filial on aurait pu naître.
>
> A drift of lace sensing the sky
> in the vague dawn, implies a curtain
> half-drawn intended to deny
> a bed was ever there for certain.
>
> All this tangling and unwinding
> at the window becomes one white
> influence making for the light
> and seems more latent than defining.
>
> But with the gilded dream he's in
> adept of the saddened mandolin
> from whose expectant hollow dumb
>
> womb of music might there not begin,
> of such that reach upward, to come
> to birth some new being akin.

8 From which comes 'Surgi de la croupe et du bond', set to music by Ravel in 1913.

This is a remarkably musical text – so much so that anyone not knowing *Improvisation II* but familiar with the work of the composer in general would in all probability be led to think of the resonant sonorities of vibraphone and harp, celesta and bells. This sonnet plays on the intangibility of an expression that eludes the hand that aspires to grasp it.[9]

It will immediately be obvious that we are here concerned with octosyllabic lines, rather than alexandrines: the text is circumscribed, with half-lines reduced to a single word with its determinants and with recurring rhymes. The vocabulary concentrates on words already remarked: on transparency ('dentelles', 'entr'ouvrir', 'vitre', 'fenêtre'), whiteness ('dentelle', 'lit', 'blanc', 'blême', 'ventre'), disappearance ('abolit', 'absence', 'enfui', 'enseveli') and womb-like illustrations ('guirlande', 'flotte', 'dore', 'mandore', 'creux', 'ventre', 'filial', 'naître').

The proposition at the start of the sonnet could be summed up thus: will this piece of writing (this 'dentelle') attain the promise of fecundity (the 'lit')? The first quatrain answers in the negative. The scene is viewed from outside a room, in the fitful light of dawn (the succession of nights and days seen as life's supreme gamble). The curtains are drawn aside to reveal a room conspicuously lacking a bed: the definitive nature of this absence is marked by a full stop at the close of the first tableau.

The second quatrain is purely descriptive, as if the preceding observation had created a feeling of stasis through its lingering and disjointed description of lace curtains flapping idly against the window-pane. The final word (which answers to 's'abolit') is loaded with possible meanings only subjugated through emphasis; the image of Death is present thereafter.

The first tercet then effects a complete reversal of perspective. The inaugural 'Mais' has a forceful ring more akin to the German 'Aber' than to the English 'But'. A periphrasis personifies the poet, no longer a swan but a musician. In theory 'Tristement' implies no discontent, since it qualifies the emphasis placed upon 'Mais' following the negative tone of the first quatrain; it serves rather to allow the pun 'Triste*ment dort* (une) mandore' to launch a refrain – 'the murmured leitmotiv, the melancholy song of the old instruments' (Noulet), which is echoed in the 'viole et clavecin' of 'Don du poème'. The mandore – a sort of lute that Boulez did not feel obliged to represent by the alto voice of the guitar – is an instrument with a hollow belly, resonant and fertile as a woman's womb.

The second tercet attempts to demolish the hopes raised, of seeing the poet fulfil the fertile task which the absence of a bed had earlier seemed to preclude. Alas, the 'Tristement' was not without significance: the conditional 'aurait pu naître' expresses in a few words the renewed failure of this confinement.

---

9 It is strange to find the great Mozartian Théodor de Wyzewa commenting on this sonnet two months after its publication. However, my own comments owe more to Emilie Noulet (*Vingt poèmes de Stéphane Mallarmé*), the starting point of such embellishments as I indulge in.

Thus the whole poem takes on the overall sense of an allegory of frustrated creation – 'the dominating power of the non-existent work', as Noulet calls it.[10]

The progress of the sonnet – musically such an important concept – is then that of a preliminary negation, inverted *en route* into a plausible hope– only to be disappointed once again at the end. The austerity of this outlook is somewhat overwhelming.

'A la nue accablante tu' (Improvisation III)

This sonnet first appeared (in French) in the Berlin review *Pan* in 1895, three years before the poet's death. A particularly obscure poem even for the expert, it forms part of a final output which acknowledged neither variation nor punctuation.

> *A la nue accablante tu*
> *Basse de basalte et de laves*
> *A même les échos esclaves*
> *Par une trompe sans vertu*
>
> *Quel sépulcral naufrage (tu*
> *Le sais, écume, mais y baves)*
> *Supréme une entre les épaves*
> *Abolit le mat dévêtu*
>
> *Ou cela que furibond faute*
> *De quelque perdition haute*
> *Tout l'abîme vain éployé*
>
> *Dans le si blanc cheveu qui traîne*
> *Avarement aura noyé*
> *Le flanc enfant d'une sirène.*

> Under the storm-cloud's towering crag
> what fraught with silence runs aground
> drawn by the foghorn's obscure sound
> the water's jaws and slavering thrash
>
> admit disaster but to brag
> of masts ripped in the supreme clash
> where cliffs of basalt and lava pound
> great waves towards a distant splash.

10 It is rare to find a commentary becoming an elegy. 'From the position it occupies, one can guess that the poet has charged the word "Filial" with intent: according to the meaning adopted it can sound sorrowful, fervent, nostalgic or devout. But above all, pathetic–particularly when one considers that, throughout his life, Mallarmé had entertained the absolutely clear, pure, dream-like ideal of a supreme and unfinished work, consenting in its name to the mockery and insult of his contemporaries and sacrificing an easy fame for its sake–living only in the hope of finally becoming the son of the work itself.' (Emilie Noulet, p. 164.)

> Or was it in some lesser gale,
> whipped to a fury when the wild
> abyss, whirled out to no avail,
>
> brought forth from hoary-headed trail
> of foam to shore not ragged sail
> but a mild mermaid's drowned child.

The poem is an evocation of a shipwreck (line 5). Its overall interpretation depends on a definite and factual analysis of its grammar and logic:

What shipwreck (subject)
    you . . . by a muffled trumpet (relative clause)
knocked the mast over (principle proposition)
or that [hid] (principle co-ordinate)
which . . . all the abyss
will have drowned some . . . siren's infant (object).

The general sense of the poem is obvious: the poet questions himself indirectly as to the nature of the unexpected catastrophe that has fallen upon the world, concealing its sole consequence: the loss of the poetic object.

The rest of the text is then quite easily explained. The 'basse de basalte et de laves' – of which Boulez was to make such marvellous use in *Don* – is in apposition, giving the cause of the shipwreck: in marine terminology, a reef is volcanic in origin. Line 3 should be read after line 4 – to which it is again in apposition. The sea is the single witness to a niggardly shipwreck that consumes only a siren's infant. The tragedy of the poem lies in this absurd victim of so great a whirlwind, unregarded by an outside world unforewarned of its existence.[11] It seems that the image here stands for that of the *Livre* and for Mallarmé's final awareness that it was not awaited, nor would its incompletion even be noticed.

'Tombeau'

After the restricted forms of the three *Improvisations*, Boulez chose to conclude his reflection with an architectural structure equalling that of *Don*, thus restoring a coherent sequence to the poems. Unlike the other Mallarmé texts, 'Tombeau' does not seem to require interpretation. It is an occasional piece, written with an affectionate gravity by the austere poet Mallarmé as a tribute to the vagabond Verlaine; its meaning is self-evident.[12]

> *Le noir roc courroucé que la bise le roule*
> *Ne s'arrêtera ni sous de pieuses mains*
> *Tâtant sa ressemblance avec les maux humains*
> *Comme pour en bénir quelque funeste moule.*

---

11 This is also the subject of Brueghel's 'Fall of Icarus'.
12 Emilie Noulet comments on it (pp. 256–69). Jean-Pierre Richard (pp. 249 and 274) seems to misjudge 'le ruisseau' and, in order to give a firm base to his interpretation, makes 'calomnié' (which he bluntly feminizes) agree with 'mort'.

Ici presque toujours si le ramier roucoule
Cet immatériel deuil opprime de maints
Nubiles plis l'astre muri des lendemains
Dont un scintillement argentera la foule.

Qui cherche, parcourant le solitaire bond
Tantôt extérieur de notre vagabond –
Verlaine? Il est caché parmi l'herbe, Verlaine.

A ne surprendre que naïvement d'accord
La lèvre sans y boire ou tarir son haleine
Un peu profond ruisseau calomnié la mort.

The black stone raging in the north wind stands,
and will not yield, not to those pious hands
that bless the monument and mean to find
a pattern of the sickness of mankind.

Even the ring-dove cooing sounds too loud,
lamenting here, and darkness with its sorrow
the star rising triumphantly tomorrow
to shed a silvery light upon the crowd.

Whoever seeks Verlaine, they will not see
the vagabond sometime he was known to be.
Verlaine? He's there, look, in the grass asleep,

happy he didn't have to hold his breath
or wet his lips in a stream miscalled death,
seeing it was not really all that deep.

It is more important to draw attention to the last line – the only one used by
Boulez in his final movement. Just as only the first line of 'Don du poème' had been
used as a foreword to the work, so the use of the last line of 'Tombeau' gives an
intentional and consistent symmetry which links the two:

'Je t'apporte l'enfant d'une nuit d'Idumée!' (the first line of 'Don')
'Un peu profund ruisseau calomnié la mort' (the last line of 'Tombeau').

This linking may be seen as the very epitome of the work. The death of the poet is
in no way prevented by a poem cursed from its birth. But this Styx is shallow, and
the poet's description is to be short-lived; the dark flood is only an unjustly
maligned stream: death is the half-open door to the real life of the work. Verlaine
is to be saved from oblivion, and this connection with the theme of 'Remémoration' now makes the latter seem to serve not only as a title to the work but as the
foundation stone of an arch which likewise concludes with an evocation of poetic
destiny. To take one of its own expressions, a chain of 'amitié neuve' is thus forged
between Villiers de l'Isle-Adam, Mallarmé, Verlaine, Debussy and Boulez.

Index